An Amazing Human Journey

Remembering from the Subconscious Mind

Volume Two

SHAKUNTALA MODI, M.D.

Strategic Book Publishing and Rights Co.

Strategic Book Publishing and Rights Co.
12620 FM 1960, Suite A4-507
Houston, TX 77065

www.sbpra.com

For information about special discounts for bulk purchases, please
contact Strategic Book Publishing and Rights Co. Special Sales, at
bookorder@sbpra.net.

ISBN: 978-1-62857-509-5

The essence of spirituality and the guiding force behind human endeavors is extremely important. Without it, human efforts can go wrong, whether political, social, scientific, or just every part of human interaction and human life. Most of all, we need to learn from the mistakes of the forgotten past. We are facing the same situation now in this lifetime as they had in Atlantis. We need to understand what has happened in the past and the choices we face in the immediate future. We are in a similar stage of development as Atlantis was in its Golden Age. Humanity at large has to understand what has happened in the past, of the choices that have to be made, and of the need for spirituality in human life. Humans cannot and will not survive properly without this understanding. We have the choice now to maintain, enlarge, and expand that Golden Age to the entire Earth or, by making the same mistakes of using technology without spirituality that Atlantis made, turn the continents into living hells.

OTHER BOOKS BY
SHAKUNTALA MODI, M.D.

Remarkable Healings: *A Psychiatrist Discovers Unsuspected Roots of Mental and Physical Illness*

Memories of God and Creation: *Remembering from the Subconscious Mind*

Prayers for Healing and Protection: *A Gift From God*

An Amazing Human Journey: *Remembering from the Subconscious Mind* **Volume One**

TABLE OF CONTENTS
Volume Two

Volume II

INTRODUCTION

For readers who have not read *Volume I* of this book, this is a brief summary to assist in comprehension of what follows in this volume. Most of the information in both volumes is given by my hypnotized patients.

Plan for the Development of God

According to my hypnotized patients, the original plan for the first couples on Earth was to pass on knowledge to incoming souls through the spiritual joining of two souls while out of their bodies. While they were spiritually merged, their learned spiritual, physical, and emotional knowledge and qualities could be passed on to incoming souls before they entered the body. This way, the incoming souls (the newborn babies) did not have to start from scratch every time, but would continue on to where the previous generation had advanced. This way, their energy field would grow exponentially and everybody and everything it enveloped would evolve too; first on their planet and then to other races on the other planets.

The first humans were never able to carry out the original plan of soul merging, that is, the joining of two or more souls in the spiritual realm and passing on all their learned knowledge to the new incoming souls. Instead, they got into physical sex and reproduction first, because they were influenced by Satan and his demons. Physical reproduction would have come naturally because it was part of the scheme to produce new bodies, but it was not supposed to be the primary focus. The primary

1

focus was for spiritual development, the spiritual joining and passing on of knowledge to the incoming soul first, and then two beings would have been ready to produce a physical body.

Satan was there, trying to influence and prevent the first humans from carrying out God's plan. The breakdown of the original plan happened when Satan played on the first couple's emotions and convinced them that sexual intercourse, lust, and physical pleasures were important. Had the plan been followed completely, through spiritual merging of the souls of two people and passing on of knowledge to the next generation enabling the next generation to start where the previous generation left off, in about thirty or forty generations, human beings would have evolved to become masters very quickly and would be ready to return to the main body of God shortly after that. But Satan and his demons tricked those who were the first humans, who had everything they needed to be successful, just not complete knowledge. They fell for Satan's trick and became firmly rooted in the physical body, which slowed down their spiritual development. Currently, the incoming soul starts from zero. The only thing that has been developed is that the culture exists, and it can pass on these values to some extent. Since the first couple failed to carry out the original plan, the progress of mankind was extremely slow, as each soul had to relearn from scratch during each incarnation.

According to heavenly beings, there were a few planets where Satan did not succeed at all because their vibrations were very high and Satan and his demons could not tolerate the higher frequencies and could not get close to those planets. There are other planets where they have succeeded, to greater or lesser degrees. Satan has succeeded full scale in perverting only one universe, his own universe, which we call hell, and it has the lowest vibrations.

Heavenly beings, through my hypnotized patients, say that the desire for spiritual merging is built into the human race and we need to reestablish the spiritual joining in humans. There is still considerable influence from the dark side, but it is possible to reestablish the ability to have spiritual children through spiritual merging without physical sex. It does not have to be the couple that is creating the body that influences the soul. Those who are too old can mix, merge, combine, and influence somebody else's incoming soul. They can develop a spirit child that will be born into a physical body. It will have their spiritual knowledge, their spiritual characteristics, and be someone else's physical child.

When the child is born, after receiving the spiritual knowledge by the spiritually merged souls, they do not start at ground zero, because the newborn child already has the knowledge infused into him or her. As the graph develops, there will be spiritual joining by thousands or tens of thousands or millions of couples, and this could pervade the whole planet and even the entire universe. Everybody who is within their spiritual fields also gets evolved, including other humans, animals, and inanimate objects.

Here lies the importance of humanity. According to the heavenly beings, we are a unique race. We have the potential to transform the entire universe. There are only a few other races scattered around the universe that also have this capacity. We could be the end of creation. It is still possible for us to go back to the original plan of spiritual joining and the passing of knowledge to the incoming souls. We can enlarge the spiritual field around us, and everybody and everything in it can get spiritually evolved. Gradually, this could spread all over the planet and even the whole universe. We can take everybody back to God with us. According to the heavenly beings, even some of the highly evolved races in the universe do not have this capability. They are limited to developing within their own race. There is a little bit of spillover from them to their surroundings, but not the ability to spread and cover others in their field.

Alien Intervention

Human kind was evolving painfully slowly after the first couples failed to carry out the original plan. According to my hypnotized patients, there were eight alien races that contributed to the significant changes in the human race. The first alien race came to Earth about a million years ago. All of the eight alien races were divinely inspired and none of them meant any harm to humanity through their genetic modification. Their intent was to improve humans, and that did occur, but there were also some unintended changes, which were both positive and negative.

Most aliens look the same now as they looked when they first came on Earth. The first and last two alien races are human-like in appearance, while the rest are in humanoid forms; that is, they have a head, a body, arms and legs, and walk upright. These eight alien races are divided into two groups because there was a wide separation in time between the two groups and the extent of changes they made that affected mankind. The first alien group includes the first three alien races, and the second alien group includes the other five alien races. The genetic changes that were made by the first three alien races of group one affected the entire human race. The genetic changes done by the second group of five alien races were close in time and did not pervade the whole of humanity. The changes the alien races instituted are still shaking down through humanity and still coming into fruition. Some of the alien races of the second group also did spiritual teachings and gave different technologies to human beings.

Heavenly beings, through my hypnotized patients, state that the brain of today's human is not the same as the brain of the original, ape-like humans. There were genetic modifications done by the aliens, plus the changes that came through natural evolution. Although alien genetic manipulations in humans brought about many positive changes, they caused some negative changes, too. Some of our chronic medical disorders are due to the tampering of the aliens. As advanced as they were in genetics, they did not completely understand what they were doing, therefore, not everything worked out for the better.

According to the heavenly beings, there were total of five major genetic modifications done on human beings by different alien races.

1. In trying to develop spirituality in ape-like humans, the aliens did genetic modifications in the temporal lobes of the brain, which are considered to be more important for spirituality. In the original brain, they were a little more than a streak, a thin layer, and after the modification, they became a distinctly bulging part of the brain. All three alien races of the first group and the first, second, and third alien races of group two modified the temporal lobes of the brain. The aliens hoped this modification would help humans with spirituality, not realizing that spirituality was already there in the ape-like human beings. These ape-like humans did become more spiritual due to the change in the temporal lobes of the brain. They related more completely to the existence of God and it helped to speed up their spiritual evolution.

2. According to the patients' reports, there is a mushroom-shaped area in the center of the brain, from the left and right and almost in the center, between front and back. In that area is located a group of cells that help us focus and concentrate. The second alien race of group one, the Epsilon Eradante, recognized that this concentration center was necessary for development. They decided to improve that area to aid us in our spiritual development, and it did work. It became definitely bigger and, yes, people can pay attention and concentrate better. It did speed up the developmental process.

3. According to heavenly beings, the conscience center is a part of the brain on the top half of the forehead, slightly on the left of the center of the forehead. We have not identified that center yet and do not have any name for it. This center is responsible for the sense of right and

wrong. The Sirians, the third alien race of group one, genetically modified that center. As a result, altruism developed in humanity, leading to an expanded sense of right and wrong, which includes a part of society, a town or country, or all of humanity, and not just an individual. The negative effect of this modification was bad after the development of conscience center. People developed a sense of ownership and possession and the concept of stealing, and a sense of right and wrong was developed. The Sirians also did genetic modifications to develop emotions, communications, and hearing to better hear different tones.

4. The fourth and fifth modifications were refinements that made the spiritual centers (temporal lobes) more active. Fourth genetic modification was done about 250,000 years ago by the first alien race of group two. This was a telepathic race and they did it in an effort to improve our psychic abilities. The psychic abilities were already there and were previously increased and amplified by other races, but in this change, they were trying to refine them. They also worked to develop the spiritual centers.

5. The fifth genetic modification was done on some humans about ten thousand years ago on an island in the Pacific Ocean, and then they were allowed to mix in the general population about two thousand years ago. This genetic manipulation was done by the short, stocky, human-looking alien race five of group two on the temporal lobe of the brain to improve psychic ability. When the modification was judged to be stable, after eight thousand years of observation and study, then the people were transferred back to the general population. It spread through the general population and is still spreading through the mainland. That is why we have such heavy alien activity right now. They are keeping tabs on us to see how this modification is spreading through the cultures around the Earth.

Gross Physical Changes

Due to the genetic modifications done by the alien races, some physical changes were set in motion. Because of the enlargement of the temporal lobes and the brain, the skull was enlarged and the forehead, jaw, and the whole face were pushed forward. We also became taller but less strong, and have less hair as compared to the original ape-like humans.

A series of steps, both natural and imposed by others, caused the changes in humanity. Through all these five modifications, humans have developed emotional, intellectual, and spiritual abilities that even surprised the alien races that did modifications on humankind. We can concentrate better and step outside ordinary time and space and access power and information, which many of them cannot. These races are still observing and checking to see what happens to us.

Evolution was preceded by refining the nerve structure, and the brain actually got a little smaller because it works better. Finally, we wound up with the modern human, with the spiritual centers developed with the expectation of the spiritual life. We have a better-developed attention span and are more spiritual than our predecessors due to the genetic modifications done by the aliens, and also due to natural evolutionary changes. Over the last several thousand years, most of the changes in the spiritual nature of humans have been due to natural evolution.

Heavenly beings, through my hypnotized patients, report that we became something of interest in the galaxy because we are the race that is entering the spiritual phase. Most of the alien races have never seen this happen. They have gone through their own evolution, through their own experience, but they did not have the science and the tools at the time, or the understanding, to really study it. Every other race they met had already been developed, so this is the first time anybody is having a chance to watch a race developing.

There are some unique things about us humans. First, the depth of spirituality appears to be unusual as to how very spiritual some of us can be. This in part is due to the third race of the first group tampering with the spiritual center. Some feel that the genetic manipulation the third race did to enhance feelings was responsible for the emotions in humanity. They are surprised that we are such an emotional race and it plays such an important part in us. We already had some spirituality and some emotions, but they did not know it.

This is the main reason for all the interest on Earth. Not that there was anything that different about Earth, but because, before, nobody ever watched the development of a primitive race. That is an advantage of being a latecomer, to see the development of spirituality.

Through their genetic modifications and spiritual teachings, mankind became more spiritual, thus creating a larger spiritual field around them and the Earth. The larger the field becomes, the faster the general overall spiritual, emotional, and intellectual development of mankind will occur. Some of the aliens are startled to see psychic gifts popping up in humans. This gives aliens cause to rethink their understanding of the universe.

Heavenly beings state that there is a danger of doing genetic manipulation on your own race and not being sure what the outcome will be. You can have an intended outcome, and you may accomplish it, but you may make changes that you do not know, do not understand, and may terribly regret later. There have been races that have made themselves extinct by manipulating their genes; like grays are at the verge of doing now. Of course, people who make these changes are never there to reap the horrors that come. The genetic changes still rattle down through the race. Without observing, without recording, it takes about three generation to forget something completely because you do not experience it and know it.

Alien races are quite upset and quite leery of human efforts to tamper with genes without sufficient observation to know what a gene does or how it changes things. They are deathly afraid that negative characteristics can be introduced into the human race and may result in its destruction. They are

shocked and dismayed that humans created genetically modified foods without a thorough understanding of how that particular gene interacts inside the human body, without having
the full knowledge of their intended effects and the way to
get those effects.

Lamuria

According to my hypnotized patients, about 200,000 years
ago, N-hante, the alien race two of group two, found the
Earth. These aliens were spiritual and were divinely inspired
to help humankind to speed their spiritual evolution, but did
not know it consciously. These aliens selected, from the area
where Iraq is now, a group of people of all ages that was
cohesive and could survive together and provide support to
each other. They transported people, their livestock, tents,
and all their equipment and supplies by the spaceship to the
northwest part of Lamuria. The next morning, when people
opened their eyes, things were changed all around. They were
outside the tents, which were stacked up. The animals were
there but the land was changed all around.

The aliens did two genetic modifications. In the first modification, the aliens changed different genes to increase the size
of the temporal lobes by increasing the cells. In the second
manipulation, they modified the genes to cause more nerve
connections in the temporal lobes. There were also changes
set in motion that caused a decrease in the size of the jaw and
reduced the number of muscles and made them not as heavy
as they had been. This was a side effect and was not intended.

The tribe members had children who were different. They
accepted them, and by the time they were adults, people
were used to them and they did not stand out as glaringly
different. The tribe people lived out their normal lives. Each
generation was different in appearance and more spiritual.
It took about five generations until the gene was fully
expressed in humans. Then came a time in which the gene

had to spread sideways, as they married people with different genes. After a time, the gene had pretty much spread throughout the whole population, with everybody having the gene, either active or inactive. The Lamurians began to spread and settle in different parts of the continent and crossed the dry region in about tens of thousands of years, to reproduce and spread.

Alien race two of group two also provided a great deal of spiritual teachings to Lamurians. They taught them about prayers, meditation, and the proper way of living. As a result, the whole society became very spiritual, psychic, and could communicate telepathically. They were very simple people who did not need much and did not care for materialistic things and technology. Because of their spiritual practices, the society was free of demonic influences and illnesses. They did not need any hospitals.

Before the Lamurians left the continent, around 80,000 BC, and before the Atlanteans arrived in Lamuria, the third alien race of group two, called Kicks, began to teach the Lamurians. At this point, the Lamurians were completely self-contained because they had no outside contact and they had everything they needed, both externally and internally. They had no desire to leave their island-continent and explore. They did not have any way to go to other lands because they were not technologically oriented. They had what they needed without developing new technology. By now the whole continent was sparsely populated.

Kicks, alien race three of group two, decided to educate and help the Lamurians and prepare them for explorations outside Lamuria. They told the Lamurians that there were other inhabited lands to the east where they should go and teach about Divine. They also taught them that they should learn a new way of trading, by using money and making a profit. The aliens taught them how to build a boat, how to sail, and gave them courses in capitalism, free enterprises, trading, and making a profit, which was a totally foreign concept for the Lamurians.

They taught the Lamurians the different languages of people in various lands. They were told to spread the word of Divine and teach others of various spiritual practices. The aliens also told the Lamurians that they were different than the rest of the humans because they had special genes which made them spiritual and they should spread their genes for the benefit of the rest of humanity.

Only people with high telepathic and psychic abilities were sent out as traders and spiritual teachers. When they went to South, Central, and North Americas and Atlantis, and had affairs with different women and had children who had superior Lamurian genes, which spread all over through the years.

Around 80,000 BC, Atlanteans went to Lamuria to trade, and some of them settled there. According to the heavenly beings, there was intercession by Satan. He influenced people in Lamuria. Lamurians did not have any flaws, and except for the few selfish people, they were peaceful and happy. A few selected Lamurians, aided with Atlantean technology, were trying to take over the rest of the Lamurians and the Atlanteans were there helping them, leading to the destruction of Lamuria.

The destruction of Lamuria began around 80,000 BC and gradually escalated, and by 70,000 BC, almost all of it was gone except a few mountain peaks, which are now known as the Hawaiian Islands, Fiji Island, and Easter Island. Lamurians had known that the continent would be destroyed in a few thousand years and had a choice to leave and settle in other parts of the world. Some of them migrated east, to South, Central, and North Americas, Atlantis, Europe, and Africa. Most of them chose to go west, although it was farther away, because people in Asia were more spiritual than in the Americas, Atlantis, Europe, or Africa.

According to heavenly beings, most of humanity has the Lamurian genes and approximately 5 percent lack them.

After the second manipulation, the aliens were surprised to see very strong evidence of psychic phenomenon, and this came as a real jolt to them because they did not have a tradition in their own race of psychic happenings. They were puzzled. They realized very quickly what the implications were. This human being was capable of entering fully into the spiritual realm, effectively working and communicating in it, and obtaining information through it. They thought they were working with dumb animals when, suddenly, they observed evidence that these beings were actually capable of spiritual abilities that were vastly superior to the aliens. This was astonishing to them and they recorded it in their experimental results.

The alien races that were studying us suddenly found that we are kind of unique, first, due to the psychic phenomenon surrounding mankind and its spiritual development, and second, the intensity of the emotions with which we live sets us apart from everybody else in the galaxy as far as they knew. We were a human race who has everything, although not too bright, not too big, but very unique.

Psychic ability is still spreading throughout humanity, according to the heavenly beings. It did not develop in all humanity at once. These aliens were working with Lamurians and they helped only that group. Psychic ability developed only in Lamuria and not in the rest of humanity in different parts of the Earth. Of course, everybody on Earth had his or her own spirituality. So there was spiritual and psychic development going on all over the Earth, but it was intense in Lamuria. There were other people coming from South, Central, and North America and Atlantis to Lamuria later, so the genes got mixed up and confused the aliens. It took them a while to figure that out. It ended up with a substantial gene swap that was unintended by the aliens. The genetic material is still being spread around the Earth. It is not uniform among humans yet, but there is more spiritual development, more psychic ability, and more psychic improvement coming as this ability is refined and established in mankind.

Atlantis

My hypnotized patients state that about 130,000 BC, people came from different parts of the world to populate Atlantis. Before that, there were no humans there; only plants, animals, and birds. People from South, Central, and North America settled in the south and central part of the west coast of Atlantis, while people who came from Africa and Mediterranean countries settled on the southeastern coast, and people from Europe settled in the northeast of Atlantis.

People who originally came to settle in Atlantis from Europe, Africa, South, North, and Central America brought their own religion and culture with them. So, in Atlantis, the religions varied from region to region, and eventually got all mixed up, depending on which tribe you were dealing with. Some religions and gods that were imported, but the vast majority were homegrown. In the beginning, there were multiple gods, and each of these gods was generally worshiped in a particular area. Originally, they had a tribal god and, in general, would have one head of that temple, with the priest under that person. If the areas were large, there would be one head, like bishops, who would control many local temples.

In Atlantis, there was a very strange spiritual culture. There was a hallmark characteristic that it was impolite to speak of religion, spirituality, and of your own spiritual development. They had a twisted sense of the word "spiritual" because it was not open for discussion and they were embarrassed about it. When something is not discussed or traded back and forth, it becomes undefined and not refined. In temples, a priest would talk vaguely about spirituality, but would not talk about how it would help them develop spiritually.

Culture also differed from place to place, till it all became unified in time. Artwork varied from place to place, with a lot based in the old culture of the tribe. These various forms spread all over the continent and merged till, over time, it was all one mixture. The northern part of Atlantis, which was richer, was remade more often. The poorer part, the agricultural south, was less blessed. Much older buildings were found in southern Atlantis than in northern Atlantis. Atlantis flourished more than any of the surrounding countries because it was self-contained. Also, it was almost impossible to attack Atlantis with any force at all.

Initially, life was very easy in Atlantis. The land was fertile, there was plenty of food to eat, weather patterns were good, and there were abundant natural resources. The population grew rapidly. People were free and independent to begin with. That is, each person was doing what he or she thought was best, regulated by small group regulations. Later, as the tribes consolidated and rulers developed, laws were established and means of enforcing the laws were set up, like the court system. They had all the freedom to do what they wanted to do. This continued for thousands of years, till electronics came, which developed in Atlantis around 80,000 BC, around the time Lamurians came to Atlantis.

According to my hypnotized patients, Atlanteans perceived that people of Lamuria were not exactly like them. Lamurians were more advanced spiritually and mentally. They were able to use their psychic abilities and telepathic senses. These abilities were developed because of two things: first, their personal spiritual development and, second, that society accepted them. If society rejected them, they would not be so common and they would be considered strange. As different segments of Lamurian society in Lamuria used the same talents, it created the spiritual field around them, and the spiritual development built on itself. So, when the first person used psychic perception, it made it easy for other people to follow. When they all used it, the spiritual field around them increased; that added to their own abilities and made it easier for folks around them to do it. The spiritual field and abilities became simply a part of the life and not an odd thing.

Lamurians got the idea across to the Atlanteans that these things happen naturally when you are developed spiritually through prayers, meditation, worship, personal connection with God, and the right living. But most of them did not believe it. When the Atlanteans perceived that the Lamurians had spiritual gifts, they saw relationships between the spiritual gifts and agriculture. The Atlanteans had trance-inducing drugs, which they considered to be spiritual drugs. People considered a drug-induced trance to be a spiritual experience, a way to leap into spiritual development and to enter the altered state without having to develop themselves spiritually first.

Atlanteans began to grow more drug plants and use them, hoping they would be a shortcut in developing spirituality, rather than developing it through prayer, meditation, and worship. They mistook these trance states that were induced by drugs as true religious experiences, not realizing that the drug-induced trance states lower the vibrations and open the energy fields for entities to come in, while spiritual trance states raise the vibrations, which bring them closer to God and also protect from spirit possession.

Atlanteans developed the idea that it was possible to reach these elevated trance states by other means without developing spiritually. This led them to experiment with electronics to see if they could develop spirituality. Since they were unsure of what the Lamurians did and said, they developed the concept of electronically-aided spirituality and developed the electronic devices for it. Since the owners of the society, the rulers and the ultra-rich, controlled the technology, they were the ones who got to use the so-called spiritual devices to dominate and control other individuals.

Alien race four of group two came to Atlantis around 70,000 BC and alien race five of group two came around 50,000 BC and gave different technologies to Atlanteans,, allowing them to make faster technological advances. The Golden Age in Atlantis was between about 70,000 till 50,000 BC. During this time, Atlantis had a strong organized government and people were cooperating with each other all over the country. It was the most powerful nation on Earth, with trade and information flowing back and forth with explorations, settlements, and colonies. In this time period, there was rapid technological, medical, and architectural advancement, and many things came into being.

It was a positive, happy, highly functioning, and fairly balanced society at this time. Everybody seemed to have plenty, from the economic perspective. It was a good society from a cultural, social, environmental, and medical perspective. There were lots of theaters and fine music. Even average and lower class people had a comfortable lifestyle. Everybody had education and a chance to go to college if they chose. There was a lot of harmony in the society and rulers cared for their people. It was a pretty happy, productive, positive, and contented society. They had more emphasis on science and technology but little emphasis on spirituality.

Until about 70,000 BC, Atlantis was a functioning unit and people were prosperous and happy. Things began to change gradually when different people developed various ideas, such as: putting neck implants in people, first to communicate with them and later to control them; breeding special kids; breaking up family units by separating males from females and children from parents, etc. These ideas gradually spread all over the country. This began around 65,000 BC. By this time, the situation had been set up where the rich and powerful were in solid control of society. The rulers began to regulate the family, by putting economic pressure on the family, controlling their wages and income so the family could not have an easy life.

As time continued, the system in Atlantis got more and more rigid and the ruling group separated more from the common people, until they were thinking of themselves as different or better, and the common people as being more like beasts of burden who were to serve them. The rulers committed heinous crimes, such as taking away people's free will to live out their own lives; taking away the concept of marriage; breaking up family units by separating children from parents; and breeding kids according to rulers' specifications. Males and females were separated from each other and were not permitted to grow up with normal interaction. They were kept in different dormitories till they were put together as a mating pair to produce children and then separated again.

The final insult was when rulers began to treat human beings as total abject animals and began to butcher and eat them. This was the unforgivable sin, the denial of the human spirituality. The growing selfishness in the ruling class caused a growing disregard and dehumanizing of humanity, which was possible because the ruling class and the whole society were lacking in spirituality. The people of Atlantis were literally captive slaves of the ruling class for about the last 30,000 years, with the help of their technician class, which also ended up being controlled. They successfully maintained their control from about 50,000 BC till about 20,000 BC. People were literally born into slavery.

The tall, thin, human-like alien race four of group two regretted giving technology to Atlanteans who misused it. So they helped in freeing the people of Atlantis by interfering with the power supply, and all of a sudden, the whole population was free of control, including the technologists in the palace, who killed the guards and set out to destroy the mechanism. The whole ruling class and the technologists were wiped out by the angry people. Many people went to the coast, boarded ships, and headed east to Europe, Mediterranean, Africa, and Asia Minor. Some of them headed for Central, North, and South America, but most of them went east. As they settled into new lives, they totally rejected the memories of Atlantis, its technology, and the horror of it.

After the dispersion from Atlantis, things went downhill rapidly. People underwent a complete revulsion and avoidance of technology, and in three or four generations, they completely forgot that the technology had ever existed. The great-grandchildren absolutely had no knowledge of it, because the parents and grandparents did not speak of it. Once the technological descent began, people abandoned the cities and went back to the Stone Age. This was rapid, and humanity was literally reduced to wandering the Earth, living in caves. They lost agriculture, lost practically all their skills, and had to redevelop from scratch. It happened worldwide.

In Volume II, you will read what happened to humanity after Atlantis till now, how humans progressed very slowly spiritually and technologically over the years till God sent many spiritual teachers and masters to sprout spirituality on Earth. You will also read how many alien races were inspired to give us different technologies over the years and also during the present time. You will read how we all incarnate on other planets and why, and different reasons for the current abductions by aliens and our future interactions with different alien races.

You will also read in this volume that we humans are not alone in this journey. We have had many different types of souls working with us and helping us along the way, beings such as insects, animals, plants, elementals like Undines – the water elementals, sylphs – the air elementals, salamanders – the fire elementals, and Earth. Also, beings like gnomes, mermaids, and fairies are working with us, even though most of us cannot see them. Insects, plants, and elementals bring a lot of Light to Earth because they live short lives and are not very creative. As a result they have very little dark energy and spread Light on Earth.

Also, you will read how astrology plays an important role in our journey and how intricately we are connected to the masters of our solar system and how they help us with everything we do every day.

You will learn about the mysteries of different monuments and power places on Earth, and the crop circles, and the important role they will play during the transition of Planet Earth and the human beings from the third dimension to the fifth dimension.

So, come with me on this amazing and at times shocking journey and learn how we have evolved into an unique race that has the potential to take the whole galaxy and the universe to God.

Chapter 7

HISTORY OF MANKIND FROM ATLANTIS TILL NOW

In this chapter, we will discuss the aftermath of Atlantis when, after leaving Atlantis, people totally rejected technology. The Atlanteans did not want anything to do with technology. They wanted to live a simple, primitive life, and in few generations, they went from a technological society, which was a very sophisticated civilization, to practically being cavemen. This happened worldwide. They gave up technology and living together in big cities. They spread out across the countryside. For a period of time, people insisted on being primitive and non-technological.

Then as thousands of generations went by, they began to lose the dread of technology and the fear of advancing civilization. They began to rebuild, and for a long time it appeared as if this civilization came from nothing. When civilization returned and larger cities and rulers came in to play, around 12,000 BC, people had stories of their ancestors. The histories their ancestors had been provided by mouth, but with no real perception of what the generations went through. So they were not as frightened by it as their parents and grandparents had been.

Lots of memories were forgotten. The most sophisticated and technological stuff was completely gone. There were small memories of it here and there, but nothing really on which to build. The society started to reclaim itself literally after the Stone Age. Spirituality after Atlantis was very low all over the Earth, and after the Ice Age, God and heaven sent many spiritual teachers and masters to sprout spirituality all over the planet. God also inspired different alien races to give different technology to our scientists.

Atlantis Before the Destruction

According to my hypnotized patients, the people of Atlantis were literally captive slaves of the ruling class for about the last 30,000 years, controlled with the help of their technician class, which also ended up being controlled. They successfully maintained their control from about 50,000 BC till about 20,000 BC. People were literally born into slavery. The rulers committed heinous crimes, such as taking away people's free will to live out their own lives, taking away the concept of marriage, breaking up the family units by separating children from parents, and breeding kids according to the rulers' specifications. Males and females were separated from each other and not permitted to grow up with normal interaction. They were kept in different dormitories till they were put together as a mating pair to produce children and then separated again. The final insult was when rulers began to treat human beings as total abject animals and began to butcher and eat them. This was the unforgivable sin, the denial of the human spirituality.

As mentioned before, Lamurians brought spiritual knowledge to Atlantis about 80,000 BC. Lamuria sank about 70,000 BC, ten thousand years after they taught spirituality to Atlanteans. At the beginning, Atlanteans did not understand that the Lamurians were communicating mentally, did not understand about their foreknowledge, and when the Atlanteans caught on, it was a tremendous revelation to them. They tried to duplicate it through technology, rather than through individual spiritual development. It was not good because it was not a spiritual gift.

The Lamurians who had these powers and abilities were incapable of enslaving anybody. They were spiritually developed and spiritual people do not do that. But the people of Atlantis were not spiritually developed and did reprehensible things to damage and control each other with technology. Atlanteans did the same thing when they went to Lamuria, which partly was responsible for Lamuria's destruction, in addition to the earthquakes and volcanoes.

Atlanteans had water power, wind power, solar power, and they also broadcast the power through crystals. Crystal vibrates at a certain frequency, so they used it to attune their power wave, and then broadcast the power waves to all the other crystal sets at that same frequency. They could put a little crystal on a small device, and the electricity would come to it and they could run it right out of little crystals.

Lamurians also used crystals for healing, but never to control or hurt others. Strangely, the spiritual development that Lamurians brought to Atlantis was part of the reason for the big problems. Misapplication of the spiritual knowledge caused a large part of the problem. Atlanteans did not have the spiritual background when they gained spiritual powers through technology. Here were these tremendous powers, technologically amplified, and not controlled by spiritual people. This was when the real evil started. A very spiritual person could not have done what these people did.

Accidental Freedom from Slavery and Escape

As described before, it started with the electrical power failure, when the power was interfered with and shut off by the fourth alien race of group two. It started in one area, where two power supplies failed, one after the other, and there was a noticeable gap in the power. The technician who was temporarily freed by the power failure threw the switch and turned it off because he was in the position to do it. All of a sudden, people were no longer controlled and they realized what their lives had been like; they knew that they had been kept as slaves. They also found out who their owners were. It was as if the people wised up all at once and took possession of the buildings, the towers where the masters, lived and started to kill them. Similar incidents happened in many cities of Atlantis.

Atlantis was also in physical turmoil. There were volcanic eruptions, earthquakes, and the land was sinking part-by-part and city-by-city. Once freed, people began to leave Atlantis. Mostly they left by boats and they sailed off in all directions. They went to North America, Central America, South America, Europe, Egypt, and Africa, depending on what side of Atlantis they were coming from. As Atlantis was going through its last stages, literally dying, people were leaving as fast as they could. One of my patients recalled a past life in Atlantis as follows:

• *"I am an eighteen-year-old female living in the city of Yadrilst, in the southeast part of Atlantis, on a peninsula between a river and an ocean. My name is Geneisha. This is about 26,455 BC. I am living in a laboratory complex. A long time before I was born, there was an uprising here and the people killed all the rulers. Then many people left the city. A large number boarded ships and boats and left, while others went to other places in Atlantis. I heard that my mother and father were in the dormitories, and when the control system broke down, they were freed. When my father saw my mother, he raped her, and my mom became pregnant with me. Then they kind of stayed together. My father left a few weeks after my birth and I stayed with my mother. When I was sixteen, my mother went on a boat to another country but I chose to stay in Atlantis. There are only a few people living in the city by now.*

"I grew up here after the control was gone, so I do not have repugnance for Atlantis like my parents and the others did. When I found the laboratory complex, I was fascinated by it and have been living there since. Here, Atlantis is unpopulated and civilization has broken down.

The people are gone, for the most part. There are only a few others and myself left in the city. I am not educated but I am fascinated by technology. I examine the photos, books, notes, and videotapes to try and figure out what technology was here.

"A ship has come with people from North Africa looking for treasures of Atlantis because they heard fantastic stories about how Atlantis is made of gold, how there is wealth in the streets to be picked up, and that there are all kinds of precious metals and jewels.

"First, they looked for gold and jewels and found very little of anything. Then they came to the technology lab. I tell them about what types of technology Atlantis had. I tell them about some of the wonders of Atlantis and about how they could send voices from here to far away, how they sent energy through the air, and about the machines that are still here. People in the expedition take a large portion of the lab supplies, such as the machines, books, charts, pictures, videos, and they also take me because I told them I am a technologist. Even though I cannot read or write, I can tell interesting stories. When the ship came close to the first island, which is heavily populated with people from Atlantis, the word spread from the dock that the ship was carrying a load of technology, and within an hour, there is a huge crowd of Atlanteans who had settled here, trying to get to the ship and burn it. Then, when they hear that there is a technologist on board, the crowd really gets nasty. I am terrified. Now they want to kill everyone aboard and then burn the ship. So the captain decides to sail away. The island was part of what is now known as the Canary Islands.

"The captain, the crew, nor I knew much about Atlantis because we were all young, and we were surprised at how the Atlantean settlers reacted. We are short on food and water, so life on the boat is getting tough. We are moving toward the Mediterranean and land in Africa. The crew is instructed not to tell anyone about the technology or

the technologist. The captain goes and talks to some people who tell him that the technology is worthless and they will not pay anything for it. These people did not want anything to do with it. It breaks the captain's heart. Looking around, he realizes that local people do not even use the technology that they already have, such as hammers, saws, and axes.

"The danger at the last port drove me and the captain together, and we are soon sleeping together. Time after time, when people find out about the technology, they try to kill us, so the captain eventually orders the machines to be thrown into the water in the interest of self-preservation. Then we go to Egypt. The captain is talking to some of the priests who are interested in burying the remaining books, pictures, and videotapes in caves to honor the memory of the Atlantean civilization as it used to be. They know people do not want technology at all and life is getting simpler and simpler. Machines are not being replaced after they break down. The captain sells about seven books, twelve eight-by-ten prints, and two videotapes at much less than he anticipated.

"The captain and I are living together in Egypt, but we are not married. He gets violent and beats me and then leaves on trade missions, so I am alone most of the time. I feel very out of place. I have light skin and light brown hair, and most of the people here have dark skin and dark hair. I stand out in a crowd. I sit at home and eat. I gained a lot of weight. I have one son and one daughter by the captain. I feel a nagging emptiness. I feel I was robbed of my technology. Being fat gives me status with the local people.

"At the age of twenty-nine, I go to the temple and see the statues of animal heads with human bodies or vice versa. I remember the captain talking about the priest to whom he sold the books and I ask the priest about them. He takes me aside and whispers that they are safe and put away. They are being preserved for the future.

He explains to me that if they try to bring them out, the people will destroy them and all of us, and so they have done the best they could. They have preserved everything and hidden them away, and he cannot tell me where they are. In fact, they have built a secret structure and only one priest knows where the books are taken and only one priest knows who did the construction and only one priest knows the exact location, so nobody can give the whole thing away. The structure is really hidden and not intended to be found at this time.

"He explains to me that there are maps that are hidden showing the location of the material that is buried. I am disappointed but I know I cannot do anything about it. I know what the priest says is true, that if I try to talk about the technology or claim to be a technologist out loud, I will be killed. There are many Atlanteans here, scattered around, and they do not want to hear about technology. They do not even want to connect with each other because that is how they grew up, in dorms being controlled through devices. They feel that Atlantis is dead and it should stay that way. They do not want to think or talk about Atlantis or technology. They do not want to remember. The local people have heard stories about Atlantis from traders and they are horrified too, so they do not want to talk about Atlantis either. It is just an accepted fact. There was a great revulsion brought on by the thought of Atlantis and what happened there. I also talked to the priest about the concept of life after life and wonder if it is true.

"By this time, the captain has made a lot of money and is out sailing most of the time. My children are married and on their own. They grow up as Egyptians. They work with mud and stone. Nobody uses any metal tools or machinery anymore. They are totally rejected by people, who are not passing any knowledge of them to their kids. I am all alone, overeating all the time to stuff my feelings, and have gained a lot of weight.

"At the age of fifty-four, I die on a hot, dry summer day while walking up a hill. I get chest pain and die wanting water, falling with my face in the dust. As I am dying, I think fatter is still better because society likes it. After a while, I see a white Light and angels in it who take me to heaven. They take me to a place where a being is sitting. I talk to him about how violent my husband was and how I hated him when he knocked me around. Also how bitter I feel about losing my technology and how unhappy I was with my life. I did not feel that I belonged anywhere and felt no connections to anybody. After venting my feelings, I feel better.

"Then I am sent for cleansing on a beach, as I did in life on Earth. The attendant asked me to take my clothes off so I can clean better, but I refused to do it. As I go under the water, my clothes disappear, and as I come back out, a different set of clothes appear. I come out slimmer than I was when I went into the water. Then I am sent to another room for my life review. I am astonished to see the different animal-head gods I saw in the temple of Egypt, and I ask them if they are real. They tell me that they are the representation of God here in the Light, but those statues were not God; they were just stone statues. Since the Egyptians thought of them as gods when they prayed to them, they, who are just different aspects of the one true God, responded to their prayers. There were nine of these animal-head gods who were there helping me to review. They were just taking these forms, which the people in Egypt believed in, to make people feel more at ease in heaven. They explain that they are here to help me review my life and not to judge me in any way. They tell me that I need to look at what I planned before entering into that life and how I did.

"As I look back at Atlantis from heaven, I see what happened in the city to cause the uprising before I was born. Alien race four of group two interfered by beaming through two different directions and caused an electrical problem. A

part melted, got soft, and separated because the temperature increased. As a result, the current was interrupted and the machines stopped working. A technologist reached over and turned the switch off, causing a loss of control of the people. As soon as the control was interrupted, the first thing people experienced was a momentary loss of balance and jarring. Then came the realization that they had been controlled and what had been done to them, and a sweeping rage overcame them. They focused on who was responsible for it. The uprising began first at the palace. All of a sudden, anger erupted in people and they killed the rulers. Then the second wave of the revolt came from the common people in the dorms. They broke free and killed the rest of the people in the palace.

"The machines were broken and destroyed before the technologists could get them repaired. Everyone was blaming different people. The junior priests blamed senior priests, junior technologists blamed senior technologists, and the common people focused on the rulers. Junior technologists killed their supervisors; then the common people came and killed them, and then they began to fight with each other. There was a medical crisis for days due to the rioting and violence toward each other from all the anger erupting. Many people headed to other parts of Atlantis and others went to the docks and got rides on ships and boats and some stayed there in the city and set up households.

"When the rioters went to the palace, they found bodies of the rulers and others who were killed during the revolt. They also found cooked body parts. The common people had no knowledge of the rulers eating people and they were horrified and talked about it for a while. I see that there were about 150,000 people living in that city. When the revolt happened, it went down to 50,000. There were only a few hundred people left in the city by the time I was eighteen.

"I see from heaven that my mother and father were living in their dorms, totally controlled. After the control was

gone, they were out on the streets feeling normal sexual impulses for the first time. When my father saw my mother on the street, he grabbed her and dragged her off and raped her because he probably did not know any other way to deal with his feelings. But then he stayed with her because it seemed like the right thing to do at the time, but then he left her four or five weeks after my birth. I was brought up by my mother in that abandoned city. There were many empty dwellings and we could move anywhere we wanted, and we changed houses pretty often. There were thousands of dwelling places but only a few hundred people.

"When I was sixteen, my mother was sick of Atlantis because it was a bad place with revolting memories. She left Atlantis on a boat. I chose to stay because I was not revolted by Atlantis. I was born after the revolt and I was fascinated by some of the things I found in the technology lab. I began to collect the material and tried to figure out the technology, but I did not succeed. I got the ideas but not the facts.

"The heavenly beings are saying that humanity cannot afford to repeat the flaws of Atlantis. According to my plan, I was to get the story out about what had happened there, almost like a history account, with the technology material to back it up, and get it out where it could be preserved and found sometime in the future and I succeeded in doing it.

"My husband's unreasonable violence was set in motion as a karmic make-up for some of the tortures I did to him in the past lives. I was supposed to diffuse his anger and get a relationship going. Also, I was to experience in another way the helplessness I had inflicted on others in a past life. I experienced helplessness by moving to a foreign country and by losing the technology material, and also by the abusive behavior of my husband. I see from heaven that my husband's mother was a prostitute. He was raised on the docks and often slept under the docks. She often beat and starved him.

"From heaven, I see that many problems came to me from that life to the current life, such as my weight problems, arthritis in my knees and ankles because of the weight, feelings of being disconnected and empty inside, feelings of being an outsider, and sinus problems. I also have teeth problems because of the beatings and having my teeth knocked out, and thinning hair because of having my hair pulled out of my scalp, and pain in my feet because of walking everywhere. I also have skin problems due to sunburn.

"From heaven, I see that the priests put the technology stuff in chests and sealed them and put the chest into a stone container and then buried in an underground chamber. Since then, the ground shape has changed. The chamber is on the Gaza Plateau, seventy-five yards east of the Sphinx, just ahead of the front legs, and is filled in with dirt. The priests also buried histories of places, commercial records, stories, myths, religious records, and anything else they could find. The chambers are interconnected. There are several chambers just packed with such things and fully preserved. They coated each page with beeswax and then coated the books in beeswax and sealed them in jars, hoping that someday someone will find them and read them. The Sphinx was already there, and is more than 30,000 years old, but the pyramids were not built yet.

"I see that I am the one to point the way and help in finding the buried information. I will participate in the search and its dissemination because there will be attempts to suppress it."

Dispersion From Atlantis

As mentioned before, Lamuria sank in about 70,000 BC, about ten thousand years after Lamurians and Atlanteans were in contact. Lamurians had already colonized in South

America, North America, Central America, and Atlantis. The destruction of Lamuria was known to the people of Atlantis. According to my hypnotized patients, as Atlantis was sinking, most of the dispersion was to the east of Atlantis. This was for several reasons. First, the primary seaports of Atlantis were on the east coast. The majority of the large ships and the transportation sources were in the northeast. So the majority of the ships headed toward the port they knew the best. The boats made multiple trips. The majority of the Atlanteans went to the Mediterranean Basin, settling in the areas around Italy, Greece, the coast of Asia Minor, Egypt, and some in North Africa. Some of the Atlanteans went to the west coast of Europe, what is currently Spain, a few to Portugal, and a few further north to France, England, and Ireland. There were small ships in other parts of Atlantis. Some did go to South America, some to Central America, and a few went to North America. The power grid was maintained in Atlantis for a period of time and still had the air-transmitted electric energy power after the overthrowing of the masters.

One of my patients recalled a life as follows.

• *"I am a forty-four-year-old female living in a tribe in Southern Michigan. My name is Wada Harily, and this is 15,220 BC. I live with my parents and siblings. We are a peaceful tribe and we trade shellfish, shells, and stone beads that we make with quartz stones. Everybody is helpful and acts civilized, and there is no violence in our society. We do not have any technology. Our tribe has refined features, more like Asians. We are short, with straight black hair and reddish skin.*

"There are stories about a tribe called the Arquay moving our way. We hear that they are nasty. They make war and kill people. I feel that maybe it is a trade gimmick, but it turns out to be true. They would rather take by force than trade peacefully. I hear that these people came from Atlantis. They are vile and violent people. These are the

upper class people who sailed out of the northwest part of Atlantis and were carried along by the currents. It is a mixed group. There are Atlanteans who moved here and they mixed with native people. These tribes of Atlantean-Indians attack, torture, kill, rob, and occupy the land before moving to a different place.

"When they came close to our place in Michigan, we heard stories that you cannot talk to these people, so we were prepared to fight. When they attacked us, we fought, but we lost. These attackers have dark brown skin, short brown hair, and long, straight noses. They catch and tie me down to a stake. They build a fire around my feet just for the fun of it. As the fire reaches my feet and I try to move, they laugh and beat me. They cut open my back, break my ribs, and take out my kidneys. Others are poking at me with sharp sticks. I am scalped with stone knives and my eyes are poked out with sticks. I die of bleeding and pain, asking God to remove my attackers from the face of the Earth.

"After the death of my body, I want to get away from these people. I see my mom in a bright Light and she takes me to heaven. I am taken to a room where there are two Light beings waiting for me. They ask me to talk about my death. I tell them about the terrible torture. I feel like I failed because I could not change them. The rest of my life before was fairly good. After cleansing, I am sent to another room for a life review with three Light beings.

"From heaven, I see that I felt they could be changed to work, to create and trade rather than just steal and destroy, but I was wrong. This also became our tribe's biggest drawback because the other tribe did not show any mercy, and we were not prepared to fight.

"One of my personal goals in that life was to promote a more complete use of the animals that were killed, to avoid more killing, and making sure that everything that came from the animals be completely used. I also tried to find a way of preserving meat and hide so it would not rot.

I succeeded in this. I got the distribution system set up in our tribe; that is why we did not need to hunt as much. But it had a drawback. We did not have any weapons to fight that violent tribe.

"My group goal was to create a respect for civilized life. The lesson we needed to learn was that even though we promote spiritual life styles, we have to maintain a balance to survive, to protect, and to compete in the world, and until everyone comes to the same understanding, we are still going to get renegades.

"From heaven, I see what happened to the Atlantean culture after the sinking of Atlantis. Few of the ruling groups escaped and the many who went to Europe and Africa did not survive. They were killed because the people there had much more knowledge about what had been going on, while the Indians in North America had no knowledge of it. They landed in what is now northern New Jersey and began to attack, torture, and kill people and take whatever they could. They were there for about five hundred years. They continued to take over different tribes since nobody defended themselves. They made no attempt to join with any other tribe. The big surprise came when they ran into another group in Seneca and met a tribe whose members were similar to them, with the same language and customs. Then they found a third group like themselves. They had all come from Atlantis with the north current, but landed in different places in North America and spread by attacking and taking over. Another group of Atlanteans landed in Canada and settled there. In time, these Atlanteans intermingled with local Indian tribes, but their language and attitudes were different from ours."

My hypnotized patients state that most of the people were gone by the time the final destruction occurred. The destruction was caused by the submersion of the lock of land on which Atlantis was located. This was at a time of rising sea levels, and as parts of Atlantis submerged into the sea, the pressures were built up for many, many years. When the final break came, it was violent and catastrophic. New volcanoes did emerge and erupt. The plate on which Atlantis was situated did bend and stretch, tearing the land apart. As the plate bent and submerged, the sea rose around the land and terrible earthquakes and many new volcanoes sprouted into existence. There was a lot of noise and confusion and shaking of the Earth. Of those who were left in Atlantis when the end came, none of them could escape.

The Atlanteans who escaped were very troubled for a couple of generations. Most of them were common people. Most of the rulers had been murdered, and many of the technicians and priestly class were also killed. Those who responded quickly and ran straight to the harbor and went on the ship without preparation survived the best. Those who waited had a harder time, because there was a lack of transportation

Those who were not wiped out by flood or tidal waves escaped to Spain, Portugal, and to North Africa. The ones who made it to the Mediterranean Basin were pretty safe. They did experience the fluctuating water levels but were saved from the tidal waves. Most of those who went to Spain died there. Those who stayed on the coastal areas did not survive. This reduced the number of the Atlantean survivors and it may account for the lack of any indication of the remains in the Central, South, and North Americas.

According to heavenly beings, the very basic cause was that the crust block on which Atlantis was located tilted and dropped and took Atlantis under the water. People were totally controlled by the demons and they did not turn toward God and ask for help. So God could not do anything. Actually, the demons took the underpinning from underneath Atlantis and let it fall.

Atlantis and Trade Routes

This knowledge was given by an angel named Namesh, through my hypnotized patient. Angel Namesh claimed to have special knowledge and has worked extensively with people who make their living on the sea by traveling, trading, or by fishing. According to him, it may not make sense to the readers that a country that is in contact with only the fringes of Europe, Africa, and South, Central, and North Americas could have so much influence all over the world. How did the news of Atlantis spread from culture to culture? How did Atlantean influence and downfall become known and affect so many people in so many different places? They never really crossed any of the Americas; they never made it deep into the inland areas of Europe or Africa. How then did their influence and the knowledge of them spread around the world and their downfall have such a profound effect on everyone?

The real-life, horrifying tales make very interesting telling for human beings. The information came out of Atlantis during its downfall, during the Dark Ages and during the worst of times. The news was carried around the world on trade routes. We are not aware that there were extensive trade routes around the world at that time. People believe that, at that time, humans were primitive savages and incapable of moving across continents or oceans, but it is not true.

According to the angel Namesh, a civilization existed long before the current civilization. Ocean-going travel was possible and was engaged in. This appears to be new information and people might wonder why is it that nothing shows up on the face of the Earth to indicate that these things occurred. However, information to this effect does occur, but it is disbelieved. It is not accepted as belonging to the time period when Atlantis existed. One of the reasons is that there have been profound changes on the Earth since the time of Atlantis.

The continents do rise and fall. The sea level does change. Atlantis existed during the ice ages. During the last ice age, the sea level was drastically different. Things within hundreds and hundreds of kilometers of the shore have disappeared completely. During the very coldest part of the ice age, there were huge quantities of water locked up in ice sheets. Much of the land on which mankind lived is now on the ocean's bottom. All of the works, all traces of mankind, have been obliterated. The areas that were mineral rich and literally gardens of fruit and honey are now under the sea. Indications of any ocean-going ships, which were comparatively primitive by our standards, are gone. Monuments and cities that were built have been covered over. Some of them have been found but have been misinterpreted. There is proof that these objects were created a long, long time ago, forty-, fifty- or even one-hundred thousand years ago, yet they are ignored because it is believed that it could not possibly be true. Man could not have been created that long ago. Yet, it is true.

At that time, the climate belts were different and habitable areas were also different. The north part of Africa, what is now the Sahara Desert, was a lush, green, growing area. The belt of dry area was substantially smaller and further south. Vessels easily sailed around Africa and trade routes existed from Africa into Asia and also into the Indies. From China, trade routes went north, then across the Pacific Ocean to the Americas. It was not uncommon for men to travel back and forth between the continents.

The trip across the North Pacific was much easier than the trip across the South Pacific. The traffic tended to be one way, to go from Asia to North America. Very seldom did travelers actually make the round trip. There was travel from Europe and Africa to South America, and when Atlantis was not in the way, to Central and North America.

These trade routes at certain periods in the past were well established. Information and goods flowed freely. Human curiosity was no less at that time than it is today. Atlantis, at that time, was one of the leading jewels on the Earth. People all over the world knew of Atlantis. To some, it was a fairy tale; to some, it was a living neighbor with whom they engaged in trade. The tales of Atlantis sparked wonder in people and it was thought of as a golden land and a wonderful place to be.

When Atlantis entered into the Dark Ages and the people of the world began to hear horrific tales of how the people were losing their free will and being controlled, it turned people's hearts and they rejected this information. It was hard to bear, yet the tales were repeated again and again until they spread across the continents. The true wonder was that people continued to go to Atlantis for trade, and since the profit was great, it was a wonderful incentive. As Atlantis became more and more withdrawn, more and more under the control of its rulers, the danger to the outside world that Atlantis represented before grew less and less. As the tales from Atlantis became even more horrible, the word spread around the world, following both the land and sea trade routes. The tales entered deep into the human psyche and became a real part of human psychology. Though Atlantis had previously been the golden jewel in the crown of creation in the history of civilization, it became the depth of depravity.

When Atlantis finally collapsed and the great slaughter of the noble classes began, people flocked away from Atlantis. The fact that there were survivors to recount the horrors blew a fuse in the collective human consciousness. Everything that Atlantis was, everything that it ever stood for, was rejected. It was pushed so far aside that humanity entered a period of psychological gap, thinking this can no longer be nor will we let it exist. The history, the culture, the technology, and the civilization were all rejected. People all over the world slipped from a civilized state back into a stone age where the technology of making things and using sophisticated techniques disappeared. They went back to the primitive hunt-and-seek form of existence.

This happened over the course of two generations. First was the generation that did the initial forgetting, and the generation after them did not get the knowledge of the culture from their immediate ancestors. So the drop-off of humanity was like falling off a cliff. The population also decreased because of Earth changes due to the ice age. As the climate warmed and sea levels rose because of ice melting, there were floods all over in which many people died. The fertile lands along the sea, which had been seacoast plains used for many different crops, were covered by water and mankind was forced to move inland.

This was a time of great hardship because the climate belts were shifting. The crops that grew in a given climate belt now had to be grown in a different climate belt where people were not used to raising these crops. There was a drop off in the food supply but plenty of water everywhere. Life was difficult at that time and the changes were profound.

The melting of the glaciers and great ice sheets affected everyone on Earth, and the changing of the climate belts happened everywhere on Earth. The rising and falling of the land was occurring everywhere. The story of Atlantis and what happened was known worldwide. It was not just limited to those areas directly in contact with Atlantis. These changes began around forty thousand years ago and continued for a long time, until most of Atlantis was gone under water, about 20,000 BC.

As the glaciers melted, water collected. When it was finally released, the flood was tremendous and caused terrible effects, such as cutting valleys through the land, and God have mercy on anyone who was in the way.

Those who were in the right location and were wise loaded their possessions and their animals onto an ark (a boat) and escaped the dangerous situation. The story of Noah's Ark was about Atlantis, and entered the human consciousness in terms of the evil on the Earth before the arks sailed, and everyone knew the story of Atlantis. Everyone knew of the evil that was practiced there and that cannibalism had become a way of life. There was total control of society and the people had no free will. These things were reported by those who traded with Atlantis. For the most part, they were free to wander around the coastal cities when they made their trade stops.

The rulers of the coastal cities were glad to trade with them. Things had deteriorated in Atlantis to the point where they no longer had some of the luxuries they had had in the past. The traders were welcomed and the Atlanteans were pleased to pay for them.

It was terrible for outsiders to see how the noble classes lived as compared to the tortures and indignities of the common folk, who had become like cattle. Originally, it was behind closed doors, but then it became an institutionalized way of life, with total control of the population. There was nothing to fear. The population was not able to rise and revolt. Atlanteans did not think of controlling people who came to trade because they were supplying luxury items to them.

Traders and travelers still did not have specific information about what was going on in the noble houses, but they could see what was happening on the streets. They could see that the people had been forced to move closer to the cities. There were vast areas of the country that were not inhabited, and farming and the raising of animal had decreased dramatically. The ruling classes wanted everyone under their control to be close enough to the transmitters to be fully controlled. They could not afford to have a population in the open countryside. If one lord tried putting transmitters there, the lord of the next city would destroy it. He would not want to take a chance of his population coming under the other lord's control. Jealousy and individual self-interest kept the portions of Atlantis outside the cities free from control.

The rulers could not afford to have people living in those areas where they could not control them. Some of that was farm land, so farming dropped off and there was not much food. It became a serious situation, and as the population of Atlantis declined, the ruling classes began to eat them. For some, murder and cannibalism came first, and for others, as the food supplies were drying up, they made use of a handy supply of human meat. The shock to humanity was so great that such a tragedy had a worldwide influence.

Mechanism of Mass Amnesia After Atlantis

It will not make sense to some people that, after Atlantis fell, there was such an intense psychological reaction to the pain and suffering that within two generations mankind had completely renounced all Atlantean technology, science, and history, and literally started out from scratch again. In the space of two generations, they went from a technological society back to the Stone Age. It will be hard for most readers to believe that this could happen. I know I had a hard time believing and understanding it too.

During one session, a heavenly being named John, who is enlightened and had a lot of experience with Atlantis, stated, through my hypnotized patient, that he was here to lend his knowledge and expertise and will help us with a lot of information about Atlantis. He gave the following information about himself:

• *"I think of myself as John. I have had many names and many different lives. We have many names in the universe but only one name in heaven. We become the same person in heaven when we return. John is my chosen name. My original name by which I am known in heaven is Maltaguize. The soul comes into existence knowing its name after it is separated from God. I have lived many lives in multiple universes and I lived many lives in Atlantis. I overcame the ill effects coming from the lives in Atlantis, but most humans are still struggling to overcome the bad effects from Atlantis. Most humans have resolved at least half of their problems. It has not been that long since Atlantis was destroyed and humans are making very fast progress. I am enlightened, but I might come back in the universe to help. I am here to help you understand what happened to humanity after the destruction of Atlantis."*

John, through my hypnotized patient, explained that we really have to understand the psychological devastation that mankind suffered in Atlantis; otherwise, it will not make sense to us that things could change that quickly. Before the fall of Atlantis, there was a thriving trade network in the world. There was an exchange of goods and an exchange of ideas. People were moving from place to place, intermingling with groups and cultures, and there was trade between Atlantis and modern day Spain, Egypt, Africa, and the Near East. Then all of a sudden, everything was cut off and there was no more trade. The culture that was capable of so much disappeared from the face of the Earth.

Even during the Ice Age, trade existed and ships would sail. Even in areas where there was ice, frequently the ice would be inland and the coastal strip would be populated. Then maybe there would be two glaciers with a wide strip of green ground between them, stretching far to the north, where people would roam and hunt animals, which were in abundance.

We have to understand the extent of human revulsion to what happened in Atlantis and the renunciation of everything that made Atlantis what it was. It is sad to realize how trade stopped; ocean sailing ships were allowed to rot and air travel was allowed to disappear. Advances in medicine, electronics, and electricity disappeared. People just would not use them. They would not teach their young about them, and they reverted to a more primitive culture. At the end of the second generation, mankind was practically back to a Stone Age culture.

This will not make sense to many readers, and it is really important to understand how severely this affected humanity. There was literally a total mass amnesia and Atlantis disappeared from history and from human consciousness. Mankind forgot what the technological advances were, what tortures the Atlanteans went through, and how trade with other parts of the world was allowed to disappear from the face of the Earth. Everything was forced out of the human mind as if it never existed.

The primary mechanism for the worldwide amnesia was that the soul rejected the darkness and sought the Light. Turning against that what was so dark led to a healing time, a time of connection to Earth, a time of connecting to nature, allowing the collective healing of the human psyche. People deliberately tried to purge those memories from their souls. By disowning those soul parts that contained those awful memories, and setting them aside, people hoped that they would be safe and protected. As John was saying, the patient perceived the Egyptian canopic jars. The Egyptians, when they entombed a body, would remove the internal organs and put them in separate jars so they would not rot or decay in the body. Then they placed these canopic jars, as they were called, in the tomb along with the mummy. This was a symbolic expression of what John was saying about separating out the soul parts of themselves with the traumatic memories and putting them into spiritual containers, thinking that they were safe, but they were not. At this point, according to the patient, Ascended Master John, who was giving this information, was literally tearful and sobbing.

According to John, it was a desperate attempt to get rid of the evil that was in Atlantis, and those soul parts had to be purged for their own purity. Unfortunately, it was not inspired by the Light but was from the darkness. It was a satanic plot to make people give away the soul parts that held memories of Atlantis. People tried to protect the soul parts at the subconscious level in these spiritual canopic containers and separate them from the main body of their souls, but they were grabbed by the demons and stored in hell. From there on, the demons used those soul parts to manipulate and influence those people in future lives over and over, repeating the same Atlantean behavioral patterns. It was a satanic plan.

The result was a total amnesia throughout mankind, because they got rid of the soul parts that held memories of the Atlantean culture and evil behavior. This was the soul mechanism to get rid of those memories. By that time, almost every human being on Earth had lived in Atlantis. The intensity of the intent and the sheer determination caused a total purging of memories by giving up those soul parts containing the awful memories, and thus created total mass amnesia throughout the humankind.

The healing and destructive powers of the mind are startling. In this case, it was a choice of fragmenting to purge out that portion of the soul that held the memories of Atlantis. The patient described the mechanism as follows.

- *"I see that all the memories of Atlantis are pushed out in the portion of the soul part that was going to be separated. It looks like a brittle crystal, and when it is detached, instead of coming out in a nice neat chunk, all of a sudden hundreds and thousands of parts are floating around here and there. They look dark. Many of them were pushed out of the body. I see slightly less than half of the soul from each person was pushed out and grabbed by the demons and stored in hell. As a result, mankind developed total mass amnesia about Atlantis. They became more vacuous, spacey and kind of distant. There was no desire to own things and there was no reason to pass on the knowledge. There was a desire to purge the Atlantean knowledge and the memories."*

John is saying that, you are divinely inspired to heal every human being who ever lived on Atlantis by cleansing, healing, and bringing their soul parts back from Satan, his demons, people, places, and hell. Almost every human being has lived in Atlantis and benefited due to the healing you are asking for them, and as a result, they will have a chance to grow and evolve faster.

When you prayed to God and requested the angels to locate and bring back soul parts of every human being who ever lived in Atlantis, from Satan, his demons, people, places, and hell, and integrate them with whom they belong, after cleansing and healing, I saw it all happening on a massive scale. I see almost every human being is receiving the soul parts and healing.

It is possible to go through more world changes in the future, and it is up to us to develop ourselves spiritually now, not just to prevent it, but if it is not preventable, through spirituality we can modify the effects on the human race.

The Great Forgetting and Descent of Mankind to the Stone Age

Mankind was obviously in a very high technological state at the fall of Atlantis. However, it was not uniformly spread around the globe. In fact, the highest of the technology was limited only to Atlantis. By the time Lamuria and Atlantis were gone, the other continents were nearly the same as they exist today. What little technology had come from the aliens to Atlantis disappeared. The technology that Atlantis had exported to different places also disappeared.

After Lamuria and Atlantis were destroyed, people of Europe, Africa, the Mediterranean Basin, South, Central, and North America were all in communication, at least right after Atlantis sank. Then the survivors of Atlantis, with their rejection of technology and the fact that the natives of the other countries never had the heavy-duty technology, caused a rapid drop of technology. Within three or four generations, the descendants of Atlantis knew very little about what Atlanteans previously had. They were not even aware that they descended from Atlantis. Most of the amnesia developed by the survivors was due to the psychological rejection of Atlantis and its technology, but some of it was also due to the brain function being interfered with, due to implants.

After the dispersion from Atlantis, things went downhill rapidly. Some of the technicians survived, but nobody wanted to use technology again and they did not pass on the knowledge. Others were of the general population who had no knowledge about technology. They were too fresh from the effects of the evil. They underwent a complete revulsion and avoidance of technology, and in three or four generations, they completely forgot that the technology had ever existed. The great-grandchildren absolutely had no knowledge of it, because the parents and grandparents did not speak of it. Once the technological descent began, people abandoned the cities. It was rapid, and humanity was literally reduced to wandering the Earth, living in caves. They lost agriculture, lost practically all their skills, and had to redevelop from scratch. Times got hard, food supply was not great, and the weather turned colder. The population did decline and it was hard for mankind, as described in the following case histories:

- *"I am a twenty-four-year-old female. I have a child. It is about 14,400 BC. We are trying to walk over a mountain in a group in Turkey to go to the other side and see what is there. As we are crossing the mountains, there is an earthquake. I am scared stiff about the earth shaking. I've never experienced that before. I hear the rumble, and as I look up, I see a rock sliding towards me, but I stand stiff, as if I am paralyzed. My child is with my mother, and my husband is walking ahead with the group. As the rock falls on me, my head is crushed and I die. I go to heaven after a while.*

  "From heaven, as I look back in that life, I see that this lifetime was generations after the destruction of Atlantis. Technology is completely lost. Mankind is all fragmented and there are no memories of Atlantis, as if it never was. People have abandoned cities and are living in groups in primitive ways.

  "From heaven, I see that my headaches, neck pain, and eye problems came from that life to the current life."

***

• *"I am a woman. I am wearing animal fur. It is 13,000 BC. We are in Australia. My skin is darker. We have a hard life. We don't live long. We are fearful, so we do not interact with other tribes. We stay to ourselves. We do not fight with them. We live as a tribe and we are focused on survival. We do not have a strong sense of lineage. People appear inbred. We do not have marriages and we do not keep track of who our grandparents were. We live in caves. Men do the hunting and women take care of the babies. We use fire. We do not have any other facilities or technology. We travel in the tribe and sometimes we see other tribes. Otherwise, we do not have any contact with other human beings and have no knowledge of any other civilization.*

"My hypnotized patients state that it was from about 20,000 BC to 15,000 BC when, after leaving Atlantis, there was the total rejection of technology. They did not want any technology around them. They wanted to live a simple, primitive life. In three to four generations, they went from the technological society that was a very sophisticated civilization to practically back to being a caveman. It happened worldwide. People just gave up technology and did not want to live together in big cities. They spread across the countryside. There was farming in small villages. For a period of time, people insisted on being primitive and non-technological. Lots of memories were forgotten. The most sophisticated and technological stuff was gone completely. Small memories of it here and there, but nothing on which to really build.

"People went back to primitive farming and hunting, and manufactured simple stone objects. They even abandoned the cities and the villages and moved into the wild. It was a complete rejection of technology and society. In four generations, mankind had returned to a pretty primitive tribal state. They separated one from another, mixed in with the indigenous people who were already there. Technology and civilization of Atlantis was pretty well forgotten in four generations.

"As the generations went by, they began to lose that dread of technology and the dread of advancing civilization. Society started back literally after the Stone Age. Metals came back fairly quickly, and those who had the memories of metals and how to extract them and use them had a real advantage over anybody else. They began to rebuild, and for a long time, it appeared as if this civilization came from nothing. When the civilization came back and larger cities and rulers came in around 12,000 BC, people had stories of their ancestors. The histories their ancestors had given by mouth, with no real perception of what the generations went through. So they were not as frightened of it as their ancestors were.

"This produced part of the illusion that before the cavemen there was nothing, because the population got to be so small that we do not find many traces. We find very old monuments but we think they could not possibly be made by cavemen. We do not think these old monuments could be 100,000 years old, because we know there were cavemen 15,000 years ago. So there is no question in our minds that humans could not have possibly built the monuments, because they did not have what it took."

Ice Age

Heavenly beings, through my hypnotized patients, stated that there had been many ice ages on the Earth. The most recent ice age began about 100,000 years ago. There was a slow buildup of ice and snow in the northern regions and in the high mountains. Then about 80,000 years ago, the ice started to break up and spread out across the globe. About 30,000 BC, the ice had reached its peak expansion, spreading to all the high mountains, expanding from the north to the land south of it, and expanding from the south into the north. At this time, Atlantis did exist but it was further south of the ice sheet origin.

This ice age occurred primarily because the sun put out less energy. The climate of the Earth cooled; snow fell and did not melt so that there were the huge sheets of ice-packed snow spreading over large areas, coming out of the high mountains to cover the lowlands, coming from the north to cover the more southern portions. This ice and snow reflected the sunlight, so less energy was kept on Earth. The ice sheets kept advancing until there was a change in the climate on Earth, and when it began to warm up again, the ice started to retreat. This ice age began when Atlantis still existed, but there would not have been any ice sheets there, anyway. It was too far south.

The glaciers spread slowly. It was a worldwide event, with the ice expanding and habitable land getting smaller. This happened primarily because the average temperature of the Earth decreased and there was less sunshine. The moderate climate belt of Earth shifted and the extreme cold belt moved farther south. As the glaciers grew and the sunlight decreased, the extreme cold areas expanded even further south. Finally, all the warmth that was there was locked in the narrow band of land, and times became very hard for the people. There was a scarcity of resources, and climate condition was less favorable, so the population of the Earth declined. Life was harder, especially without technology.

The ice sheets began to retreat about 30,000 BC, and by 15,000 BC, the Earth started to shift into a warmer climate. Life became easier and civilization began to reestablish itself. By this time, people had forgotten all about the previous civilization. There were only occasional stories recorded in some repository of knowledge somewhere.

After the ice left, mankind once again slowly expanded all over the globe. Their numbers increased and people started to live in communities again. They began to build villages and then cities. People were agriculturally inclined, raising crops, but were quite primitive in social structure. Generally, there was a king ruling over a city. The king originally assumed power because he had the support of a group of people who were able to fight for him and he controlled by the force of arms. Very few kings were democratically elected or appointed.

Evidence of Atlantis Existing

When Atlantis first sank, there was a lot of matter going into the ocean. Some climate changes also occurred during this time period. It was cold in the north and glaciers did form, which made the habitable band for humanity narrower on Earth. After the Ice Age, humanity went back to the civilization mode and started to rebuild their societies. All of a sudden, it looked like civilizations were springing up full-blown from nothing, but that was not the case. Humanity was there and it was civilized. Humans were in small groups in villages. When they decided to reestablish society, they moved together. When they did this, all of a sudden, it seemed that civilization was there and there was no place to show where it came from, no observable developmental process.

When we look at some of the old things that are around, chances are that some of the things were built of long-lasting stone, and they were not destroyed over the years because the land was high. We are looking at things that are twenty, thirty, forty, or fifty thousand years old.

According to my hypnotized patients, monuments and massive structures were built during Atlantis. The Sphinx in Egypt was carved out of living rock, the bedrock itself. This was during the period of time when Egypt was a moist, green land. The Sphinx turned out to be of soft rock that eroded fairly rapidly, and within a few thousand years, it was obvious that the Sphinx was deteriorating. In order to protect the Sphinx, it was covered with dirt. According to heavenly beings, the Sphinx was carved about thirty thousand years ago. The Sphinx preceded the pyramids by an extended period.

Archeologists and scientists have a great deal of difficulty in dealing with the incongruities they keep finding. They find evidence that some things are much older than they could possibly be. Humanity descended from a high technological people to literally Stone Age savages living hand to mouth. The human race barely survived and then built itself back up. It was as if the purging was necessary to get rid of Atlantis memories, sort of a cleansing by fire. The Stone Age began about twenty thousand years ago. At this time, there were already great monuments on Earth. There were cities of stone and plenty of indications of astronomical alignment that these things were actually done in real antiquity (old times) and not within modern memory.

Search for Remains of Atlantis

Heavenly beings, through my hypnotized patients, claim that some of the evidence of the existence of Atlantis could be found on the islands of the Atlantic Ocean. These islands are separated by dozens of miles, but were geologically joined before Atlantis was ripped apart. There is identical geology from one island to the other, separated because of what happened when the plates on which Atlantis was located buckled and settled. These areas also have moved since the destruction of Atlantis, toward the southwest, as the crust plate is moved.

According to the heavenly beings, much of Atlantis is buried too deeply to be found, and the central eastern coast of the mountainous area is primarily what is showing above the sea level now. The traces that are found on the sea floor were from the uplands, the higher areas that were not much populated and did not have many signs of human habitation. The areas where we can find evidences of human habitation are in and around the Bahamas, Virgin Islands, Cuba, and Hispaniola. By going to the deeper areas around them, we can find more evidence of human habitation in areas that have not gone under the crust block yet. They will not be found by visual surface inspection because they are covered with debris, which settled at the bottom of the ocean over the years.

Heavenly beings, through my patients, state that the evidence can be located with electronic exploration techniques that will require considerable interpretation before people understand what they are looking at, which is the network of temples, houses, and apartment buildings. There is an area south of Puerto Rico, Virgin Islands, and Hispaniola where, about nine hundred feet down, is a very nice community still pretty well preserved, but deeply buried under silt, and it can be found. People may not understand what they find. Only advanced analysis can lead them to the understanding that this was a living community that had been submerged.

The islands in the Atlantic Ocean are the mountainous areas of Atlantis. There was not much population there, and as a result, there were no signs of civilizations, except some paving blocks, carved pillars, carved stones; nothing that would be considered conclusive proof. These proofs are further under the ocean, in the area that was the coastal plain, a comparatively flat land or uplands where there was a sizable human population. The areas that had the most people and the most artifacts are so deep in the Atlantic Ocean that they can never be found.

Evidence of Atlantis can also be found in North, South, and Central America. There were tidal waves, which caused considerable destruction. If we look in to the southern United States and the Yucatan Peninsula in Mexico, we will find evidence of massive tidal waves all the way into the jungles of Venezuela and northern South America. Most of the tidal waves went to the west because that was the direction the crustal plate settled. There was also some damage to the east. It did hit Africa and Europe but was much weaker in terms of the waves.

According to the heavenly beings, we can find evidence of the catastrophe in North, Central, and South America, along many miles inland of the current coast. We can find boulders and rocks that do not belong there. We will find evidence of great deposits. There was much physical damage caused when the waves came in and ripped up forests and carried the trees along with it. When the waves reached a valley and died in the mountain chains and all settled together, they left huge layers of thousands of fossilized tree trunks intermingled with a lot of sediment and the boulder. This is particularly noted in southern United States and in the mountains of Central America.

My hypnotized patients state that there are valleys in Georgia, Tennessee, and North Carolina that are filled with this deposit. If we drill into those valleys, which appear to be plains now, we will hit areas of layers of boulders, left-over fossilized tree trunks, and lots of silt deposits. Tidal waves moved inland till they hit mountainous areas, and before running out of steam, caused tremendous destruction. The worst of the damage occurred in South, Central, and North America.

Patients under hypnosis reported that, after the dispersion from Atlantis, people developed selective amnesia. They rejected Atlantean culture and technology and went back to being primitive, and in three or four generations, memories of Atlantis were totally forgotten. They did not pass on any stories; they did not talk about it, did not write about it, and did not pass on any knowledge of technology. What was written was by the natives, and these are the records that can be found in some places. They were primarily preserved in Egypt, and some of them may be found in jars stored in caves. Some of the records were made in Spain and many other places, but they decayed and are lost.

Atlanteans did not want to keep records. They were literate and could read and write, but they rejected the experiences so thoroughly that they did not write down what happened. Only the natives of Egypt and other countries who lived there all along and were not subject to the trials and tribulations the people of Atlantis went through were willing to do the writing and recording. They wrote what they learned from people who were there and who had seen what happened. They knew from common conversation at that time, and when Atlantis broke up, they wrote down what they heard and knew. It was as accurate as an objective reporter can write about an event he did not live through.

One of my patients gave the following description of a life in Egypt:

- *"I am a twenty-three-year-old male priest living in Egypt. My name is Rafractos and this is 14,988 BC. I am about five feet ten inches tall and have brown skin. My head is shaved except for a small pigtail in the back. I am named after the god, Ra. My parents dedicated me to the temple of Ra. I was their fifth child, so they gave me to the temple as soon as I was able to walk because there were too many mouths to feed. In the temple, I am brought up as a priest and I am taught the different Egyptian languages from different areas in Egypt. Finica are the people who trade; Hiscos are the people who live to the side of Egypt and the people who live up the Nile.*

  "I am initiated into the priesthood by age thirteen. I am scared because I had heard that people died during initiation and I did not want to die. During the initiation, the prayers are said and incense is burned. Many priests are pulling my hair out. I feel suffocated by the bodies of the priests that are pressing close to my face. After the hair is pulled from my head, except for a small patch in back, they give me something to drink. Everything becomes hazy and appears to swim before my eyes. What I see is that my spirit is out of my body. I see god, Ra, is welcoming me. He is reminding me of my plan for this life, such as to reestablish some technology and simple things that mankind needs to live better, to make it easier to establish spirituality and to integrate history. I am to help remind people that mankind is an ancient race and there is an interrelationship with the past and what is going on today.

"I come out slowly, feeling thirsty. The other priests tell me that I died and am reborn. They asked me if I saw the god and I said yes. They tell me that now I am a priest and that I am to live with the recognition that I have the authority of god. After that, the decision was made for me to be a historian.

"As a priest, we are not permitted to marry but we can have women for sex, and we do. It is the best of all possible worlds because we get to enjoy women but do not have to keep them. Sometimes we go to them and sometimes they are willing to come to the temple and enjoy the way we live for a while. We are not allowed to live with the women, but if one stays at the temple for several months, we enjoy her and then she leaves. Sometimes the women come during the day but have to go back. These are married women who come to the temple for a short time and have to get home to their husbands and children. They feel that in having sex with us they get blessed.

"If the woman gets pregnant with one of us, the child cannot be claimed because we are not allowed to have children. The child has to belong to someone else. The general attitude of the public is that contact with a priest, by having sex and even just conversation, is blessed, and the people benefit from it. We are also allowed homosexual relationships. We do not have women priestesses at this time because we do not believe that a woman can be spiritual.

"I am trained as a scribe to keep records and am trying to read and write so I can keep Egyptian and world histories. I have access to the treasure trove, all the accumulated records we have. Most of them are copies and the originals are put away. We have copiers here and their job is to reproduce what we already have. They are taking the originals and copying them now. My job is to read the copies to learn the history and to write down current events. A priest from our temple regularly goes up and down the river and travels to different places and

talks to the people and reports their conversations to others and to me. As the reports come back, it is also my job to work into the narrative what is going on in Egypt and in the neighboring areas. The attitude is that there is nothing anywhere else worth knowing and this is the true civilization and the rest does not count. The Finicans, the traders who sail the oceans, insist that we should also go to the other places.

"I get the reports and work them into narratives, working with several other priests. There is an older priest who oversees, works with us, and sits in on our conferences. When I have time, I read the old records. Some of them are hard to understand and we have to ask the old priests what a word exactly means and how to understand some of the characters. I realize they seem to have it memorized. They really do not read it. It seems like the stories are passed on by word of mouth. I do not ask the old priest because that would be embarrassing to admit.

"As I read the records, I cannot believe some of the stuff. These stories I am reading tell fabulous tales of great cities with huge numbers of people. We do not have that many people in all of Egypt. The old priest tells me that this was how things were before the world changed. He tells me that the world goes through different cycles and when a cycle comes to an end, people start all over from the beginning. The stories tell of incredible civilizations and great bodies of water, sailing ships and people flying in the air. I have a hard time believing it. I ask the old priest about the originals and I am told they are hidden away and only one person knows the location. I have access to copies of all this history.

"At the age of twenty-five, I am sent on a tour with the old priest and my two helpers, to see all of Egypt. We start in the south and go up the Nile where the black people live. We bring trade goods. We know their language. The black people here are like savages. From here, we go all the way back down the River Nile by boat, zigzagging *from one side to the other and stopping at every village with more than one hundred people.*

"I am talking to people, learning about them, visiting other temples, meeting other priests of Ra, visiting temples of other gods, sometimes being taken to see secret things. We keep going down through the Nile Valley, all the way to where the rice grows and there is a different way of living. It is fast and noisy. I see the Sphinx on the plateau. We visit some pyramids in the upper valleys. As I am visiting, I write down everything. Then we get to the last temple in the capital and I get the word that I am to travel east to the coast and go inland with the travelers and then further up the coast. When I find the port where the Finican people dock, I am to send messages back and maybe I can come back on a ship myself.

"I have traveled here for three more years, so I have been away from my temple for five years. It is a long, slow walk zigzagging back and forth from the seacoast to tiny settlements, tribes, and inland groups, and meeting everybody along the way. I write reports on everybody and everything I see along the way. I am now passing the home of the sea traders. It is a rich city called Tier, which is the capital of the Finican people. They worship their god, who looks like a fierce, fat man. They have secondary gods; one looks like a man with wings. It is surprising that we traveled past the civilized world and still have found civilized people. They are not killing each other and are not savages.

"I am approaching the ship and sailing back to Egypt. It sure is different out on the ocean. We visit some islands. I write down everything I can. We zigzag to the mainland and back out to islands until we reach the Nile. When I get back home, I find a manuscript in what looks like my handwriting, which I wrote a long time ago.

"I am looking at the recent history and thousands-of-years-old history and find things are pretty consistent. I really think that the old history is accurate and what the historians wrote about really did happen. They don't say

that it happened here, but in another country. According to the Finicans, the traders, there was a wonderland in the ocean called Atlantis and people could trade with them. I learned about the interrelationships between people, languages, stories, legends, and myths. I am writing about what I discovered on my tour but I do not know if I will live long enough to finish it.

"This history is important and more people need to know about it. They need to understand what happened. As you put the stories together, they paint a wonderful picture that turned awfully grim. I have written all that and my conclusions. People I met during the tour had stories but they were different in different places. So they all had their own point of view, or there was no real agreement about what happened. Atlantis must have been a wonderful place to begin with and then it became a terrible place.

"Stories were about all the murals and miracles Atlanteans had for everyday life and how bad it got to be, such as how people were zombified, just walking dead, how cruel the rulers were and how the whole country sank. People say it all got so bogged down with wickedness that it just collapsed and the ocean swept away all traces of it. The story came from more than one place. It could be that people made up the story and spread it or it could be true. It was so long ago and I wonder if there is any real proof in those hidden records. I never knew where they were hidden. Only one person knows, and I do not know who he is.

"At the age of forty-four, I become very sick. I am just coughing and coughing and feeling very tired. Some people avoid me because I have the coughing disease and people die with it. I am getting thinner and coughing blood. As I am dying, I have fever, chills, coughing up blood, and a huge weight loss. People do not come around me because they do not want to get it.

"I die thinking that I wish I knew where the records were hidden and what the real truth is. The next time I will not wait until I am too sick to discover the truth myself. I

*wrote a lot but did not get to finish my conclusions. I am
feeling sad about the writing I could not finish because
of my sickness. I believe in the afterlife and that you get
judged on what you did. My spirit comes out and I am not
sick anymore. I am taken to heaven by the angels.*

"*During the review of that life, I see that part of my
personal and group goals were to reintroduce some
technology to humanity. Not electronics, but some of the
simpler metal technology. I was supposed to find this in the
old books and bring it out into the open so people could
begin to make and use these things again. Part of that did
happen by accident. When I was with the traders, I told
them about glass and ceramics. They reinvented them and
they had glass objects to trade. So that technology at least
was brought back again.*

"*I was also supposed to talk about the history of
mankind and help people understand their position in time
and space, that there was a long history behind humanity,
and the things did not get where they are today from out of
nowhere. Part of the study showed me that people have a
simplistic view of history and where they came from. I was
developing into quite a political and economics thinker.
It's too bad I did not get to live longer and write more.
But I shared it with two younger priests with me and they
continued writing it after my death.*

"*From heaven, I see that my thinning hair, lung
problems, dry skin, and calluses come from that life to my
current life.*"

Atlanteans also had airplanes, which flew low and slow. They
were not the primary means of transportation. It was difficult
to power them far away from land. They were most effective
close to land, where the power was strongest. They did not
have a portable source of power and could not load a gas
tank and fly an airplane across the Atlantic Ocean. That is
why boats were more successful. Boats could use transmitted

power that came from crystals, and sails. They did not put big power stations in other countries and did not want other countries to have that much access to energy and knowledge. It was a way to control other people.

According to my hypnotized patients, in India, there were aircrafts that flew, but without a compact, strong power plant, powered flight was not practical. Gliders and other non-powered flight did exist. Several other places, including Atlantis, Lamuria, and Egypt also had gliders. They were not useful for commercial transportation or for carrying a cargo without a compact power plant.

Atlanteans were controlling people all over the world, and where they could not do it by trade economics, they did it by force. They generally controlled politically and economically, but sometimes they had to do it by force. They did not share their power and technology with others, wanting the exclusive control of knowledge. Atlanteans refused to train people from other countries.

Heavenly beings claim that the Greek writer, Solan, accidentally stumbled upon a manuscript in an Egyptian temple which told the story of Atlantis. This was the one that was copied just a generation after Atlantis fell. So there was still plenty of first-hand knowledge about Atlantis around, but from no one who had been there. The information is sort of fuzzy and not exact, but still it helps to get the idea that there had been a continent called Atlantis.

Sprouting of Spirituality

After Atlantis was destroyed, spirituality was very low everywhere. People had lost sight of individual spirituality. They worshiped certain nature spirits or animal spirits or, in some cases, more abstract sky spirits. In some areas, there were people who were more in touch with the memories of Atlantis, at least as far as religion went. They continued their worship of multiple gods. In Atlantean time, these were recognized as different aspects of one God, which had been forgotten by this time.

After thousands of years, people continued to establish more of a social structure. There was the redevelopment of the written languages, mathematics, the beginning of crude science and technology, and there was improvement in farming and farm equipment. The states combined into small nations, which combined into large nations, then into more prosperous commercial centers. People began to seriously question the nature of the universe, the nature of God, and the nature of the spirit. The first modern monotheism began. As described before, monotheism existed about 100,000 years ago in Lamuria with the realization that there is only one God and He is a spiritual being.

In some places, people began experimenting with their individual spirituality again. They perceived that they had spirituality and they worked to develop it, particularly in India and some in China, where they became more serious questioners. As the population increased, trade routes grew. Wherever there was trade, people sometimes traveled back and forth and chose to go see what life is like elsewhere.

Teachers spread out from the various centers where there was spiritual awareness. Generally those who practiced spiritual awareness realized that the sharing was a great spiritual practice, a great virtue. So they did this without pay, for their own benefit as well as for the benefit of those they worked with. Missionaries traveled the trade routes and their spiritual ideas spread from city to city. Various spiritual practices came back into being in different places.

One patient recalled a past life as a spiritual teacher as follows:

- *"I am living in southern Siberia. This is about 15,000 BC. My name is Edoor. I am twelve years old, living in a tribe. We move from place to place. I am thinking about how people got on Earth, about God and the universe. By the age of fourteen, I am teaching and preaching about spiritual matters. A group of medicine men decide to take me and train me. After a year, I am moving from group to group teaching about spiritual matters and people are paying attention to me. Every day I am inspired by new ideas and understanding about spiritual matters, and within me, I know it is the truth. Everyone, including the spirit people, are listening to me and agreeing.*

"Occasionally, people complain about my preaching and not doing any work. At the age of twenty-eight, another spirit man, who was jealous of me, kills me by stabbing me repeatedly in the chest, arms, shoulders, throat, tongue, and hands. As I am dying, I am thinking that I am right and that I would do it all over again at every chance I get. I also have a sense of disgust for false prophets, those who claim to be spiritual but whose actions are not. As I am going to the Light (heaven), I am thinking that now I will find out what really happens. I thanked that man for killing me so I can experience the truth.

"From heaven, I see that it was a life of accomplishment, which I am also continuing in the current life. I kind of founded modern religion. The concepts of it included the Supreme Being, the afterlife, a need to worship, and directions for setting up rituals, prayers, etc. This was the first modern organized religion since the destruction of Atlantis. It spread east, west, north, and south in Asia. The heavenly helpers are all happy with my accomplishments and are saying it was a very productive life.

"Many positive traits came from that life to the current life, such as the drive to share my messages and the resolve to do it again at every chance I get. I see that my throat problem now came from that life because I was stabbed in the throat and all over, and also speech problems because I was killed due to my speaking out about spiritual matters. My neck and shoulder pain and thyroid problems are also due to stabbing. As Dr. Modi requested the angels to bring all my soul parts back, which I lost in that life, and to

*integrate them with me after cleansing and healing, they did
that. Then the past life personality was integrated with me."*

Heavenly beings, through my hypnotized patients, claimed
that India was one of the leaders in the forefront of spirituality
because they did not have to overcome all the negativity of
the Atlantean saga. They did not rise as high as the cultures
around Atlantis did and they did not fall as far, either. They
were able to maintain more of their civilization, their culture
and thinking. When the weather improved, their spirituality
climbed at a faster rate. They were higher than the other
people of the world.

Many masters were sent to India, where the ground was
fertile. You do not plow and sow seeds on rocks. You go
where the ground is able to bear fruit and plant the seeds
there. There is no use to plant and plow on a brick sidewalk.
Some of the seeds will drop on the dirt and will sprout, but
it is not a great place to grow a crop. India was a fertile land.
They were the people who had not lost everything in the
decline of civilization and it was the best place to start the
resurgence of spirituality. Heaven sent quite a few masters
back to Earth, and India got many of them. As a matter of
fact, all of Southeast Asia, including China and Tibet, did.

According to the hypnotized patients, the seeds of the
Indian teachings showed up in what is now Egypt, in all
the cultures of the Mediterranean Basin, in Palestine, Israel,
Syria, and all the way across the near east into Asia, but did
not travel so successfully to the east, to China and Japan. Of
course, they had some of their own spiritual development to
build on. So the strongest spread of the Indian teachings went
to the west, while teachings of Buddha, from India, went to
the east.

The development of the religious thoughts and spirituality
began in small groups all over the Earth; still, the development
of the individual components of spirituality was left to the
east in Asia. In Europe, there was very little recognition of

more than just worship of God. The ideas of meditation and developing spirituality stayed in the east and were spread from there. The little centers of religious and spiritual culture started to spread from the area in which they began until they were accepted by a larger group. They then spread around the world.
. · Major teachers started different movements. Master beings were placed in various locations and founded movements that became extremely important in the history of the world. There were the beginnings of the Jews in Babylon, the beginnings of religious movements in China, Japan, Egypt, and various other locations in the world. In some places, it did not land at all and other places, it bounced once or twice before it went on.

There were spiritual understanding and spiritual development in other places, too. In the western parts of North and South America, spiritual and religious practices developed separately, mostly because of the sparsely inhabited dry and desert-like zones in between communities. There were not many people there because there was not much water.

There were centers of spiritual development in North America, Mexico, South America, and Central America. Some of the primary religious cultures were Mayan and Aztec. The Shawnee spiritual culture developed among the American Indians. These cultures related to the cycles of life, to the cycles of heavens, and symbolically re-enacted them in ritual. There was a perception of altered states and there were spiritual people and teachers in each group. A few of the spiritual people were charlatans, but most of them were sincere and actually trying to be spiritual.

People under hypnosis report that, in some of the above groups, there were some spiritual practices that became definitely nonspiritual, such as the concept of sacrifice, which turned into blood sacrifice and the murder of captives. This led to the wars of conquest, to get more captives, and it was very detrimental for the people in the end. There were also cultures in South America whose followers became military conquerors and failed to carry out their spiritual mission. This was a great drawback to the people. The spiritual mission was the most important part. Military conquest was not the goal of the heaven, but the people developed a common source of government and military conquest developed out of it. Even the common source of government originally had a religious basis.

In North America, the Shawnee culture developed and spread to some extent, while in South America, people managed to develop rather odd peculiarities in religion which made it unacceptable, especially the concept of sacrifice and self-damage. People found it very hard to find spirituality in those practices, and religion and spirituality never became popular. American Indian culture spread here and there in a spotty transmission; some tribes would not adopt it, while other tribes beyond them would.

Shamans and medicine men made up small groups of spiritual people. They worked with spirit and were the people responsible for mediating between the spirit and the people. Most of them did not relish this position, but it was something that had to be done. They had to work sometimes with very negative beings. After the Ice Age, there were no major religions in North, South, or Central America. Instead, there were local groups of various religions that never developed a very strong religious basis that everybody could adopt. In Africa, it was much the same, where the religion spread out on a tribal basis and failed to spread into other groups and tribes.

According to heavenly beings, very few masters and religious teachers were sent to North, Central, and South America, and Africa, but still they were given religious practices that got twisted and perverted and failed to spread. The problem was that the ground was never prepared to receive the spiritual masters or the teachers. People did not establish a way for the masters to come to them.

The same situations existed from the northern European coast all the way to Siberia. Heaven did not find individual tribes developing enough spirituality for a master to come and sow the seed and harvest the crops for a spiritual religion to develop there. Instead, they had nature worship, animal worship, and had practically no concept of a more sophisticated God. Even if the masters were sent to the areas in North, South, and Central America, Europe, and Africa at that time, for the most part, their teaching would have died. They would have no more success than a local medicine man because people were not prepared for the message. Unless the ground is fertile and ready to receive the seed, the seed does not grow very well, so it's no use to send masters to an area where people are not ready to receive them.

Heavenly beings, through my hypnotized patients, claimed that spiritual development goes way back in time, farther than most modern authorities are willing to accept. They place Moses about four thousand years ago, perhaps six thousand. But in fact, the beginning of Jewish religion was over ten thousand years ago, when Abraham, the founder, came. In India, spiritual development was in full swing fifteen thousand years ago. There is a distortion of the time scale, as we see it from an Earthly point of view.

There was a master sent to Egypt and Persia. In India, China, and Japan, multiple masters were sent. These areas were not affected by the Ice Age and people in these areas in the east did not have much contact with Atlanteans, but had some contacts with Lamurians. Most of the spirituality in India originally began there. The mountains were a big barrier between India and the rest of the world. Some of the spirituality spread from Lamuria to China, Japan, and India.

The history from the time of Moses, from six thousand years till now, is pretty well known. It is a part of the world history and part of the world culture. According to the heavenly beings, we need to move time back a couple of thousand years. Society and cultures are older than what people think.

Role of Aliens in Recent Development of Mankind

Heavenly beings, through my hypnotized patients, mentioned that as the human race was gradually redeveloping, from time to time aliens were implanted into the culture to provide specific ideas or specific help to cause the advancement of mankind. Very often, the person who was an alien was sent to cause the culture to extend and was an associate of a known human figure. According to the heavenly beings, Thallus of Mellitus, a Greek man who lived on the island of Mellitus, came up with the first atomic theory. He was actually an alien of race four and not really a Greek.

My hypnotized patients state that the aliens would encourage these very talented individuals to develop their insights and make use of them. We are speaking of people like Pythagoras, the mathematician, and Archimedes, the physicist, engineer, and mathematician. They published their own works with a lot of encouragement. They did almost everything they were given credit for, but beside each of them was an alien, appearing as a human, who encouraged, provided hints or directions, and guided their development, but the humans did the work.

According to the heavenly beings, this method of helping is continued in the present day. For example, the technician who worked with Marconi on the development of the radio was the one who actually made suggestions to Marconi and helped him to think it out and build it. Almost all Marconi's work had a lot of aid, encouragement, and help from the aliens. This was one of alien race five. These aliens kept a low profile and stayed in the background.

When the aliens first came to Earth, they revealed themselves and literally handed technology over to humans who were not ready for these beings from flying crafts. As a result, there were social repercussions, coupled with severe psychological impact upon humanity. It was a tremendous jolt to humanity to find that they were not alone in the universe and that there were such vastly superior beings. They questioned their individual worth, asking, "If this race is so far advanced, why do we even bother to exist?"

After the aliens figured this out, they stopped direct intervention in which the spaceships landed in the middle of a village and the aliens got out and spread all around. This was a different point of view. Nowadays, people say, "Well, if flying saucers really exist, why doesn't one land on the White House lawn with the movie cameras running?" The answer is that aliens know better. They know how badly it worked the last time and how mankind was affected by it. As a result they will not do it again. They do not want to damage mankind again.

Back about 70,000 years ago, alien races were appearing to mankind and that created bad consequences but there were also good results. Mankind was receiving technology. Later, the aliens developed their method for interacting with humanity in which they came as humans and guided very intelligent and spiritual human beings into making the discoveries. This way, they were sure that humans would develop to the point where they could utilize the discovery effectively.

If we come upon a very primitive human and give him an antigravity device, he will never understand it. He does not have a background for it, but at the proper time, as in the case of Marconi, once the understanding of electricity had developed, an alien was sent to this brilliant scientist to help figure out how he could make electromagnetic waves and send them through the air, detect them, and use them for transmitting signals.

Heavenly beings, through my hypnotized patients, claim that there are more examples of humans who were helped and the way in which they were helped. The development of writing and the inspirations for developing an alphabet in India, the reception of the written alphabet in Greece, and the creation of a written Greek language with the understanding of it were aided by the aliens. The individuals who actually did the work are gone, but they were human and they were aided, inspired, and encouraged by aliens living among them. This was a planned maneuver by the aliens to get writing back into use.

Another primary example was during the time of the renaissance, 1300-1400 AD, when the aliens worked to inspire the artists. The aliens did not paint pictures, but an alien would do things to show a better way to weave canvas into a paint receiver or a better way to stretch canvas. They also provided some of the clues that enabled the pigments to be developed. The aliens' feelings at the time of the Renaissance were that there had been enough technological development and it was time to develop the spiritual and emotional aspect through art for a while, to counterbalance the technological development. They were inspiring this emotional development and trying to balance it with the development of art.

According to the heavenly beings, mankind is nearing the same point again, when we have all the technology we can handle and technological progress will diminish. It will not come to an absolute standstill, but there will be a big drop off in technology as the aliens withdraw their support, their aid, and start to emphasize arts, literature, humanities, and spiritual development again. It will change our focus. Instead of helping technologists, they will help artists. These are not aliens taking human forms in human incarnation, but are the aliens themselves, who look like humans and exist amongst the humans while they work with them. Alien races four and five of group two can pass for humans. They often keep a low profile. Even now these aliens are among us, inspiring us and providing knowledge and technology.

Heavenly beings, through my hypnotized patients, claimed that races four and five of group two helped us with solid state electronics, with the development of the computer, and with the realization of the atomic power. They are still interacting with us and living among us during the time when they are doing this work. Other than that, they prefer to be where they are more comfortable, where they do not have to pretend all the time. Other alien races are just observing, but the alien races four and five are still making technological interactions with us.

Chapter 8

DEVELOPMENT OF SPIRITUALITY IN HUMANITY

According to my hypnotized patients, after the breakup of Atlantis, religion and spirituality was extremely low. People took their local religion to the new lands with them. They lost sight of their aspect of god as being part of the whole, the one God, and went back to worshiping multiple individual gods. To develop themselves spiritually was foreign to these religions. It was not recognized that people could do this and was taken out of the religions. After the Ice Age, there was an effort by God and heaven to bring spirituality to people. It was an act of mercy by God. There were many masters and teachers who incarnated in various parts of the world at different times, and many religions started after these masters. Later each religion founded by these religious teachers broke up into many sects. There was and is a heavenly plan to promote spirituality on Earth in different ways, such as psychic abilities; through travel, trade, commerce; charity; by divine inspiration; physical and intellectual development; and via different mass communication medias such as radio, television, motion pictures, news medias, books, and internet; by understanding past lives; and by sending new teachers on Earth. This is the subject of this chapter.

Spirituality From Atlantis Till Now

At the end of Atlantis, spirituality was in an awful shape. First, in order to accomplish their goals, the ruling class had to pervert religion and spirituality. They fastened upon the least spiritual and the least developed portions of religion to emphasize, so that they could break away from any control by religion, yet they could use religion as a means of control. As described before, the Atlanteans had a very loosely organized religious structure. They started out with deity worship from different places, and it was not until the Lamurians came that they started to see all the different deities as being different aspects of one God.

As Atlantis aged, as it grew and developed, Atlanteans went from a state of local religions to a unified religion. They went from worshiping a series of local deities to an understanding that there is one God and seeing each of these local deities and religious groups as being part of the whole and grouping them all together under one umbrella. As religion came under centralized control, it was odd, because it recognized all the diversities and each area continued to emphasize one aspect of one God. Once there was a centralized control mechanism, the ruling classes found it very convenient to exercise control of the masses through this religious structure. As organized religion grew and became more powerful, the individual's relationship with God diminished. They did not teach it, they did not emphasize it, and religion became formal and meaningless.

As mentioned before, Lamurians came to Atlantis before the control. They were telepathic and had psychic foreknowledge, which Atlanteans did not understand. Atlanteans realized that something else is going on with Lamurians, and they began to duplicate psychic ability with technology, and later used it to control people. Atlanteans did not have the concept of individual spirituality. They had some formal practices. They had an idea of a good life, but it differed from people to people. In some areas, if you fought war well, then that was a good life. In other areas, if you treated humanity decently, that was a good life. If you did your job well, or if you were more sincere in worship of God, that was a good life, but actually doing something spiritual yourself sort of died out.

The priestly class had its own power base, just like the ruling class, only it got there by different means. Birth was the primary way into the ruling class, especially after the lower classes were tightly controlled. Before that, it was possible to get in by the accumulation of the wealth. After that, it was impossible for others to break in. The masses were too tightly controlled. Meanwhile, the priestly class could break into the ruling structure mainly by being mean and nasty. The use they made of religion marked them for the command structure.

At the break-up of Atlantis, most people abandoned religion, as they abandoned technology. There were some members of the common mass who carried it over after the escape. Those who carried on their local religious group, the prior local understanding of God, before the total control, took religion to the new lands with them. There was a conglomeration of people from many different parts of Atlantis who had a multiplicity of seemingly different religions. They lost sight of their aspect of God being part of the whole. So they went back to individual gods. Sometimes these show up like a Greek or Norse god, where they had about fourteen major gods, each dealing with one aspect of life, plus a bunch of minor deities.

The same religious group showed up all over the place. After the escape from Atlantis, the folks were all living together. Out of a hundred people, you might have fourteen different gods being worshiped. They integrated into a pantheon, and somehow one god got accepted as "the lead god" and the others became "co-gods." But again, the idea of the individual spirituality did not carry through. The gods existed, they held formal worship, but to develop individuals spiritually was foreign to these religions. It was not recognized that people could do this. This had been taken out of the religion.

Religious teachers started to arise after the dispersion from Atlantis. After the Ice Age, there was an effort by God to get the word back to people. There were different masters who incarnated at different times in different parts of the world and brought different understandings of the truth. It was usually not all the truth, but enough to move people to better understanding and realization. This was an act of mercy on God's part. Sometimes the masters were religious teachers and other times they were not. They were also philosophers and political leaders desiring to set up a better organized form of government. They began to redevelop the idea of individual spirituality and personal spiritual development.

With the few worldwide religions, each following one of those masters and teachers, came the concept of individual gods again. Each religion founded by these religious teachers broke up into many sects, sometimes along the national lines and sometimes along lines of religious understanding, but never for any great reasons. Whenever anybody discovered a difference or realized the difference, instead of incorporating it with the original, they tended to just splinter off and form a new sect. This often occurred due to demonic influences, because fragments do not stay together, and this gives you something to disagree about and fight over.

So, there was this continuous development. More religious teachers were sent, stressing individual spirituality, how to develop it, giving moral codes, and sometimes rituals of worship, and satanic influences continued to split them into different sects. Different groups, not understanding each other, emphasized different aspects until they got to the point that many could not be sure that any religion was true.

Religion

There are multiple definitions of religion, according to heavenly beings. The simplest is, "Man's attempt to systematize and put into practice what God has revealed about himself, the universe, and man's purpose in the universe." Another way of thinking of religion functionally from the point of view of heaven is, "It is an organized way of thinking of God and it is put into terms that human beings can understand."

Religion is a formal organization, while spirituality is individual development, which can be developed spiritually within a religion and can also develop spiritually without a formal religion. They are not intertwined to the point that they must be connected. They can exist completely separate from each other. There can be those who practice religion but do not develop spiritually a bit because they do not have connections established with God. They do not love their neighbors and do not benefit from the practice of religion. So religion is sterile and empty for them. Some formal practices that they go through do not benefit them at all. They do not grow in love for God, do not grow in love for humanity, and do not grow in love for themselves. They do not increase the flow of spiritual energy in themselves. This is a sterile practice of religion with no benefit to the individual and it does happen.

There are also rituals in personal spiritual development that can focus attention on God and the person's connection with God. Spiritual practices such as prayer, meditation, yoga, tai chi, and formal rituals can help develop the connection to God. They also help to develop appreciation for the other members of mankind or appreciation for self. These rituals are practices that benefit the individual immensely. To practice good works can make up for previous bad actions or gain benefit for future incarnations or even in the future of current life.

We can practice religion or personal spiritual practices alone or together. Perhaps it is more beneficial to practice both together. The more time we spend in contact with God, the more time our mind is fixed on God, and the more often the name of God is on our tongue, the stronger our connection with God is. Even when we use the name of God in anger or frustration, it is still beneficial. Sometimes what is thought to be cursing is not always seen like that by heaven. A person who tends to be negative, who uses the name of God in vain, or who blasphemes, has turned his thoughts to God for that instant, and a little bit of Light gets through to that person. In order to curse that way, a person's mind gets connected with God, which may someday serve as the basis for a permanent and closer connection with God. Even this slight turning of the person's mind to God is beneficial and may provide the link by which the Light can eventually break through to this person and change his or her habits. So even while cursing, the name of God is praised rather than cursed.

Religion is a good thing as long as humans think in a spiritual manner and it helps to keep people working on their own spiritual development. Religion becomes a bad thing when hate, negativity, and exclusivity become part of it, which is often inspired satanically and not by God. Religion becomes less applicable when it becomes mechanical, stilted, and formalized so that people do not enter into the religion or spiritual development with body, mind, spirit, and emotions. Unless men develop all of these, the actual practice of religion is not as beneficial as it can be. Some religions become so formalized that the emotional element is left out or negated and the mind becomes the important part of religion. When this happens, religion does not serve mankind as best as it can.

From Satan's point of view, religion offers an opportunity for him to enter it, pervert it and to advance the viewpoints that are contentious, causing division, power grabbing, and political intrigue. The more formalized a religion becomes the more open it is to satanic influences.

If love is in action in a religion, then it is a good religion, one that is fulfilling God's purposes. In the Christian domain, Jesus gave two commandments, "Love God, and love thy neighbors." Very simply, this is the essence of religion. In loving God, we develop ourselves spiritually, and when we put that into action and develop love for our neighbors, our community, and ourselves, we grow faster spiritually. Self-love is one of the most frequently neglected forms of love.

Spirituality refers to the connection between God and the individual. A personal connection and practice of spirituality deepens and intensifies this bond. Spirituality can be developed in many different ways or in a combination of them. Even the practice of religious ritual, which seems like a very formalized and non-emotional practice, can be a valuable aid in developing spiritually, because as the ritual is practiced, the connection with God is intensified.

Habits of right living, love of humanity, of self, and of God are things that can intensify the spiritual connection. To be honest and not eat meat for religious purposes can also help to intensify the spiritual connection. Physical exercise done for our own benefit, to develop our own bodies and to keep us healthy, is an act of self-love and, believe it or not, this is also part of spiritual development. It develops love for self. Physical exercise also opens the energy centers and meridians, and God's Light and energy can flood through them and remove blockages and thus allow the body to function in a healthy way. But Satan can promote extremes. To run beyond the physical body's capacity and to be destructive to the physical body by any kind of excessive exercise is not a godly act.

According to the heavenly beings, to abuse the physical body, as in excessive religious zeal or penance to atone for past sins or to punish yourself, is not from God. It is satanic in origin, just as pulling hair out, putting needles in the skin, or extended fasting to the detriment of the body are not from God. For a healthy, vigorous young or middle aged person, a one-week or ten-day fast can be very beneficial, by relieving the physical body of the need of providing fuel for itself, to allow the metabolism to shift to a neutral state, and to allow the spiritual to become foremost in the body's energy usage. The dark side inspires extended fasting by presenting to these people as the ultimate in spiritual development, except that God does not see it that way. God has created all the beings of the universe to function in a certain way. To go too far beyond the functioning of the body is detrimental to the body and not in keeping with God's will.

Development of Formal Control Structures and Organized Religions

A book of dogma was being developed in most religions, and competing control structures were developing. The more the satanic influence, the tighter the control structures, such as, "You cannot get to heaven without us," "They are the essential ones for salvation," "Unless you belong to this religion, you cannot return to God," "Only through Jesus can you go to God," etc. Emphasis on the old religion was stamped out by incoming religions. Each time a formal religion takes over, they have to stamp out the concept of individual spirituality, to make it less important than the formal structure. They interpose the priest between people and God so that people must have their church and their priest to commune with God. In every religion, strengthening the individual's connection with God should be the most important goal, but it often gets left out and the religious priest becomes a middleman between God and the people, which is not good.

Generally, the more satanically influenced the religion is, the more fundamental and more demanding it is. "Everyone must believe in this to be saved," "My religion is the only correct religion," or, "Scriptures of my religion are the only ones from God." When we find this inherent in any religion, we have to know that we are looking at a structure that is designed to control others and is inspired by Satan. A true religion will recognize that there are alternate paths to spirituality and God, and that the true ideal of every religion is to develop individual spirituality in their people. There is no such thing as one religion for everybody, mainly because we are different people with different degrees of development.

Religion and Spirituality in Healing

Practically every religion has within it the culture of healing or the thought of healing and of curing all human ills with the religion, such as the laying on of hands, praying, sacramental healings with blessings through various means, the focusing of group prayers, and channeling God's Light through the priest (a teacher of any religion) into a church, synagogue, or temple, etc. A priest can form the intent for the entire group in a worship place to be healed and to serve as a conduit for the energy to heal and make it much more effective, just as a group of people can serve as a conduit for God's love and energy to the Earth. Similarly, a clergy person, while preaching, can pray for everybody in the worship place to become a conduit for God's energy.

God can pour healing energy into an individual down through his or her silver connecting cord and that healing energy spreads through the person's body and can heal one or many physical problems. This person can be in a church, temple, synagogue, mosque, at home, or in a hospital praying for healing. Sometimes God would like to pour his healing Light into a person but something in the person is blocking its access. In this case, the laying on of hands by another person can heal this person. In this case, God's healing energy can pour through the silver connecting cord to the hands of the person who is laying his or her hands on the person needing the healing and can remove the blocks. Also, the healing can come to the person through people's prayers and compassion. God's Light energy can also be built up in one person and can be willed to the one who needs the healing.

The act of healing can be beneficial to the healer as long as the energy comes from God and the Light. There are forms of healing where the energy comes from inside the person during the healing. This drains the person who is doing the healing because it takes the energy and spirituality from them, which is not good. In a way, it is an act of love, but it is also self-destructive. If somebody uses this self-draining method of healing and accepts payment, they are in the same position as someone who donates organs for money. It is self-destructive for no spiritual benefit and therefore wrong all the way. The intent of many people joined together in prayer and each of them sharing a little bit of their energy with the sick person is an act of love and not destructive because it can be restored easily. All these healing methods are valid, especially here the healing comes from God and the Light.

Psychics can use a crystal to focus their energy and their thoughts upon another person. As the crystal tunes into the vibration level that the person needs, the healing energy comes in various frequencies and the crystal helps the psychic to focus upon the proper frequency for the problem that the person has. This is a case where the healer is using his or her own energy without drawing the Light energy, and the crystal is serving as the focuser to get the energy attuned at the right frequency for the person who needs healing. The crystal is serving as a conduit or a transformer between the healer and the one who needs healing. In this case, the psychic is donating the energy and is also operating through the crystal to attune to the proper frequency for the person to be healed.

According to the heavenly beings, these are healers who do not know any better. They have not been properly taught the techniques and are not in touch with their heavenly guides. When God's energy goes through the healer to the crystal and then to the person who needs the healing, it is better because, in this case, both the healer and the person who needs the healing are benefited when God's energy goes through the crystal and then to the person who needs the healing. The effectiveness of the healing is the same.

Healing can occur directly through prayers, and God's healing energy can come directly through the patient's silver cord and heal. The benefit of having an external healer, whether a crystal or another human being, is in the case where a person has blocks set up, whether it be confused thinking, a past life problem, demonic influences, or any other reason that causes the healing energy to be blocked. Then using the crystal, prayer power from other people, a healer to lay on hands, or another healing method with the person can circumvent this. These methods can effectively heal the person even though they have blocks against the energy coming from God.

Energy can be more finely tuned to the problem the person has with the use of a crystal, and both cases will benefit. With the use of the crystal, we would expect to see the benefit more quickly because more of the energy is tuned to the proper frequency. Generally, tuning is done by the interaction between the person being healed and the psychic ability of the person doing the healing, with the intervention of God acting at the crystal. It is a joint effort. Primarily, the psychic person who is sensitive does the tuning. In the case where both are sensitive, then both of them are tuning the crystal. In this case, there is likely to be little or no intervention by God because it is not needed.

A person who demonstrates little psychic talent, can serve as a functional healer with a crystal simply by praying that God's energy flows through him or her to the crystal and then to the person who needs the healing, and letting God take care of the tuning. It can be effective, even though there is minimal interaction between the healer and the person being healed, with the majority of the action is coming through God.

Psychic Surgery

Some psychic surgeons are actually religious teachers in disguise. Some are genuine and some are fake. This works, but not for the reasons usually given. It is a spiritual healing, not because they cut through your abdomen with their fingers and come out with a chicken liver. That is fake. Psychic surgery is actually like a hands-on healing. It is like a battery, a group of people directing their spiritual energy to the task.

Promoting Spirituality on Earth

My hypnotized patients state that God and heavenly beings are trying to spread spirituality on the Earth and in the whole universe by establishment of religion. Even though many religions get twisted and perverted, they are still the fundamental way of establishing spirituality. Normal, everyday religion has a part in the scheme of things. There are many ways spirituality was and is spread on the Earth, such as psychic ability; travel, trade, and commerce; charity; spiritual inspiration; mass communication; physical development; spiritual development; sharing and learning spirituality and religion of different cultures; teaching and sharing spirituality with the races of different planets; resolving and understanding past lives; and sending new teachers on Earth.

Psychic Abilities

By allowing a window into the spiritual world through psychic abilities, people can look through that window and experience the spiritual world acting in ways that the physical world cannot and in ways that are beyond physical experience.

Following are examples of how psychic abilities were used to spread the spirituality:

- *"I am a thirty-two-year-old male living in the south of Siberia in a forest. It is 15,628 BC. I have married into another tribe. I came to the tribe when I was sixteen years old. My wife was widowed and older than I was. She asked me to come and live with her at her house, and when I accepted, we were considered married. It is a matriarchal tribe where the husbands follow the women. The men are more flexible because they can hunt anywhere, but the women's social positions and farming are established in this group so the women do not move. The husband can do his work wherever he is, so the husband moves and joins the wife's tribe. They exchange men. The women are the tribe. They start out as children being born into the tribe. If they are female, they will stay with the tribe, but if they are male, eventually they will go to a different tribe to live with a woman. This also helps eliminate warfare. One tribe does not want to attack another tribe because they have relatives in it. So it ends up as a cooperative unit. There are no property rights for men because the women have all the property.*

"I had always been very curious about spiritual matters since I was young, but the shaman in the tribe I came from was very secretive. Everything he did was undercover. In my wife's tribe, the shaman is very open and I spend many hours talking to him about what he knew, how he learned it, the difference between living and the dead, etc. I am fascinated by the information.

"We have wooden tools and absolutely no metal and no good weapons to defend against wild animals. Life is very hard. One day a tiger jumps on me and gets my head in its mouth and begins to pull my hair and scalp, and snaps my neck. Its fangs go into my head and puncture my brain and I die. My spirit is very confused after it comes out. I do not realize that my body is dead. My spirit is still running away. I begin to feel something is wrong when I realize that I am at a treetop level and not on the ground. I keep wondering what happened, so I go back to my body and watch it being eaten by the tiger and realize that I am dead. I am surprised because I do not feel dead.

"I go back to the tribe and contact the shaman because he will know what to do. The shaman is aware that I am there because he can feel my spirit. He makes a tea, drinks it, and retires to his hut to go into a trance to talk to me. I tell him what happened and where my remains are. He tells me that I need to go to heaven (Light) and not to hang around the tribe or move into anybody's body. It would be detrimental. The shaman does ask me to come from time to time from heaven to let him know what else goes on in heaven. It was a way to get spiritual information to the tribe. He points out the Light to me. I see my aunt, who died of a heart attack, who takes me to heaven.

"I am taken to a reception room in heaven where I talk to a Light being about how I was killed by the tiger

and then about the hard life I lived, with the cold, the blizzards, and the scarce food. As I talk, I feel better and relieved. Then, after cleansing, I go to the review table. There are three Light beings. One of the beings makes a comment about how horrible my death was. I brushed it off by saying that I had died worse deaths before. It is as if my memory has already come back and the death by the tiger has come into perspective after the trauma of it was released by venting and cleansing.

"From heaven, I see that my group goal was to get spiritual information to the shaman, who is also part of my heavenly group, to increase his understanding of things such as the process of death and dying, the existence of the spirit and what we do in heaven, so that he can pass it on to the other shamans and to the tribe. My goal was to live the life, to be a friend of the shaman, and after death, to supply the shaman information.

"The Light beings are reminding me that this needs to be carried through. I have to pass on the knowledge to those who are still living on Earth and I can do it through the shaman to whom I am connected because I have already gone back and talked to him once, so now it will be easier. As I look back, I had communicated with him many times after I returned to heaven. Sometimes by thinking about him and sending him information and making the shaman inspired. This is done through a shared soul part. The shaman had given me a soul part of him and I gave my soul part to him. I even go to visit the shaman as a Light being and meet with him in spirit.

"From heaven, I see that my group purpose was to establish a way that I could pass on information from the Light (heaven) into the universe through the shaman quickly, easily, and accurately. I also see that I planned my early death so I could go to heaven and communicate with the shaman from heaven while he was still living on Earth and he could pass the information on to others. My individual goals were to increase personal spirituality by

participating in this plan. I planned to develop spirituality on Earth and then develop more spirituality by running back and forth between the two worlds with information."

- *"I am a forty-one-year-old black woman living in Africa. My name is N'gaian and this is 21,020 BC. I am an advisor to the chief of the tribe and I must have an overall picture of everything to give good advice. The chief is not very bright. You have to sketch out everything for him. He will make a good decision but he has to have a complete understanding.*

"I am a healer and I work with herbs and potions and other things that grow here. Sometimes the plants are effective and heal, but at other times, it is the power of the mind that makes the suggestion of healing. Often there are spiritual things that are causing problems and they need to be healed spiritually. The worst case I have seen concerned a man who was possessed by a demon. I helped the man by removing the spirit and pushing it into a tree. It keeps the demon relatively harmless. I have also dealt with possession by human spirits. I am a psychic but I do not tell people about it. I can see, hear, smell, and know, and I can reach out and heal from a distance.

"I have two husbands. There are more men than women in our tribe. According to our culture, the senior husband is the father of all the children. I have seven children and the older ones help the younger ones. I have traveled all over this country in spirit [out of body] and I know what is where and who is who, what actually happens, what things are like, who is in charge, and who is doing what, so I can counsel the chief.

"I often travel out of my body when I am sleeping; at other times, I go on purpose. I burn herbs, smell the smoke, and then lay down. They tell me that my eyes roll up in my head and my body twitches, but I don't know. I am not there and I do not look back. I go out of the body

purposely to an individual, just go sight-seeing, or to do anything I wish. I also see angels, who are a lot safer than demons because they do not try to overtake you.

"I also travel in spirit to Atlantis because of the stories I have heard, such as how rich Atlantis was, how powerful and wonderful it was, how they used to go out and trade, and how they even sent out armed forces to establish colonies. I have been to Atlantean colonies and culturally they are no longer Atlanteans. As I travel to Atlantis in spirit, I have seen the darkness on this land. They no longer send out ships and their land gets poorer, and there are fewer people. I have seen what happens to people and I see tremendous suffering, terror, and horror. The first time I traveled to Atlantis out of body was when I was eight years old and heard tales being told around the fire.

"I saw rulers eating people. I saw a lot of darkness everywhere. There are devices being put in people's necks to control them. Everybody looks poor compared to the old stories. Atlantis was the land of milk and honey and overflowing with all things good. They had strong and vigorous people, and now it is just full of slaves who function like zombies and are unable to do anything on their own. The rulers are torturing people. The government is split and they have gone to a town by town tribal system.

"When I come back into my body, I tell these stories to my people, but not how I learned of them. As far as they are concerned, I am a spirit person and I am supposed to know this. I traveled to Atlantis many times in spirit while out of my body to see how it was from one end to the other. There was evil all over the continent. It was fragmented and broken into little pieces. Sections have disappeared into the ocean and the civilization is almost non-existent.

"We have a conflict with another tribe. They want to use our grassland for their cattle because theirs is drying out, but if we permit this, we will not have enough to feed our own cattle. We are fighting to keep our ancestral land

while they are fighting for their lives and want to take our land. The advisor of the other tribe, Oogro, wants dominance. If we can get him out of the picture, maybe we can decide something rationally, but then that would not be the right thing to do. One night, Oogro actually leads an attack while negotiations are ongoing. We attack back and win. We capture their chief and dictate the peace terms. We do not throw them out.

"We, the spiritual counselors, have a series of conferences with the surrounding tribes discussing what we know of spiritual matters. Most of the healers felt that our jobs, positions, and talents kept us on the side of good and positive so that life was good for the people, except Oogro, the evil counselor of the tribe who attacked us. We have conferences to understand what the nature of spirit is, what is it like, what is the difference between good and evil, and all types of things which can be very important. There are also military counselors, social counselors, political counselors, and farming counselors at these conferences. The head of every group has to be spiritual, including the military. It is the king who represents the common people and we all have to be able to explain to one common person, who makes the decisions. If the king has full understanding, then he keeps all the people happy.

"We have meetings of the counselors of up to seven tribes to get this spiritual understanding and perspective. We meet for a period of several weeks at a time, after everything is planted and before the harvesting. We discuss many things: God, are there other heavenly beings, is there evil and what is it like, why are things structured the way they are, and by what powers we travel around and see.

"We are trying to gather what we know, write down the parts we all know, and agree on what to tell the people. We put down parts that only a few of us know, explaining that these are not experienced or acknowledged by everyone. We are examining all that we know. It is consistent year

after year, and we pass it on to the people and to our apprentices. I have two of these who learn with me. I teach them how to go into a trance and what to do and not to do while in a trance.

"We all came to the conclusion that there is some higher power who is in charge and causes things to happen, although the higher power mostly observes what is happening and helps when asked. Also, that there are many lesser beings who have a portion of this divine power and can and do use it to help us. There is good and evil, and it is possible to distinguish between them. We try to pass this on to the common people verbally through stories, by making rounds through all the villages and tribes. As a result, because we did it that way, all the tribes in this area develop the same religion and have the same spiritual understanding. Over the years, the effects were profound. The system of right and wrong was set up, the understanding of God, understanding of good and evil, how evil can act and influence, what good can do about it, and the different ways of healing were all passed on. We believe, and are pretty sure, that the soul survives after death and we are pretty sure that the soul goes to God.

"We spiritual counselors decide that we will shave our heads in the center from front to back to distinguish those who have spiritual talent and commitment to do the work of God. It is not a personal decision. It is the spiritual group's decision. It was one of the conclusions we came up with during those conferences.

"I am dying at the age of sixty-seven of an infection with a fever, swollen belly, and aches and pain all over. I think I ate some bad food and have stomach pains. My spirit comes out after the death of my physical body. I do not feel dead and I am not sick either. I see my healer-teachers who died a long time before but look younger. They take me to the Light (heaven) and to the cleansing place, and then I am taken to a room for a life review.

There are four healers who tell me to look back at my life purposes, which I planned for myself before incarnation.

"From heaven, I see that the dramas were being played all over the Earth at the time when Atlantis was going through its final throes. Life was continuing as usual in other places. I planned to counterbalance Atlantis, as a group and personal goal. I have lived and died in Atlantis in different lifetimes. I traveled in Atlantis in spirit from Africa. I know of the evil in Atlantis, which was really heavy and overworking in the world. I came up with the idea of improving spirituality and improving goodness as a counterbalance to that evil, also to show that evil can be overcome without becoming evil and that good can overcome evil on its own. We can overcome evil people without resorting to black magic, just using the forces of good. This was an important lesson I learned in that life. I also planned to have my spirituality bloom free and full. Life as a healing counselor or a "Stone Age psychiatrist" was practiced for some of my future lives. These were my personal and spiritual goals. I see that I succeeded in achieving my personal and group goals.

"From heaven, I see that many of the people who were there as spiritual counselors along with other tribe members belonged to my heavenly group, including Oogro, who got to play the part of a villain in that drama. The group members were scattered in all the tribes, which was a real group effort to organize this religion, to get it to the people and to set up a training program for future counselors. We can foresee when the tribes will be united into one and the local ruler will not be the supreme ruler; instead, there will be a single leader over all the tribes. I see many people who were there in that life and are also here in the current life.

"I see from heaven that many of my problems came from that life to the current life, such as the thinning of my hair in the middle of my head and GI tract problems. I see angels bringing soul parts to my hair and other parts

of my body and integrating them after cleansing and healing."

Travel, Trade, and Commerce

Travel, trade, and commerce can be spiritual activity and have a spiritual purpose. Consider that an allegory for the development of the soul, as to how the soul develops through interactions with others. The following life is an excellent illustration of it:

- *"I am a twenty-three-year-old male living on an island in the South Pacific near Australia called what sounds like Labuvanua. This is 6021 BC. There are seven kings ruling in cities on the island. Mostly the cities are located on the coastline, and there are mountains inland. For practical purposes, it is a circular kingdom, a circular island, because it is difficult to cross the mountains. So most of the people live along the coast. I married at the age of nineteen and have three children. I am a trader. I collect things that are made here and take them around the island and trade them. I am from the south part of the island. I usually do not start out going west. I go east and go around the island counterclockwise. I want to avoid the king on the west side. I do not like the feelings I get from him.*

   "The trade routes are pretty well established but there is considerable flexibility in going from one area to another. There is social interaction while traveling these routes. I am thinking about what it means to be spiritual, and as I go around, I study with different spiritual leaders who are also kings. These rulers seem to be multifunctional. They are the secular rulers and run the government, and also they are religious leaders handling the rituals and the spiritual aspects. They also serve as spiritual

teachers. They conduct classes and answer questions. It is a combination position. The head spiritual leader does not have a city but has a little village in the mountains in the middle of the island.

"By the age of thirty, I have developed a better understanding of spiritual development by talking to these spiritual leaders on the trade routes. The ruler or the king of a city is not necessarily a native of the city. When a king dies, the other kings get together in the capital city and choose someone from the population who goes to that city and becomes the king. The people of that town do not get to choose their own leader. He is sent by the ruling counsel and has all the qualifications to be the spiritual head and the ruler. So the city government and the spiritual leader are combined, and there is a great deal of spiritual interest among the people.

"People from the trading class are frequently chosen to be city rulers because they are known to all the leaders and known to many people in each city. They know the customs, how the civil government works, trade routes, rules, and the roads, and can handle diplomacy with other cities. They have to be personable and get along with people or they do not last long as traders. We study with each of the spiritual leaders or the kings. So we have a great spiritual background. We know the religion and spiritual beliefs of each city.

"Trading is actually the best training for becoming a king. Traders also carry the news, the gossip, and the history from place to place. We are also historians and news broadcasters. We are not inventors. We also formed the hospital system and did the healing. We know the economic systems, so we are the economists, and also further the cultural integration, and have had experience in civil government. Traders also make up the banking system, broadcast system, and mail carriers. If you want to transfer money or mail from one city to another, the trader takes it. Anybody could become a trader, so we are

self-selected into this class. We also live a common life, so we know how it is to be an ordinary man.

"I am in my late fifties and for quite some time, I have bypassed the city in the west on the peninsula. Years ago, when I was young, I used to go to the peninsula, and several times, I sat with the ruler to learn what he had to teach. I decided I did not want to learn from him because it did not feel right. After a while, he died and the new ruler was worse than the first one.

"I am captured by some men from the peninsula city I had been avoiding. I am taken to the ruler. There is a feeling of evil in that place and the ruler has organized an armed guard. I knew the ruler before, when he was a trader. The ruler is upset with me because I do not come to his city. He has me beaten and throws me out and told me not to pass through his kingdom again.

"It takes me a couple of weeks to heal. Then I go on trading again, starting around the island. I am wondering if I might be selected as a king of a city. Of course, it crosses every trader's mind and I am at an age now when people are selected for that job. My kids are all grown. If I were selected as a city ruler, I would be living in that city.

"I wonder what effect the evil ruler will have if I am elected as a king. As I am cutting across the tip of the peninsula, there are men waiting for me and they drag me down to the evil king again. I explain to him my feelings about his kingdom but he does not want to hear me. He pokes a finger in my left eye and blinds me. I bleed to death after a couple of weeks, thinking that I hate evil. He disrupted my life mission and I am disappointed that I did not get a chance to be a ruler.

"My spirit hangs around for a while. Demons try to trap me but I avoid them and go to the Light (heaven). There is a group of thirteen beings here, a mystical number, at a table. They are all masters. Two of them were city rulers when I was a trader, but they are enlightened now. Many of these masters have been on that island as city rulers.

I am telling them how I had lived a long time, prospered well, done everything that I was supposed to, yet before I had a chance to move on to the final step, I was killed by that evil king, and how bitter I am about it. I wanted to achieve the leadership of a city and the evil king cut short my chances.

"One of the masters asks me about the purpose of that negative city and the ruler. Why was it allowed to exist on an island with such a perfect system? He is telling me that it was to recognize and accept the evil and know that it has its place. It is permitted to exist for the same reason it was allowed to come into existence; to provide something against which to engage and to grow. Everyone who deals with the darkness is actually following God's plan. It is a way to develop against it. A weight lifter does not develop muscles just like that; he must use heavy weights against his muscles to make them grow strong. Similarly, the dark provides the resistance for us to work against and, in doing so, develop spiritual muscles. I could not ignore it because it is part of the human condition and something we have to engage in to grow spiritually. Dealing with the evil also gives us a chance to grow and develop, and provides something to overcome. I can continue with that growth and development process by overcoming the little flaws that developed.

"Becoming a king would have given me a chance to apply all these skills at once, such as leadership, civil government, spiritual leadership, spiritual teaching, and healing, and all these things can also be done in the Light (heaven). We can progress in the Light in the same way that we progress on Earth. Of course, it is less effective because we do not have human conditions and evil to overcome here in heaven, but still, practice can be done.

"I am also made aware that even the evil king played a role as planned. Evil was permitted to exist and have a strong hold on that peninsula and it was allowed to influence every trader and ruler who came there and everybody who lived there. It was not a pleasant place

for anyone who was spiritually perceptive, but we had to grow. By avoiding that evil city, I deprived myself of a chance to grow.

"After cleansing, I go to a room for life review with three heavenly beings. From heaven, I see that one of my primary personal goals for that life was self-development, to develop myself, to get my vibration rate developed, and that island was an ideal place to do it. I had the misconception that evil was to be bypassed rather than confronted for spiritual growth. The economic system on that island with the trade system was consciously designed and maintained by the city leaders and they knew that anyone who was assigned to that peninsula would be overtaken by evil. When they had to assign someone there, they chose someone who was altruistic enough to be willing to go there and fight with that evil.

"I see that the island still exists and there is still a tradition on the island to help each other develop, but the trade system has disappeared over the years. There is a very little change in the island geologically. It is still basically an agricultural place. It was a great island for group work because the group members were involved so directly in helping each other develop.

"I needed to learn about dealing with evil because that helps with spiritual growth. I needed to deal with evil and use it as a developmental tool to exercise against, not to cooperate with and make it a part of my life, but as something to fight against.

"I see from heaven that many of the people who were there are also here in my current life. Also most of the traders and kings were part of my heavenly group members, including the evil king. It was an excellent group plan, to develop and spread spirituality all over the island, and was very successful.

"I also see that many of my problems came from that life to the current life, such as eye problems, aches and pains all over my body from the beating, and pain in my

feet due to all the walking I did as a trader. Angels, on your request, Dr. Modi, brought all the soul parts back that I had lost due to different traumas, and integrated them with my eyes and different parts of my body."

Politics and Spirituality

In spiritual or political work, our personal or any form of organized religion must be involved in charity work. On the other hand, the political arena must attract each person in terms of what they can do for other people and not for themselves. Politics must be treated as a charity venture in order for it to be effective; that is, we have to do it for the good of other people. Without that point of view in politics, it will be meaningless for them to take political action without the thrust of being for the good for all.

Charity

A group in heaven can develop spirituality through a series of lives that interact to produce a society in which there are local rulers, politicians, religious leaders, traders, police, and general public who can cooperate to spread spirituality by taking care of the hungry and homeless, so people are able to develop their own spirituality in a society and on a continent. People can plan a series of lives in one area, one country, or one continent, trying to develop the spirituality of that place by helping and taking care of each other. This is part of the progression of how the heavenly groups are trying to develop spirituality in keeping with group plans as part of the overall plan of God.

One of my patients recalled a past life as follows:

- *"I am a thirty-five-year-old female living in South Turkey. My name is Heira Dectus and it is 1177 BC. I live with my husband and seven children. At the age of seventeen, I lost my first child a few months after his birth. As a result, I went through a severe depression, which was kind of an internal spiritual crisis. I became more spiritual because of this. I do not have enough to give to the poor because I am poor. I am using my determination and energy to create a charity to take care of people.*

"I got the local temples and the government involved so that more people will be active and give more. I made it institutionalized and a regular part of city life. There was at least a yearly collection for the poor. I also try to distribute food so that nobody starves. This was putting my spirituality into action, taking care of other people. After I collect all this money for the poor, I hand it to the government officials, but I am not really sure that it would all go to the poor. I am realizing that some of it is handed out for political favors and they are getting all the credit for it.

"I am dying of a wasting disease at the age of forty. My hair is stringy and most of it has fallen out. I am delirious with a high fever and chills. Many people are getting sick because of the bad water. I have bloating, weight loss, fatigue, and my teeth are loosening and falling out. I pray and give offerings to God in the temples but my prayers are not heard. I am upset about it; that I honored God and made offerings and it is the priests who are getting fat. I die thinking that I will not let them get away with it. I paid for my healing and I did not get it. God owes me.

"After the death of my physical body I do not feel dead, so I want to learn everything about being dead. I pay attention to other spirits around me. After a while, I see two angels in the Light who help me up to heaven. They take me to a reception area where a Light being is sitting. He welcomes me and wants me to tell him about my life. I am talking about the terrible shaking and weakness I felt while dying, and the frustration of my doing the community work and everyone else taking the credit for

it. I feel better as I talk about it. Then, after cleansing, I am sent to a room for a life review. There are three beings waiting for me. They want me to look at my life.

"From heaven, I see that our group was trying to establish a spiritual place, a place where spirituality could spread out to the surrounding territory. The group planned to increase the spirituality in that area and then let it diffuse from there. So my being spiritual was part of the group purpose. At the same time, it fits in with my individual goal of being more spiritual in life. I see that the death of my child was planned so that the tremendous pain of the loss of a child would lead to the spurt of spirituality. I see that the child was also a group member who volunteered for the early death.

"I also planned to build a foundation for the spiritual part of what I was doing, taking care of other people and helping them survive. It was also counting toward fulfilling parts of God's plan by building a foundation for the care of the poor. From heaven, I see that it was the first organized effort made with political and spiritual people together on Earth. Nobody had organized such a plan before. I got the temple and the politicians involved. I knew they were going to steal some of the money but I hoped that most of it would go to the poor. I made it a self-sustaining system.

"Raising seven kids was also a part of the group goal, to raise kids who were independent, energetic, and self-directing. It was a hope to get them into some political offices and some of the priestly spots. As I look back from heaven, one of my sons became a priest, one daughter became a priestess, and two sons became politicians. I feel I succeeded in fulfilling these goals fairly well.

"I see from heaven that I was afflicted with typhoid and also with malaria. As a result, many problems came from that life to the current life, such as my weight problem, thinning of my hair, teeth problems, bone weakness, memory and comprehension problems, leg problems

because my leg nerves were damaged, and circulation problems due to blood vessel inflammation.

"From heaven, I see that the child I lost in that life is the same soul who I miscarried in this life. The soul made the sacrifice with love because it knew I needed to do this and it was willing. The soul thanked me for the opportunity to help me. I see that when it is done with love, the soul develops positive karma in accepting the short and not necessarily happy life for later benefit in the physical and spiritual universe. Also, the soul was balancing the karma from a prior life. There were other people who were there and are also here in my current life and many of them are also part of my group in heaven.

"According to the heavenly guides, it was a very successful fulfilling of the group goals. Here, many group members were working in association with me to achieve that group goal. This was a very large-scale effort. Many times before, the group members involved in an effort like this were relatively small, which makes it much more difficult to achieve. This was a unique circumstance and it resulted in a very successful change in the behavior of people. I achieved the group goals, my individual goals, and helped in fulfilling God's plan for human development in the universe.

"It was the first time that the scope of the plan was so broad and so much went into it to make it self-sustaining. It was the most successful implementation of this idea. According to the heavenly helpers, I acted like a spiritual teacher because I involved my own spirituality in creating the plan and also involved the priests of the temple to make it a spiritual experience for the believers of those gods. This made it a real spiritual mechanism. It was spreading the act of spirituality in every aspect of society, including politics and religion, and was done very well. This is an example of a spiritual teacher, someone who put her spirituality into action and did it publicly and involved other people."

Spreading Spirituality Through Mass Communication Media

Different communication media can play a major role in spreading and developing spirituality in modern times. Development of mass communications through writing, music, radio, internet, television, and motion pictures can serve as a means of communication so that the knowledge of spiritual information and experience are spread.

Spiritual Inspiration by Human or Divine Beings

Sometimes literally a touch will inspire the spiritual development in a person, or other times a person is inspired by a human without even knowing what is happening and without being on a spiritual path. It is rare that a person is not on a spiritual path after they are touched and inspired.

Then there are those who are directly inspired by a divine or heavenly being or beings, such as a saint or a master, and are put into action that way. Heavenly guides, angels, masters, higher selves, and God also inspire a person when he or she prays or meditates for help and guidance.

- *"I am a sixteen-year-old girl. I live with my mother and father. I am the caretaker of the higher life. At age three, I was given information from within that I would be teaching people about the higher knowledge, about the truth that we are governed by our creator who is greater than anything we know. It is my purpose to see that others understand this, that nobody has to suffer. It is an unconscious agreement. We want freedom from the tyranny of the dark master who enslaved us. He is not of love and Light, nor fully dark. We are suffering terribly because he wanted power. It was nothing to him to have one of us*

killed. We were free people until he came into our terri-
tory and took over our territory.

"When I was eight years old, twelve of us took an oath
that we would account to no one for what we know to
be true. It is never discussed openly about what is going
to occur. We know it is beyond our understanding. I am
also clairvoyant, clairaudient, and clairsentient, and also
have an inner knowing. I see different Light beings and
get guidance from them. I am only a child but I know that
I will be standing in front of the ruler and declare that we
are going to be free. I know this has to occur.

"At the age of fifteen, I know it is time to take action.
We taught people that there is a greater Light and a
better life. I lead a rebellion against the king. I stand up
to him, rebelling against his tyranny, greed, abuse, and
oppression. By now, more people have joined our group. I
am telling the king, 'The time has come to end your reign.
You are an oppressor of spirit. You dominate, control,
and crush people's spirit. You will no longer be allowed
to carry on like this. We will take our kingdom from you,
which was ours originally. You stole our kingdom, our
divine right and freedom, and made us your slaves. On
this day we take our freedom back with the knowledge
that there is power which is greater than you have ever
known.' He is not saying anything. He is just looking at
me. I know he can call his soldiers to kill us at any time
but I have no fear. I think he is shocked.

"It is the knowledge of the truth that spreads among us
and saved us that day. There are many more supporters
than we knew. It even infiltrates their soldiers and we are
given all the support we need to drive him away. The ruler
sees people rising in our support and he is outnumbered.
There is a greater Light in charge and it is spreading in the
whole group. I do not see a physical battle but a spiritual
one. I am seeing God's Light spreading throughout our
community and even people in his army stand up in our
support. I see some Light going through the king, too. He

just gets up and walks away. He and his army leave our community that day, but somehow I know they will come back and his hatred for me would be intense, but it does not concern me.

"There is great celebration and joy in our community. We all have a sense of satisfaction that we got our freedom back. We are back to a peaceful existence. I continue to teach the community about the higher knowledge of the greater gift of life. I want people to have all the information I know, because a day will come when I will have to leave.

"We are preparing for the celebration when we will declare our freedom publicly. During the day of the celebration, I go by myself to pray. There, I am caught by the king's soldiers. I am blindfolded and taken from my community to the king. He keeps asking who I am and why I continue to rebel against him when I have no army. He wants to understand what it is that I have, why I could defeat him. I tell him first he has to get beyond his darkness that drove him to corruption and greed. I realize that it is beyond these people to understand what we carry within ourselves, that the word of God is within our souls. It is with His holy power that I can do what I do. I do not have any power of my own. I tell him that there is a greater power than him that rules creation, and that is where my power comes from and it guides me. He has no power over me. He should connect with that higher power and live peacefully and let others live in peace and harmony, too. He must serve for the general good.

"He gets angry with me for telling him what I think. He sends me to a dungeon. There, they torment me physically and spiritually. The king torments his people, too. So I teach his people the knowledge of God and their hearts change, too, and they let go of their darkness. After a couple of weeks, I am blindfolded and hung. My spirit leaves the body just before I am hanged. I see angels in the Light and they escort me to heaven. I am happy to be home.

"After cleansing and healing, I go for the life review. There are masters and guides all around the table. I recognize them and we are happy to see each other. From heaven, I see that it was not I alone who did it, but was an effort of the whole community. I was just the one who was speaking for everybody. We fulfilled our purpose of educating people about higher knowledge. I see that we could have reached more people if we had worked quietly and not announced the freedom day. I could have gone to other communities and taught there, too. There were people who joined our community by word of mouth.

"I taught people that by ourselves we have no power; it comes from the greater source, God. It is His will that everybody be treated equally and honorably, so we all can stand together for the greater good. Wherever there is oppression, we must stand up to it.

"From heaven, I see that many problems came from that life to my current life, such as trouble in expressing and speaking, and my difficulty in seeing, sensing, and hearing."

Sometimes people are inspired through the experience of nature. They can see the power and presence of the majesty of God in nature such as the sky, the stars, the planets, the galaxies, the small and submicroscopic world, and how parts interact with each other. To realize how complex the normal universe is, via the birds soaring, waterfalls, plants, oceans, mountains, and the interactions between them, serves as spiritual inspiration.

When somebody does something unintentionally which comes from a past life or some association with something else that has existed, it is as though they get hit with a bolt of lightning and suddenly they are inspired by the experience. It can happen in many different ways, as memories are opened up, or they can be inspired directly by the presence of God or other divine beings from the Light. They can even get inspirations from someone else's life who is more spiritual.

Physical Development

A physical cult can also be very real. This is a different aspect of spirituality, one that we scarcely think of as spiritual at all. It is taking care of your body, which is also a spiritual task. The body is a temple of God and we are taking care of the life that God has inspired. So taking care of the body is spiritual as long as it does not become a form of body worship. It is a form of spiritual development. Here we are talking about athletes in general, about long-distance runners, weight lifters, walkers, etc. If we are to develop spiritually, the physical body must be a component of it.

But we cannot develop spiritually at the expense of our physical body. To fast is a spiritual practice, but to starve for weeks is spiritual excess, inspired by the demons. Similarly, any physical exercise within limits is a spiritual practice, but any kind of physical activity in extreme is inspired by the dark side. To have a body that functions smoothly is to be desired, but to beat your body as a religious ritual is an extreme, inspired by demons, and is not spiritual.

Intellectual Development

Intellectual development is also spiritual, such as to study religion or any subject, physics, chemistry, biology, or anything else, and to develop a very fine understanding of that which is spiritual. The study of science, including psychology, biology, physiology, etc., can contribute to spiritual development. Studying the natural world in any form will create spiritual development as one becomes more in touch with God's spirit within the creation. Even though a scientist may profess to be an atheist and believes there is no God in anything, the truth of the matter is that he is becoming more spiritual and actually recognizes God in everything more easily. To develop humanistically is even better. The study of man, man's philosophy, and psychology are spiritual topics. We need to extend the idea of spirituality with physical and intellectual developments.

It is broadening the understanding of spirituality beyond things like praying, fasting, meditation, communication with God, etc., to the physical and the intellectual development of the body. There can be multitudes of individual religions, and as long as each of them is based in love of God, they are all right. Simple love of God demands tolerance for other paths and that no one believes themselves to be more correct or more true.

Sharing and Learning from Spirituality and Religions of Different Cultures

Different cultures coming into contact with each other and examining the spiritual content of each can be a part of a heavenly (Light) group plan, expressed here on Earth where the group plan is put into effect. Spirituality develops here by perhaps two or three groups working together in the area, and each of them, in their own way, developing spiritually.

America is one of the greatest examples of a melting pot, where people of different countries, different cultures, and different religious beliefs come together and intermingle with each other sharing, learning, and growing spiritually. Similar things are happening all over the world.

Sharing and Teaching Spirituality Among Races of Different Planets

Spiritual development in the universe also carries on between inhabitants of different planets. Alien races have served as teachers for each other. The Earth people in the future will also serve as spiritual students and spiritual teachers, to help inspire other races. Spiritual development between cultures, between individuals, and between planets where as one alien race mixes with another, intermingles, and swirls together; the understanding goes to both. Spirituality begins in one person of one race and in one culture of one race, and will spread to other cultures, to other nations, and finally to other races on other planets. It is a long, complex development in which things become more complex, only to be refined and simplified again, so that the understanding is more direct and less complicated and simplified, but still within reason.

These methods to spread spirituality were used before, during, and after Atlantis. They are effective for developing spirituality in different races with a variety of intelligent beings and even with unintelligent beings. By proceeding with God's plan, they will be spiritually developed simply by following it, because God is in the plan, God is part of the universe, in the universe, and is the universe.

Role of New Age Spirituality

According to heavenly beings, the change in the thinking of development of individual spirituality comes about with the advent of New Age type of thinking, where New Age people tend to stress the development of the individual as a spiritual being, even returning to the old religions that had been stamped out by formal, organized religion, to diminish the influence of old religion in their life. People really need to make an effort to develop spiritually. It will happen eventually, even without anybody doing anything, but it will take so much longer. We need to develop individual spirituality and get people back to individual means of developing, such as prayers, meditation, yoga, self-made rituals, and self-made contact with God.

There are also flaws in New Age type of thinking. Lack of intensity and the lack of purpose is a real drawback. The flaw is that people are not intense enough about it. They do not work rigorously at it, and many of them are willing to turn their path over to someone else rather than carry through on their own. They flock to New Age teachers to create an exclusive religion, although it is not a religion. Those who do not teach that there are multiple paths to follow are generally false prophets. They may be teaching a valid spiritual message, but if they are claiming exclusivity, then they have been influenced by the dark side.

The reaction of the formal religions, especially those that are really controlling and those that do their best to remove participants from personal spiritual development, are most vigorous in denouncing anything that has to do with the New Age. Heavenly beings state that there is no such thing as New Age; the New Age is simply the old age of medicine men, shamanism, and others revived. In the New Age, spirituality should be individual, each person developing individually, setting up their own rituals, their own standard of living, and living by it. All the hallmarks given earlier of personal spiritual development apply here. That is what a person should be striving for, whether they do it inside an organized religion or outside of an organized religion.

Heavenly beings, through my hypnotized patients, state that many of these New Age people are reviving the old religions to distinguish between themselves and the organized religions. Those who cry out vigorously against New Age religions and the New Age emphasis on individual spirituality are those who are most controlling and most negative themselves, and are definitely influenced by the dark side. God does not want control over anyone. God wants us to control our own life and our own spiritual development and not create any formal structures, other than those things mentioned before, such as to pray, to meditate, to communicate with God, to practice good works in our life, and to give our time and sustenance to maintain other people to help them. We can make up our own rules and rituals. We do not have to have any set path; anything that draws our mind towards communication with God and to permit the communications to be two-way is just wonderful.

Occurrence of New Teachers on Earth

Heavenly beings, through my hypnotized patients, claim that, in the past and also in the current time, there are new teachers being sent to Earth. Many are here at this time. Some are working within the old religious structures; some are working outside formal religion. Most of these spiritual teachers are very quiet and unassuming and not showing off. These teachers are popping up all over the world.

Every religion on Earth contains some elements of God's truth. It does not matter what religion or where. Every religion on Earth started with a message from God and that message is true and valid and applied in particular to the people of the time and place from where it began. It is always true that the message comes for a group of people, in a particular time and place. When people, time, or the place changes, it does not mean the message is appropriate for the new time. Then, it is necessary to send new teachers. It can become impossible to insert a new religious teacher to an area because of the strength of fundamental beliefs and the political control that groups can exert.

- *"I am a forty-year-old male living at a university for higher knowledge in Mesopotamia in 2 AD. There is a big group who live in this area. Our purpose is to teach others that there is more than just the physical world. I am extremely psychic. It just dominates my life. I teach selected people from the society about higher knowledge. They are supposed to go into the society and teach them, but it is very hard because they do not understand it. I am worried whether I should teach these people or not. There is darkness spreading in the society. I can see dark influence in some of them. I keep getting visions of mass destruction. I sense something drastic is going to happen to us. I feel anxious and agitated. I talk to other people of my group but they do not see it as much of a problem.*

"I see that you, Dr. Modi, are like a leader of our group. You are the Light bearer. Your vibrations are so high that it raises the vibrations of everyone else. There are some people from the community I am teaching who are upset. I can tune in to their minds. They are planning to attack our group and take over our group. I see them being influenced by demons. After a while, there is an uprising. Outsiders are coming in this university area and killing our people. They put a black bag over my head and cut it off. My spirit is out of my body. I see that most of the people of our group were killed. I am shocked to see what they did to my body. Spirits of other people who were killed are also here. We are all taken to heaven by the angels. We are also healed, together as well as individually. Angels are healing my neck with the Light and fusing my head with me. We rest for a long time. I feel guilty because I was not able to stop the killing.

"We review our lives with the whole group. What we learned as a group is that our screening process was not effective. We were supposed to select people from the general population and educate them about the higher knowledge and then they were supposed to go and teach the general population. But they were influenced by the demons. They wanted to be in control, so they came and killed most of us, except for a few higher beings, the masters, including you, Dr. Modi. Your purpose was to hold and maintain the vibrations of the place and the people. I see that you and other higher beings escaped and lived in the society, quietly doing God's work without drawing the attention of people. You chose to leave the body at the age eighty-two because your work was done. You did not look old and did not die because of any disease or old age.

"I feel we accomplished a lot and educated the society about the higher knowledge. I see many problems coming from that life to this life, such as throat problems and blockage of the third eye, which is healed by bringing the soul parts back."

Understanding and Learning from Past Lives

According to heavenly beings, we can achieve the fuller understanding of God and the cosmos based on the understanding of the past lives. Those who do not understand what has come before are condemned to repeat it, such as using technology without spirituality, and repeating the mistakes of Atlantis. That which is past is also an introduction to the future.

What we end up with is a big structure where we have the experience of the spiritual, use of the spiritual, and the development pattern of lives, so that hopefully each life is a bit more evolved than the one before it. The occasional falls from grace when we create negative karma gives us feelings that we have to make up for that shortfall and do something extra. We plan our path in the Light (heaven) with full knowledge of everything we have done before, in every life.

This is a time when Atlantis can be reproduced. The scientific technology is becoming available again, and if individual spirituality is not developed, we can go down that former road very easily. We must get individual spirituality going. We have to cut back on the power of organized religion, particularly of those who are controlling and are critical of others, and get our political leaders and the ultra-rich into spirituality. The actual teachings of the founders of most religions were that everyone has to develop an individual relationship with God. But organized religions became controlling due to the demonic influences. They lost the focus of real teachings of the religious teachers who started a particular religion, by twisting the messages of the spiritual teachers.

Chapter 9

PRESENCE OF THE SPIRIT IN THE UNIVERSE

Here, the first concept we have to understand is that each and every individual has a soul and that soul actually is a part of God and is made up of the substance of God. So, as each being acts in the universe, it is really God motivating and acting. Even the evil acts are as God operating. It is a perversion of the parts of God, that is, Satan and his demons, because they are also part of God. A portion of God was negative, dark, and evil, and had gone with Satan, as explained in detail in my book, *Memories of God and Creation*. All that is left with God is love and the positive Light. In this chapter, we discuss how we can refine and convert dark, evil, and negative parts of God into positive, and different methods to evolve ourselves faster.

Purpose of the Spirit in the Universe

Part of the purpose of the universe is refining the substance of God, converting the dark, evil, and negative parts into the positive. It is as much an educational experience for the evil and dark beings as it is for us, to convert them into loving and positive beings. By going through the developmental process, even dark beings can become all positive and Light. We can think of everything that happens in the universe, be it good or bad, positive or negative, evil or saintly, as being acted through the being of God. This thought will discomfort some. One of the purposes of the universe is to purify the dark and convert it into the positive Light and loving part of God.

Heavenly beings, through my hypnotized patients, state that many of the dark demon beings that I have helped by converting them into the Light had reached the point where they had learned enough, where they had experienced enough to be ready to change back to the Light. I was chosen as the mechanism for their conversion. They have already learned and seen the difference and the benefit of the positive ways through millions of years of experiences, both the negative experiences with Satan and the more positive experiences here in the universe before going to the Light. Some of them changed spontaneously when they suddenly realized that they can revoke and rebuke Satan and leave his service and go back to God, but that is much more difficult for them.

According to the archangels, many of the demons who were sent my way have been nearing that point, and they have been sent to me in particular so that I can convert them into the Light, heal them, and send them back to the Light (heaven). The one demon who could not be changed into Light was the one who was not ready to go to the Light. In that case, I need to simply ask them to be bound in space for a period of time, as I have been doing. They need to be bound in space for a limited time. They still have to live through the universe, to get ready to change back. They cannot be changed by the angels in the space, but somebody from the universe has to help them.

The concept that God is responsible for the evil acts of the universe will upset many religions and people. They have to understand that when the partitioning occurred in God as described in my second book, *Memories of God and Creation"* all those parts of God that were dark and negative left with Satan, but they are still parts of God. Everything in the universe, seen and unseen, including Satan and his demons, has come from the God of love and Light. Every being, basically, is good and loving, and all that was dark and unloving went with Satan. We can adopt as the basis of our behavior that everyone is intrinsically good and anything we see occurring that is evil, dark, or negative, is due to Satan and his demons influencing that which is basically good.

A tiny Light of good, a human soul, can be influenced by a massive amount of darkness of evil. This is how everyone in the universe, even though basically good, pure, and Light, gets influenced, because of the tremendous amount of dark energy that Satan can bring to one tiny point of Light, that is, the human soul. We can think of Adolph Hitler as basically a being of good, which is a difficult concept for many of us to accept, but it is true. Joseph Stalin and all the mass murderers of history were basically part of God, the bright, the Light, and the loving. The evil and negative part came through the influencing of Satan and his demons. So everything that exists physically in the universe is of love, Light, and good, and is from God.

Another way to think of the actions of the presence of the spirit in the universe is to think of a lump of coal as being part of the substance of God, and when that coal is burned and the energy is extracted from it, this is God in action. When we take a pill and the pill has some curative agent in it, we have to remember that the pill is also a part of God. The harsher part is to realize that when a bit of metal is made into a bullet that is used to kill people, that bullet is also part of God. The important point being made is that God has set up the universe by certain rules. These rules are necessary to accomplish God's purposes. One of the purposes of the universe is to cleanse, educate, and purify those parts of God that have negative leanings, to convert them to the positive and bring them back to God.

God created the universe because he wanted to spread out the qualities and the virtues through all of God, to make all parts of God the same and equal. Here is an understanding of how and why each individual soul picks its experiences. Each individual soul has to go through the experiences that will develop those qualities that are attributes of God, such as kindness, love, perceptive, etc. Anything you can say about God, is a quality of God. At the same time, there is Satan trying to influence this part of God and trying to turn it into the negative, so that it will not develop in the positive manner.

In the cycle of reincarnation, each soul keeps comparing itself against that basic standard we are all trying to achieve. We pick our experiences in the universe based on what we need to do to achieve that standard. When we are in the Light (heaven), we have a clear picture of what we need to do, as an individual and as a group to promote this process. But when we are born and take on the trappings of the flesh and blood, we go through the forgetting, which is necessary as part of the refinement process.

If we remember everything, then the learning will be very ineffective. There is a free will for each being. In order for this to do us and God any good, it has to be spontaneously developed from within. It is not efficient to try to incarnate in the universe with full knowledge. In fact, it will retard the whole process because we will never learn anything and there will be no real development of the universe. Forgetting is an act of will on our part. We know we must forget, we know we have to make it, so we choose to forget.

If we come back with full knowledge, then we know what to do and how to go about it. This way, we do not learn anything and we simply repeat what we already know. There is no learning and no development. If we come back from heaven without the full knowledge, the knowledge we develop here in ignorance becomes ours. In the universe, we can extend our qualities; we can develop them, we can improve them, and we can be closer to God's ideal than if we simply repeat what we already know. The first and the most important point to know is that we must be basically good, because we are here in the universe in the physical form; therefore, we must be from the part of God that is the Light – the positive part. All the negative parts went with Satan. No negatively leaning part of God is left in the Light. Whether they are good or bad, positive or negative, whatever their effect on humanity, it is for the better or the worst, these beings are basically the beings of good.

The presence of God in the universe is the fundamental, underlying concept, and what that means to the universe. Whatever happens, good or evil, is an act of God. Every being in the universe, everything that is physical in the universe, has to come from the basic good because the negative parts are already swept out of God. Satan is influencing the basic good. He could overwhelm it and make it negative.

The Refinement Process

To understand the nature of the refinement process, we have the comparison between the ideal and the present state of the soul. When in the Light, souls can look at themselves, how they are shaping up, how they are comparing, and how well they are doing in the universe. In the Light (heaven), there is extensive learning and teaching occurring. Those who are more advanced or those who are on the same level as us may be our teachers. We are teachers to those on our level and those who are below us, that is, those who are not as developed as we are. There are several purposes of the teaching and the learning. First, to give us a complete idea of what qualities we need to develop and to what extent. Second, to give us subconscious knowledge, so when we go down to Earth, we will be shown by our heavenly guides in which direction we need to go.

According to the archangels, this is the area where my work is exceedingly valuable, because it utilizes hypnosis to access the subconscious and brings forth this programmed information for the human beings to know it. This is why this work is so important. I will also be helping many of the aliens, to get across the concept that they too carry information in their subconscious and it can be accessed, and I will also help the aliens to do it. This process works for humans on Earth and it also applies to the alien races in space.

As the teaching and the learning are going on in Light (heaven), it is helping to solidify this information in our subconscious. Through the normal course of events, as we are reincarnated, the programmed information will prompt us to go through with the actions we need to take. This is why the subconscious mind is not part of the great forgetting; only those things we know up front are part of the great forgetting.

The first great forgetting occurred when we were formed or created by God and separated from him, and we immediately forgot that we are God. This is what is called the "first forgetting." This is the same as being born on Earth, and then we forget most of the knowledge from before. This is called the "second forgetting." We cannot accomplish our purpose if we have full knowledge that we are God. We will be able to access the Godly power, we will be able to go through the whole thing, but we will still end up exactly the same way as we were. We will not do any developing or changing.

A part of God is in heaven with full knowledge; that is the God and has full access to the power of God. Now down here is a human being who has gone through the refining process, through the development process, and who realizes exactly the same thing – that he is a part of God and as a result he has access to all the powers of God. What would we do if we have access to the full power of God? The answer is nothing. We will not short-circuit the purposes of creation because we know that the creation was set up for refinement, for the improvement and development of God. If we short-circuit it by using the powers of God, then we will ruin the purpose of creation.

The development of the qualities has to be accomplished while on Earth or in the universe. It is not so much knowledge as it is a way of being. In the refinement process, anything that is an attribute, a way of being, a way of doing can be part of the refinement process, such as to be more loving, kind, merciful, generous, enduring, internally stronger, etc. These things are all positive. The refinement process would be developing them and every other good thing we can say about God. This is what is meant that God created the universe as a part of the development process. The universe was a way for God to develop.

The refinement process means taking something that already exists and improving and increasing it, like when we take a metal ore, put it in a furnace, melt it, raise its temperature, and treat it very roughly. We may throw in a flux to help it dissolve or we may put something in it to chemically change it. In most refining processes, we remove oxygen, and in other refining processes, we might remove sulfate or phosphate, or whatever it is. We may want to convert it from one chemical product to another. This is the same thing that happens to us on Earth and in the universe. We put the part of God – our soul – into the fire – the universe. It is treated roughly, it goes through difficult times, and it is refined, just as we take the metal to the furnace and heat it and refine the metal. We change it from one form to another, we get rid of the impurities, and we make it better than it was originally. The same analogy applies to the parts of God that are the souls.

The process we go through here on Earth cannot be too gentle; otherwise there will be no development. What is set up is the best of all possible worlds for our purpose. It is a bitter journey. It cannot be the most gentle and most loving place in existence, because it would not provide the impetus, the hot fire, and the changes that are needed to develop portions of God.

How To Speed Up Our Spiritual Development

There are things we can do to speed up our spiritual development, and things we can do to help it. First, we can attune ourselves to the world of spirit. There have been many different ways developed all over the world to do that. We find them popping up in religion and popping up in popular culture. To develop spiritually, first we have to recognize God and develop ways to worship God. If we really stop and think: does God need our worship? No! God does not need our worship. Then why worship? Because we need God's help. We need to get in touch with the spiritual realm, we need to pray, and we need to think in a spiritual manner. To worship God is to benefit ourselves because we are the ones going through the developmental process. The closer we are to God, the more and faster we will develop. The more we are in tune with our subconscious mind, the faster we will develop.

There are ways to access the subconscious mind other than hypnosis, such as meditation. In meditation, we reach many different objectives at the same time. We develop our powers of concentration and we develop our singleness of focus. We develop the ability and the determination to make ourselves do what we want to do, what we need to do, and get in touch with the spiritual realm and allow God to speak to us and guide us. Meditation is one of the most valuable practices. Even if a person goes into it with no knowledge of what he or she is doing, without any idea of trying to develop, it is fantastically powerful for that person. In fact, it may even be more powerful for them than for someone who knows exactly why he or she meditates, because they have no preconceived notion. They have no idea about what will happen, and when it happens, it is a startling revelation. It is a real confirmation of the fact that the spiritual is the real realm of the universe.

When we worship, we attune ourselves to the spiritual world; even the rituals of worship help as long as the intent is to connect with the spiritual world, although some of the rituals are pretty silly. The rituals bring us closer to God, but they do not have to be elaborate and confining. It should be free flowing and does not have to follow a rigid pattern. Rituals are not really necessary for those who do not feel comfortable with them. It is the thought and intent behind the ritual that is important, which is to get in touch with God. Every prayer is an act of worship. It is turning our mind to God. Prayers can be formal or informal. Praying does not have to be rigid and it does not have to follow a pattern. We can express ourselves as long as we are communicating with God.

If we define worship as an act of turning our mind to God, then we can really see that prayer, no matter how informal, is as much an act of worship as any formal ritual enacted by thousands of people, following precise patterns and using exact words. The end result is exactly the same. When our mind is turned to God, it is turned toward the world of spirit. It is getting in touch with our essence, with our higher selves. The fact is that we are spiritual beings and even our physical body, which seems to be separate from our souls, is also part of God. The soul exists inside the body, but the body is part of God, too.

The body exists in the physical realm, using chemical elements. The spirit – the soul – remains in the spiritual realm. It is not part of the physical realm. It interacts with it. The soul is never a physical being but it is always a spiritual being. The body has a dual nature – spirit and matter. This is because it is split between spirit and physical.

Anything we do that helps us to develop spiritually is an act of worship, particularly when done with the hope or the intent that we will develop. This intent does not have to happen at that second. We can make a general statement, "Anything I do that is for the better and will help me develop spiritually, I intend it to be an act of worship to God," and then whatever happens is an act of worship. When we have tragedies or any kind of suffering, we should know that there may be a higher spiritual purpose for it and we need to accept and deal with it, as an act of worship to God. Then it will be more beneficial.

As people develop and realize their God-like nature, they do become God and have access to the full powers of God. Then they can be ready to go back to God if they so choose, or they can stay in the Light or continue to work in the universe. Many make this choice, realizing that none of us can really be free until everybody is free.

The concept of sacrifice, giving up things or doing things for our spiritual development, such as the practice of fasting or denying yourself in any capacity, is also a way of directing ourselves toward spirit and we can control it and make it as effective as we want. Any type of sacrifice that is in extreme and causes physical damage is not spiritual. Societies that stick pins in themselves or tear their flesh as a religious sacrifice are not spiritual, because it results in physical damage. Religious saints who beat themselves or are beaten with whips, or pull their hair as a religious ritual are not making a spiritual sacrifice, but are inspired by the demons.

Choosing less of something is usually a form of sacrifice and an act of worship to God. We can sacrifice in a tiny way over short periods of time, but not in a way that will damage us physically. Fasting or cutting down the amount of food or certain types of food is considered an act of worship and takes us closer to God, making us spiritual in nature. Fasting also removes blocks from our spiritual channels (the meridians and energy centers) as a side benefit. But extended fasting for weeks or months is not good because it damages the physical body and is a perversion introduced by Satan. The main focus of the sacrifice is spiritual development by getting closer to God and entering into the spiritual world.

Denying ourselves anything, like making a choice such as, "I really would like to sit back and watch TV, but instead I will read this religious or spiritual text which will turn my mind to God," is an act of sacrifice. It benefits us in two different ways. First, just making that choice is an act of worship. Second, reading the spiritual or religious book puts us into a state of spiritual development.

Another example of worshiping God is Reiki healing, which is also spiritual. It is real and it does work because during Reiki, the power (Light) flows from God, through the person giving the Reiki. It helps to be attuned, but you do not have to be attuned. Anyone can do this form of healing. To be formally taught and attuned is first a sharing of knowledge, and second, it is an act of worship. Every time we do Reiki, if we do it in spirit, it is an act of worship. Similarly, other types of healing work, such as energy healing, hands-on healing, vibrational therapy, massage therapy, magnetic therapy, and others can also be worship to God.

Heavenly beings, through my hypnotized patients, state that there are many ways to develop spirituality, such as prayers, worship, meditation, and also the work I am doing, which is hypnotherapy. When done with spiritual intent, hypnotherapy can be a form of worship, where people can get in touch with the spiritual part or aspect of themselves. Anything that leads to spiritual development is all right. For example, suppose a person is living a life, and at the end of that life, he is hung. If this hanging helps him to advance spiritually, then it is an act of worship. Similarly, the different trials and tragedies we go through in life are kind of acts of worship to God, because they help us develop spiritually. The crucifixion was an act of worship for Jesus because he gave up his life for others.

Heavenly beings point out that doing this type of hypnotherapy work with my patients for hours and hours at a time, and the time I put in writing the books are acts of worship. It is a sacrifice of my time; it is a choice between writing and other things I can do. It is an act of worship in multiple counts. First, because I am learning and teaching, these activities bear their own spiritual development. Second, to have my mind on the spirit as in this work with my patients and doing the writing, planning, and actually performing it, is another form of spiritual development. The subject matter of the book, the fact that it is about spiritual topics is the third form of getting closer to the spirit and developing. This way, my whole life is dedicated to God and becomes worship to God. So one activity here carries three different forms of development. All I have to do is to perceive it, recognize it, and admit it. Any time we focus our attention and devote our entire being to something positive, it is a form of meditation and is a worship to God.

Earth Religions

Earth religions come in all varieties. All of them hold some grain of truth, some part of God's knowledge, some part of God's truth. Every Earth religion has suffered some corruption from Satan and his demons. There are hallmarks by which we can recognize those things that are from God and those that are from Satan, so that we can differentiate between them. Things that come from God tend to be loving, supportive, and promoting of love and good will among the people of Earth. Those things that come from Satan have an element of meanness in them. Exclusivity that tends to promote separation among mankind, such as feelings that one religion is better than another, or the idea that the master in whom I believe in is better than yours. Anything that is mean, hateful, and demeaning to someone else comes from Satan.

Heavenly beings say that for a religion to allege that it is the only real religion that provides the way to God is a mark of evil. It does not mean that the entire religion is evil or that it should be discarded. It means we should discard that part and pay no attention to it because that is the part promoted by Satan. A true religion will promote loving and healing between all mankind, between humans and beings who have understanding.

Each bit of God's truth that is given to mankind is given in a particular time, to a particular culture, in a particular place, and it is most suited to that time, place, and culture. Of course, the truth is true everywhere, but what is given in religion is tailored for that group. This does not mean that it is suitable for all groups, for all times, and for all places. Nor does it mean that it is unsuitable. It means that it must be judged according to the standards. This particular part of a religion for everybody always, or is that part of the religion good for a particular group or culture in the year it is given?

Religions have been created in a developmental manner; that is, as mankind has evolved and advanced. This does not necessarily mean that one religion supersedes a previously given religion. It just means that it is best for those people and at that particular time, and at some time in the future will come another of God's revelations for a particular group at a particular time. God is not intending to create conflict between religions. He is intending to keep the flow of divine knowledge coming so that those on Earth, those in the universe who receive some portion of the truth, will know that there are other parts of the truth out there and that it is good to study all religions. Not just the ones we are born into or the ones known as the best in their areas, but to look at what is true in all religions and also what is false and satanic in all religions.

The understanding of certain animal species is limited but it is human-like in its nature. These animals should be subject to a great deal of respect as our spiritual and physical cousins, in particular the whales, dolphins, great apes, chimpanzees, and orangutans. These all have human characteristics to one degree or another, and should be treated with respect as fellow spiritual beings. There is a spiritual bond between them and us. They too participate in spiritual life, the same way we do. Their discrimination is not fine, their spirituality is not as deep, but it is real.

Such things as dietary laws and rules are of a protective nature. For the most part, they are not of spiritual significance. To refrain from eating meat is different. In eating meat, it is necessary to kill an animal. It is abuse of an animal. According to the heavenly beings, to use the parts of the animal that dies on its own is not sinful. It is the proper use of the animal. To kill the animal for selfish purposes such as for food or use of the skin or other body parts is a questionable use of the animal.

Place of Religion in Everyday Life

Religion is a formalized system of information, practices, and beliefs that are taught and passed on from one generation to the next. It is a generalized system because it encompasses everything. It covers a wide range of spiritual practices. A religion can change an entire society, not just one individual at a time, but hundreds and thousands. This makes it a very potent force in the universe, and very necessary for the existence of the universe.

A part of the purpose of religion is to develop society as a group. As we have come through the ages, society has grown and developed in keeping with religious thoughts. The very fact of having religion in society tends to make society responsible to human beings and to God, and people are more likely to treat their neighbors decently.

Religion may be for individual development, but in a much larger sense, it is for general social development. According to the heavenly beings, Satan's most favorite place to bring in perversion or dark influences is in the field of religion. It makes him very happy to be able to do it. It is easy for Satan to interfere with religion because it is spiritual and Satan is a spirit being. It is right up his alley. Also he puts a lot of effort into interfering because if he can influence religion negatively then he can affect the whole society. This is a real victory for him, and through centuries, he has succeeded very well in this.

According to the heavenly beings, at times Satan has succeeded more than the Light has. It fills him with glee to pervert religion. He inserts in religion anything that condemns others, anything that judges and criticizes others, and anything that is negative toward other human beings. These are all due to dark influences and are inserted in different religions by Satan and his demons, and are never from God. The sacrifice of a living being as a religious ritual is certainly inspired by Satan and his demons, and the higher the being who is being sacrificed, the more dark the deed. Human sacrifice or physical or sexual abuse in the name of religion are just inexcusable.

As a society goes into its developmental process, religion can help. Religion can also help an individual human being because it gives him or her an organized framework to be spiritual. There are those who have to have something organized for them because they cannot do it on their own. Anything that is inspirational or spirit-directed can be part of religion. It does not have to be part of a formal religion.

Some religions say that you cannot be a member of their church unless you give up all other churches. This is not from God and is arrogance on the part of that religion, according to the heavenly beings. Religious leaders who are very dogmatic and rigid in their beliefs are generally inspired by the demons. Any religious leader who says this is the only way and you need to come to him to get to God, as has been taught by many religious leaders, is inspired by the demons. Real spirituality is directly between an individual and God. That is the important part of spirituality. Each and every person has their own spiritual responsibility. We cannot give that responsibility to a religion or religious leader. We have to develop it. Religion can help us in that by giving us focus, an idea, a point from which to start, or a framework in which to operate. Of course, religion must be showing the positive aspect.

If a religious leader is to be sacrificed or permitted to die as part of the underpinning or undermining of his religion, as part of his own spiritual religion, and he thwarts this by leading an army in the battle, then he suffers grievously. A negative act does not resolve into a positive spiritual gain.

Positive aspects of religion are that it makes society more spiritual and contributes in the development of every member of society. It influences society and has positive effects for every person in society, whether they believe in the religion or not, whether they use religion or not. In a pluralistic society like the United States, we have many different religions. There is somebody doing something in every religion all the time. The effects of it on society are good, even though some of the religions are pretty negative and critical of other religions.

Negative aspects of religion are that we can tell a religion has been influenced by Satan and his demons when it tends to be negative, condemning, judgmental, makes claims of exclusivity, is violent in its own behalf, and attacks other religions. Satan and his demons often brag about influencing religious leaders to cause wars, crusades, and jihads. Negative religions and religious leaders can bring less Light and more darkness and can cause wars. Religions and their leaders, who believe that their religion is the only true religion from God and their religious figure is the only one from God, are satanically inspired.

Many great religious teachers who were connected with the Light have taught persons to develop individual spirituality, do your own praying, your own meditation, and your own worship. We do not need a church, temple, or a religion; we do not need a preacher, but we do need to be involved with our own spirit. We need to be spiritual ourselves. A good teacher will teach us and help us along. He will also tell not to rely on him;, we must be our own source, which is inside all of us.

Religion, Spirituality, and Society

Society is composed of a group of individuals. As people develop spiritually, they each have a spiritual field around them, and their own personal development will affect other people. Many people feel that only religion is necessary for their development. They are wrong. They must develop spiritually, individually, through prayers, mediation, charity, and helping fellow human beings, and even animals, one way or another. As these individuals develop, others around them will be influenced to develop. Similarly, religion can cause spiritual development for the general population. As more and more of the population develops greater spirituality, the political and other leaders of the society will also become affected by it. They will become more spiritual and their actions and decisions will become more spiritual. But it does very little good if there is a single spiritual country on the Earth and the rest of them are not spiritual. It becomes a process of developing everyone, everywhere, as fully and completely as possible.

As more individuals become spiritual in different countries, so more and more leaders of those countries develop in spiritual orientation. When all of the population and all of the leaders reach a high degree of spirituality, we will see an unprecedented increase in cooperation, decent treatment for all people of the world, a drop in crime, a drop in wars, and a decrease in the number of actions taken by companies to literally steal money from the customers. There will be an overall improvement worldwide.

Individuals and society can match up, but the individuals need to develop first. Very few people ever think of it, but as the individual can do good work and increase their spirituality, society as a whole can do the same. To feed the hungry, clothe the naked, and shelter the homeless can be undertaken by society acting through its political leaders. As individuals develop spiritually by doing good works, the same is true for society. If society does good work and if society takes part in spiritual development, society as a whole gains benefit, and not just the ultra-wealthy.

There are spiritual assessment tools for judging the extent of spiritual development, and if used properly, they could even be used for making an attempt of assessing the spirituality of a society or a nation, by asking each individual the following questions:

- Do you practice a religion?
- What part does spiritual faith play in your life?
- What spiritual practices do you do?
- Do you pray? If yes, how often?
- Do you meditate? If yes, how often and for how long?
- Do you donate your time to any causes, such as raising money to fight a disease or giving to others? How much of your time do you put in, in terms of total

time available, or in terms of total money available? This can take the form of church support, money to a charity, volunteering for any sort of community groups or organizations, or teaching and helping others to develop spiritually.

- What religion do you belong to, whether Christian, Moslem, Jewish, Hindu, etc.? There are some individuals who really do not believe that they have a religion. They may not have a formal religion as such, but they may be spiritual with a group of spiritual practices and even some rituals that they engage in.
- Do you have experience with clairaudience, clairsentience, clairvoyance, claircognizance, or any other type of psychic experience, such as healing and participation in healings?
- What spiritual and religious books have you read?

Evaluation: The highest point total goes to practices that are used for individual development. The higher point total is given for the longest time spent in the practices. Group practices will receive a lesser weight and those things that are done in a group maybe one-half an hour a week, would weigh the lowest. Anything that is individual, involving his or her own time and sustenance is more valuable than anything else. How do we evaluate or rate them? It is like voting. When we enter into individual spiritual practices, we are actually getting into the big leagues, because that is the most direct and fastest way of development.

Individual spiritual practices include: formal religious practices evidence of worship like donating time and money; religious, spiritual, and/or psychic experiences such as vision, sight, sound, and feelings that come up during prayer or a ritual; and increasing spiritual knowledge. All this can give a general assessment of the individual's spirituality and thus of society and the nation.

Development of Humanness in Humanity or Spirit in Biology

Heavenly beings, through my hypnotized patients, state that all religions were, in some way, inspired by God. There is no such thing as the one true religion. People have grown, matured, adapted, and changed at different rates, at different times, and in different places. All the religions have the truth that God gave them, suitable for their development at certain times and living in some particular place. Religion and knowledge of God are formalized into a series of teachings and practices.

Religions grow and are dynamic. The truth is that God's knowledge is unchanging. People's understanding of it grows, develops, and changes. Because people develop and also change, they grow and they mature spiritually. The same religion is not suitable for all people, at all times in all places, nor is one religion suitable for the same group at all times in their development. We can develop spiritually by using the following practices.

Worship: With time, the form of worship changes. The more people develop and understand that they are part of God, the more their worship practices will change. In some, the form of worship of an external God can change to the form of worship of God within, an understanding that they give credence to God by celebrating the spirit within them. (A creed is a statement of beliefs.) According to heavenly beings, some formal religions became too centered in intellect and thought, leaving out the emotional side of people in religion, which is not good. We need to involve the whole person emotionally, mentally, intellectually, and physically.

What we are really looking at is Satan affecting religions, perverting the understanding and changing the religious beliefs. As soon as religion begins to crystallize and the series of beliefs and understandings about God is passed on, Satan is already there to pervert and modify the understanding of people. As a result, the information God is providing to people is twisted and perverted. The parts of religion that seem biased, such as, "We are the only true religion given by God and there is no other religion; no other God but ours," is a good indication that Satan has influenced that religion. Anything in a religion that is mean-spirited, critical, judgmental, or petty is derived from Satan. No religion is totally destroyed by Satan. All religions have an element of spiritual truth in them and developed practices that will bring the individual worshipers closer to the spirit of God.

Understandings of God come and go. The rituals involved in worship change. For example, at some times, in some places, people believed that blood sacrifice by the murder of an animal was pleasing to God. Over time, that has evolved into an understanding that personal sacrifice or sacrifice of something that is not alive is more desirable, such as fasting or giving up some food, the amount of food, or having fewer of things.

Some religions use celibacy as a sacrifice, and thus it is an act of worship. Celibacy as a sacrifice is to refrain from sex as a form of worship, and is all right, but otherwise, it is a perversion by Satan. Giving up things would be in the same category as fasting, which is contrary to human nature but still acceptable. To be celibate for no good reason is contrary to human nature. To starve without religious and spiritual purpose is not a good thing. Anything that goes against the normal functioning of the human being, for no good reason, is a negative thing. Self-mutilation or self-damage is usually satanically inspired and is not in keeping with God's will.

Worship must be in keeping with the emotional and spiritual aspect of the worshiper. For instance, abstaining from meat or animal products can be practiced by anyone of any religion, whether it is done for a day or a certain day of the week or whether it is all the time. This is a sacrifice that contributes to spiritual development.

Prayer: The concept of prayer is not the same in every religion. Some religions stress formal worship, the recitation of patterned prayers, while others stress the more personal talking to God. Usually, the more informal and direct conversations with God do the worshiper the most good. If the prayer is more intense, directing the person's heart, mind, and the emotions to God, it is more powerful and effective. The more direct the communications with God, and the more specific the prayers, the better they work.

Anything that turns our mind to God is a prayer. When we say prayers, it involves only the mind. To say a prayer out loud involves at least two channels, sound and thinking, the cognitive and expressive. Both are effective. Generally, the more channels we are using, the more effective prayer is. The more completely involved the worshiper is, the better it is. Prayers can be more powerful when emotions are involved because then you are using two of the channels, the cognitive ability and the emotional. Playing spiritual music and singing devotional songs with rhythmic dance or rhythmic movements is more effective. Singing is much more powerful than just praying. The more channels, such as emotional, physical, auditory, tactile, and with music, that are involved while praying, the more effective it is. Informal, specific, and emotional prayers are better than patterned prayers.

Prayers that utilize more sensory channels, such as auditory, visual, and tactile are more effective than prayers that utilize a single channel. Using multiple channels does the worshiper more good and makes it easier for God to answer. For example, many people rock or dance while praying. Other practices to call attention to yourself, such as clapping hands, ringing temple bells, playing music and expressing yourself through the dance, like an Indian woman singing, dancing, and playing a finger instrument. Some meditate and pray at the same time. Tai-chi, Hatha yoga, Indian classical dances, African religious dances, South American dances, and dances from all over the world are based on communicating with a higher spirit and are acts of worship. Those who are opposed to dancing and who believe that dancing is sinful and who seek to limit it in normal life are satanically inspired.

While dancing, we involve multiple channels, such as mental, physical, and emotional all at the same time. A complete human being is involved in worship. Anything that liberates the joy in the human being is good. According to the heavenly beings, even the Middle Eastern belly dance, which seemingly worships the body, has a divine inspiration behind it, since the physical body is also a part of God, and it is part of God's plan that human beings be sexual and sensual beings. It is essential to the development of God. Properly used with proper intent, even the dance like a belly dance ,which seemingly is worship of the body, can be a religious dance, as long as the intent is not to hurt anybody. It will depend on who, what, when, and where.

To pray in the spirit, as in a meditation, is many times more effective because we are actually in touch with the spiritual. We are seeing the hierarchy of effectiveness. Some do the spinning dance, which involves the intellect, the emotions, and physical movement, and they also do it as a meditation and enter the spiritual realm. The same can happen with tai chi and Hatha yoga, and depending on the intensity of the concentration, it can become a meditation.

Repeating prayers is powerful. There is a focusing of the thought and this gets into a meditative state. Decrees are formal religious statements repeated quickly. They are official statements of understanding and belief of God. Like any patterned prayer, they have value. According to the heavenly beings, there must be an emotional involvement and not just the words. Words without emotions are not as effective. If we tape them and play the tape back in slow speed, we will be shocked to hear that the words are not always formed completely, and sometimes the meaning is changed. Other factors, as mentioned before, are more important than the speed of prayer.

When God intervenes or creates something as a result of our prayers, it is us joining God as a co-creator in that act of creation or whatever he is doing. This is a great means to develop the soul, to develop spiritually by joining in God's action. God does not need our help, but it does make us a participant with God, as a co-creator with God. By praying for something that God does, we join with God, and this develops us spiritually. For example, when we pray for development of humankind or of an individual, and it occurs, then we have joined with God in that creation. It is like conscious co-creation, where we have the ability to act in concert with God. Here is humanity with two natures, spiritual and physical, and there is God up there in the Light, all spirit. It is like our spirit and God's spirit join together to accomplish a task. The net result is very beneficial for us to join with God in any task. We join together in the same activity.

Mantra: This is a short word or phrase that has some meaning to the spirit. Mantras are more powerful when they are in keeping with a person's emotional makeup. If you start a mantra and it does not feel right, then do not use it. Search until you find a mantra that suits you emotionally and resonates in your being. With the mantra, you have to be able to pronounce the words and you have to be able to understand its meaning. Emotion is the most important part, and the mantra we use has to appeal to our emotional makeup.

Healing: Heavenly beings state that any means of healing by spirit, whether by prayers, laying on of hands, crystal healing, magnetic healing, Reiki healing, religious faith, medical practice done by a doctor who is doing God's will, and healing through spiritual means, as I am doing, are all forms of worship. These are all forms of spiritual development.

Pluralistic Society: From the concept of religion to the concept of spiritual development of the people within a group, a pluralistic society has a better chance of developing than a monotheistic society, according to the heavenly beings. A country that tries to have just one religion is actually a detriment to itself, because there is only one form of worship in the country and all the ideas are the same. When there is only one religion, there is no cross-understanding and practices become tilted and formalized. As a result, people do not grow or develop rapidly.

In a country like the United States, there are many great religions; many of the minor world religions and many types of Christianity are represented. When ideas of worship, ideas of God, cross-fertilize, people learn from each other as long as they all accept that these are all different paths to God. Then they can utilize this information to improve their own spiritual practice and increase their own spiritual development. It is a very valuable aspect for spiritual growth. According to my hypnotized patients, a Roman Catholic can learn from a Protestant neighbor of the importance of human emotion in religious practice. Roman Catholics stress intellect and leave human emotion out of religion, while Protestants stress emotion in religion.

Caring for Another Human Being: The concept of grace, a gift that God gives to all humankind, means that in caring for someone else, we develop spiritually. The sharing of time, money, love, and care with another person is a spiritually developing experience. When a person cares for another individual, such as an older or disabled person who is no longer on his or her feet and is not able to take care of himself or herself, the caretaker grows spiritually. It is also a spiritually developing experience for the person who is being taken care of.

As each individual develops, society develops, because each spiritual field enforces the other; so we become more spiritual simply by associating with people who are spiritual. Society is developing spiritually at the same time as the individuals in it develop. If a society is set up so that we do not let people starve, do not let people be without adequate shelter, take care of the children, educate them and house them, then society is gaining merit and developing spiritually, and that is shared by all participants of society.

Development of Heavenly Group: Groups working in the Light are like another society. We have portions of God that are interacting with each, both in the Light (heaven) and on Earth. They are working for certain spiritual purposes. This is certainly a society in development. Just as individuals develop through their spiritual practices, so does the heavenly group, which develops through the spiritual changes in humankind. Each and every member of the group participates in the development. Groups develop faster than individuals. Even interacting for spiritual purposes, as in group meetings or smaller meetings in heaven before and after, are spiritual practices. When we are incarnated on Earth, the members of a heavenly group also interact with each other on Earth, and the distance can be across the world.

Society on Earth

Each society has a leader, by birth, by appointment, or by election; whatever means society uses. The leaders of society may not be particularly spiritual people, but as society develops, the leaders also get pulled into it, or occasionally pushed out in front. Frequently, leaders are too busy or too self-centered to do their own spiritual development, so their only chances are being pulled along by society. Various politicians in high offices have their time taken up by other things, and spiritual practices are not a prevalent part of their life, just an occasional thing.

There are different degrees of spiritual development in the leaders. Some actively engage in it, but most do not. Their primary method of spiritual development is through the spiritual development of society. Society as a whole has practices, such as welfare, job security, unemployment programs, giving help overseas that help other people, that go toward the society's spiritual development and the development of its leaders. Life is like a game. There will be positive movements and there will be negative movements, good and bad things, but the important thing about our efforts is that we keep trying. It is not about physical life, but about spiritual life. It is important that we keep trying to develop.

One nation developing will pull along the other nations and cause them to develop also. The final extension is from the development of the world, the Earth, to the development of other races on other planets. Some of the alien races that came here and began the development were divinely inspired, and it was actually part of the divine plan for them to do so. This is something that the human race is contributing to, in terms of their spiritual development. There is enough of a field around our planet to help contribute to the development of other planets. We are no longer just the receiver; but we are a contributor now.

The concept of spiritual development extends from the individual, from the concept of religion, into the concept of society developing, nations developing, the world developing, and the whole universe developing. We also have the concept that the groups in heaven are also societies and also contribute to spiritual development. First, the group as a whole, and then the individuals within it, because they are doing spiritual work that is like a worship of God, and those things that contribute to God's purpose. This is how spiritual development spreads, and in the parallel line, society in the Light (heaven) also develops. Group membership in heaven is only for those who are incarnated.

According to the archangels, only those who go through the surface of the world, the surface of the universe, who incarnate and partake in the universe, are actual group members. Angels also have their associated groups in heaven, with common interests, common tasks, various aspects of the universe, and of God and creation that concern particular angels. Their teaching tasks are generally assigned. They do not just go out and start teaching souls; they have an assignment to do so, and without the assignment, they do not enter into that part of the universe. Angels also have free will, but they have chosen to follow God. Angels are the associates to the human groups. They only contribute.

Religion of Alien Races

According to the heavenly beings, when we come in contact with the aliens, they too will have their version of God's truth, because this is what is revealed to them. Some groups may not be overtly religious but there is spiritual understanding within that group. An alien race may be devoutly religious and their entire lives may be spent in spiritual exercises, yet we will find different religious groups within the alien race suitable to the people who are there at the time. Their religion will also evolve and new truths will be given to them. When we contact an alien religion, we need to judge it by the same standard we use for an Earthly religion. The parts that are of God are recognizable by love, faith in others, an innate truthfulness, rightness and goodness of the race, and a demonstration of God's love for all parts of that alien race and living beings.

We need to use the same criteria in examining alien religions. When we find something that is true in that religion, we need to accept it. When we find something that is false and promotes hate, fear, contentions among the groups, which claim to be the only right way, then we need to reject it as part of Satan's work. Most alien groups already recognize the truths about religion, that a religion is created for a certain group for a particular time. In their dealings with other races, they accept their religions with the same belief, that this is a portion of God's truth.

Not every alien race acts this way, though. Some alien races have the same flaws as Earthly religions and assume that their truth is more true or better than anyone else's and should be spread across the universe so that all races can enjoy this truth. In general, these races have a satanic influence behind them, which tends to lead to some negative effects from contact with these beings. Negative technology is given; negative parts of the religion are promoted, and the interaction between the races is not based on respect or love but is based in terms of taking advantage, literally stealing resources, handing out technology, intentionally or not, which will be damaging without forethought, without thinking through the effects of their actions.

This is part of what has been seen with the two human-like alien races, four and five of group two, who gave so much technology to the human race. The dark side influenced them, even though they were not aware of it. Some negative markers in their culture tell you that this is a satanically inspired group. Even though they act like reasonable, decent people, they hold a lack of respect and a lack of love. "We are better than they are so we deserve more." The technology was traded without finding out what the effects might be. This is the negative part, even though there are no objective religions where you can point and say that this is their belief system, this is whom they worship and this is the structure of their religion. Still, it is a form of their religion. Both alien races have had their religion but with the dispersion, their religion sort of died down. Both races acted toward humanity with a superior attitude, without respect for other spiritual beings, without even recognizing their own spirituality. They were selfish but not all evil.

In the gray alien race with almond eyes, there is a strong satanic influence, but they are not aware of it and are not totally controlled. Just like in humans, we see people who have strong satanic influences, while others have less, and still others are clear. We can tell the difference between them by how they act and what they do. According to heavenly beings, the gray aliens' connecting cords were blocked willfully by them because they did not want to hear from God because it was inconvenient. The satanic influence for them is more comforting than contact with God.

They do not have the advantage of something we have going on here on Earth. We have examples of people who are so thoroughly evil that it cannot be missed. These people serve as a great lesson to us, showing the evil that is possible, so that we can tell the difference between good and evil. We have this great gradation, from saints to Hitler and Stalin.

Alien races four and five and the gray races do not have these extremes. They all tend to cluster toward the negative side, not extremely evil and not quite average, but from average to moderately bad.

The fifth short stocky alien race of group two chose to give up emotions and spirituality after they began to travel in space and did not want to take emotions in space with them. They intentionally chose to get rid of their emotions. According to heavenly beings, it was not that Mr. Spock from the show *Star Trek* had no emotions, but his emotions were controlled and were sublimated to logical, rational thinking. There are many races in the universe like him. Not so with this fifth alien race, in whom emotions were eliminated. They are not there anymore.

When, during a session, we healed them and opened their connecting cords to God, they felt confusion and bewilderment. Even though the emotions were coming from the Light, their brains have to readapt to them. The layers of the brain that they used for emotions have been taken over and used for other functions, intentionally and consciously. So the emotions had no place within the brain to reside.

The new change will be most successful with the very young, because their brains will develop normally to what their race used to be, while the old aliens will be dealing with sensations and feelings they cannot adapt to, but it will not harm them. It will give them an interesting point of view but may not have any great changes. They are getting heavenly guidance with what they can handle. Only the very young will be able to incorporate those emotions into the proper brain structures. It is the children who will remake this race. These children are getting the emotions from the Light, which will go to the proper places in their brains. The other things they plan for those brain structures will be partitioned out across the brain and replaced by emotions.

In the grays, we are seeing the other extreme. Their brains were not changed that much. There were more extremes of good and evil occurring in the grays. Since we did the healing for their race, they are getting guidance from the Light. The extremes are widening; that is, the evil are staying evil, but the good ones are becoming better. It is moving the average of the race toward the good side. In the grays, there is also a very strong willful component. They chose to be blocked through their own wills and rejected the Light. They also got rid of their emotions through genetic modifications.

Archangels say that the DNA template changed on both races after we did the healing. The effect in both races is the same; that is, the adult brains are not really changed. The brains of the young and those being born will undergo the change. But there is a difference between the gray race and the short, blocky fifth alien race. The fifth alien races have used those brain structures for other purposes. The members of the gray race still have their emotional structures in their brains and they are still at least partially available, because Satan has been using those centers to get the negative feelings and negative emotions into them. They were not permitted to go completely blank and that is why the grays are so much more evil than the others. Now that they are getting positive emotions from the Light (heaven), those brain structures are there to receive them and that is why we are seeing the immediate, wide range of reactions. Many are changing toward the good.

The short fifth alien race genetically altered their brains slightly. There was a combination of factors here. Blocking the Light was partly due to the genetic modification to eliminate emotion and also due to satanic influence. So it was a choice on their part, aided by Satan.

This is why it is important to be extremely careful in any genetic modification, whether it is with a human being or a non-human being. It is not something to tamper with and not something to take lightly. It must be very carefully planned out for at least a hundred years or more, with all types of experiments to test the thoughts and the theories that cannot get loose in the environment. A small change can make a profound difference in an organism and it must be fully understood in all its ramifications over generations before we dare to spread it all over creation.

Following the *Star Trek* analogy, the gray alien race followed very much the same procedure as Mr. Spock's people to eliminate their emotions through control, training, and rationality. There was very little in the way of genetic modification. As a result, most of the brain structures for emotions are intact, and not taken over for other functions. They were able to be much more strongly influenced by Satan and became much more evil. The training that eliminated the emotions and replaced them with rationality, similar to Mr. Spock, was directed with evil intent to get rid of emotions, not for the betterment of everybody but for selfish motives. The Vulcan race on *Star Trek* did this for an altruistic motives, to eliminate strife and war in their society and to treat everyone equally and even-handedly. According to heavenly beings, there are many races in the universe similar to the Vulcans in *Star Trek*.

The gray race did the extensive genetic modifications on their own race, which affected the emotions, but they did not eliminate the brain structures or use the brain structures for other purposes. The short stocky fifth alien race of group two changed the structure and function of the brain responsible for emotions, and also through will and practice, while the gray race did it mostly through will, practice, and some genetic change. Some of their genetic modifications were to that end, and some of the genetic modifications were for other things, such as to reduce their physical size to make it easier to travel in space, to reduce their requirement for food mass, air, space, and everything that is in short supply so that they could exist more successfully in spaceships.

Originally, while on their planet before its destruction, gray aliens who were creating genetic babies found more Light in the beings of other planets than in their genetic babies. As a result, they created machines to suction the soul parts from beings of other planets to put in their own genetic babies. According to the archangels, this was a self-defeating thing.

They tried to eliminate emotions and then stole soul parts connected with emotions from other races. They did not understand that spiritual Light in the soul parts is connected with emotions. It was a complete lack of understanding of how things really worked.

Even though these alien races have no religion, the way they are and how they treat other beings is their religion. They show a lack of respect for other beings and gave technology without due regard for the consequences. This is all religious in nature, negatively influenced by Satan. How we act, how we function, and how we treat others can be called spiritual. Our spirituality is lived and our religion expresses itself in our daily lives. If our religion is not what we practice in churches, temples, or mosques, then perhaps we better examine either the religion we are practicing in church or the way we are living our lives. Our expressed religion and our learned religion are far different.

There are many alien races that made the decision, like angels, that they will follow God. There are those planets where the first couple, the so-called Adam and Eve, did not fall, and they are growing and developing very rapidly. Their main drawback is the rest of the universe, even though their field of energy is nourishing others. It is like the material universe is an anchor to them.

Stepping Outside the Boundaries of Organized Religion

Over many years, communication from the Light (heaven) to Earth has been a one-sided thing; the God-sent messengers, prophets, and masters incarnate through whom He had given ideas. In current times, we are not requiring God to place ideas in our head, not requiring the master to be sent. Instead, we are entering the spiritual realm and get the information directly, such as by going to heaven and getting the information straight from the Akashic records or from heavenly beings. It is like sending the master or some spiritual being into the body, complete with the information that they need or at least have easy access to it. Only in this case, we are doing the work of a master and we are doing it in the same way, but by going to the spiritual realm or by being in the spiritual realm and bringing back the information directly from the Akashic library or from the heavenly beings during meditation or under hypnosis.

If you think of the pattern that has been established over the years, over eons of time, then what we are doing now is going outside the pattern, coloring beyond where the lines or the limits are. The thrust of this section is intensifying men and women's individual spirituality, until he or she can enter directly into the realm of the spirit and partake in this information-gathering in comparatively large numbers. Right now there are very few who are getting any information at all this way, primarily, my colleagues, other trance workers, and Light workers.

Part of what I am teaching in the book is that it is possible for others to go to the Light (heaven) and experience it directly. They do need a guide. They need someone who is knowledgeable and experienced, who can help them pass through the rough places. This is not advised as a casual everyday parlor experience or even a bedroom experience. This should only be done by people who have developed their own individual spirituality through the practice of formal religion or meditation, devoting a good deal of time to spiritual thoughts, prayers, and ritual. It requires self-cleansing beforehand, then going on into the Light (heaven) and gathering information more directly and returning to Earth.

Of course, there will be as many interpretations of the information as there are people doing it. That is, people will come to the Light (heaven), they will be given the information, then they will indulge in the regrettable human tendency of trying to interpret what they are given and make it something else. In some cases, there is meaning behind it, something that can be extended from it. But in most cases, what is given is just what is given. There is no interpretation.

Part of the purpose of this section is to encourage people to develop spiritually and to go to the Light (heaven) to get the information directly. According to the archangels, it will be part of my purpose to teach people how to do this and to serve as a guide. This is part of body, mind, and spirit healing. These techniques will eventually be used in body, mind, and spirit clinics, even in the hospitals. They will become better known and more accepted.

Archangel Gabriel warned that it is important that we guard against Satan's intrusion and that people should be constantly reminded about the hallmarks of anything inspired by Satan. For instance, anything that is petty, mean-spirited, damaging to another, not loving, must be kept out of this movement. This cannot be permitted to be part of the new religion of actively accessing the information yourself. There is to be a new religion on Earth, and it is from this work, directly accessing the information from the Light (heaven). This is extremely important and necessary information.

Of course, there will be many interpretations. Masters will be interpreted as gods. People will not look far enough into what is happening. They will stop with the partial under-standing. So there will be varieties. However, it is not neces-sary that there be an organized religion with a structure, since everyone with sufficient training can access the information directly. We do not have to have a primary official religious leader, and we do not have to have any intercessor with the Light (heaven). People can do it themselves. We do not have to depend on divinely inspired revelation or on a particular book of revelations for information. We can do it ourselves.

Archangels, through my hypnotized patients, state that we are to be a nucleus around which this is built. We have to establish a new religion. This will be a difficult road and has to be walked in the Light. No mistakes can be made. We have to have individual spirituality, through all the modali-ties given. As people develop with prayer, meditation, and other spiritual practices, they should go to the Light (heaven) and obtain spiritual information directly. We have to change the focus from formal organized religion, which is standing between people and the divine, to spiritual knowledge gained from direct access to the spirit.

First, we establish ways in which individuals can develop their own spirituality, working through organized religious ritual, worship, recognition of existence of God, prayer, meditation, and all of its forms, as well as through the benefits that will come to the individual for being part of the society that has gained merit in spiritually. Merit is gained from being part of the group that does good works on Earth, and the benefits that come from being part of the group that works in the Light and on Earth.

These are the main categories: the worship done by society; the good works done in organized groups in society; and the work done by the Light (heaven) groups working on Earth and in the Light. The people must understand the benefits that come to them from each of these groups as they develop their own spirituality. People also need to understand that undeveloped members of society, those who devote no time to helping others or participating in their own spiritual development, also improve by being a member of a society that does these things even if they do not, in particular, think it is a good idea.

Heavenly beings, through my hypnotized patients, have consistently told that these means of spiritual development need to be taught to individuals and need to be taught in an organized and coherent fashion to speed up spiritual development of individuals and society through the effects they will have on the leadership, leading to the development of society as a whole and of political leaders and the rich. This way, the whole country will develop, which can affect other countries, leading to the development of the world, and even spreading to other planets. It teaches individual responsibility as well as individual actions to have direct access to the Light (heaven) and to that which is divine. It provides a direct experience of that which is spiritual.

Chapter 10

MYSTERIES OF MONUMENTS AND POWER PLACES

There are many monuments and power places all over the Earth that are full of mysteries, such as structures like the Sphinx, pyramids, the Great Wall of China, Stonehenge, the Taj Mahal, etc. People often wonder how they were built and what their purpose might be. Some of my patients under hypnosis recalled living a life when one of these structures was being built. They gave amazing detailed information about how they were built and why.

One bit of information that was common is that most of these monuments were built with the help of alien beings from other planets. The Sphinx and pyramids are also a repository of information, history, and knowledge. Also, since there are no natural vortexes in Egypt, these structures were created in a way to create powerful vortexes under them. Heavenly beings, through my hypnotized patients, claimed that most of these monuments and power places are either built to create vortexes or are built on vortexes all over the Earth. During the transition of the Earth, from the third dimension, to the fifth dimension, all of these vortexes, along with the vortexes we have created recently under every home, building, street, and everywhere, in and around the Earth, will be activated together. The energy will be very strong and will push the Earth to lift up and move into the fifth dimension.

Building the Sphinx with Sound Tones

One of my patients under hypnosis recalled a past life when he carved the Sphinx with sound tones, as follows:

- *"As Dr. Modi asked me to visualize a closed door to enter a time tunnel to a life in Egypt, where I was assigned to build the Sphinx, I see a big, heavy door made of wood. It has a big, heavy ring that is flat on the top. The door is curved on the top; it is like that "Ali Baba" door. The door is hard to open. I am just opening it a little bit, and squeezing through and closing it as I enter a big tunnel. The side walls of the tunnels are changing a lot; they are shape-shifting. They are changing into different tunnels. Some are very beautiful; some are with the holes in the Earth, and others are made up of blue-and-white Dutch tiles. The bottoms of the tunnels are sometimes made up of earth, of wood, of tiles, or bricks. Other times, it is invisible, like a reflection in water. It is like a multi-dimensional time tunnel.*

  "What I get is that this tunnel is what you go through to access a consciousness of multi-dimensionality. I also see that it could be almost like a library of information stuck on the sides of the tunnel. I am also seeing a tunnel of gray granite with carvings of animals and humans. In this case, there is a light on the top, which becomes the higher tunnel. It is changing all the time to make me aware of the history of all the different eras and qualities of human life on Planet Earth. There are these symbols of possibilities. It is almost like the tunnel is a museum with different eras of humanity, so that when you go through it, you can know all the different possibilities that are brought in to the basic human body. There is a lot that is physical and very heavy.

  "There are no books in these tunnels of libraries; it is more a kind of knowledge. The tunnel is like a birth canal,

with a particular kind of birth that is a multi-dimensional consciousness and a spirit that will be born when it comes out the other end. It is not a normal tunnel; this tunnel is a lot of different things. It is a magical tunnel. For certain people in certain lives, they come through this multi-dimensional tunnel before coming into the body. Sometimes, it could be a birth canal. The wombs of some women have this capacity to change into the multi-dimensional birth tunnel or canal when a particular child is going to come. Right now, there are many such children being born.

"As I come out of the time tunnel, I see myself as a male wearing a brown toga made of a soft cloth and I have a heavy gold necklace around my neck. I do not like it.

"I am a twenty-seven year old servant. I have medium-brown skin and I live in a desert in Egypt. I have knowledge of the future. I live in the slave quarters of a ruler. It is about 30,000 BC. Time is more flexible, so it is hard to tell the time. Time became more solid around 15,000 BC. My name is Rotarian, and I am not married. We are all males living in this dormitory-type of living place. Females live in separate quarters.

"My job is to be sure the sound is maintained, so the spaceship or the beings that are coming from another dimension can glide in on the sound that I make. I train others, also, but I am more like a director of an orchestra. The aliens in spaceships give me mental instructions because they do not have bodies like I do. My body is created to be able to make the sounds. When you combine the body with the understanding of consciousness, it is called the calling. You have to have an acceptance of the new information capability; that is why that tunnel had all the information. I am the only one who has that capability. The other humans with me can recognize it and do it, but I have to direct them. I have to set the original tone and they copy me.

"I was about four when I came here. I was discovered because the wise man knew about my ability to hear *instructions from the extraterrestrials and to physically create a form out of the body that would be like a bridge, because we are speaking through time and space now. It is to create bridges for all of humanity so the creative evolution can happen. At this time, there are very few people on the planet. We did move back and forth in time so we could take information from the future. The past, we already know.*

"I was playing outside with a top. I was making a sound that would be like a spinning sound. At that time, there was more telepathy between humans who had different capabilities. Many of the humans who were born would be like archetypes for later evolution. There are very few of us. So those who were adults heard that there is a child who is making a sound. I would make different sounds and they would hear it from a distance. They found me and gave my mother some valuable stones, and my mother gave me to them for the greater good.

"Then I was taken to the construction site. They made the bricks out of the baked earth, like an igloo would look like. When I got there, I was all alone. The women were nice to me and the big men were my teachers and assistants of the rulers. The ruler and many assistants had different talents: the talent of sound and communication with the aliens, and the ability to create energy forces, like a beam, with the sound. I am learning from them and then they learn from me because I have more ability than they do.

"Once I reach puberty, the sexual urge comes but is not to be manifested in procreation. It is needed to channel the energy of the spine into the mind. It has a lot of creative life force in it. The sounds that come out of me have much more power because they have within them the capacity of creation. Then from there on, it is all an experiment to see what to do with it because it is very powerful. At first it is out of control. I am able to break things with my sound and create a hole in a big wall. It is necessary to learn to

master it for the different purposes with the breath. The breathing and the intention are very important. I am a bit rebellious; I do not want to be in class day and night. I just want to feel the sexual energy in my body.

"Initially, with the sound, I am able to knock down the trees and buildings. They decide to make it more creative and I am able to carve a design in the stone by making small sounds. They take me to a cave where there are huge mountains of rock, and I am carving designs in these rocks with the sound. I can make the sound to create laser quality; a very refined carving which can cut right through. I am about twenty-two at this time. There are other extraterrestrial beings of Light who are working on the evolution of humanity. I have this ability to build, in the physical form, a symbol of life on Earth that will contain within it the history of evolution up to this point so it will not be forgotten. The rock's basic structure will be altered and it will become like a receptacle of history, like a library. Stones and rocks are libraries and the geologists know this.

"I am still in a rebellious stage. I want to be with women and be sexual and experience my body. I am free enough that sometimes I disappear and come back. They want me to stop it. That is when they put the heavy gold chain around my neck to weigh me down. They are saying that I have to do it. It is a job for humanity and I have to do it, the same way I was given up by my mother. I have to give up my personal life and the heavy gold chain around my neck is a reminder. It is a combination of interesting work, but I am also frustrated and unhappy because I want to be free, and I know I can never be free. I am not able to adjust to it and have to stay in this uncomfortable condition of wondering what is going to happen next, but it is also very interesting. There are three elements of positive, negative, and intermediate, and they keep on switching back and forth inside of me.

"So we begin the project. I am the only one who knows how to do it and what to do, and there are other slaves

who can also use sound to carve, but I have to show and tell them what to do and how to do it. The other teachers are making sure I stay focused. I will do the main cutting and the other slaves can lift the stones and put them on the beam of my tone with the sound to a certain extent. Sometimes they can cut and other times they have wider range. It is like an electronic conveyer belt; the beams created by different tones are of different types, such as a laser beam that can cut through very smooth and straight, while the other is a wider beam that can lift and put things on like a conveyer belt. The sound (tone) is like an electromagnetic channel in the air. It is almost like what comes out of the satellite now. It is electromagnetic energy.

"In this project, there is a level of consciousness required at every stage of the creative development. The idea is to have a very large symbol of humanity on Earth at that time. The extraterrestrials from the future gave me the blueprint. They give me information through mental telepathy, but I never see them. I know that we have to build this huge representation that will be hollow inside, because it will be a library or a time capsule. It is supposed to be a huge symbol of animal and human. The stone has the memory within it, and if you touch the stone and allow yourself to completely dissolve in your mind, you are fully receptive. When you touch the Sphinx, you can understand part of your own role in the evolution of life. Then you can come back to know whatever you need to know.

"There is an ability in the stones of the Sphinx, and we know it when we are putting it together. My job is to cut the main part. The slaves are bringing the rocks and I am cutting out the huge sections. Some of the other slaves are making the tone at the lower levels but cannot do the laser carving. They can do the wider tone, so the heavy rocks will fall on each beam and move from one place to the other. There is a time limit, and even though we are moving time around, we are also fixing time. We are

moving time in our minds, like imagining. By building the Sphinx, we are solidifying or fixing the time. The Sphinx is one of the first structures created that is intra-dimensional but mostly physical. It is made of stone, and the quality of the stone has a much longer lifespan than the humans.

"It is all an experiment in evolution. Whatever we do in building the Sphinx, we also give life to it. It is a being and has a consciousness of its own. That is why people are so impressed with it, even though they do not know why. I am feeling tired because I have to go in deeper and deeper understanding. What I see is that aliens in the Light are using my body and vocal cords to make the tone sound as if we are one. One thing that happens in evolution is the sense of oneness, which is tied into telepathy where you become one with the other being, in this case the extraterrestrials.

"I am outside the Sphinx watching it. It is almost in an etheric form before the actual stones are placed. Now we are putting the stones in the etheric mold. As I look at it, I see that it is a joint venture here. It has to do with the abilities I have and abilities the workers, extraterrestrial beings, and Light beings have. We are working at different levels in creating the physical form that is a representation of the planet to this point.

"I see the stones are square shapes at the beginning, and when they are put on the etheric form, it takes the form of that part because stone is also a combination of etheric and physical. It is just amazing to see. My sound tone can do lots of things. I do the finishing touches on the Sphinx with my sound tone, like a sculpture. The purpose of having a lion's body and the human head is to show the oneness of consciousness and Light, and proper balance. If we meditate on the Sphinx, we will receive the balancing energy that we need. That will continue to be part of its purpose in the ongoing evolution of humanity on Earth. We are aware of this at this time because we can see into the future, and we understand human nature.

We do not know where the evolution will go. The demonic interference will slow it down or speed it up.

"The Sphinx is a symbol of correct balance of human nature, as far as we can see, but simply as being human, we cannot see everything, which is a gift for humans – a forgetting.

"Although the Sphinx is constructed of stones, its message is very flexible. It is a true message for humanity about balance. Its front paw is stretching forward, the back is straight, and represents the past. The whole body is the present, with the stretched paw in front as the future, and the body is resting. The lower part, the back part, is of the animal. It is only the breast and the front part that are human, and the rest is an animal. It is important to understand the animal nature of humanity which is what we are – the divine animal.

"There was a flexibility and elasticity in time between 60,000 BC and 30,000 BC, during which the Sphinx was built. The timeframe given in books about when the Sphinx was built is much more recent, so it is very difficult when you work with the flexibility of time because you also work outside of time.

"Those people who are making pilgrimages to the pyramids and the Sphinx need to understand that they can receive messages from direct meditation in situ, by putting their hands on the stone or meditating on the quality of the energy of the pyramids and the Sphinx. They will then receive in their own language the quality of that inter-dimensional energy. Once humans contain the consciousness of that, physically, it will transmit to other humans. It will go across the collective consciousness to those who are ready to receive it. It is all a question of accelerating consciousness of the multi-dimensionality of life and how to use it.

"Regular tourists will pick up some energy, but usually their consciousnesses are very limited. They need to slow down and absorb the energy in silence and allow it to come

into their dreams, whether they remember them or not. It will come to them if they meditate or sit quietly. Similarly, when people desire to reach out and touch a part of the Sphinx, that will happen. Their etheric hand will reach out and touch it and they will get the information.

"There is a door at the bottom of the Sphinx somewhere, part of which is hollow. It is access to the basement or cellar and to all those underground structures, but people do not know it; some people work there.

"My higher self is saying that you can charge the energy so people can feel the awe. When Dr. Modi prayed for it, I saw angels cleansing, healing, and shielding the Sphinx and the pyramids with a triple compression chamber of crystalline Light, mirror shields, rays of blinding white Light and the violet shield. She also requested that people be aware of the energy and awe of the Sphinx and pyramids. I see that people will get the non-verbal understanding of multi-dimensionality and the flexibility of the past, present, and the future, including the guides who work there. Multi-dimensionality means that people will not be so afraid of death. They will not be so surprised at a lot of signs they have received and ignored. There are plenty of signs that the angels and people's higher selves give them about their own power of manifesting, creating, and understanding beyond what they think they know of multi-dimensionality.

"The etheric energy almost has its own life, which is created by thoughts, intentions, and ideas. So when the stones were brought up by the sound to create the Sphinx, they were square but changed to any form they needed to be. The stones, sound, consciousness, and etheric energy all work together. The purpose of the Sphinx is to create a balance of nature. Everything in nature is one; humans and animals have oneness in them. It was later thought of as a turning point in history. It will be less etheric in form because humans have to do more with themselves and their human element. They will not be able to get that kind of

help anymore and will have to carve the rock themselves. They will not even have the sound to make them or the laser beams from the extraterrestrials. The Sphinx was meant to last for thousands of years. They decided to have a human face so people would take it more seriously.

"We simply use our minds once we understood that nothing is really solid. The minute you understand that a solid rock is not really solid because it is an attraction of energy that pulls it together, but there is a belief system that it is solid, so it becomes solid.

"What I get is that a new Sphinx could be built that will connect with our higher selves, who are connected to all higher selves of all aspects of the creator. It will not be in the form of stones; it will be an individual creation of humans for the understanding that there is one humanity within all diversification that exists on the planet. This is a complex idea.

"Although parts of the Sphinx are eroded, it does not matter. The etheric form is still there. At some point, someone will remember how we put it together and they will be able to even recreate it with their mind. They can visualize the stone covering the parts that eroded and recreate it. It is like when people lose a leg but still can feel it, even though it is not there anymore. But it is not necessary. There are plenty of other miracles happening right now on Earth that we are ignoring, like crop circles.

"When you go near the Sphinx, it will tell you if you have the sensitivity and interest and if it is the right time. These are decisions that are made at many levels about what is the right time.

"When I began to build the Sphinx, I was twenty-two. Now I am thirty-eight and it is finished. It looks like a physical structure but still has an etheric energy in it; it is a multi-dimensional being. It has a multi-dimensional energy. This means it has history that goes beyond space and time. I feel old and sad because my work is finished. The wisdom is in its walls. The Sphinx is a combination *of the etheric history of humanity up to that point, and it was necessary for the extraterrestrials to come and create the next stage of evolution, which was to build a solid thing on Earth that represented where we come from and what our highest hopes are. Once that is built, some of the doors are closed to the etheric connections because they are in the Sphinx. They are in people, too, but they have to discover it themselves. We will be in another stage of evolution and will not have much etheric connection now. There was more etheric help before; it is like the parent letting the child leave the house when they are still very young.*

"After it is done, they take the gold chain away from me. I did not like it; it made me bent because it was too heavy. Now I do not know what to do with my life anymore. I do not have to live there with the ruler. I go to find if my mother is still alive, but I learn that she died a long time ago. I just walk around, and after a long time, at the age of forty-five, I find somebody to marry. I live in a nice place by the river. I have slowed down and changed my whole life. I do not make my sounds anymore. We have two children and I spend a lot of time meditating. I sculpt dolls from wood with my hands.

"I am dying at the age of seventy-three with lung disease. I lived a quiet life. I never told anybody about my gift of sound tone and me creating the Sphinx. The Sphinx is a historic, etheric being in the physical form.

"From the age of four years until I finished the Sphinx, I had one purpose only: to learn the sound and to do the work the ruler and the extraterrestrials wanted. When the work was complete, I was sad because it was like a death with the end of an era. I had greater awareness of everything.

"I died very quietly; I just stopped breathing. I do not have any special thoughts. My soul comes out of my heart. I see beautiful, angelic Light beings around; I look all golden. We all move up and there is beautiful music being

played with violins and harps. Now we are in heaven. [Smiling] I see an etheric Sphinx here. It is almost moving and smiling at me, like it is saying that I did a good job. It is like a being.

"I go through some kind of Light tunnel, and the Light goes through me and dark things fall out. It is more than I thought, almost like I emptied coins from my pockets.

"Then I go to a room where there are five people who are my friends. We do not talk very much. But we have psychic communication. We are outside of time and do not know what the future will be, only the general plan.

"Then I go for the life-review. It is like reporting to a large auditorium. There is a long table and there are ten people sitting around it. These are different masters, and about three hundred people around who are like students. These are the people who are going to be spiritual guides. I am reporting about different things, including how I felt. It has to do with attachment and non-attachment. It happened when they took me away from my mother at the age of four. How attached I was with her; I did not have that later in life. The heavenly helpers are compassionate and let me cry.

"As I look back from the Light, it was 30,682 BC when I began to carve the Sphinx. There was a fluidity of time, and time was stretching then. I see now that the importance of the Sphinx is laying one's hands on the stones of its form and having the conscious intent to search the insights of the history of all humans who ever lived. The imagery is more for the mental connection that people will make; the psychic connection is in touching it and tapping into the history that is needed. The history is not necessary on any large scale because each human has a different part of the history; only what you need, not all of it.

"I am seeing everything on so many levels. Even if the Sphinx did not exist anymore, it will still be there with the intention of the concept. So it can be found on the etheric level, in a crystal, or simply in the intention that is locked in

there, and then people will find what they need at the right time. They will find something buried in a great big chest that has an electronic protection around it. People will find them in different parts when they are ready for it, so there is no specific place.

"I am seeing that underneath the entire Sphinx different types of knowledge, information, and history are stored. I also see a long tube or tunnel underground between the Sphinx and pyramids near it, including the Pyramid of Giza. The storage places are everywhere. Some of them are connected and others are not, and they are equivalent to metal boxes. People will recognize them when the time is right, in whatever way possible. I see all these black metal boxes. They are etheric and physical like the Sphinx is, so people will find what they need when they are ready and in whatever form. The purpose of the Sphinx is the creation of forms with whatever the intention is. During the transition to the fifth dimension in the future, there will be a great opening toward the ending.

"People are slowly gaining more understanding of the connection between spirit, life, eternity, the oneness of all things, and the similarity of design. It affects people's lives on a mass scale and is happening now, but they do not see it as much. People are complaining right now and everybody is very confused and uncomfortable. There is a tremendous transition happening, and 2012 is a point of marriage of physical and etheric, and it is changing people.

"When people are conscious, they will see the purpose of the Sphinx differently. They may feel like a new person and may not notice it. They will not realize how different they are from one day to another. The Sphinx and the pyramids are not isolated. They are part of the network of creative energy all over the entire planet. People are awakening to their spirituality, and nature is awakening because people are. Everything is interconnected. It is already happening.

"The lesson I needed to learn from that life was not to be so isolated from other people. It is one of the problems I bring from that life to the current life. Also, there is some kind of confusion between superiority, uniqueness, and isolation. I do have that in this life. I also do not have any deep connection in the current life as in that life. Physically, I have breathing problems, as I did in that lifetime.

"I see my brother now as a ruler in that lifetime. Dr. Modi was a part of the extraterrestrial alien consciousness out of time. She was a part of overall consciousness. Her individuality dissolved with others and they all made it possible. They all were holding the vision because they were together. She was also helping me to make the sound to sculpt the Sphinx.

"When Dr. Modi prayed to God to flood all of Egypt, including the Sphinx, pyramids, all the storage places for history, and the people who were in that life and the current life with the crystalline Light, I saw crystalline Light flooding the whole of Egypt, then and now, including the Sphinx, pyramids, all the tunnels and the storage places, the whole land, and all the people who were there in that life and here now, cleansing, healing, and shielding Egypt and everything and everybody in it with the triple compression chamber of the crystalline Light, mirror shield, and rays of blinding white Light.

"I forgive the ruler and all the teachers for not being loving and caring, and for being emotionally aloof. I also forgive all those people who separated me from my mom. They all accept my forgiveness. Although I loved my wife and children, I was kind of emotionally distant to them, so I would like to ask for their forgiveness for not expressing my love and affection to them, and they are completely forgiving me.

"When Dr. Modi asked for all the soul parts of me and everybody who was living in that life and of the Sphinx and of Egypt, I saw many soul parts coming back

to me and other people from Satan and his demons. I also saw soul parts coming to the Sphinx, and it looks like it has more emotions. The etheric parts of the Sphinx are coming back to its broken parts and it looks better. Angels also shielded the Sphinx, pyramids, all of Egypt, and everything and everybody in Egypt in that life and the current life.

"On Dr. Modi's request, angels brought back all our past life personalities and integrated with us after cleansing and healing them. I see about two hundred past life personalities we have healed before, are integrated with me. I also see many of Dr. Modi's past life personalities, about three hundred of them, being integrated with her after cleansing and healing them.

"Sphinx in heaven is looking much smaller now. I see that when you asked the soul parts of the Sphinx to be brought back, a lot of Light was going from the Sphinx in heaven to the Sphinx on Earth."

Construction of a Pyramid

One of my patients under hypnosis recalled a lifetime when people, with the help of aliens, built a pyramid long before the Pyramid of Giza was built. This pyramid is underground now and not visible on the surface.

• *"I am a thirty-year-old man living in Cairo, Egypt. My name is Anaya, and this is 12094 BC. I am married and have two sons, ages ten and twelve years. I do not have a lot of money but everybody respects me. I am very knowledgeable and powerful. I perform rituals and ceremonies. I am an advisor to our king and people. I am next to the king and advise him in court-related matters and guide him. I am very calm, centered, with a strong physique and shaven head. I try to be as just as possible.*

"I am about forty-five-years-old now. There is a famine in the country because of lack of rain and hot weather. I advise a ceremony and an offering of a panther to fire to get some rain. We go to an open altar and we pray to fire for rain, and sacrifice the panther. I pray for the release of its soul.

"After a few days, a stranger comes to the court with a plan to build the pyramid. He says that the pyramid will attract the clouds and rain and we will never have famine again. He appears like one of us but there is something weird about him. I cannot pinpoint what it is but I can sense it. I think about his proposal, and convince the king that we should accept the idea. It appears very convincing and also we are quite vulnerable at this time. We know it will take a long time but are hoping for the best. He asked for very little in return. He just wanted some control and say in the kingdom.

"So we started the project. So far, we do not have any pyramids in Egypt. The man is a chief engineer. He has his men, who live in tents, and we also provide men for help. First we laid the foundation a few floors down, and then they begin to build on the top of it. These people have some technology by which they make stone blocks with sand.

"Our people who work for him felt something strange, as if they are controlled by him and his people. It is like we are ruling and they are dictating. It takes a longer time than they said, and the more time they spend with us, the more control they have over us. They are gradually telling us how to rule the kingdom. When I realize what is happening, I plan to go to the king and discuss it, but they find out about it and suddenly they become tyrants. They imprisoned me in the underground level of the pyramid, in the cellar. It is very beautiful here. They made special chambers and compartments in the lower levels underground. It is like a maze for a specific reason, but they refuse to share that information with us. You can get

lost in it. I also see some carvings and some inscriptions on the wall here, and they are painted with gold and silver paint.

"I am becoming more and more defiant. I want to go out and tell everybody. At the age of sixty-three, I try to escape but they catch me and behead me. They bury me there in the wall. My last thoughts are, "I should have paid attention to my gut feelings. A lot of people are under the influence of these people." My soul comes out of my heart area. I am still very angry, so I hang around them. I get the sense that they are given information and orders from somewhere else. They have these huge machines and they are getting signals and all types of messages. I do get the sense that it is for some higher purpose.

"I see these angels in the Light. They are smiling at my anger and confusion. I go with them to heaven. After cleansing and healing, I go for my life review. There are six Light beings waiting for me. They tell me that maybe the engineer builder did not present himself properly, but overall their intention about this project was good. My gut feeling was correct. They were not from that area. I was hindering them in their work; that is why they killed me.

"From heaven, I see that it was a smaller pyramid, and the aliens who were helping from the spaceships above were Martians. They look like robots with red eyes. They appear to be very strong, well-built robots with a little human touch in them. They are half robot and half beings. They do not seem like actual Martians. They are about six feet four inches tall, but are mostly robots.

"From heaven, I see that there is a huge energy vortex under the pyramid. They were channeling the energy into the maze from the core of the Earth through some technology and creating a vortex. It takes about fifty years to build it. It is a very powerful place and people can do many things there, such as healing and preserving. I see that this pyramid is underground now and is not visible

on the surface. I see that there are about a total of twenty-five pyramids above and under the ground. There is a pattern to the way they are spaced out, their direction, and the way they are built. They will be a powerful source in lifting the planet to the next dimension. When they are all activated together, the energy will be very strong and push the planet into the next dimension. All the pyramids together create a bigger vortex. These pyramids are in the center of the Earth and all the others are scattered all over the Earth.

"I get the feeling that the Sphinx also has a role in this. There are vortexes in the water also, and they will open up, too, and will cause a lot of calamity because water will be a very powerful source.

"From heaven, I see the lesson I needed to learn was not to get distracted no matter what the situation is. Always listen to your gut feelings. Killing animals or any living being as a sacrifice to God is not right. It is always wrong.

"I see that our people were doing just the labor, carrying the sand bags and stones that were easy to carry. I see that the aliens were sending the beam of antigravity energy from the spaceship to cover the whole area, which makes everything lighter than they are.

"I realize that many problems came from that life to my current life, such as pain and stiffness in the neck because I was decapitated.

"When Dr. Modi requested everybody who was there in that lifetime, including myself, every person who took part in building the pyramid, aliens on Earth and in spaceships who were helping in building the pyramids and vortexes under them, and the whole of Egypt to be filled with the Light, a brilliant white Light came from God and removed everything that was dark and did not belong there, and healed and transformed all of Egypt, all the pyramids and temples, vortexes and everything and everybody, including everybody who was there in that lifetime. Then all the

soul parts that we lost in that lifetime and all the other lifetimes, soul parts of all the aliens who were helping and also to all the vortexes, pyramids, and the whole land of Egypt, and to everyone and everything in it were brought back, transformed, and integrated where they belonged. I see my head is coming back to me, and also soul parts to my heart and all over the body are brought back and integrated with me after cleansing and healing them and me. Also, soul parts of the panther are brought back and integrated. Then angels shielded everybody with a triple net of Light, violet shield, metallic shield, mirror shield, and rays of blinding white Light. Angels also shielded all of Egypt, all the pyramids, temples, vortexes, homes and buildings, hallways, attics, basements and underground, and everything between them with crystal shield, metallic shield, mirror shields, and rays of blinding white Light, and created the centers of Light all around them."

Life in Egypt to Build the Pyramid of Giza

Under hypnosis, a patient recalled a past life in Egypt when she was abducted by aliens, who prepared her to build the pyramid of Giza as follows:

• *"I am a twenty-two-year-old male with a brownish complexion. My name is Rajak. It is about 5000 BC. I live on a farm outside of a village in Egypt. I am married and have two children: a boy and a girl. I work alone on the farm and take care of sheep. I am lonely and bored. I wonder what else there is, and about all the mysteries of the universe. One day I am farming and thinking there has to be something more to life, and as I think this, I feel some beings around me but I do not see them. They call me by my name and talk to me. I am scared but also interested in what they are telling me. They are saying that I am chosen for a special work. In the next few years, I will be prepared for the work and will be uniquely qualified for it. I will be open to new ideas and many gifts will come to me. Over the next eight years, they come to me and communicate telepathically about once a month, but I cannot see them. They usually come when there is no moon.*

"Sometimes I have visions of what will happen in the future, about the pyramids, which will be like satellite receiving towers, a communication system. At the age of twenty-five, they are showing me a movie about me with a jackal's head, which will be a bringer of wisdom, and I should not be afraid of it. They are telling me that I will have a higher status and will be wealthy. I will be able to bring people back from the dead, heal people, and build massive things. I am shown that my children will join me but my wife will die. I feel sad about that. They show me these movies about my future once a month, to prepare me, until I am thirty years of age. One time they even try the jackal head on me. I feel anxious about it and have difficulty breathing. They are also giving dreams to my children to prepare them. My wife is becoming depressed because I am becoming more distant. She also had a dream of me with a jackal head.

"At the age of thirty, they take me to a spaceship. I am sitting on a chair in the middle of a crystal room seeing the movie of my future on the crystal walls all around me. It is like a panoramic 3-D movie. They are showing my future and how I am going to change the world. I am going to bring a new civilization here. I am seeing myself with the jackal head and coming into power. I am going to start a new religion and civilization and I will be given the knowledge by the people here. My children will become the rulers and my grandchildren will have a privileged life. I also see how I am going to be remembered. I am seeing that I could also lose everything if I do not follow their instructions. I am seeing different scenarios, such as I am very rich living in a palace. They are also showing

my future lives, including my current life. They are also showing me other planets and beings on them. I get mentally exhausted and overwhelmed watching the movie and I fall asleep.

"As I look back under hypnosis, in that life, I see that when I fall asleep they begin the process of putting the jackal head on me. They anaesthetized me. They put the shell of real jackal head, without any brain, on my head. They fuse the skin, and all the blood vessels and nerves are attached together. When I wake up, I am hurting all over. When I touch my head, it does not feel like my head. I am terrified and I scream. I try to pull it off but I cannot. I realize that I will be like this for the rest of my life. I am crying, thinking I will be treated like a pariah, an untouchable. I do not want anybody to see me and I do not want to see anybody. I look up and see a being that looks weirder then I do. He is about seven and a half feet tall. He is humanoid with two arms, legs, a body, head, and grayish yellow skin. He has a big head with no hair and prominent brow ridges, with sunken eyes, and almost looks like a skeleton. He has a smaller mouth and not much of a neck. He has long fingers, and he is wearing a purple robe. I feel a little bit comforted by this being. Although I was prepared by those other beings for years, I do not feel empowered. I still do not see the beings who were communicating with me telepathically. I can feel them but have never seen them.

"The being in front of me is doing some energy work on me and talking to me to calm me down. I sleep for days. It is also a kind of denial. Now, as I look back under hypnosis, I can see that these beings are programming my brain, which makes me more mechanical, but I still have some independence. They are putting information in my brain and also modifying some emotions. My body is still human but I feel stronger and muscular because there is this energy flowing through me. I feel overwhelmed with all these changes in me, so I just sleep most of the time

for weeks. Then when I wake up, I feel more accepting of what they did to me.

"I try to eat and swallow with the jackal head on. It is difficult in the beginning, but gradually I am able to do it. The tall being is helping me. He is teaching me how to control my emotions and how to use my body. He shows me how to govern, how to pull in my own power to sustain my core because I will be isolated. He teaches me how to understand different languages because the beings put a chip in my brain. This being also teaches me how to levitate things, how to manifest whatever I want, and this is how people will think of me as god. He is teaching me how to build the pyramid and for what purpose. I am given power tools, like the Egyptian symbol of Ankh.

"This being is also showing me how to send messages intergalactically and how to get messages back and forth. It is like in stores when we get our credit card swiped electronically and we sign on a little pad and it appears somewhere else. He also teaches me telepathic communication and how to make healing sounds. At this point during the session, I began to cough a lot because my throat was irritated, and I saw a device that looked like a beetle was put in my throat in that life. It was put in to make healing sounds. It is big and irritating my throat. It is an iridescent greenish gold color and large, about as big as my fist. On my request, angels are removing that device and putting a new silvery Light device, something smaller and more concentrated. Angels took the alien device to heaven.

"The aliens also wired my brain and put chips in it. I am the only one on the spaceship who is being worked on. The alien being is also teaching me how to heal with my hands, how to tap in to people's minds, and how to tap into different planets and their beings, because the aliens are building pyramids in other planets, too. They will be used as satellites and also as military outposts. He is also teaching me how to read auras and do color

healing, and how to manifest things by my willpower and to access knowledge. I see that I have laser eyes. They also put a self-destruct device so they can destroy me any time, which was ultimate control. They also put a tracking device in me so they know my whereabouts.

"The aliens altered my DNA so I can live for more than two hundred years. They also make me taller. As I look back under hypnosis, I see that I am lying on a table. The aliens have an image of how they want me to be, above me, on a photographic plate, and I get conformed to that specific image. I am actually seeing a pneumatic pump and they are pumping air into my knees, hips, back, neck, elbows, and all the joints. The air is dense so it acts like a big cushion. First, they stretch me and make me about seven feet tall. Then they give me something like steroids to make me muscular. I see them putting a disk in my brain and downloading information into me from a computer, such as different languages in Egypt and other areas, how to build the pyramids, and where to get materials for it.

"They put a crystal shield around my heart so I can remain detached emotionally. They also tune up my sight and hearing, like turning a dial, so my sight and hearing will be sharper. It is like using a television dial to sharpen the image or a radio dial to sharpen the sound. They also made my sense of smell sharp through another dial. They are also putting heavy weights on my chest and I am having difficulty breathing. They leave the weights on for months at a time to put me in a state of suspension so I cannot totally oxygenate my body. It is like a physical form of decreased awareness while they work on my DNA. They are also taking some spinal fluid from my coccyx to change my intracranial pressure.

"After all the preparations, the aliens send me down through a beam with another being. People are gathered in the marketplace and watch me descending from the sky, but they cannot see the other alien who is with me. I feel disoriented. People are terrified and they drop on

their knees as I come down. I tell them who I am and that I have been taken by a god and transformed into a god. People are horrified of me and try to get away from there. I manifest a shield around them so they cannot escape. I call my wife and children. My wife is terrified, but my children are not as afraid. Kids come, but my wife is frozen due to fear and cannot move. She has turned white. I lift her out and bring her in front of me with my willpower, without touching her. I tell them who I am and that I look different but I am the same person and I love them. I talk to my family about what I am going to do to advance civilization, while people are suspended in time. I manifest a palace overnight across the river so my wife and children and I can live there. My wife is still afraid of me, and after a few days, she kills herself by cutting her wrists and bleeds to death.

"All this time, people are learning how to farm. I contact the people of the surrounding areas in Egypt and they send representatives from their areas to me. I tell them that I am a god and I am going to advance the civilization. I create holographic pictures of pyramids for them to see. I tell them that they will be used to bury the dead and honor the gods and they will have a higher purpose, but I don't tell them what it is. I choose some people to be my helpers who will be the priests and who will help set up a religion. These people are the link between me and the people.

"I also select people who will help me build the pyramid. The aliens provided laser tools to cut stones and equipment to levitate the stones and carry them to the site of the pyramid and place them where they need to be. People do not need to carry the stone, like it is shown in the movies. I taught about a hundred and twenty priests how to use equipment to cut stones according to the specifications and levitate them. They transport them to the site and put them where they need to be, under my instructions. Then the workers cement them into place.

What I see is that I have connecting cords going from me to these hundred and twenty priests, and the power and instructions are going from me to them. They know what the dimensions should be, how to hide the doors, how to stack up the rocks, how to hide different chambers inside, etc. It took about two hundred years to complete the pyramid.

"My son dies at the age of thirty. He falls from a horse. He had a child, a girl. My daughter gets married to one of the priests, who did it because of the power and prestige he would get. I also saw that he was responsible for the death of my son, so he could become the next in line for the royalty. I saw his ulterior motive and had him killed.

"I lived for two hundred and forty years. My daughter died when she was fifty, and also my grandchildren and great-grandchildren all died within the normal life span. At the age of two hundred and forty, I was lifted out by the aliens. People watched me ascend and thought of it as ascension. It spread my legacy to others and the younger generations. I am taken back to the spaceship where aliens unplug what looks like an energy source, and I die. Two angels come and take me to heaven. I am glad that my body died. I was tired and depressed after watching all my family die before me.

"I feel like my mind is completely wiped out and erased. Angels are taking out all the devices and enhancements from me. I just sit there for a long time as the angels heal me. They have their palms facing me, sending the healing energy swirling around me and through me in a clockwise direction. I sit there in a suspended state. They are also healing my DNA. I feel weak, disoriented, and amnesic. It takes several months to heal me because every part of my body and DNA was changed. After a long time, I see my family. It does a lot of good to be reunited with them.

"Then I am taken to the review of that life. There, I see God sitting on a throne and many other beings are there. They are telling me that I suffered well. I

cannot understand it at this time but it was something that needed to be done and I have done well. It is not about me and Earth, but it has galactic implications for the future. They were saying that I am really strong and had faith in God. Most people could not survive it physically, emotionally, and spiritually, but I did. They really honor and appreciate me for my willingness to serve for the higher good and this will reach out far into the future. Pyramids will have great implications in the future. They are saying that I will be greatly rewarded in future lives and I will not have to face such a hard life again.

"From heaven, I see that the purpose of this life was to lay the groundwork for this dial which will be dialed in 2012 AD. It is a template for the connection to the whole universe and the different worlds. By having this demigod appear, people were able to advance much more rapidly. The aliens did not want to come down and do it themselves. It had to be somebody who was willing to do it. So they had to find the right combination of a person who was willing and able, and I was it. I was one of the first humans; I think differently and I had very powerful memories. I am able to tap into ancient memories. If I did not do it at this time, they would have to wait for a long time.

"From heaven I understand that the pyramid will be a kind of disguise. It will be a tracking place, a time capsule, and will have a military purpose. Pyramids will also have something to do with astrology. The little capstone and cornerstone were built at a very specific time and movement. The pyramids are supposed to be tombs for superficial human understanding, but the real reason is that pyramids will be the seat of great power and vortexes. They will be used for communication. I am seeing a dial being twisted. It is like the movie Stargate, which is about traveling through different dimensions. In the movie, there is a star gate, which is like a portal.

This dial in the pyramid is something like that. It is also a repository of information. All around the universe, they have places where they keep their history, knowledge, and information. It will be used for that, too. It also has military significance. The aliens can defend and launch attacks from here, and it could also be a refuge. They can come back and make a stand here. Something significant will happen in the future, and something in the sky, like a dial in a clock or a light timer, will click in place. When the dial is in a certain place, then something will happen around the pyramids and other symbols of Egypt, even the Sphinx.

"I see that there is some information under the Sphinx that will be discovered. That will tell us about the alien intervention that helped humans evolve much faster. It will be proof beyond doubt. It will happen in the near future. Then there will be total darkness on Earth for three days. There will be no moon or sun, and there will be blood on the moon, which will be an optical sign, and everybody will be able to see it. I see everybody, regardless of their faith and religion, all over the world on the ground, praying and asking for answers.

"Then I keep getting the feeling of something turning, and then all the pieces go inside an open hole inside of the dimension. It is foggy and it is hard to see. I see alien troops come in through the hole. They look like military. I see all the humans on Earth uniting and not fighting with each other.

"I see this turning of the star gate. I see something below the paws of the Sphinx opening up. There is a tunnel and the chamber in which there is some information that will blow the world apart. The aliens will come down and show the diagrams, the pictures, and the hologram. It will be in the news. We will discover the roots of our past just in time before that star gate opens. It will not be in pyramids, but will be close. It is not in existence now, but will be in a space in the air. Then all of a sudden, all

these military beings will be coming. They look like aliens with military weapons. There are lots of them and they are moving like troops.

"Everybody on the planet will see and know it, and everybody will turn toward the religious leaders. We will all unite and will pray and talk to God. We are afraid of some kind of galactic invasion. I see Archangel Michael, Gabriel, and all the other angels all around the Earth in a big stand. I see a lion that is bigger than the regular lion. It is running around and roaring. It is one of those four types of beings spreading the infection, influenced by the aliens that we worked with before. [This will be described in a future publication.]

"Then I see the four horsemen of the apocalypse standing on a hill watching all this, and they will be rushing in. Earth has this massive religious revival and the rapture comes after that, and some people are being lifted out to the different dimensions. I believe the pyramids in Egypt will have an important role. The Earth and all of humanity are being watched by all of creation. I get the feeling that we are a proving ground so this does not have to happen in the entire universe. We stepped up to do it when the Earth and we were created so Armageddon doesn't have to be everywhere.

"The natural disasters began with the tsunami in East Asia. That was the beginning, and more will happen all over, off and on, but the last three years will be the worst. I also see an asteroid hitting the Earth and there will be much destruction, but we will survive it.

"Many of us will go to the pyramids, and just by being there, something will shift within us and also something will click in the dial, which is on the side of the pyramid on the ground. It is as though things are locked in certain ways in us and something will open up in us and it will affect that place, too, because that dial will shift a gear. There are other places on Earth, such as Machu Picchu and Australia, where similar things will happen.

"I see many people who were there in that life are also here in the current life. The hundred and twenty priests who helped me build the pyramids were all first humans. There were a total of two hundred first humans who were there in that life and helped me in different ways.

"There are many problems that came from that life to the current life, such as throat problems because they hooked the jackal head on me and put in a device; eye problems because they tightened the optic nerve to provide more acuity; difficulty in expressing myself because of the jackal head and also because of the devices in the throat; difficulty in breathing because of the jackal head and the weights on the chest; an enlarged heart because of steroid-type substances being given to me; and joint problems because they stretched my body and also because they put air in my joints and muscles. My abdomen distension is caused by them stretching my body and pumping air into it. There is also a difficult marriage, because I had to put intergalactic responsibility ahead of my family in that life and also in the current life. I also have memory problems in this life, because of the different devices the aliens put into me and the programming they did. I lost a lot of soul parts from my brain during those procedures. I blocked a lot of memories of being close to family and friends because of the physical changes. I compartmentalize my feelings and memories a lot, and as a result, my mind-heart connections are affected.

"In that life on Earth, I never saw the aliens working on me. From heaven, I see that they are like humans, but are very tall, about eight to ten feet or so, and very thin, but the alien I saw had primitive features. He had pronounced brow ridges and ends of his fingers were like spatula fingers.

"From heaven, I see that in the future, when the dial in or near the pyramid is turning, there will be an

opening in the galaxy and these tall, thin aliens are going to send this robotic army to protect the Earth. What I see is that some other aliens created them and these tall, thin aliens modified them to protect and fight the battle for Earth.

"When Dr. Modi prayed to God to heal everybody and remove all the negative entities, devices, and energy, I saw white Light flooding through everybody, pushing out all the entities, dark devices, and energies, which were taken to heaven after transformation. When Dr. Modi asked the soul parts of everybody to be brought back and integrated with whom they belong, I saw people on a time square and everybody's soul parts were brought back from Satan, his demons from people, places, and darkness, and integrated with whom they belong after cleansing and healing. I see lots of soul parts coming to me and going to every part of my body, most of them going to my brain, heart, lungs, scalp, hair, neck, throat, bones, skin, muscles, gastrointestinal tract, and even to the DNA, because the aliens modified almost every part of my body. Angels also cleansed, healed, and shielded all of us and all the pyramids and other monuments in Egypt and all over the Earth."

Alien Beings Helping Build the Pyramid of Giza

One of my patients under hypnosis recalled a life as an alien being from the higher level of consciousness, and gave the following information about how the pyramid of Giza in Egypt was built and how he, with other higher level alien beings, helped in planning, designing, and building it. Being a third dimension being, we may find it hard to understand the information because he was from a very high level of consciousness and dimension beyond time and space. They do not have time as we know it. As a result, the being had a hard time explaining things from our point of view:

• *"It is a gray metal door to a time tunnel, an enormously huge building. As I go inside, it looks like a basement of a factory building. It is like an extraterrestrial construction factory or a place where projects are planned and built. There is a long passageway in front. The whole place is a time tunnel. When I come out of the tunnel, I see myself wearing a space suit. I am both male and female. I can be either, depending on my plan. At this time, I am a man in a space suit. I am from a planet close to Mars. It is a parallel reality. My name and age are irrelevant. But I am picking my sex, clothes, name, and age because we need to communicate with you on a human level. I will call myself Vernon, and I am forty-two-years old, which seems like a good age, but I am ageless. We do not have death like humans experience. We have transformation and resting period.*

"I am part of the multi-dimensional planetary association that is way beyond the comprehension of humans. We can tap into any point of history but it is more complex than that because we are part of the history. We are part of the entire creation and we are responsible for everything that happens on every level, which is actually everybody, because everybody is a part of God and everyone is responsible for what happens on every level, but people are not aware of it. There are different experiments operating to enhance the flow of creativity in the creation.

"The reason I have come out of the tunnel at this time is because I have a past history. I have been a human; I have been a spiritual helper and a part of the Alohim levels of creation.

"We are about to embark on the beginning. The Sphinx has been already created as an inter-dimensional portal and symbolic demonstration of human and animal life, and a sense of permanence within a multi-dimensional mystery which is the past. There has been a great mystery within the pyramid because it is necessary for people to

keep the concept of mystery to keep their mind and heart open. The Pyramid of Giza is directly behind the Sphinx, and the shadow of the Sphinx, so to speak, and the first of many of the pyramids. Again we are working outside of time, so some pyramids may have appeared before. The Pyramid of Giza is a kind of storehouse. It is a deliberate storehouse of history, information, and the energy of evolution, which is inside it. People can move inside and when ready, they can tap into the levels of their own individual evolution. It is about individuality within the group.

"One of the reasons why pyramids are created in this shape is because it is a very stable form. The shape reminds people of their own experience, even though they are not aware of it. When they enter it and when they are ready to receive this information, they will have this enormous infusion of their participation and their role in the eternal evolution of God. But it will all be presented in human stories and dramas.

"So, I am getting ready to come out of the tunnel to go into the spaceship to go to the Earth commander, so to speak, and also the human representation of leadership in Egypt, who will be responsible for receiving information telepathically and in physical form. We are creating some physical designs. Building the Pyramid of Giza is a joint effort between us and the humans. We represent many extraterrestrial aliens. We have more of the eternal lives but we still change to take on a life on another planet. We are very evenly balanced.

"I am a part of the thread of the Alohim responsibility to keep incarnating in different forms and to monitor the development of the evolution on Earth as well as on other planets. This is the point in history that we move back, because it is part of the experiment where the humans need to forget more of their origin so that they can see how much of it is intuitive to their structure. It is about creating their individuality within a group, so individuals can

have more creativity within them rather than being simply group-minded. These different civilizations that develop, to some degree, on their own, means that they can destroy themselves. We do not want them to destroy themselves. They have free will and they do not remember that they are eternal. We are talking about humans.

"It is hard to tell what year this is according to Earth time, because we live out of time. It is about 7200 BC, but it changes according to the astrological movement, so it may be 20,000 BC, because it is flexible. It really does not matter to us. We simply watch how the energy progresses and what we believe humans need to work in cooperation, since there is free will. We have no power; we are only advisers.

"We have a group of people observing Earth and its history, and we decided it is time that humans forget more about their origins, so they can become more Earthbound and more individualized. People were ready to forget that they are part of a larger group and that they are part of God. When you forget that you are one, you lose your individuality, and this experiment on Earth is to develop this individuality so there will be more detailed creativity.

"We found a leader on Earth we could communicate with and who agreed that it was a good idea and that they were ready for it. Most of us in our group have an Alohim connection; we designed the pyramid. Some of the humans remember some of the sound techniques. The pyramid is very solid on the top of Earth and points up to the heavens, which is infinity, and then the stars are all over the sky, from the visual point of Earth. This is all designed with the symbols of Earth. Astrologically and from the point of energies within the Earth, the vortexes exist at various points.

"The Alohim is at a level like the Christ level. It is a spiritual level of creation and responsibility. So there can be one or two or billions of Alohim splitting into one or two or three, because we understand that we are gods; we

know that we are one and we also know that we are many. We can move into individual streams, depending on what we need to do.

"This has evolved from the beginning, if you wish to look at things in linear time. There is a limitation in different areas to allow greater uniqueness or greater details. We have created death in human lives, which will change in the future, but at the moment it gives you another chance.

"Right now I am a creator of Earth and we are concerned with it, but since I am a part of the Alohim concept, we can access creation of form in all the worlds of form. We are not individuals in a sense that you understand individuality on Earth. We can move from one individual to a group consciousness somewhere else and still know what our history is. The questions you are asking and the answers you are getting are all about why this pyramid was built. You were one of the builders. You are also one of us – the Alohim – but you have separated out to advance the experience of the Alohim, of Earth. Now I am up in a spaceship and I am looking down and look at day one, day fifteen, day one-hundred or six-hundred, or any other days. I can look at the progress on any of those days because I am out of time. All of us on the spaceship look back and forth in time and guide humans with what they need to do and why. Each creation is discovery. Walls have spaces in them that will carry different sorts of energy, cooling, heating, or breathing. The bricks and materials of the Earth all have an organic component.

"There are about twelve of us right now, but it changes from time to time. We are all different aspects of Alohim. We have developed different things coming out of the Alohim idea of creation knowing that we are fingertips of God. We are all working as unique individuals, but we are also part of a group. We can become one because we are also evolving in linear time to some degree. What one knows, all know, and we each will use it differently, and

then we move back and forth. The truth is that all people can access the Alohim level. There has been exclusivity, but actually it is like the Christ level. Christ is the spiritual level that everybody can achieve, depending on their evolution in consciousness. The number 144,000 is connected with the Alohim.

"I have a lot of abilities. I can become one or many; I can go back and forth in time, but I have to respect the free will of people and the linear time of Planet Earth and the connection to you and others on the Earth who are involved in building the pyramid, which is a storehouse for historical information. It is stored underneath in the ground. It is also etherically possible once you reach that level of belief to be able to access it just by going in time. You can visualize a library inside and take out a book and read it. That is the power of a lot of these spiritual vortexes. When you are ready for it, you can manifest a different level that exists on an etheric level.

"We have a connection with the ruler in Egypt who recommended an architect-engineer who is a part of the advisory counsel to the ruler. He is chosen to construct the pyramid. The designs are made and we have communication back and forth with the ruler and other humans who are working on building the pyramids. Some of them are using sound techniques, which were used with the Sphinx, so that the stones would be cut exactly the way they need to be and raised and put where they need to be. If sound does not work, then we send beams from the spaceship. Some people can create a sound beam and use it like a conveyer belt to carry stones, and if that does not work, then we send the laser beams from the spaceship to carry stones to the pyramid construction. That is the reason we have to bring the spaceship so close to Earth.

"Sound comes before Light; it begets the Light. At this time, there are some people who can make those laser sounds, but not like the person who created the Sphinx with his sound and created the powerful laser beams.

That is why we have to send the beams from the spaceship to do the job. So it is necessary to learn other techniques. Like now, you do not have the spaceships near the Earth to help, so you developed your own laser beams and you developed your own sound. The whole idea is to cut humans loose to do on their own, because they still have the memory and the knowledge but they are not so aware of it. It makes them more creative. It is a problem-solving, challenge.

"This is the reason for the separation-creation of Satan – the Lucifer – and the whole demonic network. They are here to provide interference so that creativity could work around it. Now all those demons will be put out of the job. That is why you are transforming them into the Light and returning them to heaven. They had a very hard job without any pleasure and fun. When every demon returns to heaven, we should thank them and have a big party in heaven.

"Stones are brought from the surrounding areas. There are a lot of slaves to do the other work. They are not treated as badly as humans think. When the pyramid is completed, the spaceship, along with all of us, went back and never came back again. Then other pyramids were built, but they never had the etheric perfection of the Pyramid of Giza. The stones are taken to a certain place by the workers, then the laser beams from the spaceship will move them from one place to another and then lift them and place them where they need to be.

"As I told you before, the base of the pyramid is a square. It is very solid and represents the Earth. Four is always the number of the Earth in numerology. The solid, flat, square ground is a most solid thing. It is not going to tip over under the pyramid. They built separate chambers that are connected to the Sphinx and several other pyramids, which will be built later. There are passageways underneath. The shape of the pyramid goes up to certain height that is imposing and points to heaven that represents infinity. It also

works with gravity and antigravity. It contains energy in a particular way. The shape and numbers are very important to all structures. There is energy in numbers. There is energy in letters and there is energy in every single thing that exists. So there are combinations of energy.

"It is for humans to understand intuitively. The ones who go there are the ones to understand it. They will be driven to go there and they will understand the purpose of it. It is a link from the past that had superior knowledge to subsequent evolution of humanity. Once you are able to understand it, then there will be a kind of dissolution and recreation of humans and of Earth, the way memory disappears and is replaced by knowing. The old knowledge will dissolve and will be replaced by the greater understanding that it will go through all humanity that is capable of it. The ones who are not capable are already set up to live in their own environment. We do not know exactly what will happen to them.

"The purpose of a pyramid is to create an etheric-physical combination that people will understand and be able to recognize the ancient knowledge. Many humans have the knowledge in bits and pieces but no one has it all. The way the human experiment is designed is the essential solitude of an individual.

"Pyramids will seem to disappear to some when their purpose is served, but not disappear for others. There will be a division of perception on the planet during a certain period of time, with different levels. Some will not have as much in common with the whole as they do now. Right now, there is a commonality with every one of the six billion people on the planet. This is the lowest common denominator. The highest is intra-dimensional or multidimensional unity, but some of the most ignorant (in terms of scientific knowledge) people also have that. Then there is a morality code that is part of the basic human equipment for every human, regardless of where they are or what their education level is.

"There will be a way to use the pyramid once there is a greater understanding, but the satellite system that is used on Earth now is not very different from the way pyramids are set up all over the planet. There will be an understanding of what the ley lines are doing and the vortexes, where the different churches and other worship places and spiritual centers from eons of time have been built. People will feel that those locations will be good places to do it.

"Once the pyramids are built, all our jobs on the spaceship are done. My time on Mars was already incorporated by others there. So we have kind of a ceremony and we step out of the body. I go back to heaven and I see my friends. I do have a cleansing, like a checking at the airport, to make sure that nothing alien comes in. It is like going through a shower. It was necessary to lower our vibrations to communicate with people on Earth at lower vibration. The Earth is set up deliberately at a lower vibration so that time would be stretched out and people can somehow rediscover things they have already known, but in their own way. So it would open up new areas for the Light, but the lower vibrations also contain a lot of demonic influences, leading to anger, hate, resentment, jealousy, and competition. These are essentially stumbling blocks and people get annoyed, upset and hurt each other or find another solution.

"I rest after cleansing on a nice hammock. After resting, now I have a Light body. Then I go to meet my friends. There are four of them. They are all enlightened and belong to the Alohim group. They are spiritual leaders. They have taken on many lives as people who were blind, deaf, mute, and crippled. This is related to the whole plan. We are part of the group who were the original planners.

"Then I go for my life review. There are about 250 lives I have lived so far. I am reviewing my soul history before the time I incarnated five or six times as hu-

mans, but not as a baby. I incarnated as an emergency on Earth. We are trying to understand the Alohim level and how time works. You can stretch it or not, because we are creating time. I have not done a lot of progression in this life as an alien being. It was a short life and, as an alien, I did not have the need like humans have emotionally, so it was a way to feel the Light and love of God all the time. It was like a little vacation from being human.

"From heaven, I see that the Pyramid of Giza is a beacon. It has a quality of energy that is grounded through the ground. The Giza pyramid was a prototype for the other pyramids and therefore that quality of energy is grounded in the consciousness of the Earth for all time, within the exploration of linear time. That life was successful and also a gift because it can be accessed from other lives. The very fact that this is possible is very important.

"There is an etheric energy within the physical structure, such as the walls of the pyramid, because it creates a bridge of etheric energy in the physical structure. Otherwise, etheric energy is separate. In the Sphinx, etheric energy is all around like a pattern.

"I learned I can be happy. I do not see any problems coming from that life to the current life. As I look at myself as that alien being, I appear very thin and like a grasshopper. Even the face appears like a grasshopper. He has a long face and black, beady eyes, big whiskers, two antennae, and is standing on his legs."

Alien Beings Guiding People to Build Pyramids on Different Planets

One of my patients recalled a past life as an alien being who was helping to build pyramids on three different Earth-like planets that were far away from each other:

• *"I am an alien being. I look like a big bird, like a vulture. My legs look like human legs and I have a vulture-type head with a really long beak. I have two wings and two arms, which are hidden under the wings. I can fly. My chest is broad like a human's, but covered with feathers. I have two sets of sexual organs, female organs at the bottom and male organs at the top. We do not self-impregnate. The male organs are pulled into the body and they come out when we need them. Sometimes we have to be a man and other times a woman.*

"I am on a planet far away from Earth. I am being sent to seed this Earth-like planet to build the pyramids, which will have libraries within them for future development. It is preparing a place to which we can go someday, if we need to leave our planet. We go to two other planets that are also like Earth; all far away from each other, almost creating a triangle. They are all like Earth. If something goes wrong with our planet, then we can go to other planets. Our planet is old and is vulnerable to diseases. We have been close to extinction more than once because of sickness. We have also been invaded several times.

"I am sent with a group of six people. I am in charge of the group. It takes a long time to go to this Earth-like planet. After we finish our project, we are supposed to go to the second and then to the third planet. We know it will take a long time to finish the projects on these three planets and we will not be able to go back to our home planet. We gave up everything to follow these projects.

"There is an urgency about this mission, and there are forces that do not want us to complete it. They are going to try to stop us by destroying us. These other beings look like big beetle bugs. We are about ten to twelve feet tall, but these bug-like beings are about two or three times bigger than we are. They can also fly like us, but not as fast. They lay eggs in us, and as we grow, they grow. They occupy and live off of us like parasites and then we, the hosts, die. They look like scarab beetles, which are iri-

descent green. Their heads and jaws are big and they are scary and ugly. They stand on their hind legs and look like bugs rather than humanoid beings. They make a humming noise that is loud and scary.

"I see a bright light and a light beam in the darkness of space. The ship is behind the bright light and going over a thread of a light beam. I feel that the thread is like a meridian in space. It looks wavy, and the light is going along that wave. We live in our spaceship above the Earth-like planet. The spaceship is made up of metal and looks like a disc. It is round. It is skinny outside and gets a little fatter in the middle.

"We have surveyed and are mapping out the space where the structures will be built. The ground is prepared. We give a few humans on that planet the visions of pyramids and how to build them. We gave them special gifts and knowledge that they could levitate things, and people think these 5 percent of the people are gods. We want them to build. These are the 5 percent of the population who are the important people of the town. We guide people to build structures like three pyramids in an Egypt-like place and step pyramids in a South American type of place. We are also giving humans the knowledge about how to create the hanging gardens.

"We beam people up on the spaceships. Then the humans are put on a table. We have little robots who work on them, and I am overseeing the whole process. They scan the human beings on the table with the light like an MRI machine to see what is going on with them. We can tell how many years and days they have left to live. We change and heal the minor problems in their body. The robots put tracking devices in these people so we can track them and give them information and knowledge. Then we send them back on Earth and they do not remember anything about being on the spaceship.

"The human being who is in charge of the project has a nice home, is married, and has a boy and a girl and some

extended family members. After the device, the person is able to receive information much easier. We give him a vision of the pyramid when it is completed, like watching on television. He can project the holographic picture, which other people can also see with him. They can walk around it but cannot touch it. It was projected through the person's eyes. People were in awe of it and wanted to cooperate in building the pyramids.

"The leader on Earth, who is responsible to build the pyramids as he receives more knowledge, is becoming taller and stronger. The pyramid is to be built in about two hundred years. There is a dedication ceremony for the pyramid, and he dies right after that of a heart attack.

"After the pyramid is completed, we go to a place like South America, where another group of our race is building pyramids with the help of people there. Then we all go to another planet far away and build pyramids there, too. After that, we go to the third planet and do the same thing. I understand that these three planets will be the ones where, during the Armageddon, survivors from different planets will go. It took a long time to finish the project. I die after that of some lung problems.

"My spirit goes to heaven. There, I look like a human rather than a bird because I am a human incarnating on another planet. I go to a rain chamber where I get cleansed and healed by the Light rain. Then I review my life as the bird being. I watch my life on a movie screen. The beings who are helping me review my life are telling me that I was a seed of knowledge and information. I was giving the people of those three planets special knowledge about how to build the pyramids. I was given that knowledge from heaven to seed in people of those three planets. These planets, including the Earth, are the intergalactic beacons with repositories like libraries and landing towers. They will be the places like Noah's Ark for the universe. There are many more planets throughout creation besides these three planets where similar structures were

built and are beacons of Light and will be used like Noah's Ark. Those places are repositories of knowledge and are pristine power places. They will also be the places where things can be preserved, such as knowledge, information, species, etc.

"From heaven, I see that our planet was destroyed while we were far away working on our project. I did not know that it happened while in the body, but I felt sadness. The bug type aliens blew our planet and everybody on it into pieces. On Dr. Modi's request, angels brought back the soul parts of every being on that planet at the time of the explosion, and reintegrated them with whom they belonged, after cleansing and healing, and took all the beings into heaven. The angels also brought all the soul parts of the planet and integrated them together, recreating and healing the whole planet and shielding it with the crystal shield. I am watching it like a movie in reverse, with explosions and everything shattering into pieces and then all the pieces flying back together.

"From heaven, I see those beetle beings standing near the star gate trying to get in and invade those planets, but they cannot get them to open. On Dr. Modi's request, angels cleansed and healed all those planets, including the Earth, and all the pyramids and similar structures, including the star gate near them, and put crystal shields and violet shields around them and on the inside and outside of the star gate. The angels also cleansed and healed the beetle beings, who were very dark and in spirit form. They claimed to be outside the vulture beings' planet when their race blew it up with a nuclear bomb. The beetle beings' planet was also destroyed due to heat and volcanoes erupting. It was also recreated, healed, and shielded by bringing all its soul parts back. All the beetle beings were collected from all over creation by the angels, then cleansed, healed, and taken back to their section of heaven. They were all in spirit form.

"I see that the reason we were preparing those planets was so we could go there to live if something happens to our planet. I also see that all these things are interwoven. I see a grid and a pattern that overlaps because there may be more purposes that are higher. They might have to do with the prophecy and evolution and the hope for the future.

"From heaven, I see many problems coming from that life to my current life, such as breathing problems and loneliness. I also see the positive achievements, such as bigger missions and saving lives on an intergalactic level, etc. On Dr. Modi's request, angels brought back all the soul parts of me and everybody who was with me as vulture beings, and integrated with all of us after cleansing and healing.

"From heaven, what I see is that the planets where the pyramid structures were built are Earth-like planets with human-like people living on them, but were not Earth. I also see that the human to whom I was giving the knowledge on that Earth-like planet was a part of my soul from my soul pyramid, living two separate lives on different planets. I also built pyramids on our Earth when the aliens put the jackal head on me. I was chosen to build pyramids on many other planets to seed the knowledge. I see that the same souls were involved in building the pyramids on different planets. Most of them were the first humans. It was really orchestrated by God.

"I also review my life as the human being who was in charge of building the pyramids on the Earth-like planet. People followed my suggestions and instructions because I showed them the vision of pyramids we would build. Aliens did not put any animal head on me in this life. The aliens already excavated the land by removing the loose sand, and it was leveled. It was staked out with strings. Then I set the four cornerstones by levitating them and putting them in those places.

"I see that I die right after the dedication. I was about two hundred years old. I was considered a god. I go to

*the Light, where, after cleansing and healing, I go for life
review. Here many people are sitting and telling me about
my life. They are telling me that I had a mission and I
fulfilled it successfully and set the civilization on a path.
They are saying I did a great job.*

*"I see that in the life as a human who built the pyra-
mids, I was pretty much led. I did not make any independent decisions. Five percent of the people in that village
who were given the information about how to build the
pyramids were first humans of that planet, and I was chosen as the leader.*

*"I see that problems which came from the human life of
the leader to my current life are feelings of isolation, sadness, and eye problems because the vision of the pyramids
came through my eyes to project this hologram and made
both of my eyes weak."*

Building a Pyramid in St. Louis

One of my patients recalled a past life in St. Louis when she
helped in building the pyramids there as follows:

• *"I am an eight-year-old girl living with my parents on the
other side of the river near St. Louis. My dog is running
into the water. I run after him into the icy water, where
I twist my ankle. I am drowning. My father comes and
brings me out of the water and resuscitates me. When we
go back home, people think I am special because I survived. I spent a lot of time with my mother for the next
ten days, almost regressing to a younger age. I want her
to hold me. I am sitting on her lap curled up in the fetal
position. I am non-responsive. They let me be that way. I
feel there is Light going through my head and healing me.
After about ten days, I feel strong and healed and people
think I am different. They consider me a holy person be-*

cause I have visions of the future. My father is a shaman. I go in a trance and I tell my father about the future. We will have seven years with an abundance of food, but for the next seven years we will have no food. We need to build the pyramids because they are stairs to God. I tell him how to build them. My father has the power to see that it is done. I also tell him that we need to preserve and store food for the future.

"My father finds some caves close by and decides to store food there but does not tell other people. During the seven years of famine, a lot of people of the other tribes are starving so they come to us for food. We share some food with them but not all because we have to save for our tribe. I am about fifteen years old at this time. We begin to build the first pyramid. I meet a nice young man. We spend three days together and get married after a while. I have a baby boy. When I am pregnant, I do not have any visions. Two years later, my husband gets killed by a bear. After that, I feel all his physical, mental, and spiritual power coming into me. I think his spirit came into me, which I did not realize at that time. I am seventeen years old at this time. The rest of my life I dedicate to becoming a shaman and taking care of my son.

"By the time I am thirty-five, we built seven pyramids. The way they are built, I see a pentagram there. They are all of the same height and they build an altar on the top of the five pyramids where we sacrifice [as an offering] grains. We keep the fires burning at the altars all the time. When the fires are burning at the altars of all five pyramids, I see a pentagram between the fires, which is for protection. Each pyramid has a person who is the keeper of the fire, who is responsible for keeping the fires going. It is considered a sacred duty."

"After my death, I go to heaven and get cleansed and healed. I see that, at the age of eight, when I was sick after drowning, my spirit was being taken by aliens into a spaceship, where they healed me. They also put some kind

of communication and tracking devices in me. Then they beamed me back to my body. After that, they continued to heal me with the Light and communicate with me. They also gave me knowledge of the future and how to build the pyramids."

Construction of The Great Wall of China

One of my patients had pain in her shoulders, arms, and fingers for a long time. As she looked at the reasons for her pain, she recalled a past life as follows:

- *"I am a sixty-one-year-old male living in China in 1745 AD. My name is Chingshua. I am a medicine man. I practice martial arts and I am very fit. I have a lot of knowledge about herbs and other medicines. I heal all sorts of ailments. I know the basics of human health. I know how to use medicine, yoga, meditation, and martial arts together to balance the body and keep very fit and strong. I am sixty-one but I look like I am twenty-one years old. I am very strong.*

    "The king has ordered the building of a wall so others cannot invade our country. One person from every family was ordered to go to work at that project, and I do not want my children or grandchildren to go there. It is like slavery. We were just given meals but not money. I have been working here for six years. They began to work on the wall about ten years ago. I transport cement and other stuff from one place to another. There are thousands and thousands of people working here.

    "They are beating people with sticks or their food is held back if they do not work faster or if they make a mistake. A few times, when I tried to help people with my medicine, they beat me. That did not bother me. I still try to help people whenever I can. One time when I tried to

help someone, they stripped me naked, beat me badly, and took away the few things I had. Then they cut my hands and dumped me. There is a woman worker who put a blanket on me. I tell her to get some herb and put them on my wounds. I heal some and I walk back home with great difficulty. It takes a long time.

"My family is shocked and angry about what they did to me but I am still calm. I lived to ninety-one years of age. I feel bad that I could not pass on my knowledge because I feel my kids and grandchildren are not ready for it. I just choose to die by leaving the body. I do it in meditation. I will to separate my soul from my body; first the lower part of my soul separates and then the rest of the soul comes out of my body. I know I need to go in the Light and I do.

"After cleansing and healing, I go for life review with a few Light beings. They tell me I did my best under the circumstances. From heaven, I see the king's people also killed the woman who helped me. They suffocated her. I see a lot of workers being hanged. There is a lot of darkness there controlling everybody. From heaven, I see I needed to let go of my guilt about not being able to help.

"I see that many problems came from that life to my current life, such as aches and pains due to beatings, pain in the shoulders, arms, and fingers. In the current life, I have an intense desire to do the healing work, also.

"From heaven, I see that the woman who helped me is a family member in the current life. She was a woman from Iran living in China. She married a Chinese man.

"On Dr. Modi's request, God is sending a powerful tornado Light throughout China, the Wall of China, and all the people who were involved in building the Wall of China, and everybody who is living in China now, removing and transforming everything that does not belong with them. Then everybody's soul parts are brought back from Satan, his demons, from people, places, darkness, and from each other, and integrated with whom they be-

long after cleansing and healing everybody and their soul parts. I saw a lot of darkness all over China, especially when the Wall of China was being built, which was all transformed and taken to heaven. Now it is all Light and shielded.

"I see soul parts coming back to my hands and fingers, heart, all the chakras, back, and all over the body. Then the angels cleansed, healed, and shielded all of China, including the Wall of China and the vortex under the wall. Angels also brought back past life personalities of everybody who was there to build the Wall of China and all the others who got healed and integrated with whom they belonged. Then on Dr. Modi's request, God flooded all of China, and everything and everybody in it with violet liquid fire and let it blaze into intense flames nonstop twenty-four hours a day. When Dr. Modi asked to bless all of creation and everything and everybody in creation with the divinity, I saw a burst of Light flooding with calm, peace, serenity and spiritual wisdom.

"From heaven, I see that it was the king's idea to build the Wall of China to protect China from an invasion. The main difficulty was the height and transporting the material there. They got people involved from every household. The wall is about one hundred miles long. It took about twenty years to build it. From heaven, I see that alien help was involved in transporting the material. They were helping from their spaceship with an antigravity device to carry stones and other materials. I see some energy beam is coming down and covering the whole area where people are working. It covers a wide area and makes everything there light and easy to carry around for humans and animals. I see that on the spaceship there are only robots and no aliens. The spaceship is not very big. The aliens are on their planet and control that spaceship with a satellite. These aliens look like large crickets, about seven feet tall. They walk on their six legs but they can also be upright.

"From heaven, I see that the king and aliens planned in heaven to work on this project together. On Earth, in life, they did not know each other but they both were guided by the heavenly beings. It took about twenty years to build the wall. Stones are basically brought from the nearby mountains.

"As I look back from the heaven, I see a big vortex under the area where the wall is built. Basically, the height of the wall is giving a lift of over one-hundred miles which will help during the transition, by pushing the vortex from the bottom up and helping lift the Earth in another dimension. I see that pyramids, the Taj Mahal, Machu Picchu, the Great Wall of China, Stonehenge, the Grand Canyon, and many other places all over the Earth will help during the shift of the planet into the fifth dimension."

Construction of the Taj Mahal

One of my patients had pain and weakness in all her fingers and arms, and aches and pain all over her body. She also had trouble finishing anything she started. Under hypnosis, she recalled a past life when she was hired to do carving all over the Taj Mahal:

* *"I am a twenty-five-year-old male. My name is Arayan and I live in India. My father, myself, and many others are building what is now known as the Taj Mahal but it was not called that name at this time. We live close to the place where we are working at this time. We are given a small place to live and two meals a day, and they promised a big reward from Raja Sahab, the king who is building it, but we have never seen him. The construction began in 1637 AD.*

  "We are good at carving and did it in many palaces. The basic structure of the Taj Mahal is already built and we are hired to do the carving all over this building. They

began to build this monument about seven years ago, and we have been working here for about three years. We are given instructions about what to carve and we just follow them. We worked there for about seven years. We are whipped a lot so we would work harder out of fear. I have a sister who lives with me and my father and cooks for us.

"Now the building is almost completed. I am about thirty years old at this time. There is going to be a big ceremony and the king is going to come here. We are putting on final touches. We are told that the king is going to reward us generously. We all watch the king's procession coming on an elephant. All the workers, which are in the thousands, are sitting in one section. Town people are also coming to see the maharaja, the king. He has arrived but we cannot see him clearly because we are all sitting in the back, far away from the maharaja. He is very happy with the building and admiring it. He is throwing a lot of gold coins toward us and then everybody is given more coins.

"After a couple of years, all the workers are taken behind a hill away from the town in an isolated area. We have no idea why we are being taken there. When we reach the place, they tie people's hands a few at a time, and then we hear people screaming. We do not know what is going to happen. We are scared and panicking. Then they take my father, me, and others by force behind the hill. There everybody is screaming with pain. Blood is flowing everywhere. They grab me and put me on my knees by force and tie my hands. I scream and try to free my hands but cannot, and before I know it, a man chopped my fingers off. They are still moving on the floor. There are whole piles of cut fingers all over, still moving and bleeding. Then they let us go from the back of the hill. We are having profuse bleeding and intense pain. Some are becoming unconscious and many die of bleeding, piling on top of each other. It is a very grotesque sight. We are all just shocked. Why? We did such a good work, why would they do this to us? Later on, we are told that the king did not

want anybody to build a similar monument so they cut all the workers hands that did the carving.

"My father becomes unconscious and dies. I also become unconscious with pain and bleeding. When I come to consciousness, I just continue to walk but do not know where. There are dead and unconscious people all over, lying in blood. Few of us make it out of there. Eventually, I see a bullock cart and the people in it put me in it. Then I pass out again. They take me to their village and bandage my hands and nurse me. Gradually I gain my strength back after several months. I tell people what happened. Nobody knows about it because it was done in secrecy. People here are kind and compassionate. They gave me a small place to live. I do not talk much and remain by myself most of the time. I learned to use my legs in place of my hands.

"Everybody loves me in the village and they become my family. Kids often come to visit me and I have a good time with them. I die at the age of sixty-five with lung infection, thinking "Why were we treated so brutally when we did such a beautiful job? I will never specialize in anything and do it perfectly. I am ready to leave because I am tired." My spirit comes out of my crown chakra. I am free of pain.

"I see the Light and go in it. I am still very angry. I talk to some angels and tell them how cruel and unjust the king was and what he did to hundreds of us. We devoted our lives and why would he punish like that? He was a coward because he did it in secrecy. Angels are telling me to look at the positive side. To see how much love I got from the children and town people. By ventilating my anger, I feel better. Then I go for cleansing under a waterfall. A lot of darkness comes out. I see a lot of demons and devices coming out of me. Also soul parts of other people, including the one who chopped the fingers, and the king and queen's soul parts, too, because it was their desire to cut workers' fingers off so nobody could build another

monument of such beauty. Theses soul parts are cleansed and kept in heaven.

"Then I am taken for the life review. There are twelve heavenly beings waiting for me around a table. They tell me I need to look at my life. There is a glass screen in the center of the table and I can look down through it and can see my life. I can see the whole sequence of events happening like in a movie. I see that we lived in a village where everyone had this carving talent. I began to go with my father to his work and he would teach me how to do things. Then I began to work with my father. We worked in a few palaces and temples before working on what is now called Taj Mahal.

"From heaven, as I look back, I see that originally the Taj Mahal was built by a Rajput king whose name was Rana Ranjeetsingh, who was very pleased with us and rewarded us well with gold coins. It became very famous and people came to see it from far away. After a couple of years, the Mogul Badshah Shahjahan heard about the Taj Mahal and invaded the place and won the whole territory. He named it Taj Mahal after his queen Mumtaz Mahal. He also, on Mumtaz Mahal's prompting, ordered thousands of people's fingers to be cut off so that nobody could build another monument like that.

"I learned the lesson that no matter how hurt or damaged you are, there is always a place for love. Also the more you share, the more you get.

"I see one of the family members in my current life was my father in that life. I don't see the king or queen in this life.

"From heaven, I see that many problems came to me from that life to the current life, such as aches and pains all over the body due to beatings, pain in the fingers and the arms, weakness in the hands, and not being able to finish anything I begin.

"When Dr. Modi prayed to God to send the healing Light to me and everybody who was in that life, including

my father, all the people who worked on building the Taj Mahal, everybody whose fingers were chopped off, those who were tying and cutting the fingers, Shahjahan Mumtaz Mahal who ordered workers' fingers to be chopped off, and all the village people who helped me, the Taj Mahal, and the place where hands were cut off, I saw everybody being cleansed and healed. Then angels brought my and everybody's soul parts back from Satan, his demons, from people, places, and each other and integrated them with whom they belonged after cleansing and healing. I see soul parts to my fingers are coming back from the place where they were chopped off; literally, fingers are flying back to me and all the others whose fingers were chopped off. Also from places where we were whipped at work, from the Shahjahan and Mumtaz Mahal who ordered for the fingers to be cut off and to different parts of the body.

"I also see that later, when I found out that Shahjahan and his queen were responsible for our fingers being cut off, I was very angry at them and my soul parts fragmented, and the demons latched on to them and took them to Shahjahan and his queen. Also their soul parts came into me and all the others when our fingers were butchered off. In that chaos, all the people whose fingers were cut off and all our soul parts were going to everybody there. All of them are taken back from me and everybody else, and all our soul parts are brought back from them and people who tied and cut the fingers, and integrated with whom they belong, after cleansing and healing the soul parts and us. There is a lot of activity occurring.

"Now I am at the Akashic library and have a book about the Taj Mahal. I see that a forty-one-year-old architect named Muhamad, in Chandigar, India, had a dream in 1635 AD. I see that the dream was given by some heavenly beings. In the dream, he was given the vision about a monument or a building and how it would look. This place would have a lot of energy. He was guided by the heavenly beings when he was designing the building. There is

an energy vortex in the area where he was supposed to build the building. There is also a river in the area, part of which flows through the vortex and it feeds the vortex.

"The architect approached the Rajput king by the name of Rana Ranjeetsingh, with the blueprints of the monument he dreamt in about 1635 AD. King Rana Ranjeetsingh was interested in art and liked the idea, so he agreed to build the monument. From the Akashic library, I see that the king was also inspired by the heavenly beings. The construction began about 1636 AD, and finished in about 1649 AD. People came to see it from faraway places.

"Shahjahan, a Mogul Badshah, also heard about this monument and how beautiful it was. So he invaded that area and won. I see that in the rooms below there are mantras and other Hindu writings and also writings about the king who built it.

"When Shahjahan took over, a couple of years after it was built, he decided to dedicate the monument to his Queen Mumtaz Mahal and named it Taj Mahal after her. He changed the Hindu script at a later time.

"It is a powerful place of energy because of the vortex. I see from heaven that, as the Earth evolves and gets ready to go to the next dimension, this high energy monument, along with the others, will help the Earth to move into the fifth dimension. The specific shape of the Taj Mahal will help magnify the energy and project it upward when the time is right.

"From heaven, I see a lot of energy coming to the rooms and in the dome of Taj Mahal from the vortex under it. There are many other buildings and structures which together will help Earth move up into the fifth dimension, such as the ancient religious and other areas that are built on very high energy vortexes, such as Stonehenge, Machu Picchu, the Grand Canyon, the Wall of China, the pyramids, places in Brazil, ancient churches, temples, mosques, and many other places all over Earth. There are *vortexes all over in the oceans, which will also help move the planet into the fifth dimension. I get the information that we should all pray for cleansing and healing those places and the vortexes all over the Earth and around it."*

Mystery of Stonehenge

One of my patients under hypnosis gave the following information about Stonehenge from the Akashic records. She described when and how it was created and what purpose it will serve in the future:

- *"From the Akashic Records, I see that about two million years ago, Stonehenge was created as an anchor of energy because the Earth was going through some major shifting, as the Earth shifts about every million years. I am seeing that tectonic plates were moving and land was shifting around. So a group of Light beings decided to anchor the Earth by putting the stones in strategic places and stopping the Earth's movement.*

  "I also see some alien beings who have antigravity devices helping these Light beings in moving the stones. What I get is that these aliens are Pleideans. The stones act as an anchor to stop plates from moving, and if one section of the tectonic plate is anchored, then it stops the movement of all the plates. The stones were taken from under the Earth where they were erected. Then, through prayers and intent, they created the vortexes underneath.

  "The formation of the stones is able to attract Light energy easily and sucks it in and surrounds the area with it. The vortex brings the Light energy up while the stones bring the Light energy down. This collects a lot of Light energy there and stops the plates from shifting. The stones have a fine crystalline quality in them. That is how they attract the Light energy.

"From the Akashic Records, what I see is that in the future people can go there and ask for information about what to do and where to go, and they will get the answers from heaven."

Grand Canyon

Under hypnosis, one of my patients from the Akashic Records, gave the following information about the Grand Canyon and its formation:

- *"From the Akashic library, I see that the Grand Canyon was formed when there was a great earthquake a couple of million years ago. It just ripped the whole area of the Grand Canyon. It had to do with the planetary alignment of Earth and other planets, causing earthquakes. Since there were lots of hard rocks in that area, it cracked but did not move. I also see that these rocks have tiny crystals that attract a lot of Light energy. There is a huge vortex there. So it is also one of those places where you can go and receive a lot of energy. Also, like other vortexes on Earth, the vortex here will also help Planet Earth in lifting up and moving into the fifth dimension."*

Chapter 11

CREATION OF MYTHICAL GODS AND GODDESSES

Some of my patients under hypnosis recalled a life when an animal head was attached to them by aliens. These were the first humans, who had planned to bring, with the help of some aliens, different knowledge and methods to advance human evolution, such as irrigation, sanitation, farming to improve the crops, different healing techniques, and information about herbs. These aliens were supposed to guide these humans and give knowledge from their spaceship. According to my hypnotized patients, these alien beings got influenced by demons and began to put animal heads on these humans, to create the mythical gods and goddesses so that people would listen to them.

My hypnotized patients claimed that one of the human beings who planned to advance human evolution with the help of aliens had cancer on his face. So the alien beings covered his face and head with an animal head. People on Earth were afraid of him but listened to him because they considered him to be a god. So the aliens, under demonic influence, began to put heads of different animals on these humans just to see what will happen, without caring about what happened to these humans and the plan for evolution. My hypnotized patients saw from heaven that alien beings put various types of animal heads on many humans who incarnated on different parts of Earth, such as China, Egypt, Tibet, Peru, Argentina, Belize, and Mexico, with the purpose of bringing knowledge and advancing the evolution faster. These were mostly first humans. Some of the animal heads—or the whole body—attached to these humans with special purpose were bird head, dragon head, turtle, jackal head, etc.

Bird Head in Egypt

One of my patients under hypnosis recalled a life in Egypt when the aliens attached a bird head on him, so people would think he was a god and listen to his advice:

- *"I am a thirty-year-old farmer living in the upper Nile Valley of Egypt. There are no pyramids at this time. I am married and have two children. It is about 10,010 BC. I am fascinated with stars. One night I am lying on the ground and looking at the stars and I see light all around me, and the next thing I remember is that I have a bird head on me and I am terrified, confused, and upset. I get the thoughts that I will help found a great civilization and give a lot of knowledge to people, and that I will be worshipped by people. But I am still terrified, trying to get the bird head off me and running in terror. I go to my house but my wife tries to kill me because she is afraid of me. My seventeen-year-old son and fourteen-year-old daughter realize that I am their father. I am crying because I do not know what to do. My daughter kisses my hand and tells me that she loves me and it's all going to be okay, and my son says that he loves me and will protect me. They both come with me as I leave.*

    "People who see me are terrified. My daughter tells them that I am her father and I am chosen to lead our people and start a great civilization. Then they listen to me. We go to the river where there are some empty buildings. I teach people about irrigation and other things. As a result, crops are better and people are paying more attention to me. People are farming and building trenches so when it floods, the water will fill up the trenches. I also

teach different healing techniques and about herbs and sanitation.

"Different priests and devotees come to me and I teach them healing techniques and then they teach others. People begin to follow me. People build many temples all over the country, which provide an energy source. There are statues of me as the bird god. The whole country is united psychologically. People are terrified of me but follow my advice. I did not disrupt the power that was already there. This was before there was any central power and the civilization was very primitive.

"I want female companionship but she was afraid of me. Her father agreed to give her to me out of fear of me. The lady is terrified because of how I look and kills herself. Her brother is very upset about losing his sister and he puts a snake in my daughter's room. She is bitten by the snake and dies. I am devastated and I rip the man apart. My son also falls, hits his head, and dies. I am very depressed and distraught, and I do not want to live. I get pneumonia and I die when I am sixty. People wrap me up like a mummy and give me a special secret burial. As my soul comes out of the body, I am shocked that my body died. I did not want to be a god but then I came to accept it.

"I had forgotten my life before the bird head was put over me, and after the death of my physical body, my soul is remembering everything. It is like cleaning the mirror and seeing and understanding everything clearly. I also remember my whole soul history and past lives. I remember that aliens chose me because I was one of the first humans. I am supposed to advance civilization and bring it out of the dark ages.

"I see a bright Light and am being pulled up from my back with my face down. I can see the world passing by and also a movie of my life. I am seeing my whole life at different ages and then I find myself in heaven. I am taken to a room where they cleanse me with liquid Light. Then

the angels take out the invisible bolts from my neck and shoulders where the bird head was attached and remove the feeling of the bird head on me. They also take out transmitting devices from my ears, eyes, and throat. Now I can breathe easily and have more understanding of what happened. I am crying with the realization of what I went through, and the angels are calming me down by singing.

"After cleansing and healing, I go for debriefing. I speak to a Light being. I am very confused and angry and questioning why this happened to me, why I was not protected, why the aliens did this to me, and why God did not stop it. I feel like I paid a very high price for something I did not ask for. There are three Light beings that hold hands and I am in the middle. They all are humming the sound OM, which is creating the Light vibrations and healing me.

"Then I go for the life review. I see the movie of my life, seeing all the events. I see that I planned for this life so I could help people with new ideas and advance the civilization by a thousand years. This was the first time in Egypt that they created the mythological god. I began a basis for religion. People built twelve temples with my statue in them because they thought I was a god. From heaven, I see that most of these temples are now underground.

"From the Light, I see that it was a heavenly plan that these tall, thin aliens would help some of the first humans to plant the seeds of civilization on different parts of Earth. The plan was to pass on knowledge and technology to these first humans. These aliens got influenced by demons and began to put these senseless mechanical heads and other things on these first humans just because they could. Later, it became completely senseless and cruel. They did not care what happened to those first humans. I also see the places on Earth where this happened were the areas that have big vortexes. Areas with large vortexes were chosen to spread knowledge by the aliens to such sites as

Egypt, Peru, Argentina, China, Tibet, Chichen Itza, Belize, the Mississippi Valley near St. Louis, etc. I see that it was done to me in two more lifetimes, in China and Tibet.

"As I look back, I see that in one case, one of the first humans had cancer of his face. The aliens operated on his face, which left a deformity, so they decided to cover up his head and face with a mechanical animal head; after that, the idea of using a mechanical head began.

"As I look back under hypnosis, I see that I was being beamed up into a spaceship by the tall, thin aliens. There, they put me on the table and examined me. They took samples of my hair, urine, and stool. They scraped inside my mouth, nose, and beneath the fingernails and toenails. Through these tests, they could tell everything about me; who I am, what I have done in my past lives, and if I am one of the first humans. It was like they could tap into my soul history.

"The aliens put a big black bird head on my head. It was the type of head you see on one of the Egyptian gods. It had a big, long beak. It looked like a hawk or a falcon. The head was hollow inside like a Halloween costume. There were some kind of electrodes in it that connected to my eyes, mouth, vocal cords, brain, and ears. These were transmitting and receiving devices, so whatever I think, feel, see, hear or say, the aliens could also perceive. They could also send messages to me.

"Before the aliens were ready to send me down to Earth, they conducted a ceremony where they ripped my heart out of my chest with their hands and ate it in front of me. They put a mechanical heart in me. They did not make any incision. They just put their hand through my chest, ripped my heart out with the hand, and replaced it with a mechanical heart that connected instantly and worked normally. There was no bleeding. The aliens could suspend the bleeding and that is why I was not bleeding. There were probes that went from the mechanical heart to find the exact place they need to connect. There was no

anesthesia, bleeding, or pain. Then they conducted a cer-
emony and ate my heart. They thought they were getting
my emotions, abilities, powers, and all the history and the
past, present, and future knowledge by eating my heart.
They only eat the heart of the first male humans and not
the females because they think females are inferior to the
males. This heart can last a long time and they can turn
it off anytime they want. Then they beamed me down to
my farm. As I became aware of my head and touched it,
I was terrified. The aliens communicate with me through
the device and try to calm me down. They tell me that I
will be worshipped as a mythological deity in the future.

"As these tall, thin aliens were working on me, I saw
other types of aliens in the background observing every-
thing. They were in spirit form. There were short and
stocky aliens who are about five feet tall, taller aliens who
are about fourteen feet tall and thinner and taller than the
ones who were working on me, and a third type who were
humanoid and about seven feet tall but had a reptilian
face and head. They were green and had scales.

"I see that my heart, eye, and throat problems came
from that life to the current life, which improved a great
deal after bringing the soul parts and integrating them
with me after cleansing and healing."

Dragon Being in China

One of my patients recalled a past life in China when aliens
abducted him and put a dragon costume on him:

• *"I am a twenty-three-year-old male living in China. It is*
about 10,000 BC. My four-year-old daughter falls into a
well and I dive into it to save her but cannot. I almost
drown and have difficulty breathing. I am feeling terrible
and angry. As I am lying on the ground waiting to die, I

see three tall, thin alien beings come. They put their hands on my back and energetically move the water out of my lungs and leave me there. I crawl back home, which is close by. I have trouble walking. My wife is very angry when I tell her about our little girl drowning in the well. She is pregnant. She is kicking me and screaming. She has a spontaneous miscarriage and she dies. I am very distraught and angry that I lost my whole family.

"As I am looking back in that life, I see the same aliens beam me up in a spaceship. I am extremely angry and feel like my head is going to explode and my insides are burning with fire. In the spaceship, they examine and take samples from my mouth, eyes, hair, nails, blood, and semen. Then they attach a dragon head, back, and tail on my body like a dragon suit or costume. They cover up my face, head, and back, except my legs, chest, and abdomen. They do something to my eyes to make them light up and glow, almost like a red Christmas light bulb. They take some of my genes for rational thinking. They harvest some of my sperm to catalog it for later use.

"They screw the whole dragon suit on me on both sides of my spine, from top to bottom. The head is screwed on the top of the spine in the back, and in the front, it just hangs down to the middle of my chest. It is not attached to anything. The aliens also put bellows under the wings, and when I flap them, the bellows push the air down and push me upward. They slit my eyes in the middle so they look like reptilian eyes. After many months of preparation, they beam me back to my home. It looks like I am flying down. I am still feeling very angry, screaming and yelling, and as I do that, fire is coming out of my mouth and it scorches the bushes. I can fly around like a dragon. I go to where my daughter died and I am crying and crying, and dragon tears come out of my eyes. They look like pretty rocks, like tiny jades. I am just sitting there depressed, not knowing what to do or where to go.

"I hear a little girl on a cliff yelling, "Help me; help me." There is a wolf there. I yell at the wolf and fire comes out of my mouth and the wolf runs away. I pick up the little girl and fly her home. This makes me happy, and instead of being a terrifying dragon, I become a good luck symbol because I help people, especially children. Whenever there are fireworks, I come because it is a celebration, but people are also afraid of me because of my spitting fire and scorching and burning stuff. I live in a cave because I might burn a house down. I feel lonely. I fly all over the country to see what is happening. I collect shiny things like gold and gems and bring them to the cave.

"People think that I am magical, but they are also afraid of me. They call upon me when they need help and I go and help. There are some older people who want to talk to me to know more about me, but they are afraid. They consider me as a mythical character, a symbol of hope, joy, and power. I guard the borders and scare intruders away. The aliens just watch to see what happens and do not care one way or the other about what occurs.

"I die of hepatitis at the age of one hundred and five. I am happy this miserable life is ending. I am praying and hoping that there is an afterlife so I can see my little girl and ask for her forgiveness since I could not save her, and also from my wife and our miscarried son. I am happy that I did a lot of good things, such as protecting the borders. I saved a lot of people and gave them hope knowing there was somebody to save them if they were in trouble. I was like a mythological protector, like a unicorn.

"I still have the dragon form. My soul is still flying around. I see a Light and I get pulled into it and go to heaven. There somehow I walk out of that dragon costume. I see my wife with two children. I fall down and hug their feet. I feel very guilty but they are not angry with me. We are all happy to see each other. I am cleansed by a circle of Light. They do it for people who are abducted. There is a sound like "Om" with it. Angels are

taking out the bellows from my back and from my stomach that aliens put into me so if I went in the water I would not drown because of my weight. The angels take out the screws the aliens used on both sides of my back and the top of my spine to attach the costume, and they remove the devices from my temples and eyes. They are also removing a device like a video camera from the area of the crown chakra and a monitoring device from the solar plexus chakra.

"In heaven, I review my life with some wise Light beings. I feel cheated out of my normal life at twenty-three years of age. I feel upset and confused about it. The wise beings are putting their hands on my head and ears to calm me down. They are telling me, "This is what you did for the evolution of the planet, so be happy that you were an instrument." From heaven, I see that these aliens were also working with other people of other planets on their spaceship. I see one from Mars and another from Jupiter, and they were working with all of us at the same time. The Mars being is short like a dwarf, and the Jupiter being is like a gas bubble. After the change, the Mars being looks like a rubber toy dog with spikes and the Jupiter being looks like a parachute.

"With me, the aliens wanted to see what would happen if they unleash emotions such as anger, and how will humans react. They were doing these silly experiments and were not interested in giving any knowledge to humans, as called for in the original plan.

"I helped the fishermen when they got stuck. I also sensed earthquakes coming and I warned people before hand and told them if they needed to move. One time, I sensed that tidal waves were coming so I scorched part of the town so that people had to leave the town and be saved from the tidal waves. In China, I am known as a protector, somebody to call upon if they were in trouble, and I am also considered as good luck. I see that dragons were created more than once. They also created turtles.

"From the Light, I see that I need to learn not to blame myself. In a way, I was responsible, but in another way, I was not really responsible for what happened. I see many problems that came from that life to the current life. My gastrointestinal tract and lung problems came due to spitting fire through my mouth and nose, and also from inhaling smoke. The fire was created in the solar plexus because of the anger, and it rose through the gastrointestinal tract and came out the mouth and nose, and I inhaled the smoke from it into the respiratory tract and lungs. Also, feelings of loneliness, isolation, endurance, and depression came from that life to my current life.

"My eyes burn all the time because of exhaling fire, and I have pain in the eyes because of aliens slitting my eyes to make them look reptilian, and then putting the red bulb-type device in both eyes. In the stomach, bellows were put in as a floatation device so I would not drown, but now it causes abdominal bloating. Also there were bellows under my scapula so I could fly. In this life, they make my scapulae protrude out a little bit.

"After angels brought all my soul parts, there was a great deal of improvement in my symptoms."

Chapter 12

CROP CIRCLES

Some of my patients recalled a past life when they were involved in creating crop circles or saw crop circles being built on their land by some unknown source or beings. From heaven, when people look back at that life, they see different reasons for creating crop circles. There are many alien races who take turns to give us messages of different types. The most basic message is that life is a continuous circle that goes on and on. There are other messages that patients were not allowed to tap into at this time and will be revealed later.

My patients saw another reason the aliens were creating the crop circles; to create vortexes in different parts of the Earth. They used electromagnetic energy beams from their spaceships to activate the vortex by pulling out the energy from the deepest core of the Earth. The beam was sent in a counterclockwise direction to open or unscrew the channel in the area to activate the vortex. These electromagnetic beams press down the crops, thus creating different patterns. These crop circles carry coded messages, besides being a vortex, which have spiritual themes.

All these vortexes will help in the future, in the transition of Planet Earth from the third dimension to the fifth dimension.

Creating Crop Circles in a Past Life

One of my patients recalled a past life under hypnosis when he was taught different spiritual practices and also how to create crop circles:

• *"I am a fourteen-year-old black boy growing up in Africa. This is about 2000 BC. My family is moving to England. We are hired to be servants for a family there. My parents meet another black couple in England who teach at night, so they enroll me in their classes. They are teaching me how to use telepathic communication and other spiritual practices. This couple told me that they are alien beings from another planet. They have a spaceship above Earth, but they also live on Earth in a house like humans. But we have to keep it a secret. I am surprised, because they look like us. They bring their hovercraft from the space-ship and create crop circles with it. The wheat crops are pressed down by the wind created by their hovercraft. The crop circles have to do with the environment and how to grow things in the future. They also have a spiritual theme. They teach me how to create these crop circles with the hovercrafts. By the age of seventeen, I grow spiritually and can create these crop circles with my mind, just by focusing and creating them. I understand that, through the crop circles, the aliens are reminding us that life is a circle that constantly goes on, and as we go through it, we are constantly evolving and becoming closer to God. It is the whole purpose of life. I am not allowed to tap into the exact meaning of all these crop circles at this time, because it is not yet time for me to know about it.*

"I teach people how to plant crops and how to grow things. I also teach about spirituality. At the age of eighty, I decide to leave my body because my purpose here is finished. So one day I lie down and my spirit lifts out of my body and goes to heaven. My family and close friends knew about it and celebrated it. There are many angels who are taking me to the Light, and many large and little angels are taking me to God, who is at the top. We are floating up to God and I feel his loving hands around me. He is thanking me for the work I did on Earth.

"Then I go for the review, where I see Jesus and many other higher beings who are helping me. Jesus is telling

me that I succeeded in teaching love to people in that life and many other lifetimes, and I will continue to do so in future lives.

"From heaven, I see that the aliens began making crop circles on Earth around 2000 BC, and I was involved with it in two more lifetimes. Crop circles are markers of events. Sometimes they indicate a landing location for a spaceship that used the grid to reach its location as an energetic propulsion system. They can be created as a by-product of a vortex creation. Crop circles are also used by some aliens to relay messages to those that can understand them.

"The purpose of some crop circles is to let people know that life is a continuous circle and it goes on. The message is very basic. Most people think that they are born, live their life, and die, and that is the end of them. This message is to remind them that life goes on and on in a circle. I see that aliens were inspired by the Light. The aliens of various planets take turns forming the crop circles. Satan is also trying to interfere with us. Currently, there are about fifteen alien races who take turns to create crop circles on Earth and educate people. Sometimes these aliens leave messages for their race.

"From heaven, I see that I needed to teach people through crop circles and spiritual teachings that life is a circle that continuously goes on. I see that my father was an alien and my mother was a human, and later I married a girl whose father was alien and mother was human. I see many people who were there and are also here in this life."

Aliens Making Crop Circles to Create Vortexes

One of my patients recalled a past life when aliens were creating the crop circles from spaceship to create the vortexes:

- *"I am in an open farmland surrounded by mountains in Argentina, South America. I am a man, forty years of age. I am wearing an American Indian dress. My name is Maya and my hair is long and braided with feathers arranged around it. I am about five feet tall, wheatish in complexion, with dark hair and small brown eyes. I am chief of the village. I am wearing a cloth around my waist made of leather. I have feathers around my belt, as well. I am carrying a bow and arrow. There are about six hundred people in my tribe.*

  "I have a family, my wife and two children, eighteen and fifteen years of age. The huts in the village are made of bamboo and dry grass. Beds are also made of dry grass. We grow vegetation on our farms and we ride on horses. I administer the village and make sure everything goes well. If there is any new project, I make sure that everything is going well. I have innate wisdom that comes naturally to me, and I have good foresight with good intuition. I can feel nature and sense things. I look for signs from nature and can foretell if there is going to be a good year for crops or a drought. I also get some information from the behavior of animals and birds, and some from nature, for example, if certain kinds of birds migrate or if I don't see a particular breed of birds. I also study the texture of the ground. I feel things that others don't feel, like nature, birds, animals; things that are obvious to me are not so obvious to others. I understand the behavior of animals and birds quite well. I do feel that horses communicate with me when I go near them. I know we understand each other, but I cannot explain how.

  "At the age of forty-five, I am out in the field and get a very strange feeling. It is a very uneasy and anxious feeling, something I have never felt before. I am out in the farmland, talking to nature and feeling nature. It is very windy. I see an area of the field in the middle that is dry and burnt. The crops in the surrounding areas are all lush green and standing. I inquire if anyone has been in the

field and done any mischief. No one came forward. It is very strange. I feel that whoever did this is probably very afraid and not coming forth and admitting the deed. After a few months, I see it again in another part of the field. So I again inquire where and how it happened, and again no one comes forward. I am feeling very angry and quite anxious, too, and don't get a good feeling about this. It is a perfect symmetrical pattern which could not possibly be made by any human, which is what bothers me more. They are circles of burned crops; no ashes, but they appear burned and dead. These crops are not standing straight, but are dead, like being pressed down by someone. The plants that grew in the burnt area have grown out to be very big crops, bigger than usual. The plant wasn't destroyed, but dried, so the seeds are intact and the plant grew and the crop that grew from it is much bigger than normal. I am very anxious and go several times to the field and inquire within the village as to what is going on or if anyone has seen any activity. I don't get any answers and my anxiety grows.

"I feel very strange when I go to that area where the crop has been burnt. Once, I go at night and experience the same strange feeling and feel as if someone is pulling me. I also hear some strange voices. I see some lights and very strange activities, so I go toward the lights, which are up in the sky. I am at a distance from the light; being more curious, I go toward the light in spite of not having a good feeling about this. I am anxious, scared, and curious. Something in me is telling me to turn around, but I keep going toward the light. There is a point when I feel a sudden jolt of electric current and I immediately step back. I become all the more cautious and anxious and put my spear in the area where I felt the jolt and the spear immediately burns. So I sense that there is definitely something going on and don't know what to do. I am all alone and on foot. Suddenly I see the light in the sky on me like a spotlight. I am totally stunned and shocked and freeze

with fear. I feel a magnetic pull in that spotlight. I feel a sudden jolt and fall to the ground, unconscious. When I regain my consciousness, I am in the village. Some people from the village came looking for me and found me, as I was missing at night. I know that the jolt, magnetic pull, and the whole incident is a warning for me, but I cannot explain the whole thing. I rest and heal for a few weeks.

"I again hear of such burnt crops in the fields from other people, and I get anxious as to what is happening and what is the reason, who these people are, and what their purpose is. Just out of curiosity, I am tempted to go back to that place. I become very quiet and drawn into myself, figuring out what to do. These patterns are a few meters in diameter. They are circular patterns. I don't want anything bad to happen to my village. The villagers are asking more questions, and I can sense fear and anxiety in their voices. I decide to go to the place where they recently found another similar pattern in the field, determined to get some answers. I do not want anything bad happening to my village and I am determined. No matter what, I will find the truth. I go toward this area where they recently found this new patch. There are about seven such patches now so far. I go alone at night, determined not to be scared and to get some answers. As I get closer, I get the same feeling of a magnetic pull, and when I go further up, I sense the electrical current. To test it, I put a stick in that area and it burns right away, so I know there is something going on in this area. Like a daredevil, I keep going and get jolted by a very strong bolt. There are lights in the sky like I saw before. I get up, gather myself, and keep going toward the patch. I get another jolt; again I get knocked down, but I get up and keep walking toward the patch. I am very close to the circle. Not realizing how fatal it can be, I step into it and get totally burnt. My whole body is burnt off. There are no flames, just ashes on the ground and I die from this.

"My last thoughts while this is going on are that I still want to know what is going on and who is doing this. My

soul is still in the field. I died at the age of forty-six. Be-fore I could even sense any burning sensation, my body was turned into ashes. I did not really get a chance to feel anything. I stay on the field with this confused feeling for some time. People from the village come looking for me, but they cannot find me. They look everywhere for any trace of me, but they find only my spear. They do not find my body. They find a piece from the crown that I used to wear, which fell off from the initial jolts. They keep look-ing for me for days, and eventually give up the search. I want to tell them everything that happened, but I am help-less because no one can hear me. I stay around for a year and then everything calms down and I don't see any new patches anymore. I wander around a little more, want-ing to know what it was and where it went. People who come to the fields avoid the burnt area totally, as they are scared themselves. I wander around aimlessly and even-tually give up everything in frustration.

"Then suddenly, I get a very comforting feeling around me. I see butterflies, as if they are trying to cheer me up. First I don't notice them, but gradually they look like little angels, putting their arms around me and pointing me to a place filled with Light. They are pointing me to heaven. I go there and feel very peaceful and light; I haven't felt this way in ages. Then it feels as if they are giving me a bath with Light at the entrance of heaven. A lot of emo-tional dirt comes out and they take me to a much brighter place, which is filled with white, peaceful Light. It feels like home and I am very much at peace. I go there and just sit around trying to absorb everything and it feels very good. I see more of these angels and other forms there, all very loving, serene, and vibrant.

"Later, the same angels take me to another place to-ward the inside of this Light. They open very large doors for me and I enter a huge hall. There are about nine bright forms and I feel very comfortable and at ease with them. Then suddenly I see my life movie, from start to end, on

the wall. Then they show me the incident where I see the
burnt area in the fields and I get very uncomfortable. I
get very uneasy seeing this and the beings sense my anxiety and they give me very comforting looks as if saying,
"Don't worry." I see the way I die. I sense at that time
that these beings are putting their arms around me as if
telling me it's okay. Whatever happened then is over and
I am fine now. I see that I was electrocuted and my body
just disappeared as if influenced by an external force.
There are only ashes; no burnt area. The plants on the
burnt patch gave bigger crops as the seeds grew back into
plants. I get a smile from all the beings to the questions
that I had when I was going through the process of dying,
as if saying that what was done was okay.

"I see that this was done by aliens and not humans.
These aliens were tall with big eyes, green faces, and flat
features. Their faces were oval; they look something like
grey aliens with thin limbs. They had two fingers and a
thumb. They appeared as a deformed version of the human body. They were making all the patches from their
spaceship, which appeared like lights. They were from
Mars and it appears that what they did on Earth was what
they were supposed to do; they were inspired by heavenly
beings. They were installing some energy in that area for
the benefit of the human race in the future. This energy is
supposed to grow as the Earth evolves and was created
by manipulating the surface of the Earth as if they were
activating the vortex under the surface in that area. They
used an electromagnetic energy beam from their spaceships to activate the vortex by pulling out the energy from
the deepest core of the Earth. They sent this beam in a
counterclockwise direction to open or unscrew the channel in that area to activate the vortex. The electromagnetic beam pressed down the crops in that area. The denser
the land, the smaller the area of the patch, as it required
more energy to pull up or activate the vortex. That is another reason why they created ten such vortexes instead of

creating one big one. All this energy together will create one big vortex. The depth of each vortex is different and each is deep enough to pull the energy out from the Earth. They have created similar vortexes in the ocean as well.

"These burnt patches are similar to some of the crop circles made by other aliens. Some crop circles are made by aliens and carry coded messages along with being a vortex. The burnt patches created in Argentina are just vortexes and are created on crops. There are no messages coded here. All these vortexes will eventually help in the transition to the fifth dimension. The energies created by Earth from the vortex and from people's prayer will to-gether move the Earth to the fifth dimension.

"From heaven, I see that some problems, like itchy skin and blocking the natural instinct, have come into the cur-rent life from this life.

"At this point, Dr. Modi asked Archangel Michael if we can create vortexes under each home and building all over the Earth and maybe all over creation, so more Light can flood to them and everybody who lives and works there can become more spiritual. Michael said, "Yes, it can be done on Earth but not in other dimensions at this time." I see angels creating vortexes under every home, building, and many other places on Earth, and also in the oceans. They also shielded them with transparent shields at the lower end and the upper end of the vortexes. I am realizing that every cell in humans, aliens, animals, and other creatures (also chakras), acts like a vortex. God is opening and activating all the vortexes in Earth and in humans and all the creatures on Earth. It appears as if light is transcending all over the Earth and the connect-ing cords of all the souls are opening up and energy is permeating through each of them. All this vortex activa-tion will help in uplifting Planet Earth in the future, dur-ing its transition to the fifth dimension."

Chapter 13

UNDERGROUND ALIEN RACES

Heavenly beings, through my hypnotized patients, said that there are three alien races living on Earth, underground, who affect Earth and humanity. The underground ranges from the center of Earth to the crust of Earth. They are as follows:

- Lestos – the miners
- Reptilians
- The fifth alien race of group two

Lestos – The Miners

The miners are a gnome type of alien being, with axes and picks. They are short, about three feet tall. They are attracted to the energy of the core of the Earth, and are affecting some of the Earth changes, like volcanoes, the underground flow of water, and a lot of climate changes. They affect the magnetic core. They are not causing it, but they affect the shifting of the magnetic field, which has been going on for a long time. These aliens are known as Lestos, and are called miners because they are mining silica and uranium from the underground of Earth. They come to Earth from their planet through the black holes or wormholes between the planets. These holes are like tunnels through different times and spaces. It is like in the movie *Star Trek*, where they step down onto a device like a pad and then they transport to wherever they want and they materialize wherever they want to. They can transport the minerals the same way from Earth to their planet in no time. They are not taking a whole lot of minerals. They think they need these minerals for their spaceships, but they do not. They have depleted the minerals on their own planet, so they are taking them from Earth. These people are not interacting with people on the Earth at all. They are in the infrastructure between the core and the mantle, which is the crust of Earth, about six miles below the Earth's surface. These miners work below that. They can work in the great heat. They are not evil but are misguided.

According to heavenly beings, their mining under the infrastructure of Earth has caused sinkholes, where the ground collapses a little, causing geysers and volcanoes. They are working under Yellowstone Park and other areas underground and are causing a lot of geological problems. Their mining underground affects the way pressure builds up in the volcanoes, and when they erupt, it causes problems with weather patterns. They are working under Mount Saint Helen and under all the places where there are volcanoes on Earth, and even the volcanoes under the ocean causing the tsunamis. They were partly responsible for a recent tsunami in Southeast Asia. They live under the mantel of the Earth, the crust, and they do not know if they are under the earth or ocean. They are not even aware of humans living on Earth. What they are doing does affect the Earth, but not immediately.

They live in the tunnels and all they do is work, according to the heavenly beings. They do eat and sleep but work in twelve-hour shifts. They do not take a lot of time off and do not socialize much, just work. Most of them are men, a few women, and no children. After several years, they go back to their planet and another group of miners is sent. There are about 30,000 of them here at one time. They have no intentions of hurting humans, like the underground reptilians who come on Earth from time to time and interact with humans.

Archangel Michael said that it is time to help them, so I asked the patient to locate these aliens wherever they are underground.

Patient: I see these miners are living in caves underground. They have some kind of laser device with which they cut the stones to build the caves. I am seeing tables, chairs, and beds made out of stones. They cut a square room in the stone where they can sleep. They really do not have a big need to own things or have privacy. Everything is communal.

The short stocky aliens also live about six miles underground but not where reptilians are, so they do not know that other races exist underground.

Dr. Modi: Look at these miner aliens and tell me what they look like.

Patient: They are thin but have a barrel chest. They need that to breathe. They are like humans, with two arms and two legs, a body and a head. Their face looks human. They are about three to four feet tall. They do not look strong because they do not use strength. They use laser devices. Their face looks delicate, with white pale skin because they are never in the sun. They have hair of different colors, but mostly red and black. They have a protruding forehead. Their eyes are slanted and the pupils are big and dilated. Their ears are pointed, their nose is flared, their mouth looks like a human mouth, and they have five fingers and toes. They can change their fingers into a crab claw. They are wearing leather one-piece tunic that looks like a dress, that is straight, has short sleeves and scoop neck, and come up to mid-thigh. There are mostly men and only a few females and no children. They stay here for a while and then go back to their planet and another group comes here to work. Their families are on their planet.

Dr. Modi: Locate their leader.

Patient: Angels brought their leader here.

Dr. Modi: Alien being, why are you here on Earth?

Alien Being: We need things we cannot get anywhere else. We need a fuel source, such as silica and uranium. We had these on our planet but we used up all of them. We use them for spaceships.

Dr. Modi: How long have you been here on our planet?

Alien Being: We have been here for more than ten thousand years. I have been coming here off and on for about seventy years. Every seventh year, we go back to our planet to our families for a year. Then we come back again and stay for seven more years. About 35,000 of us are here on this planet at this time. We do not interact with humans. We have lasers and a sound machine to cut very precisely. We are also mining on three other planets. We do not want to run out of minerals again. Our planet is close to the sun and we have light all the time.

Dr. Modi: Then how do you function in the underground where it is dark?

Alien Being: We do not like it, but after a while we get used to it. It drove some of us crazy.

Dr. Modi: Alien being, does your race have emotions?

Alien Being: Yes! We feel emotions when we are with our families, but when we come back to work on Earth, we are in a different state of mind. We just focus on our work and shift into a different state. We are all born on our planet. When we are about twenty years of age, some of us are sent to Earth and other planets to mine. Then every seven years, we rotate. Every year about seven thousand people leave and another group arrives.

Dr. Modi: How do you go back and forth to your planet?

Alien Being: We use wormholes or black holes. We use a transporting device that we beam from one place to another. We stay on this pad or platform, and we turn into molecules and, next thing we know, we are on our planet and we change into our bodies again.

Patient: Yes. I can see that, just like in the *Star Trek* movie, they step on a platform and are surrounded by a beam

222   SHAKUNTALA MODI, M.D.

of light, and they change in to molecules. Then they go through that wormhole tube and, in seconds, they are on their own planet and changing into their bodies again. I do not feel that they have much emotion.

As I look at their planet, I see these beings live underground because their planet is very hot. They live in family units. They look pretty much the same except they do not have barrel chests. They do not seem to be evil. Being unemotional helps them to stay away from their families for seven years at a time. What I am getting is that parts of their soul goes into a hibernating state because they do not need those parts because they will interfere with what they are doing. So the aliens compartmentalize them for a while. These soul parts while hibernating do a lot of internal work.

Alien Being: We have emotions but when we come here, we block them off. We ask that our emotions of love be blocked and that energy be used for either physical, mental, emotional, or spiritual development, as if it is asleep or resting and becoming stronger. It is like a split brain that does two things. Then when we go back to our home planet, we ask the emotional blocks to be opened. It is like we get to live seven years in one year. So when we are with our family, the relationship is very intense and wonderful. We have not given away those soul parts but shielded them. They are also developing.

Dr. Modi: Do you know of God or Creator?

Alien Being: Yes! We pray to him to keep us and our families safe and protected and to bless us with success.

Dr. Modi: Do you know of Satan and darkness?

Alien Being: We know of Light and dark and the balance. We know the idea of evil. We have very little evil on our planet because we are a spiritual planet.

Dr. Modi: Check and see if they really need these minerals, because they have been continuously mining for thousands of years.

Patient: I get that they really do not need these minerals. Their planet is small and they have too many people on their planet and there is not enough space. The government is using them to solve problems such as the increase in the population. This is a small planet and they do not have a lot of space and this is one way to reduce the population of the planet. I see their connecting cord to God being blocked but they are not dark or evil.

Dr. Modi: Let us communicate with the planetary leader who makes decisions. I request the angels to help us connect with the leader of their planet.

Patient: He is here.

Dr. Modi: You have been mining on our planet for thousands of years. Why do you need so much of these minerals?

Alien Leader: We use it to build spaceships. We ran out before and it caused us problems, so we want to make sure this never happens again. Also, we do not have enough room for everyone to live on our planet. We want to make sure that we do not have any more people who we cannot support.

Dr. Modi: Do you know because of your beings mining on our planet it is causing damage to our planet?

Alien Leader: If they all come back, where will they live? We have about 35,000 beings on your planet and 20,000 each on two other planets. Our planet is small. We have about 500,000 people on our planet, and we do not have much space, and we have to make sure that we have enough resources.

Dr. Modi: Can I speak to Archangel Michael, please?

Patient: He is here.

Dr. Modi: Michael, do they really need that much minerals?

Archangel Michael: No, they do not, but they think they need them. It is true that they do not have enough space. They can actually survive with technology. They can live underground and above. They can build high-rise buildings, which they have not thought of so far. They are not evil but are a little misguided. They are like on an automatic pilot type of behavior but they can come up with another way. They go into a hibernating state, where they have other bodily functions and can think. They disconnect a large part of themselves because it caused problems of loneliness, anger, and depression. Their family members' emotional parts are also shut down on their planet, so they are not angry, bitter, or lonely. When they go back to their home planet, the shield is opened up and they have this wonderful emotional opening. For workers, it is done for them, but they know about it and want it because it is easier to survive with it. When the workers come back to their planet, the family members also get shifted emotionally, as if they were half asleep.

Patient: I see that when they say goodbye to their family, they go through a chamber. It is mandatory that they do this. They walk through some kind of light and their emotions get shielded. Then when they come back, they go through another chamber with a different color of light and it activates their emotions. When the soul parts to emotions are shielded, that soul part is not dead but is still doing the work to evolve in a different direction, which they choose. I think their connecting cord to God is partially blocked.

Dr. Modi: Alien beings on their planet, our planet, and the other two planets listen to me. Do you see your connecting cord to God and is it open?

Alien Leader: Yes, we are opening the radio communication on all four planets. Our connecting cord to God is open but there are some blocks.

Dr. Modi: I request the angels to please go through these alien beings and their planet and lift out all the foreign entities, dark shields, dark devices, and dark energy from their bodies, auras, souls, connecting cord to God, and their homes, work places, and their planet. Lift them out and help them to the Light. Remove and destroy what needs to be destroyed and transform them. Open their planet's connecting cords to God completely. Scrub, scour, and fill them with the Light and shield them with the Light. Bring all their soul parts back and integrate them with whom they belong. Clamp the cords to the soul parts that cannot be brought back at this time. Shield all of them the way they need to be shielded. We pray to God to please speak to every being and guide them in the right direction for all possibilities. Tell me what is happening.

Patient: God is telling them, "Now you are awake and you will get used to the feelings again. You will be able to use more of your brain to solve your problems and I will help you. All you have to do is ask for help."

Dr. Modi: Thank you, God! Alien beings, did you hear God?

Patient: Yes! They are amazed that their life can change so quickly. I see their planet had a big dark connection with Satan, which is now cut, and the soul parts are brought back and integrated with the planet after cleansing and healing.

Dr. Modi: I request the angels to help all these aliens to go back to their planet safely and securely from Earth and the other two planets where they are mining.

Patient: They are all going to their families at their home planet. They are feeling better. They already know what they need to do.

Dr. Modi: Alien beings, remember to pray and ask for help and guidance. You all have your angels and guides, so ask them for help.

Alien Leader: We prayed for safety and protection, but it never occurred to us to pray for help and guidance. Thank you for your help and healing.

Dr. Modi: You are welcome. We also request the angels to scrub, scour, and heal the Earth and the other two planets, and the black holes between them, and the aliens' planet. Bring all their soul parts back and integrate them where they belong, after cleansing and healing them. Flood all the four planets, black holes, and everything and everybody in them with the violet liquid fire and transform and realign their DNA.

Patient: I see their planet is becoming brighter. Before, they were unhappy about their situation but they tried to make the most of it, but they did not know how to change it. I also see that every time they dug the minerals out of Planet Earth, it lost soul parts. As a result, they created problems for Earth and the other two planets, such as making the volcanoes and geysers more active because they weakened the infrastructures so the Earth changes happened faster than they would have. I see that the tsunami was affected by it.

I see the golden shining Light flooding through the black holes and the underground and the four planets and through everything and everybody. It is also going through the volcanoes, geysers, and fault lines. Then I see the violet Light flooding through the black holes, all these planets, and everything and everybody on them, healing and transforming and realigning their DNA and removing the aliens' transportation devices and shielding the black holes.

Dr. Modi: Michael, the tall, thin aliens had similar devices in Atlantis that were responsible for ships, people, and planes disappearing. Are they still there or have they been removed?

Archangel Michael: They are still there. You need to ask for them to be removed and destroyed. You can do it today.

Dr. Modi: I request the angels to please destroy the devices the tall, thin aliens left in Atlantis. Cleanse and heal the black holes in the Atlantic Ocean and all over creation. Flood them with golden and violet Light. Shield them on both sides. I request the angels to guard those black holes and underground areas all over creation.

Patient: I see it all happening, and large warrior angels guarding the underground areas and the black holes.

Underground Reptilian Aliens

During a session, a patient felt that there was a pulse of energy waves coming from a spaceship interfering with the session by influencing her.

Dr. Modi: I request the angels to collect the beings in the net of Light who are using energy waves to influence the patient and bring them here, please.

Patient: Angels brought six alien beings. They are negative and dark. They look like Darth Vader of the *Star Wars* movies.

Dr. Modi: Alien beings, why are you interfering here?

Alien Being: [Angry] We are trying to stop you. We are from this person's past on a far away planet. We want to take over Planet Earth and you are trying to stop us. There are many of us who are working on it. I am not going to tell you anymore.

Patient: He looks like a big, nasty demon being. He is getting irritated. He just wants to slap you for asking these questions. He is cursing you.

Dr. Modi: Alien being, stop throwing temper tantrums. Tell me who you are.

Alien Being: [Angry] What do you mean by "who are you"? We have been battling for thousands of years. I am very powerful. We are taking over and you are not going to stop us.

Dr. Modi: I do not consider screaming, yelling, and cursing to be powerful. I request the angels to cut these beings' dark connections with Satan, his demons, his dark centers and devices, please.

Patient: This alien being is calling on angles and demons who are engaged in a big battle. I see and feel this being is being choked by the commander he was calling. He also has my soul parts with him.

Dr. Modi: I request the angels to cut all the dark connections this alien being has with Satan, other commanders, demons, dark centers, and devices. Also, bring all the soul parts of this patient and everybody else and integrate them with whom they belong. Collect all the dark beings this commander has called in a net of Light. Dark one, how do you feel?

Dark Being: [Deep Breath] Better!

Dr. Modi: Light has been around you for a while now. How does it feel, and what did Satan tell you about the Light?

Dark Being: He told us Light would burn and kill us. But it is not burning me or hurting.

Dr. Modi: Now look deep beneath the layers of your darkness, within the core of yourself; tell me what you see.

Dark Being: White gauze, and as I look at it, it is getting bigger and darkness is going away.

Patient: He is not changing anymore. He is growling and wants to kill you.

Dr. Modi: I request the angels to please bring all the soul parts of the patient out of this dark being. Cleanse and heal them, cut their dark connections, and integrate them with the patient, please. If there are alien beings trapped inside him, bring them out, please. Cleanse, heal, and fill them with the Light, cut their dark connections, put them in a bubble of Light. Lift the dark one out; help it to the Light or bind it into space.

Patient: I also see an alien being coming out of it. It looks like a reptilian with black, greenish scales, big eyes, and bumpy head. It has two arms and two legs. Feet are bigger and webbed. They look like reptilians.

Dr. Modi: Alien being, you were trapped in a demon. Did you know that?

Reptilian Alien: No.

Dr. Modi: Alien being, are you a spirit being or a living being?

Reptilian Alien: My body died when our planet was destroyed a long time ago. We were on a planet. I was a commander. There was some kind of battle with another alien race from another planet.

Patient: These reptilian aliens are living underground on Earth and masquerading as humans. They are sucking our energy. They were on Earth before humans incarnated on Earth. They can impersonate humans. They are shape-shifters and can change their shapes. Since you are releasing so many dark entities from all over the Earth and the creation, the vibrations of Earth are rising and these aliens are having a hard time staying here. They manipulate and influence humans negatively.

Dr. Modi: Describe what this alien being looks like.

Patient: He has two legs, two arms, one body, and one head. He has a reptilian, long face with yellow eyes. He is like an upright reptilian that walks on two legs.

Dr. Modi: Alien being, tell me about yourself.

Reptilian Alien: [Arrogant] We are an old race. We were here on Earth before any humans incarnated on it. We are setting people up in power. Eventually, we want to take over Planet Earth. Our planet exploded a long time ago. We do not know why. We were not on our planet at the time. We live underground on Earth because of the heat, and also, we want to remain hidden. Our race is scattered on many planets in the universe, which we are trying to colonize. We have Earth and many other planets we could go to if necessary. We like Earth because it is green and has water.

Dr. Modi: Tell me about what you have done on Earth.

Reptilian Alien: We came millions of years ago before humans incarnated on Earth. We knew this is a planet we can use eventually. We had people mine cadmium, tungsten, and uranium. These were the ape-like humans and they did what we asked of them. We enslaved them by controlling their minds and took away their will power. Since then, we are watching and manipulating humans. We live underground because the temperature is either too hot or too cold on the ground. The temperature is more even underground, like in a cave. We also live underground because we look like reptiles and we might scare people. We stay away from them because we do not want to do that.

Dr. Modi: What have you done with humans?

Reptilian Alien: Sometimes we kidnap them and take them underground. Sometimes we dissect them and eat them. Sometimes we mate with them, but not a lot. We have some of those hybrid children. There are about ten thousand of them. We are involved with government and other human affairs such as planning who will be in a position of power. There is a shift in the vibration of Planet Earth, and if it shifts too much, people will be able to see us. Some of our hybrids are living among people and some are in positions of power. These reptilians look like humans and can regulate temperature better than we can. They have to keep up this force field to look like humans. Sometimes we can put the force field around us and look like humans, but it is hard to keep it up all the time. The hybrids can do it easier. Because of pole-shift, the vibrations of Earth are changing and the axis of Earth and the electromagnetic field are also shifting, which is not good for us. We will not be able to hide because people will be able to see us.

Dr. Modi: Tell me about these hybrid reptilians.

Reptilian Alien: They can look like humans and live among humans. They are in key positions. They come up to the surface of the Earth when they are young adults. A new identity is created for them and they get a job in key positions of influencing and they are very good in what they do. One well-known political advisors is a hybrid. He influences people positively. Whatever information we need, we get it from him. He does a good job. We want humans and Earth to survive.

Dr. Modi: Check this person and see how he looks.

Patient: [Surprised] Yes, I see him and a shadow self that has a reptilian face. It is almost in him. I see he had a human father and reptilian mother. I see other similar humans, but I do not get who they are.

Dr. Modi: What else have you done with humans?

Reptilian Alien: We really stopped them from destructive things, such as acid rain, nuclear war, and other things that would affect us underground and the water. Water is very important to us. We do not live in the water but our skin needs a moist environment. We are pretty much taking what we need. We are not giving anything to humans for their benefit. We are setting the political scheme just in case we want to topple their government. I don't think we will ever do that, but we could if we feel it is necessary. We really feed off the people's negative energy. People's negative thought forms give us energy.

Dr. Modi: Do you have any demonic influences?

Reptilian Alien: Sometimes people think we are demons because of the way we look. I look grayish green, green on the outside, with a grayish cast inside.

Dr. Modi: Have you met other alien beings of other races underground?

Reptilian Alien: No!

Dr. Modi: Check and see how their planet was destroyed millions of years ago. All the reptilian alien beings on Earth and on other planets watch as she recalls.

Patient: As I look back, I see these reptilians on their planet. They were very cold, isolated, and ruthless. A being from another planet went to that planet with a nuclear bomb and put it in the center of the planet and detonated it. It caused a series of explosions and the whole planet was destroyed. They destroyed that planet because beings on that planet were ruthless and greedy. They often invaded other planets and took whatever they wanted.

Dr. Modi: I request the angels to collect in the net of Light and lift out all the foreign entities, dark shields, dark energy, and devices from all the reptilian aliens on Earth and other planets and their surroundings. Help them to the Light or bind them into the space. Scrub and scour, take away any residue left over, and fill them with the Light. Please bring all the soul parts of every being who died on that planet when it exploded and from all the lifetimes from the beginning of time from Satan, his demons, from people, places, and other aliens. Cleanse, heal, and fill them with Light and integrate them with whom they belong. Do the same for all the reptilian beings who are on Planet Earth and other planets. Open and heal their connecting cords to God and shield them completely.

Patient: I see all the reptilian beings and their surroundings being cleansed and healed and all their soul parts brought back and integrated with whom they belonged. The reptilian beings on that planet were very aggressive. I think I was a princess on that planet. My parents sent me and many of my brothers and sisters to another planet to my uncle's place. I was eight years old and they did not tell us anything. Now I can look back and see that my parents had feelings of impending doom, that something drastic was going to happen to that planet. So they sent twelve of us to another planet to a cousin's place. We were still in the spaceship, pretty far away when the planet exploded. We could see that the planet exploded in the middle and nothing survived. It was like an earthquake, with little ripples through space. The explosion was loud. We were all telepathic, so even though we were not there, we felt and heard everything. We are like a living record. It caused a massive soul shattering for us due to the trauma. I did not want to know anything, so I willed to block it completely by creating a block around me. I just totally shut down my emotions and walked away. Now I asked God to remove that block from me and it is removed.

Dr. Modi: I request the angels to scrub and scour this person and fill her up with the Light. Bring all her soul parts back that she lost in that life and all the other lifetimes from the beginning of time. Cleanse, heal, and fill them with the Light and integrate them with her, please. Clamp the cords to the soul parts that cannot be brought back at this time.

Patient: I see soul parts coming back to my third eye and eyes, ears, heart, and all over the body.

Dr. Modi: I request the angels to locate and bring all the soul parts of the planet back, cleanse, heal, and fill them with the Light and integrate them together and recreate the whole planet please. Fill it with the Light and shield it thoroughly.

Patient: I see that the planet is coming back together. It looks like Earth but it has more cloud cover, so it is wet with even temperature. These reptilian on that planet were invading other planets and were taking anything they wanted from there. They were brutal and killed people and also enslaved and controlled them. On the planet of the being who detonated the bomb, they killed their prince, so it was revenge, but also to get rid of the whole race because they were planning to take over those planets and were very destructive.

Dr. Modi: Reptilian beings, do you understand now why and how your planet was destroyed? Was everybody of your race on Earth and on other planets watching as this person was recalling?

Reptilian Being: Yes!

Dr. Modi: Do you know of God? Do you pray and ask for help?

Reptilian Alien: We have heard about Him but we do not know Him.

Dr. Modi: We pray to God to please speak to every reptilian being about what they need to know.

Patient: God is saying to them, "It has been a long time; come home."

Reptilian Being: We have caused paranoia and fear so we can feed off their negative energy. Since we do not have any place of our own, we were planning to take over this planet but the plan was not working. We have influenced to cause wars, political turmoil, and economic upheavals. We influence news media. We have reptilians in key positions in many fields who can telepathically insert thoughts in people and make them fearful and paranoid.

Dr. Modi: I request the angels to cleanse, heal, and help all the reptilian beings to the heaven who are in spirit form on Earth and on other planets. All of you, we send you home to the Light with love. I also request the angels to lift all the reptilian beings who are living in the body and take them wherever they need to go. Tell me what is happening.

Patient: Lots of them are going to heaven from Earth and many other planets throughout the creation. Almost 90 percent of them from Earth have gone to heaven and only 10 percent are left who are living in the body. About fifty thousand are living on Earth and ten thousand are hybrids. The reptilians are taken to their sister planet by the angels.

Dr. Modi: Can I speak to Archangel Michael, please?

Patient: He is here.

Dr. Modi: Michael, when did these reptilians come to Earth?

Archangel Michael: They came while the Earth was cooling, before the humans incarnated on Earth. They could see the future and how the Earth would evolve and appear, and that it would have an atmosphere of oxygen. The reptilian beings' planet was destroyed, so they were looking for a place to live. They look the same now as they looked when they first came on Earth. They live underground in tunnels.

These reptilians live six miles underground. They live in tunnels but not like a family unit. They have females and children, but they live in groups. The females are used for breeding. The hybrid children are put in the human families. They substituted them for the human babies, which they took underground and used for sacrifice. They killed and ate them. Other times they put these hybrid beings on Earth when they are young adults.

Dr. Modi: What have they done since they came to Earth?

Archangel Michael: They are very dark. They feed on negative energy. They try to create fear, anger, jealousy, and pain in humans by sending out the vibrations that create those emotions. They do this through different media. They amplify feelings that are already there.

Dr. Modi: How do they do this while living underground?

Archangel Michael: They can live on the surface, too, but not for a long time. They shape shift. They create a thought form and walk into it and manifest on the physical plane but the vibrations around them have to support that, too; otherwise, the form begins to deteriorate. Since there is a big shift happening, with the Earth vibrations becoming higher, it is harder for them to manifest. The vibrations of Earth are changing because it is destined that humankind can reach another level in terms of the way they think, have telepathic communication, have higher connections to God, and doing what you are doing. Everybody will be able to do what you are doing now, but it is not a done deal. There must be a significant number of people ready for this. There is a magnetic pull on the planet and people who are aligned that way because they have done the spiritual work and are holy because they are aware, and then they have the opportunity to possibly be put into more alignment. This is already happening and there has been a shift for about the last twenty years. The planets are getting closer together and more people are positively affected by it.

Dr. Modi: How did these reptilian beings affect humans?

Archangel Michael: They influence those in power. They use beaming and amplifying devices. Anything that is connected to cables, such as computers, television, telephones, cell phones, radios; they can use them. It is like an electromagnetic field and they can write their notes on it and it enters on people's electromagnetic field. It usually feels like a telepathic communication. Through beaming, they can cause feelings of paranoia, anger, and hate. They work with certain races and bloodlines of people who are in power. People do not know that they are being used as robots.

Dr. Modi: What have these reptilian aliens done historically and currently to humans and the planet?

Archangel Michael: When the tall, thin aliens were creating those mythical gods and goddesses in different parts of the Earth by putting different animal head costumes on them, the reptilians were there, too. They worked on a minor level on them. They also worked on Atlanteans and all the root races, such as the brown, black, white, Chinese, Indians and all the other races throughout the Earth. These aliens were very influential in modern wars. They assisted in the development of atomic nuclear energy, which created a lot of paranoia. By the late 1950s it was believed that world was not a safe place. They helped create these feelings and amplified them. They were the major reason for those feelings. The more negative people get, the more powerful the aliens become. They are controlled by Satan and his demons, but they do not even know it; just like the gray aliens.

Dr. Modi: How did they participate in wars?

Archangel Michael: They influenced all the wars. They caused misunderstandings and amplification of greed and power. At this point, they are even trying to influence this patient through the phone. During the last session, only one-half of the reptilians were taken to the sister planet and one-half of them are still here.

Dr. Modi: What happened to the hybrid beings?

Archangel Michael: Some of them are being neutralized, inactivated, and realigned. It is like taking out a tumor. They go back in time, before conception, and realign and re-change, and the effect is as if it never happened. That part of the DNA is shifted back, as if it was a human birth. The alien part was absorbed and removed, just like we remove the devices. We deal with it like an energy device.

Dr. Modi: How did they create these hybrid babies?

Archangel Michael: They often abducted humans and mated both ways; human males mate with reptilian females and human females with reptilian males. Some of the hybrids were brought up from the underground; some of the babies were used for sacrifices and were eaten by them. They also took some human babies, killed them as a sacrifice, and ate them. They often preferred babies, but they also kidnapped and sacrificed women, almost like in satanic rituals. That created a lot of fear and a lot of negative energy, which is immediately released. It is an evil act.

Patient: I am having a hard time in saying what Michael is saying. I see a box-like device in my brain. It looks like a cardboard box. It is blocking my flow. Now I am getting sharp pain in my head and eyes.

Dr. Modi: I request the angels to remove the device from her brain and destroy it. Scrub and scour her brain and fill it with the Light. Bring all her missing soul parts back from Satan, his demons, from people, places, and darkness. Cleanse, heal, and fill them with the Light and integrate them with her, please. Clamp the cords to the soul parts that cannot be brought back at this time.

Patient: The device is not removed for some reason. I feel that a soul part of me is holding on to it.

Dr. Modi: Part of this person who is holding onto this device, how old are you and why are you holding onto this device?

Soul Part of Patient: I am eight years old and I am holding onto this device because I want to use it to block listening to my family fighting.

Dr. Modi: You know that happened a long time ago. You need to heal and be one with the older one. Do you understand? Let go of the device box. I request the angels to lift the box device out of her and destroy it. If there are more soul parts of the patient trapped in that device, free them and integrate them with the patient after cleansing and healing. Also, bring all the soul parts she lost in this life and all the other lifetimes from the beginning of time, from Satan, his demons, from people, places, and, darkness, and these reptilians. Cleanse, heal, and fill them with the Light and integrate them with her, please. Clamp the cords to the soul parts that cannot be brought back at this time.

Patient: The device is removed and destroyed. All my soul parts are brought back and integrated with me. I still have the headache and I see a silver ball with spikes on it in my brain. It is like a tracking device as well as a receiving device. It is a device that is connected to a reptilian being.

Dr. Modi: Reptilian being, what are you doing with that device?

Reptilian Being: I am beaming, blocking, and interfering with her. We put these devices in her when she was born. We make her feel depressed and hide in her work. We make her feel numb and cause her to focus on her problems and insecurities.

Dr. Modi: Do you also have these devices in other people?

Reptilian Being: Yes; in most people, we have inserted these devices. This is how we manipulate humans, by giving them different thoughts and ideas and interfering with their functioning. This is how we create the negative energy and suck their Light away.

Dr. Modi: I request the angels to please remove all the devices from each and every human being, from all the telephones, computers, radios, television, VCRs, DVD players, and all the cables and electrical connections and wherever they may be, and destroy them. Scrub, scour, and take away any residue that is left over, and fill and shield them with the Light. Bring all the soul parts of each and every human being and integrate them with whom they belong. Clamp the cords to the soul parts that cannot be brought back at this time. Do the same for all the other aliens on other planets where reptilians are influencing them. Reptilian being, do you know that you all are controlled by Satan and his demons?

Reptilian Beings: [Arrogant] We do not care. We like it. We are smarter and better.

Patient: I see angels removing all the devices from all the humans and all the computers, TVs, radios, telephones, including cell phones and all cables, destroying them and taking the energy to heaven. Then they are bringing everybody's soul parts back from all the reptilians, Satan, his demons, people, places, and darkness, and integrating them with whom they belong after cleansing and healing.

They are filling everybody and everything with the Light and shielding all with the salmon colored glass type of Light, which is a healing color and calms aliens down. They do not feed on the calm; they feed on negativity and chaos. For them, it is calming but also repelling. I see the same Light going to the other planets where these reptilians are.

Dr. Modi: I request the angels to go to these reptilians, including the hybrid beings on Earth, and lift out all the foreign entities, dark shields, dark devices, and dark energies. Help them to the Light or bind them into space. Remove and destroy what needs to be destroyed. Scrub and scour them and fill them with the Light. Bring all their missing soul parts back from Satan, his demons, from people, other aliens, places, and darkness. Cleanse, heal, and fill them with the Light and integrate them with whom they belong. Clamp the cords to the soul parts that cannot be brought back at this time. Cut all their dark connections. Do the same for all the reptilians and beings they have been influencing on all the other planets.

Patient: They are all being healed except maybe 5 percent of the reptilians.

Dr. Modi: I request the angels to please lift all the reptilians from Earth and take them to the sister planet.

Patient: Most of the reptilians are taken to the sister planet except for the 5 percent who are still on Earth.

Dr. Modi: I request the angels to please scrub and scour the underground areas and caves where these reptilian beings were living. Lift out all the entities, dark energies, and dark devices, and help them to the Light. Remove and destroy what needs to be destroyed. Flood the whole Earth and everything and everybody on the Earth, including the underground areas, with the white Light. We pray to God to please flood all of creation and everybody and everything in creation with the violet liquid fire and let it blaze into intense flames and purify and realign the DNA.

Patient: I see all of creation being flooded with the violet fire. I see most of the reptilians are healed and taken to the sister planet, except for about four to 5 percent. All the hybrid beings are also healed and the energy from their DNA is removed, but they still will act different than others. They are usually very cold and detached. They can appear as sociopaths who do not feel much and are arrogant and feel superior. They do not think of others and are selfish. Since most of the reptilians have gone and their reptilian energy is taken away from their DNA, now they have a choice. They always had a choice, but now, because of their behavior patterns and habits, the changes will be subtle. They may not be as ruthless but they will be pretty much the same in their attitudes. There are about ten thousand reptilian hybrids on Earth. They are of all ages and are placed in key positions.

Fifth Alien Race of Group Two

Heavenly beings through my hypnotized patients stated that the third alien race living underground on the Earth is called Meddac or Kubold, and it is the fifth alien race of group two. They came to Earth about fifty-thousand years ago. They look like short stocky humans. They taught humans metal work, carpentry and planning, designing, coordinating and actually building large projects. This alien race is quite comfortable living in the tunnels underground. More information is given about them in chapter five of Atlantis.

Chapter 14

DIVAS AND ELEMENTALS

Healing of Divas and Elementals and Their Dimensions Around the Earth

During one session, my higher self suggested that it is important to work with elementals, nature spirits, and divas because they are very intricately connected with us. They spread the Light on the planet. There is not much darkness in them, but it is the environment that they are in that makes it harder for them to be happy. They are not so happy when they get tired. It is like they are surrounded by mud and cannot move quickly. The darkness in the atmosphere around the elementals makes them uncomfortable. They are doing their work anyway, but they are not so happy.

Divas are like a higher self to the souls of the nature spirits. Divas are in heaven and on Earth. They can be seen by some and hold the etheric patterns for those to whom they belong.

They are the creation of God. They are like an over soul to the souls of the nature spirit.

According to heavenly beings, there are the following main elementals on Earth:

- Earth Element – gnomes, kobolds, giants
- Water Element – undines
- Air Element –sylphs
- Fire Element – salamanders
- Nature spirits

Past Life as a Gnome

One of my hypnotized patients recalled a past life when she incarnated as a gnome:

- *"I am a female gnome about fifteen years old. I feel happy; it is springtime. I am wearing a pink dress with a little apron that has a big bow in the back. I am about four feet tall and sort of chubby. My face looks like people who have acromegaly. I look like a dwarf, but my body is more proportionate. We have light brown skin and live in caves underground because we love the smell of the Earth. I am not as bright as other gnomes. I am kind of slow and retarded. I have a round face, fat cheeks, big lips, wide nose, small eyes, and heavy eyelids. I almost look like an albino mongoloid, and look different from the others. I have six brothers and sisters, and my family does not like me because they say I am slow. I have some problems with my knees and am not pretty. They laugh at me and call me "little piggy" because I have a wide nose, big lips, and little round eyes.*

"My name is Minga. I am ready for a husband and a baby. I love babies. There is a boy who likes me. He is a little bit like me and they make fun of him, too. We live in caves ten feet underground and take care of the Earth. We mostly live underground, but also built igloos above ground for parties, for guests, or to be alone. There are lots of rooms in our dwellings and we have wooden beds and furniture. We can manifest most of the things we need, like clothes and other stuff. Sometimes fairies come and they tell us magical stories of different religions, mythology, and about kings and queens. They tell us how they dressed and we could manifest it. We are not very creative; someone has to tell us things and then we imagine and manifest them.

"I know about our history. We gnomes have been here for a long time, since the beginning of the Earth. We have

a great love for the Earth. We came from some other place and did not start here. We changed ourselves when we came here for the first time so that we could fit in. First we tried different shapes, like a little squirrel or a mole that would burrow under the ground.

"When we saw the humans could do many things with their bodies, such as their hands and feet, we decided to look and act like them. We can be invisible, except a few people could see us. Our bodies are solid, but not as solid as a human body, and through our intent and mind, we could make ourselves invisible. We also get old because we are living on Earth with this time element – the progression of time. So we do get old, but we can stretch the time to five hundred or six hundred years. On average, we live for about two hundred years

"Some of the human children can see us. Sometimes they play with us; other times they tease us. Some of them can communicate with us telepathically. We love our body. We sometimes imitate an animal and can do somersaults and roll around. We work hard digging tunnels and making sure the roots of the trees are appreciated.

"We do not feel as humans do. We do not fight or argue much, and do not need many things, but they are always fighting. We are simple people. We have a type of royalty, such as kings, queens, and lords. We keep parallel with human life so we can keep the web of life that goes through different dimensions. We imitate the humans. Humans are just busy with competition; we do not like to compete. We just like to do the work, and we keep the Earth nice and loving. We know everything needs to be recognized and we recognize the stones and animals.

"Our time is different than the humans', because we are etheric and do not live in the same time zone. One year of human life is like three days for us. We move in and out of human time.

"We know all the elementals because they are like us. The diva kingdom is different than us. They are on an-

other timeframe and go back and forth. We can communicate with them telepathically. We also communicate with undines – the water spirits. Salamanders - the fire spirits, are hard to communicate with because they are so busy. We are slow like Taurus, which is an Earth sign, and we are connected to Earth. We stretch out time.

"The fire elementals help create a fire when needed. They move in and make sure the fire is okay. After the fire is extinguished, they move into the other dimension; it is a resting place for them. There are lots of dimensions, and poets, artists, and musicians of the human kind, and they sometimes move into different dimensions to get inspiration.

"We also have parties in our homes above the ground. We mimic humans mostly, and we sing, clap, and dance. Men like to march through the forest and different places and create paths between the trees to help the humans and animals. They have the intention, which manifests the paths.

"We have different groups for different parts of nature, different countries, and different lands, and they have their own leaders to maintain stability. We can also move into the future. We know a lot about the history of the Earth – the land.

"I am sixteen years old now. I met one boy and we decide to get married. We imitate humans here, too. The leader of the group gives us permission to get married and there are about two hundred people at our wedding. We imitate ceremonial rituals from different human religions and customs, and I have a veil and a bouquet of flowers. We build a separate cave for ourselves with different sections or rooms. We do not have electricity, but whenever we need to, we can boost our aura and create light. We also call up light from the Earth, which can be receptive and reflective in these tunnels. There is always communication between all the elementals and the Earth. When you are in the Earth, you understand what it is feel-

ing. We got permission from the Earth to make a tunnel. We always feel embraced by the Earth, like the arms of your mother around you.

"I have twins. We press our bodies close to each other and our etheric part is overlapping, which looks like a womb of love and Light, and it is a nice place for a baby to come into. We think about a baby and it appears outside of us in the protective space we created between us, which is oval and our size. It is all Light. As soon as we move away, the physical body takes form and goes in and out of that space, so you see it and then do not see it. It takes time for the consciousness to settle in. We are surprised to realize that they are twins. They look normal; not like us.

"I talk to flowers and other elementals and try to help them. My husband works with other male gnomes to cut the tunnels in the caves and to make the paths in the woods. We all need to sleep and dream.

"We do not deal with humans, except when we occasionally play with children. We think humans are dangerous to the Earth because most of them do not have any respect for it. Some of them care for Earth but are very busy and do not have time to take care of it.

"We help many people who are specialists, such as engineers, farmers, and forestry people. Our job is to protect the Earth, so we are always paying attention to what it needs. We are caretakers of the Earth. There are about seventeen million of us on Earth, living in small communities all over. We do not have religion or a belief system; that is too structured for us. To us, all of nature is God. We know of God and we know that we are part of the Light.

"I live for six hundred years in human time, which in our time would equal forty years. I just decide to step out of the body. As we get older, we change. We become more abstract and more refined. We know a lot about the Earth, and we do not have to have our hands in it all the time. We dream more about the structures of the universe and understand it. We do not have a reason to be here anymore.

We have about a hundred and fifty children we brought in, because we do not have to become pregnant.

"My husband has already gone, and now I am planning to leave the body. I tell my children and other people in my community, and then I meditate and leave the body. Angels come and take me to the Light. I am telling them that it was a nice life and I loved every moment of it. Then I go through cleansing, by taking a shower with liquid Light, and some dark blobs and energy come out of me.

"I walk in nature and meet my friends from before; then I go for life review with some masters. I learn from that life that it was possible to feel love almost all the time, as well as have the ability to understand people who are suffering but not to get involved with them. Here I have some understanding of the past and future lives. From heaven, I can see a larger sense of balance and the purpose of the Earth. There was very little demonic influence with me as a gnome because we were not very creative. I see the reason why I am not seeing much darkness with gnomes; it has to do with what you are doing, Dr. Modi, clearing the demons and negative energy throughout creation.

"I do not have any problems coming from that life to the current life.

"I see some of my friends in the current life were also there in my gnome life.

"I see that humans are very creative and we learned a lot from them; we just imitated them. We are like demons, who also are not very creative and are always imitating the humans. That is why they left us alone, because they could not influence us and did not have much to imitate us.

"When you prayed for all the gnomes who were living in that life to cleanse and heal everyone, I saw white shimmering Light, like diamonds, filling and healing us. All these soul parts were integrated and everybody was healed. My past-life personality was cleansed, healed, and integrated with me.

"I am seeing a huge dimension parallel to Earth for gnomes, and it was fairly dark before you cleansed and healed it. Most of the worlds parallel to Earth were influenced by the demons, and now they are all cleansed, healed, and shielded at your request.

"Archangel Gabriel is saying that many of these parallel worlds were dark and getting cleansed and healed every time you ask for their cleansing and healing. Once, they are not so differentiated, and then they are integrated. There is not much darkness now in these parallel worlds since you have been clearing and healing them, but memory of the dark time is still there. Once the darkness is also cleared from memory, then they do not remember those things and the past is re-written. The past gets changed and the dark memories do not exist anymore. The same is true with human beings and all the other souls.

"It is like when you were working with the large soul part of Satan and when you transformed him into the Light; he remembered his name as Lucifer and did not want to remember what he did as Satan. He said you have to ask the part that is still Satan and he will tell you. When these parallel dimensions are cleared and there is no darkness anymore to feed, the dimensions will collapse. There is a parallel to everything: a parallel universe, a parallel world, or a parallel thought."

Life as an Undine

One of my patients recalled a life as an undine:

- *"I am part of a group of many undines. I am born with eight others and we are like eggs of Light. We are both male and female, but our appearance is that of a female. My name is Leela. I have a human-looking form, very small and delicate. My soul came into the body when the* oceans were created. My soul can go in and out of the body at any time. Part of my soul is always an undine in that dimension. I am part of the group soul of undines with individual consciousness, so I can always ask for the undine energy. I always know who she is and feel her. I simply need the right circumstances, which is a flow of love in the water. It is the energy of Neptune, which is the energy of water. We hold the love that exists in water, the attraction of water to water.

"I am the diva of the ocean. As the oceans were created on Earth, at first there was one overall energy, which later was called Neptune. It was the name that was given to water in Greek mythology. I was there before that, but was not called an undine. I came in as the oversoul, or the essential soul; I am seen and not seen. I carry the love of water, and dance and move as other undines.

"I come when it is necessary to connect with the energies as they are appearing on the Earth. They are Earth energy, and the plant, grass, and trees begin to grow and other things of nature are coming in.

"I came out of the stream of God's Light of Neptunian energy as a diva of water. We are very playful and go up and down with the waves. I have a body of Light that is used in human form, but I can take any form necessary to operate within the parameter of what it is created to do.

"There are no parents. The closest feelings of parents are those for the god of water, Neptune. Out of Neptune comes the original essence of me as the water diva, who is the master of undines. I can change form and shape to put love, joy, and energy in the water; it is the immensity of love in nature. There are mythological stories of undines sitting on the rocks and singing and playing with love. We are the manifestations of love in the ocean and the beauty of creation.

"I am about two to three inches tall, or I can be five feet tall. I can change to any size and I like the human shape. We undines are supposed to play in the water, move the *energies around, and sing love songs to it, because we are the water. When the humans came upon the Earth, we began to take their form. Most of the human body is made of water, so we feel like a relative. Our spirit can enter the human consciousness and bring joy to them. We are in and out of the linear time, and we weave the Light of heaven in the water.*

"I first entered the undine life stream to give me a more complete experience. I am a part of the essential undine, or an oversoul. In linear time, I entered in 1647 AD. I had some animal lives for experience. Once I entered this undine life stream, it is always in me, so I can even connect that part of me with this experience and it flows through my bloodstream. I can just think about it and feel the connection. My life does not have any high or low points; it is a continuous, joyous experience. There are multitudes of us in the water. We take forms and join together to become one big undine and then split again. We laugh a lot because it is so silly and we love the silliness.

"We sparkle around the fishes and dolphins. When they jump up and down in the water, we jump with them. We imitate them and sing and dance. Singing and music is the music of the spirit, universe, and the space in between, which we bring to Earth. It is the highest quality of music. It is the musical communication of God that travels through all creation. It is the musical sound of creation. I move around the oceans, rivers, and other water bodies; sometimes even the bloodstreams of human beings, but it gets a little tricky. It is a little confined and the color is not right. We prefer the Light in the oceans, the rivers, and the lakes. The lakes do not move so much; they are more content. We go there to rest. Sometimes when there is some tidal activity in the lake, we like it there. We like the movement of water a lot.

"We play, dance, and spread love and joy. We exchange messages about love and unity with the Creator. Sometimes, if people ask us to go through them and their

bloodstream for a good reason, we do it. We are always ready for an adventure. We have a very pure understanding about what is the best thing to do to bring the love, joy, and maybe healing to people and others.

"Part of my soul is still an undine and the other part is incarnating in human form. I can access my undine very easily. I have a connection with the part of my soul that is incarnating and I also have the individual connections with all the undines as the diva. This is the way the oneness of all life is layered. We do not die like people do. We just come from the Light whenever we choose and leave whenever we want. We have a group consciousness that is connected with time and space in the linear time.

"My consciousness as Leela undine stays on Earth for about three hundred years. In human terms, it will be about fifty years. Time is different for us; we have no time. Humans have linear time as past, present, and future, and are connected with the experience of birth, childhood, adolescence, adulthood, old age, and death. It is an experience in linear time for humans. We stay here as undines as long as we need the experience to develop our soul, and we are very aware of our limitations.

"I have been very aware at every level that I have a destiny, even when I had a very long or very short life. I have always known that I have a special purpose and destiny, which directed me to make choices and decisions. Whenever life as a human became traumatic and painful, I come back as an undine to experience the boundless joy and love. As a human, I would sit quietly near an ocean or a waterfall or splash my hand in the water, I could see the bubbles and sparkles of Light and it would bring joy to me. I am realizing that I can enter into that undine life anytime.

"I needed to have the experience of unity with the other seven undines with which I came. These are the souls I worked with before. We had many negative experiences and karma with each other and needed to have this ex-

perience of boundless joy, love, and unity. It is the way the oneness of life is experienced. So as people advanced spiritually and understood more, and as they incarnated as artists, musicians, writer, and creators, they created this group consciousness because they participated in different lives.

"I leave the Earth and decide with my higher self that it is time to have different experiences. My Light goes to heaven and I go through cleansing, because although I was a Light-bearer, I have taken on some human emotions when I was in human form sometimes. That included a lot of fears and I had to release these negative human emotions. I go through a shower of Light to remove them and there was not much darkness. Then I go dancing and singing and meet other undines and beings to whom I am connected.

"I go for the undine life review with the masters of the three major religions. They are saying they represent the history of the spiritual evolution of Planet Earth and also they represent spiritual evolution in all creation. They each have female counterparts. We are discussing the purpose of my oversoul in my entire existence, as well as the insight I have brought back to my oversoul from entering into the life stream of an undine. We do not consider it as an incarnation; it just helps me to understand the quality of my soul in that life stream. What I have learned from it is the sense of continuity of all life, so it makes it possible to do my work, which I am doing at this time.

"It is a lesson of feeling and understanding the joy and awe that I could experience. It is always available to me and all the undines. I have incarnated a lot as Taurus energy because it gives very good connections to the Earth, but it is slow and a little heavy. It is necessary for me to remember this incarnation of undine life at this time. I was allowed to experience undine life so it will bring me more joy and help me recognize and even look for the Light. When I turn on the kitchen faucet, I can look for the

bubbles of Light and feel the joy. I can feel free of any tension because I am living that timeless empty space of pure joy. The movement will stretch to eternity, because when we are outside of time, we are in the eternal time, the so-called eternal now. This is the major lesson that I learned.

"Since I have a greater understanding of living in no time, I can simply experience the joy, pleasure, and playfulness. Also, the knowledge that I can change my body in and out of my life means I can shower this energy with my intention into every lifetime I ever had, every other human's, and all the life forms in all of creation up to the beginning of creation. I can do it through my oversoul, which can work as a great sprinkling of rain of love and joy in the undine life I experienced.

"The masters are saying that I can include in my prayers that all of those who have not had an undine life of joy and playfulness as part of their soul development can have the opportunity now so they can have the joy and playfulness outside of time in heaven. Their soul will provide them with that experience and there is no linear time in heaven. So if a person prays for life as an undine, part of their oversoul can come down as an undine to have an experience. Oversoul is when, over time, one soul splits into two and two into four and four into eight and so on, to live individual lives. When we go back to heaven after life, all of our memories and experiences are registered, like files in a filing cabinet, in that original essence of the soul known as an oversoul. It is the intermediary part between the individual soul and the oversoul.

"The higher self operates a little bit like an undine. It is a part of the oversoul, and every life the soul lives has a connecting cord to the oversoul. We can have access to knowledge and information about the lives of other souls who have split from the same oversoul.

"There were no negative experiences in this life. The only problem was when I was occasionally identifying with human emotions; it is cleansed completely in *heaven. I will also retain the memory of my compassion for suffering, understanding that part of the suffering is both necessary and unnecessary. It will help me further develop understanding of this paradox that the darkness is necessary and unnecessary. It is like parentheses, and even the shape or design of parentheses in language is important.*

"The masters are saying that I can draw a left parentheses, leave the space and then draw a right parentheses. These are the arms that embrace the empty space inside. Whenever I feel stress or a problem, I can draw parentheses with a space inside and remember the experience of the undine life in that space, and I will feel joy and peace. I will be living in that empty space where all creativity comes from the Light of God through you, to you. We can do it every day at any time we are stressed, or we can turn the faucet on and look at the water and see the undines jumping in and out.

"As an undine, I took the female human form, but I could also take a male form. When the undine wants to sing, they sing in the female form, because the range of the male voice is different. It is more underwater. The male would sing under the water in the darker places. The female sings at a higher pitch to the Light outside the water when it is leaping. The female would leap up and the male will dive down.

"What I see is that it is the level of original higher self of all undine lives, same as the higher self of all the insects. It is like a dimension of Light around the Earth but it is beyond our time and space.

"It is a part of my soul experience as my oversoul. My higher self is part of my oversoul that chose to enter the life stream of the undine, so that will access energy to that part of the oversoul and to all of the other lives that exists in the oversoul. I ask for it because my current life in the twenty-first century does have access to all the lives but it will be impossible to remember all of them. I do have

access to some I might need for my evolution within the limitation of my current life.

"I have enhanced the conscious options to not only me in the current life but to all my other lives. If I ask, I can examine one of my other lives and ask it if it has access to this undine life stream. I can do that with my friends in heaven and I can also do it for all of creation because the masters say so.

"I am programmed to pray and heal all of creation; I cannot pray just for myself. It is imprinted in my DNA. That has been the history of my life, my purpose, and the limitations they are putting on me to keep me from being distracted by the culture, issues, and problems. If I can understand it, then conflicts and problems will not be as painful. With this understanding, I can be very patient with myself and others.

"Dimensions are not planets; they are encircling a planet one on top of the other. Every category of soul has its own dimension. Dimensions are like parallel worlds or parallel Earths. They do not contain climates and are like spaces. Fairies exist in one of the dimensions around the Earth, which is called the Middle Earth, but the quality of their energy has a different form than beings in other dimensions. These dimensions are like bands around worlds such as Earth.

"As I look at the dimension around the Earth for undines, I see it is made up of water with small dark things floating on the surface. As the water keeps moving along with undines, the darkness is transformed with their Light. These undines are almost like vacuum cleaners. As I see this dimension around the Earth for undines, it looks like it has water but does not. It has a concept or the energy of water. It is in reality an etheric space with etheric water. This undine energy goes to a parallel dimension around Planet Earth, which is etheric and is filled with water where undines go after they leave the Earth. The gnomes live on Earth and also in their parallel dimension, same

*as the insects. The divas, fairies, and other nature spirits
all have their own dimensions related to what their job or
purpose is. Like the fairies, where they live is their own
dimension around the Earth, but they come down and live
on Earth from time to time.*

*"Every life expression or energy has an oversoul,
and when this life energy moves back and forth through
the oversoul, they do not die. They will merge into the
oversoul and then they will return to where they need to
go. They change forms at the Earth level where they live
changes. When there is more pollution on the Earth and
in the water, their form has to change, and maybe a group
becomes one so they can have the mutual intention to
maintain the level of joy.*

*"The undines bring some darkness with them from the
water or Earth to their parallel dimensions. When they
take on the human form, it includes emotions, so they also
feel some dark emotions and some of the attachment that
humans feel. Their job is to bring a lot of joy and happiness, so sometimes the group will join together when
things get tough due to negative energy. They join together
to create happiness and focus. When the undines worked
inside of time and had all these experiences, they went to
their oversoul in their parallel etheric dimension. Their
etheric places are part of the Light around the Earth, not
in heaven. It is the level of heaven in creation.*

*"These undines leave the body often, maybe two thou-
sand times in two days. That is why we can safely say that
they live in both places. They are balancing the energy
on Earth all the time, just the way insects do. They bring
the joy and happiness on Earth, so they keep going back
for instruction to their oversoul for where else to appear.
Their bodies are not dense; they are illusionary and do
not die. They can change instantly, like a shape-shifter.
They take the human form because human energy is the
most prevalent on Earth and affects everything else, and it
is necessary to help humans maintain the proper balance*

*because they have the capacity to do the major creativity
and evolution of life, but they also have the most interference because they are free to check out anything. For example, the Neptunian energy does not care about good or
bad. Humans can go into the very dark places, and if they
are focusing on finding the Light, they will. In the meantime, their journey through the dark brings many refined
changes in the ultimate creation. They do not get stuck
there, but many do. So the function of the undine is to keep
people happy and to weave Light through all the liquid
spaces. When people are connected to the Light, they are
not likely to be influenced by the dark. If there is a lot of
dark in the ocean, then undines will come together and go
for direction to their oversoul in their etheric dimensions.
They have an etheric place and a place of form, which is
water on Earth, and they shape shift between form and
pure energy.*

*"My coughing as I am looking at this life of undine is
a way of clearing out my resistance to have joy and fun,
and also an indication that I need to drink plenty of water.
Also, my voice-box was kind of blocked, so it was also
clearing it to open up the singing ability. As different human experiences, I get the feeling, like most humans do,
that I cannot maintain joy and happiness like undines do.*

*"When Dr. Modi prayed to cleanse and heal all the
etheric dimensions and places around the Earth, and
all over creation that are partially in the world of Light
and the world of form, I saw the magnetic sheets around
them sending the magnetic energy through etheric dimensions and curving around each dimension. It loops down
around, sending the magnetic energy all the way through.
Then when she asked for negative energy to be ejected, I
saw all these black arrows coming out and going in every
direction. They are caught up in the nets of Light by the
angels. Then when the magnetic switch is turned to the attract sign, I see soul parts coming from everywhere. I see
people and beings all lined up to receive their soul parts.*

It is like an announcement was made [laughing]. All the different types of elemental beings also were cleansed and healed and got their soul parts back. Then, on Dr. Modi's request, all the dimensions around the Earth and all over creation and all their beings were shielded with triple compression chambers of crystalline Light, violet shield, mirror shields, and rays of blinding white Light. They also created centers of Light around those dimensions throughout creation.

"*When Dr. Modi asked for that past life personality of the undine to be integrated with me, it was cleansed, healed, and integrated with me.*"

Master or Diva of Sylphs – The Air Elemental

I did not have any patients who had a life as a sylph, but I was able to communicate with the master or diva of sylphs and get some understanding about them and their roles in our life, as follows:

Patient: I see little, white crystalline Lights twinkling around me. They are sylphs – the air elementals. They are saying that they are not getting much attention. You spent a lot of time talking to undines, mermaids, gnomes, and insects, but not much is known about them.

Dr. Modi: Locate the sylph master.

Patient: Oh, this is the most beautiful looking being! It is a female and looks like a fairy, very thin and almost transparent, with a silver outline. Her dress is made of some silvery cloud and she has beautiful, long hair. She can be of any size. First I see her as three feet tall, and then she is expanding up to twenty feet tall. She is a Light being and dances like the wind. I see regular sylphs look like Tinkerbelle, a tiny little sparkle of Light. They are about an inch tall and can take a human shape. They hold a little

Light on their head and are similar to an undine. They are full of joy and fun, but sometimes can be fierce because of strong wind. They almost take the shape of the crystalline net of Light. All elementals are shape-shifters except for gnomes, because they are more close to the character of the Earth. The Earth is the most solid among all the elements. Fire and air are the most ephemeral or mysterious, and transparent. Now you see them and now you don't.

Dr. Modi: Master of the sylphs, tell us about yourself and about sylphs.

Master of Sylphs: We are part of God. We whistle and sing. We are absolute beings of Light. We can even be Light in the darkness. We can be like twinkling stars in the night. We love air; we are the air, and whatever passes through or whatever forces through, we allow it to pass or we can be flexible and stop it. We can dance with the wind. Many humans, women in particular, can call the wind. They can call us because we are both the air and the wind. The wind is a force that is created sometimes by other elements, such as the energies of the Earth coming out of the thoughts of humans, by the movements of birds, by temperature changes, and by the actions of the sun. We can be static in the air, but also part of the air breathed in by humans. So we stay close to you and maintain balance, as all elementals do. We maintain it as a kind of telepathic understanding. It is like a computer that always knows the temperature, the qualities of understanding, and the consciousness of humans, animals, trees, and everything that populates the Earth because there is Earth and there is us. We also go outside into space, outside the Earth environment.

Our knowledge of the temperature, the measurements of thoughts, effects of the sun, and attitude of people's consciousness has to do with the greater consciousness of humans being part of everything. We know we are like a final line of knowledge of how people are changing. Since we are part of the breath of humans, we know about their lives, desires, and feelings related to other humans who are also breathing, to the Earth, to the plants growing, and to the insects. We enter all of these. So it is necessary to have computer-like information. It is built into us. It is an extension of an explanation of how telepathy works. You humans can also have access to it as your body evolves, but you need greater discrimination or your heads would explode. There is too much information available. You have networks such as Google or Yahoo, which are like infants compared to us.

We have a very refined way of editing what we do not need; otherwise, it would be disastrous. There is a priority and all life forms have a time limitation on them. Everything breathes a balance of carbon dioxide and carbon monoxide, and we maintain that, as well. So, if too many trees are cut down, we work with the other aspect of consciousness.

Patient: I see angels and higher self are also helping.

Master of Sylphs: It is one of the reasons there is not much written about us, because a lot of the information about the other elementals came before computers. That type of information gathering, with one part of the human consciousness, gives our names and description over thousands of years, because, in truth, we are simply energy forms. As humans feel and understand us, we can take human forms. They can build stories about us so we can maintain contact with them, because the consciousness of humans is an integral part of the balance of energy on Earth. It works the same way in other dimensions where there are advanced life forms, regardless of their thoughts and forms. They are advanced in terms of creativity, original thinking, and understanding.

So our main job is to maintain balance, and we are like a computer network, where we constantly monitor what is happening. Humans mess up the balance by cutting down too many trees. We monitor the balance of human and plant life. For example, when humans plant only one type of apple, insects come to help us and eat up a lot of those apples. Some advanced scientists will say, "Let us diversify," but the less-advanced people will say "Let us use the pesticide." There is a change in overall thinking about not using so much pesticide. So we are involved in inspiring by maybe a small distraction. Similarly, you do not have insects in your room since you honored and showed your respect for them. This is absolutely essential for the consciousness of humanity to make the quantum leap, by knowing they are all part of nature. We have to cooperate because we are all advancing and evolving creatively. Now that you are helping the demonic network to be transformed into the Light to upgrade their adversarial role, the adversary does not necessarily mean to be so damaging. It could simply be a shadow, or another way to look at it that can assist the creative process. This has not happened on any large scale, but has happened occasionally.

Dr. Modi: How do you affect tornadoes?

Master of Sylphs: Tornadoes come about in an attempt to balance the dark and Light energies, and we monitor this as much as we can without interference. We have a net of Light, similar to what angels use to collect the dark souls and other things, that we use to contain them if tornadoes go too far. Tornadoes are also related to the balancing that people need to move out of the house if people have too much attachment and, therefore, too much security. That way, people will be more creative when there is a disaster, such as the September 11th event, which was a willful agreement with all those people to create this monumental shock, bring people together and create a need to show the uselessness of war by having more war. We are still in the midst of that, so we are constantly monitoring with the help of our higher selves, angels, and people of higher spiritual evolution who help with planning these events. We are also monitoring the thoughts of humans.

We cannot stop the tornadoes, but we can make them less powerful. We work in cooperation with other elementals. There are some humans who can command the wind to stop. We inspire people to move and change. We also work with the fire element, the salamanders. When there is fire, we feed a fire or we suck air out, if necessary.

We do not have much demonic influence; none of the elementals do. A lot of the demonic influence is in the animals. We do not have a life span; we are eternal. We can take a form if necessary, but mostly, we are just a spark of Light. We can change shapes, or rest, but we do not die. We are all connected telepathically via this computer-like center. Many computers are actually modeled after us.

We are influenced by the dark side because we are monitoring, so we are matching, to some degree, what humans are doing. So if humans have demonic influence, even though they are being creative, we are limited by their demonic version. We ourselves are not originally creative. None of the elementals are creative. We are the opposite of the demons. We coast along, see what the humans are doing, and counteract it, like demons will counteract to create confusion and distraction, but we will counteract to create harmony and balance. As the humans advance in their consciousness, so do we, because we are adaptive rather than creative. In that way, we also evolve. Dark demons have no interest in us because we are not creative. Their interest is in stopping the Light. The more creativity there is, the more Light there is.

The job of the demon beings is to maintain the level of separation from the Light. However, this is changing with what you are doing because it is necessary for humans to have more Light, and it is time for the demons to graduate, to the same work but at the higher level and the greater balancing. There has been, if you want to stretch the idea of balancing between good and evil.

Dr. Modi: How do you work with humans?

Master of Sylphs: We go to psychically sensitive people

and inspire them. They will feel the Light and then the Light will inspire them. It is very subtle. We do not go near people because we are doing other things. We have very important work to do, which is to maintain the balance since there is so much interference. When there was a great deal of pollution a number of years ago, we worked very hard, and most of it is improved now, except in some places. We contacted those scientists who study long-range effects and essentially inform people on the long-range perspective. If there is a danger of pollution, they will put out a warning so that politicians and others can make the necessary changes. That is the chain reaction, and we find the people that can start that chain reaction.

We understand because we are the part of the computer – the cause and effect. We have a tremendous analogy of the cause and effect. It may not be that obvious to humans but we will see a correlation. There will always be certain humans in the right place to be the crusaders for their own evolution and to bring problem to people's awareness.

We are very joyful. We love being in the wind and the air, we love our environment, and we love the humans. You breathe us in all the time. We can dance in someone's body. We can go in and come out with the air, plus we can help people with asthma. When they are struggling with air, we can give them some joy.

Dr. Modi: I read somewhere that everybody has a sylph assigned to them. Is that true?

Master of Sylphs: No, that is a very loose interpretation. We are always there but not as individuals. We are not individual consciousness. Humans always love the idea of individuals. We hold the energy of impeccable, almost distant love. It is not personal and emotional. Humans connect with individuals, with personal emotion, a concept of love. We are more of a flow of love and Light, opening up to acceptance of the wonder of Light and the feeling of safety people have when experiencing divine love, which is often not emotional. Mystics can have very emotional, almost orgasmic experiences. The kundalini experiences are a form of orgasm but are not personal in the sense of attachment.

Dr. Modi: How did you affect this person?

Master of Sylphs: I helped this person in Vietnam when she was afraid of heights. She was in a large aircraft that was flying slowly, and the whole back of the plane was open. She had a parachute strapped to her and was hooked to the plane, but she was hanging out through the open space at the back of the plane as it was moving. We were there to give her the air and joy of the experience and she completely forgot about her fear of heights. She had set up the original steps to do it to cooperate. She has the lovely memory of the air and the whole experience was very sweet for her.

I helped you, Dr. Modi, many times, too. When you were going into the water and not swimming so well, you would feel unsafe, and at that moment we would surround you with lovely breezes and give you some pleasure of being in the water.

We like to be with people at the frontier of their fear or uncertainty. When people are experiencing fear, they catch their breath and hold on to something so they do not fall. We would be there and help them with the breath when there is an opening, but they can reject it and close right down. We are not so different than the demonic energy that also comes in to cause problems. They see an opening due to trauma; we do the same thing to help, and you can reject both of us. Anytime there is anxiety, there is a tendency to hold one's breath, but if you think about us, we can come and help you. We can distract your attention from the anxiety with our Light.

When you meditate and watch your breath, we are right there with you. When you are holding your breath and your concentration to maintain that, you can go a little further. You can ask us to give visions by floating them consciously right into you. You need to recognize us the way you did the insects. We can look like beautiful insects, such as dragonflies, and can have wings like them because they are transparent.

Dr. Modi: What should humans know about sylphs?

Master of Sylphs: They should know our joy in being alive; that we are eternally alive because of the breath and air. Humans should move their arms to appreciate the air going through their fingers, and it will create sensitivity all over the entire body. To notice the details of nature and the joy of being part of life; that is as much as we can do and it is a lot. We can also inspire musicians because sound travels through us.

We are also part of the GPS system, because the information is coming through the air and atmosphere. We worked with the scientists who developed this and inspired them.

Patient: It is interesting. I can see sylphs around me, about eighteen of them in a circle, from my shoulders and up over my head, like an arch. They are dancing together. They look like little Lights with dragonfly-type wings, but not its body. They give a very delicate feeling of peace and happiness.

Dr. Modi: Thank you for the information.

Master of Sylphs: Nice to have met you.

Master of Salamanders – The Fire Elemental

Master of Salamanders: We can look like humans but we take any shape or form we like. Males and females both can wear red clothes and we can take the shape of a triangle or a little wisp of smoke. We could be pale, gray, blue, red, or other colors. We can go to the center of the Earth or into a volcano where there is fire to renew our color because it is solid. Other fires move more than we do.

We have the same purpose as undines, which is to maintain balance and make people happy when they see us. We create warmth and a common bond. When there is a tremendous fire in the forest or houses burning, sometimes it is necessary for breaking down the forests, waking people up, arresting someone, or helping people not to be so materialistic. We help them understand it does not matter if they lost everything, as long as they are alive. They can cry about what they lost, but at the same time, it gives them a proper perspective. We are all about perspective. When dogs first came to be helpers with humans, they came when humans were circled around a fire. Fire has been great for the communion of people.

We are part of fire. We are the Light beings that represent fire. We are not fire, yet we are fire. It is hard to explain. We are separate from fire and we are fire. Without us, there would be no fire because we hold its pattern. We are the divas of fire; we are the containment and the form of fire. We are like the DNA of fire. We are the recipe – the pattern – and like the divas, we hold patterns of energy. Sometimes the demonic forces can interfere with us by making people feel there should not be fire. We do our best to contain it, but it is not so easy.

When there is an unwanted fire, we will sometimes make a loud sound so people who are sleeping will wake up and get out of there. A lot of fires are because of people who are influenced or possessed by demons accidentally or intentionally. We represent a warning of danger. When lightning strikes, fire is created. We do not create fire; we just hold the pattern for it. Maybe it was necessary to create more fire so there was more air in the forest and new birth could come. We never start the fire; we just maintain the pattern of it. We have the same intention of Light, love, good cheer, and warmth. It is all of the Light, and fire is the brightest Light. It is always productive, even if not used properly. It is the understanding that the dark side can stimulate the Light and creativity.

The fire of hell is imaginary; it is not real fire. It is the effect of a lack of air on all things that is most dangerous and unpleasant for humans because they are trapped in hell. There is no Light or air, and you are burning. It is a misuse of all our capabilities, but then again, it is the correct use in that area and that idea.

We, the fire elementals, are in the band of Light around the Earth that is part of heaven. The same dimension is divided up for different elementals. We are not in actual heaven but in the Light of heaven. We are eternal; it is our space in heaven. Our dimension is a piece of heaven. It is like a piece of heaven is taken out and put here around the Earth. Everything a fire does, at many levels on other dimensions and other planets, wherever we have a connection, has the essence of fire in the mind of God, so to speak. Everything that is created is created out of the mind of God.

Each elemental has a section in our dimension where we retire. Insects have their own section, while trees and plants have a different level of heaven, because they stay. They do not die. Their consciousness moves into the other tree. If there are no trees left of a certain species, the pattern of that tree will go to a part of heaven that is like an Akashic record of the history of trees, and it is also like a storehouse of consciousness. The trees are considered a life form.

There are about twelve bands of Light or dimensions around the Earth. They are all part of heaven and are outside time and space. So there are areas, or levels, that are the level of masters of the species. There are levels within the insect world, such as the bees, ants, and all other species. We are the elementals. We each are separate, but there is also a link to the caretakers of the elementals. Everyone has a master in heaven. They are a part of the Alohim group to keep on creating the life form. They incarnate from time to time to see what they have created. There is a separate dimension for fairies, with hills, trees, and flowers that other dimensions do not have. They are etheric beings who appear to clairvoyant people.

Elementals such as gnomes, undines, salamanders, sylphs, etc., live partly in the world of form and partly in the etheric world. There is always an oversoul, like DNA, for that life form.

Life as a Mermaid

One of my patients regressed to a lifetime when she was a mermaid and gave the following information about that life:

- *"I incarnated when we Alohims were in the process of creating mermaids. I created the mermaid energy as a continuous life force, and most of my energy went back to heaven, while a small portion remained on Earth. I and other Alohims are in the process of creating different animals and other life forms, and later we came into the human form. Everything we created is still a part of us. I see mermaids are more influenced by the dark side than other elementals because we are closer to humans and have more emotions and connections with them. It is a physical link above and below the surface of the water. It is connected with one of the first creatures in evolution that emerged from the water onto land. They incorporated all the energy of the history of the entire planet.*

  "I decided to enter into a mermaid life stream a long time ago, when humans first came to the Earth. Then the undines came and then more fishes, and humans came along in the fifth stage of development and evolved early on. It was maybe the second round of humans.

  "My name is Marie. The power of God and my oversoul decided that it was necessary for part of the Alohim creator to incarnate and balance the physical and

ocean energy. I am the first mermaid and came, in human years, about a hundred years after the first humans appeared. I am about ten feet long from the tip of my tail. My upper body is female and is about five feet seven inches long.

"I operated as an investigator. I moved all through the ocean because I was setting up the formula – the rules – for future development of the relationship between humans and the water, be it water in their bodies or their connections to the life that is available as they evolve in consciousness. Some humans have always had this ability. We watch and connect with them and they can see us. We took the same emotional expressions of undines. We also have the recording of history, which we got with our connections with the whales and dolphins.

"The original mermaid came from Neptunian energy with extra form – a larger form and a greater span of responsibility. It was closer to the behavior of a human but was also partially a fish. So take the energy, say, of a dolphin or the whales, which are the more advanced fishes, into a human unity – one being. There was a great deal of intelligence and love within the dolphins and the whales. Other fishes, which are smaller, would be more reactive, more simply staying alive and working in a group. The dolphins and whales have a great sense of time and a solid understanding of the evolution of history. We are part of the mermaid and merman energy where we live forever and collect human history. We balance the understanding for all humans because they have a common thread at any given time. We have been part of the whole human history; every human has a connection with a mermaid. We come and go but we do not die.

"I have helped this person during all of her lifetimes. We appear where necessary and are actually part of all humans. When humans become aware of us in their life planning, they will incarnate briefly within us. But when they incarnate within us, they become part of our eternal *life stream. It is almost an etheric incarnation. Humans have many etheric incarnations. When they do not incarnate on the planet, they can be a spiritual guide or take on other experiences for their growth. Every human oversoul has incarnated and taken a trip with us. We do not have to show ourselves to humans. Our energy is also within the humans and we live alongside them. We can feel their needs because we are telepathic. We all are tapping into the universal history, so the choices a mermaid makes are quite different.*

"When we were created as mermaid or merman, we were a combination of humans that were developing and the advanced fish – the dolphin or whale energy. It was an experiment, like all life forms are experiments. We have an oversoul that is connected to the Neptunian energy in heaven, which comes directly from God. It is a refinement of the qualities of ebb and flow, positive and negative; we are given a mathematical description, but there is a balance between our understanding of things and our great emotions. We have a great emotional openness, which is the softest part of the humans, and the intelligence of the dolphins and whales.

"Like the undines, we also have evolved with the Earth. We have a conscious understanding; we are individuals but go back to our oversoul while living in the body, not as frequently as undines and other elementals. We are etheric but take on more of the physical forms. We are the early experiment. Emotionally, we are very different than the undines and the other nature spirits. We have the same emotional capacity as humans, whales, and dolphins, which is quite considerable. There is a great deal of love, but not so much suffering. When suffering occurs, pain occurs, and we react like humans, but we do not hold on to it. That is how we operate as balancing forces. We also do not have the limitation of time the way humans do. We do not live in the linear time. We respond to it when we are on Earth. We live on

what you call a need-to-know basis, depending on what is required.

"We all understand that we are eternal. We do not die; we transform. Whales and dolphins are much more physical and their bodies do die, but our bodies do not die; we just go to the Light. There is not much of the emotional drama as in the death experience of humans. I investigated different balances in humans between pain and pleasure, and how the demonic forces introduce negative emotions such as anger, hate, jealousy, revenge, criminal behavior, etc. We were observing all these negative points, not as bad things, but just to see how long it will take to transform them. There were humans at every level of history who were able to have the courage to create a proper balance, so they will use the negative energy as a creative inducement – toward problem solving as opposed to being caught up in a long war.

"We learned these things and were an encouragement to humans. We also represented beauty, love, and a deep understanding. We have much love and knowledge of evolution because we are eternal, so our bodies do not change or age. We are androgynous, but can take on a form of a male or female. We do not have sexual organs, so we do not reproduce like humans. We are all telepathic, which is how we collect information about humans. We appear and disappear to humans for many reasons, to give people hope and to help them understand that there are other dimensions. They need to trust their dreams, and we enter into them telepathically, but they also need to see us.

"We do not see good and evil as much as we see cause and effect. We understand long-term history because we are etheric beings and can move back and forth in time, which humans cannot do. We have a kind of dispassionate approach but we also feel the emotions of humans. We work with people within any society who are capable of understanding who we are, and that there is a larger picture involved, and we will give them courage.

"Bodies change and life changes. That is the purpose for the creation of a three-dimensional reality, a progression of time from birth to death and the different changes that take place, and the complexity of the relationships of history. All these affect everything because everything is connected. When all of this information is collected consciously, it is more of an energy progression. It is an understanding on a very broad sense of energy progression. We collect the evolutionary understanding, which, to simplify it, is how much Light and darkness is there, how much the polar opposites work in a relationship, and how love is able to wind its way through the many challenges that arise. So we go way beyond linear time. We are like divas or DNA; everything is related to everything else. We also infuse into the consciousness of all life a cellular memory that will help the DNA, because we are like another aspect of it. It is like a multi-faceted geometric form.

"As I look at myself, I see some darkness in me, including in my fingertips. I see that the dimension around the Earth for the mermaids is pretty big as compared to other dimensions. It seems dark. There is darkness in our hands because we are imitating humans; we ride piggyback with humans to understand them. I am kind of anxious about you removing the darkness from my fingers. I am afraid I might lose the connections with humans

"My oversoul explains that mermaids are part of the original stream of energy placed on Earth in different layers or different etheric dimensions to monitor and balance, similar to the insects. There are different levels of the original creation to monitor the evolution of creativity on Planet Earth. Creativity has to do with the amount of Light that any form is able to take into itself and stretch out through the hands, equivalent to the hands receiving more Light to create an idea that will take a form. Mermaids do not take on the darkness; they respond to it. They can experience without being influenced by humans

through the darkness. Humans get a lot of darkness be-cause of the density of their bodies.

"The mermaids have taken on human and fish form – the aquatic-human form to balance both the fish and the humans, but they are essentially etheric. We live in an en-vironment that has darkness, and in order to maintain life on earth, like insects, they need to relate to the humans. The human finger is the symbolic shape whereby they take on or imitate the human shape. They can balance it out in ways that are related to that level of human development. There are many levels of development within the entire human body, some much more advanced than others. The problem here was that this mermaid energy was staying at the lower level of the larger numbers of humans, imitating their limitations. That is why this mermaid was concerned that if they get cleansed, will they lose their connections with humans. Mermaids are the only emotional beings who are also etheric.

"On Dr. Modi's request, all the missing soul parts are brought back for the mermaids and humans, including to me and you, Dr. Modi. The dimension of mermaids and all other dimensions around the Earth are cleansed and healed, and all the missing soul parts are brought back and integrated where they belong, after cleansing and healing. Then all the dimensions and all the mermaids, mermen, and humans were shielded with triple compres-sion chambers of crystalline Light, violet shields, mirror shields, and rays of blinding white Light. All their con-necting cords to God were cleansed, healed, and opened. I saw their connecting cords to God becoming clear and larger.

"Archangel Gabriel is saying that every human has a connection with a mermaid. It is an evolutionary stage of the mermaid that is different than the evolution of hu-manity. There always will be some confusion or some uncertainty. Confusion is a lower level of uncertainty, so this is only a little demonstration of fear and uncertainty.

Change has been accepted and those humans who will die will die. They will not tolerate the larger amount of Light, but it happens all the time. The mermaids are feeling a false sense of responsibility. If God allowed it, it is okay."

Life as a Primrose

Sometimes my patients recall incarnating as an elemental being, because for complete evolution, we need to live all types of experiences, which need to be remembered, respected, and honored. One of my patients under hypnosis recalled living a life as a primrose as follows:

- *"I look like a primrose. I am just a being of Light but I can take form within the limitation of my experience. I am aware that I am connected to a much greater energy. I have a pink skirt and I like to play. Our main purpose is to be one and separate with the other primroses, but I also understand the genealogy of all the flowers. I am so filled with the love that creates the beauty of this flower. I am a guardian of history and development of primroses. It is a very early flower and it has no interest in evolving beyond its perfection. It maintains the fullness of itself; that is, its evolution.*

    "We like people to feel the beauty and creativity, which is there to maintain itself. When people say "I am that I am," we gave them those words. We have tiny hairs on our stem. We give people dreams of delicate beauty. Every primrose and every flower has its own diva, and then there is a hierarchy of divas for all the flowers. We are all one soul; we split and change. That is why, when we dance, we move together and also separately. Every flower has a diva and a soul that keeps it going. It is the physical manifestation of the soul. When the flower dies, we go into another seed, and when the plant dies, we join with the oversoul of

all the primroses. Then when another primrose comes, we join that one. As long as the species remains on the planet, even if it is dormant, then we would remain dormant but within time. We are also outside of time.

"The questions that relate to time and dying are a little different than for humans, because we are a pattern that moves into the world of time when the conditions are right to bring back life. If the conditions are not good, then we move to a dormant state outside of time, where we almost disappear.

"There are different levels of divas. I am realizing that I am the diva of all the divas, and then there is one diva above all the divas. I am the nature diva for flowers, plants, trees, and grass all over the Earth. There are individual divas for every type of flower, then for all flowers above that, and one for all the plants and trees, which I am. There is another diva above all of us."

Life as a Tree

One of my patients under hypnosis regressed back to a past life when she incarnated as a tree. She was crying and sobbing throughout the session:

- *"I am incarnated as a tree on Earth. Many, many trees are being cut down by people. It is making me very sad [crying] for all of these trees. Even the young ones are cut and killed, and there are little ones who are not even a foot tall being destroyed. I am about four hundred years old and I have not seen anything like this. So many trees are destroyed. It just breaks my heart [crying]. I cannot do anything but watch.*

   "Now I am about five hundred years old. There is some kind of fungus, and I feel hollow and helpless that I could

not help other trees. Everybody around me was cut off except me. I was left because I was old and had a fungal infection. They were cutting the trees so they could use the land for farming and use the trees to build houses. After about five hundred years, I die and my spirit goes to the Light.

"There are not many people who incarnate as a tree and come back and remember. Satan is aware that people do not know that plants and trees have feelings such as sadness, loneliness, and emptiness and he does not want people to know this so they can continue to destroy their environment.

"From the Light, I see that the tree already had a small vortex in it. The demons were putting the negative energy and also my soul parts in it, and the hollowness in the tree became bigger and bigger, creating a larger vortex inside the tree.

"From heaven, I see that I planned to incarnate as a tree in this life because it is my mission to help people understand what the environment needs and how to help and heal it. Also to let people know that the trees and plants also feel pain and we need to handle them carefully.

"I see that not everybody incarnates as a tree or an animal. Only a small percentage of people choose to incarnate as a tree or an animal to have a certain experience for a certain purpose. In my case, I chose to incarnate as a tree to experience the emotions of the tree in this life and to remember and educate people about it in the future.

"All my soul parts were brought back from Satan, his demons, people, places, and from the vortex in the tree. They are cleansed, healed, and integrated with me on the request of Dr. Modi.

"I see that many problems came to me from the life of the tree to my current life, such as emptiness, sadness, depression, and loneliness."

Middle Earth and its Beings

One person during a session saw a connecting cord going from me to another dimension to a fairy princess. The following is the transcript:

Patient: I see a beautiful fairy princess lying down. She looks very tired and drained.

Dr. Modi: Fairy princess, tell me why people of Middle Earth had to leave Earth.

Fairy Princess: You should watch the movie *Lord of the Rings*. The Earth was very dark and negative, and everyone was unhappy and brutal. As a result, we could not survive on Earth. There was extreme dark influence, so we all had to leave Earth except for a few who are still on Earth. Vibrations have to be high for us to survive on Earth. We are on a parallel world that is overlapping the Earth.

Dr. Modi: What is Middle Earth?

Fairy Princess: If you drill a hole through the Earth, you will not find Middle Earth. It is a different dimension overlapping Earth and exists in the same space and time. It is called a parallel world. It is a healthier dimension. We want to come back to Earth but at this time we cannot live on it because the vibrations of Earth are low. What happens on Earth affects this dimension, too. It is hard to explain. We have a lot of gifts and can do a lot of healing.

Dr. Modi: Was that parallel dimension already there or was it created for you?

Fairy Princess: It was already there. It is a very pure dimension; otherwise, we cannot live on it. We all had to leave because the vibrations of the Earth changed a lot.

Dr. Modi: What are the different types of beings on your dimension?

Fairy Princess: Dwarfs, Elves, and magical beings, such as genies, centaurs (half man and half horse), unicorns, gargoyles, dragons, special flying birds, fishes, and mermaids.

Dr. Modi: What was your work with Planet Earth?

Fairy Princess: Our job was to support and preserve the Earth and its beings. We feel the pain of Earth from pollution of the environment due to chemicals, overpopulation, and different negative actions like wars. They are hurting and destroying the planet. Our job is to bring love, joy, and harmony to beings of the Earth. Humans were invaders of the Earth. We were there first. There are many stories and fairytales on Earth about fairies and other beings of Middle Earth and most of them are true.

Dr. Modi: You have a part of my soul. How did you get it?

Fairy Princess: We are soul mates. We were one soul at the beginning and then we split into two separate souls and are living different existences.

Patient: She is lying down because she is feeling very tired. This fairy princess and other beings of Middle Earth are very empathetic and that is why they could not stay on Earth. They feel the pain of everyone: Earth, animals, trees, and humans.

Dr. Modi: I request the angels to please collect in the net of Light all the dark and other spirits, dark shields, dark devices, and dark energies from all the Middle Earth people and the whole dimension of Middle Earth. Lift them out, help them to the Light or bind them in space. Remove and transform what needs to be transformed and take the energy to the Light. Scrub and scour, take away any residue that is left over, and fill the space with the Light. Bring all the soul parts to the Middle Earth and its beings, which they lost in this life and all the other lives from the beginning of time, from Satan, his demons, from people, places, and darkness. Cleanse and heal them, fill them with the Light, and integrate them with whom they belong. Clamp the cords to the soul parts that cannot be brought back at this time. Fill them with the Light and shield them with a triple net of Light, violet shield, metallic shield, mirror shields, and rays of blinding Light.

Patient: I see all different types of beings of Middle Earth in a circle and there is fire in the middle. There are sparks coming out of the fire, which are the soul parts going back to whom they belong. The sparks are also going in their third eye.

Dr. Modi: Please flood all of Earth and the Middle Earth and all their beings with the violet liquid fire and let it blaze into violet flames. Fairy princes, tell me, how do you feel?

Fairy Princess: Less tired. We may need more healing later on sometime.

Dr. Modi: Tell me more about yourself.

Fairy Princess: We live a long life, about three hundred and fifty years. We incarnate as different Middle Earth beings. All our beings on Earth are also cleansed and healed but they need to remain on Earth. They have a purpose. They are creating magic. They are raising the vibrations of the Earth, which can only be done in a certain way. It is hard to describe.

Patient: What I am seeing is Middle Earth as one of the dimensions, in our parallel dimensions around the Earth and not in our Earth. All the parallel universes have a dimension like our Middle Earth. I see our Middle Earth in our parallel universe looks like Earth.

Dr. Modi: We pray to God and request the angels to please go through the Middle Earth in our parallel universe and lift out all the dark and other entities, dark shields, dark devices, and dark energy from the whole universe of Middle Earth, including from its kundalini, meridians, chakras, psychic antennas, and the core and the whole Middle Earth, and from all of its beings who dwell on it. Help them to the Light or bind them in the space. Destroy and transform what needs to be transformed and take the energy to the Light. Scrub and scour all of Middle Earth and its beings and all life forms. Take away any residue left over and flood the Middle Earth and everything and everybody in it with the white Light. Bring all the soul parts of Middle Earth and all its beings from Satan, his demons, people, places, and darkness. Cleanse, heal, and fill them with the Light and integrate them where they belong. Store the soul parts in heaven after cleansing and healing that cannot be integrated at this time. Open connecting cords of the Middle Earth and all its beings to God. We pray to God to please flood them with the violet liquid fire and let it blaze into intense violet flames. Transform, and realign their DNA and guide them in the right direction, please.

Patient: I see white Light flooding into Middle Earth and its beings, pushing all the dark entities and energies out of them. They are lifted out by the angels and taken to heaven. Then the angels brought all their soul parts back and integrated them where they belong. I see their connecting cords are being opened up and violet Light is flooding in and transforming all of Middle Earth and their beings.

I see the fairy princess and all the beings looking more energetic and smiling. There was a dark shadow all over Middle Earth and all its beings. It was draining their energy and causing dread, which they felt and we were experiencing to some extent. Now it looks like sunshine and there is more peace and harmony. I see a dark soul came and took their will and hope away, leaving them in deep despair, depression, and fatigue.

Dr. Modi: We pray to God and request the angels to please bring all the soul parts to the will power of all the beings of Middle Earth and integrate them after cleansing and healing. Flood all of Middle Earth and its beings with love, joy, hope, healing, and energy. Cleanse and heal all the parallel universes throughout creation. Shield them completely with the crystal shield. Open their connecting cords to God and guide them in the right direction. We pray to God to please flood all of creation and everything and everybody in it with the violet liquid fire and let it blaze into intense flames. Transform and realign their DNA and heal them, please. Thank you.

Patient: I see it happening all over creation.

Dr. Modi: Fairy princess, what else can we do to heal the Middle Earth and its beings?

Fairy Princess: I do not know yet. Right now we feel like we are waking up from sleep. But check back with us again.

Life of a Fairy Helping People on Earth

One of my patients recalled a life when she was incarnated as a fairy on a fairy planet called Silia. During that life, she and her husband chose to go to Earth to help humans. She described her life as follows:

- *"I am a twenty-five-year-old fairy, living on a fairy dimension. This is about 25,000 BC, according to Earth time. I am a female about one and a half feet tall. I have white skin, long blond hair, and small wings that help me to fly short distances. I can also walk. I live in a cobblestone house with my husband. We have been married for two years. Our home is about five feet tall and ten feet long. The roof is made up of grass. I 'see a small chimney and small windows. The walls and floors are made of granite. The whole house is one big room, with a stove and dining table on one side and a small bed on the other side. We get our water from the community wells. There is a small bathroom in the corner with a shower in the wall. There is also a miniature version of the toilet here, as on Earth. The mattress is made up of dried straw softly enclosed in a cotton cover. There are some shelves to store things. We use crystals to light the, house. We put eight-inch crystals in the sunlight and have an intention for them to hold the sun energy to light the house in the night. We mine the crystals and the granite from the ground nearby.*

"We also cook our food with crystals. Our stove is made of a wooden box, and, there is crystal top. In the center, there is a large crystal under the burner that cooks the food. We take it out to charge it in the sun every day. We only eat vegetables, herbs, and fruits. We do not eat meat.

"We do not have any schools and do not need any education. We tap into the Light for any knowledge we need. We spend a lot of time outside gardening. We put crystals around our gardens, which helps us grow beautiful flowers and lots of vegetables. We do not have to work for a living. We are happy, playful, and full of joy.

"Everybody here knows how to mine the crystals and granite. We use crystal in many different ways. Besides for cooking and for light, we use crystals to see the future, and crystals also intensify our psychic abilities. In our community, we have a circular meeting hall made up of crystals. It is about fifteen feet tall and fifty feet wide. It is used for different social functions. It has wonderful, soothing energy.

"At the age of thirty, we decide to have a baby. We do not have sex and then conception like humans. Both of us sit facing each other, praying and forming an intent to have a baby. We hold each other's hands. I see Light coming from heaven and filling both of us, and then Light is surging into me from him and I become pregnant. Then about five months later, I have a baby boy. There is no pain during the delivery, just the pressure, and the baby comes out. The baby is about four inches tall. I breast-feed the baby for about six months. He begins to walk when one year old, and talk at the age of one and a half. He can also communicate telepathically.

"I also see other beings in our community. I see gnomes who live in the trees. They are about a foot tall. They are kind of gruff, short, and stocky. They are fun and we like to hang out with them. They are good neighbors. They do not have wings like us fairies.

"There is also a being called pan, who is kind of an overseer of the community. He is about four feet tall and doesn't have any wings. He has human-like features and lives in a crystal home. Only one pan lives in our community. He does ceremonies for us. Pans act like priests for all the communities nearby.

"We are in the crystal hall for a wedding ceremony. The pan is conducting it. Everybody in the community is there, including the gnomes. There is a lot of singing, dancing, and eating. During the ceremony, everybody is sprinkled with holy water.

"At the age of about two hundred, my husband and I choose to visit Earth. We are just curious. We raise our vibrations with crystals. We cleanse ourselves with fasting for about a week to raise our vibrations so more Light can be infused. We drink just herbal tea for a week. As our vibrations rise, we become two balls of Light. We also ask pan to help us with the prayers so we can go to the right place on the Earth. We pray and form an intent and focus on that place on Planet Earth where we want to go. Fairies who went to Planet Earth before told us what to expect and not to expect. They told us that there is a lot of darkness on Planet Earth, and we need to be super-charged with the Light to do what we need to do.

"When we are ready, we raise our vibrations and become just the balls of Light. Then we pray with the pan and give our intent, where we want to be, and we are there. I see that we are somewhere in Pennsylvania. Once we touch the Earth, we become ourselves again as fairies. We do bring crystals with us. We put them in the sun to charge them. The planet is very welcoming. We run into our fairy friends who are also here. We notice some animals that are different from the animals on our planet, and some are bigger than us, so we have to be careful and hide from them.

"On Earth, we contact a few people who can communicate psychically. We share our knowledge with them

and then they are able to pass it on to other people. It is like conducting a workshop. We told them about pan – an Earth-elemental being that they can call on for help. We teach the humans we meet about the crystals, how they work, and what they do. We teach them about plants and how to energize the plants with the crystals. We teach them about meditation and how to get in touch with the Light and God. We also talk to them about the healing power of the plants, how to intensify the energy around their homes, how to heal by touch with the crystals, and how to infuse and energize water with crystals.

"While on Earth, we visit other fairies and explore different parts of the area. Sometimes we walk and other times we use our wings. We live out in nature. We manifest food and other things we need just by forming an intent. We go back to our planet after about five years. It has been a great adventure.

"At the age of three hundred, the Light in me begins to fade a little bit and I realize it is time for me to go. I tell my family about my decision. I meditate and go into a trance-like state. My family and other people in the community are gathered around me, and they are all praying for me. My soul leaves the body while in meditation and goes to heaven. There are angels who look like us fairies. They cleanse me by the Light.

"Then I go for my life review with the masters, who also look like fairies. From heaven, I see that my parents taught me the importance of the crystals and how they can keep us infused with the Light. They also taught me how to mine crystals and granite. I see that whenever we needed help, we called on pan telepathically and he always came. He was like a priest.

"I see from heaven that some of the fairies from the fairy dimension also go to Planet Earth to help. They raise their vibrations so high that they become just Light, and are invisible. Then they focus on where they want to go and end up there. This is how they come to Earth.

"From the Akashic records, I see that I chose to incarnate on Earth to learn how it is to live on a planet that is not very bright. I do not see any problems coming from that life to the current life.

"I see that my father and mother in that life are my friends in my current life. You, Dr. Modi, were my sister in that life on the fairy dimension, and you also went to Planet Earth. I see from heaven that only a few chosen humans incarnate on the fairy planet."

Parallel Universe and Middle Earth

During the next session, I inquired more about the Middle Earth and the parallel universe from Archangel Michael. He provided the information as follows:

Dr. Modi: Michael, where is the Middle Earth?

Archangel Michael: Middle Earth is a dimension. If you drill into the Earth, you will not find Middle Earth. It is a physical place but not on Earth. It is occupying the same space but in different time.

Dr. Modi: What is a parallel universe?

Archangel Michael: You can think of it like different sides of a box. Imagine each side of that box is a plane or a dimension. In the center of that box is time and space, which you cannot touch because it is empty space. The parallel universes exist at the top, at the bottom, and on the sides. They are all connected with the central space and time. Different things are happening but they are similar and they take different courses because of the vibrations. Time is like air. Everything is connected. If something happens on one side of the box, it will send shock waves and affect all sides of the box. That is why sometimes you get the effects of other dimensions. It doesn't affect you strongly, but it does affect. Sometimes the box compresses and the sides get sucked in and one side of the box touches the other side. It does not happen very often, although there are tubes or pathways between the dimensions. This can cause big, drastic changes that will be considered similar to Armageddon where the rupture happens and people go up and down or disappear. It is like big shock wave. It is a massive change and people can be terrified. It doesn't happen very often. When the two sides touch, there is much shifting and changing of energy, which leads to spontaneous combustion. Sometimes it can be a total cataclysmic collapse and then re-expansion. There is a lot of fire and energy jolting the worlds.

There are four sides to a box and then there is top and bottom, a total of six sides or dimensions. Then there are three planes within time: past, present, and future. There are a total of nine dimensions or universes. Each dimension has a past, present, and future, so it is like having nine sides. They are all part of everything. Earth has one, each galaxy has one, each universe has one, and the creation has one, and they are all embedded in each other.

Let us just say that right now the Earth plane is on the top of the box (but it is not). But let us just think that way; then the parallel universe would be one on the side, one on the bottom, one on the front and back. All of them are parallel universes. They are different dimensions but have the same energy signature. There are nine dimensions existing in the same time and space and they affect each other periodically, like nine of you existing on nine planes. Sometimes you are on a few dimensions and other times you work on all the dimensions. That is another reason why people have so many lifetimes. Not all lifetimes are lived on Earth. Sometimes souls are in one plane and at another time they are in different planes.

Dr. Modi: Like the fairy princess of the Middle Earth who is a part of my soul?

Archangel Michael: Yes! There are cords with your soul in different places, in different dimensions, and here. Satan and his demons can have influence on you in different dimensions and also on Earth, and it can have a ripple effect in this dimension. Sometimes people do not know why they are feeling a certain way and it has nothing to do with what is going on in their life here.

Dr. Modi: What kind of strengths or problems can we have?

Archangel Michael: You can get strengths and problems, both negative and positive, from those different dimensions. That is why people need to pray for all the souls in every dimension and also cleanse, heal, and shield each dimension.

Dr. Modi: I request the angels to please lift out in the net of Light all the foreign entities, dark shields, dark connections, and dark devices from everything and everybody in creation, including every dimension and their connecting cords to God and all the inter- and intra-dimensional pathways and everything in between the dimensions. Lift them up, help them to the Light or bind them into the space. Remove and destroy what needs to be destroyed. Scrub and scour, take away any residue that remains. Please bring the soul parts of all the humans and aliens who are living on several dimensions at the same time, from Satan, his demons, from people, places, and darkness. Cleanse, heal and fill them with Light and integrate them with whom they belong. Clamp the cords to the soul parts that cannot be brought back at this time. Open connecting cords to God for every dimension and everybody and everything in them, and heal them and fill them with Light and shield them with whatever kind of shields are needed. Also cleanse, heal, and shield the inter- and intra-dimensional pathways and the time and space between the dimensions.

Patient: I see a box that is curved into the shape of a ball. The surface of the ball looks smooth and colorful like a rock called peacock rock, and it is iridescent. It is bluish-purple in color. The shield looks like an ignited Light with the sun's corona outside it. I cannot see inside the box but I feel like it is flooded with the breath of air. It is a gentle wave of Light, which is healing.

Dr. Modi: Michael, is the whole box a parallel universe?

Archangel Michael: You are in the universe; you are in right now. All the other universes are parallel to your universe. They are existing in the same space. All of creation and everything you know is in your universe, and then there are eight copies going on at the same time, playing out just a little differently because of different influences and choices. They can affect each other somewhat, but not overly. They exist in the same space but in three different times; in the past, present, and future.

On Earth, people live in the USA and also in China on the other side of the Earth. It is exactly like that. You can also think of your body like a universe. A universe is made up of millions of parts all existing separately but all existing together. So you could look at it as nine universes or you could look at it as one universe with nine parts. They are all influencing each other. When you heal one dimension, you heal all, and when something bad happens in one, it can cause disturbance in all. The time space is in the middle, through which the force or energy goes across.

You are also affected by your future. Part of you is living in the future and a part is living in the past. Now you live in the present, you know the past, but you are actually living in the past, too. You are also living on the six other universes in the past, present, and future. It is actually $9 \times 9 = 81$ lives going on at the same time, but maybe not living in all places. Maybe some died and are waiting to be reborn. But there can be 81 lives for each person. Stars and planets are also part of this universe. Sometimes kids who are angry or very violent need to be on different dimensions. It is like they are trapped in the wrong place.

Patient: I am seeing that the parallel universes look like mirrors that are next to each other in a stack. They look like mirrors that are not lined up. They are like covering half-and-half. It is like a telescope. There is a round ball and next to the round ball in all directions are mirrors that are coming off it. You can see there is one mirror that is ten feet away and then eight feet and another one is five feet away. So then, when there are shock waves, they break the first mirror, second mirror, and so forth. Here, every mirror is a parallel universe and the shock waves can cause great damage to these parallel universes.

I am looking out at parallel universes that are not stacked together, but corners of them are touching each other like Michael described, as a box with six universes at six sides with their corners touching each other, and there is a space-time in the center of the box. These also look like mirrors because they are of Light and also shielded with crystal shields and mirror shields. When you are walking toward them, you see yourself walking toward the mirror, but you do not see what is in the mirror or behind it. It is important, because if you are sending out good intentions, then you get good intentions reflected to you. If you are sending out a negative intention, that is also reflected back to you.

Now I am being shown another parallel universe somewhere in creation. It is in the shape of an octahedron. It is like two ice-cream cones on top of each other, but instead of being cones, they are like triangles with different sides. They have different levels of vibration and have different purposes.

I am seeing another parallel universe. It looks like a spiral and it goes from the center out. They are on one huge center; all the parallel universes are at the periphery of the center. They each have their own center and they are rotating around the huge center.

There are many of these groups of parallel universes of different shapes, sizes, and vibrations.

Dr. Modi: Why is the fairies' dimension called Middle Earth?
Archangel Michael: It is called Middle Earth because it was in the middle time period during the development of Earth. The middle time period was from the beginning of creation to the end. That was the middle phase. Middle

Earth people were taken to the parallel universe because the darkness was increasing on Earth and vibrations were decreasing, and they could not survive on Earth.

Dr. Modi: What do we need to do to help people of Middle Earth?

Archangel Michael: You need to go to that dimension and heal them the same way you do in this dimension. Then they can send some of their energy back to heal the Earth.

Dr. Modi: Can you tell us about the different types of people of the Middle Earth?

Archangel Michael: Fairies, Elves who are tall, trolls who are short, and genies. Fairies are small, ethereal and look heavenly and attractive. They look like they can float away. They look different than humans. They have a different energy signature and feel. These are in fairy tales because people have a history of remembering them. Fairy tales and legends have these memories. Humans also incarnate as Middle Earth people, too. It is an evolutionary process. You start out as a primitive being and as you evolve, you get to a more advanced being. They are more evolved spiritually. That is why they are lighter than air and have magical powers; but not all of them, because they are also influenced by the demons.

Most of the Middle Earth people are living in the parallel universe, but there are some fairies and elves here on Earth, too. There are not many of them and they are having a hard time staying on Earth. They need to stay here and be the keepers of the Earth. They keep the Earth together.

Patient: I am seeing an image of Earth spinning and pieces of Earth flying everywhere. I get the understanding that the Middle Earth people hold the Earth together and keep it from falling apart.

Dr. Modi: The story of the movie *Lord of the Rings*: is it real?

Archangel Michael: The story is real. There are rings, but it is more like a symbol. There are other things that are symbols of good and power like that ring, things that come together and have this magical power that can bring good. They open a portal. They are not good or evil, but they do have powers. Whoever has them can wield this power. In fact, Hitler was after these kinds of things. He had many religious relics and artifacts and he was looking for the Ark of the Covenant, the Shroud of Turin, and the Holy Grail. All these things are real. The story of *The Lord of the Rings* is real. The ring was finally destroyed. It was melted for real, not just in the movie. That means it is not there anymore for the dark ones to use. There are many others things that somebody can find and use negatively.

We have soul connection with some of the Middle Earth people. Just like your higher self said, we need to go through the past lives that are involved with the conflicts and heal all of Middle Earth and their people so they can come back to Earth to live like they did before it became so dark that they could not live on Earth. They have magical and healing powers and can help Earth and its people. At present, they are living in a parallel universe because they could not live on Earth anymore. They need to come back on Earth again. So you need to heal them whenever you can.

Dr. Modi: Can you tell me about intra-dimensional and inter-dimensional pathways?

Archangel Michael: Intra-dimensional pathways are within the same universe, while inter-dimensional pathways are between different universes. Beings can travel from one end of a galaxy to the other side through these intra-dimensional pathways almost instantaneously. It is the way space is curved. So that going through one point brings you out to the other end of the galaxy instantly. In one universe, there are many different points where the curvature of space backs upon itself and brings the two points together or to close proximity. At that point, people can travel from one side of the universe to the other side by stepping through that contact point. Of course it takes technology to be able to do that. These intra-dimensional pathways can be between two planets, two solar systems, or two galaxies. When this knowledge is literally handed to humanity, humans will be able to travel great distances within this universe.

Space is not a star, not a planet, and there is nothing there but space. A space is composed of a fabric. You spread the thread of the fabric and step through to the other side. This can only happen at the point where they are actually in touch. The contact point might shift.

Inter-dimensional pathways are between two universes, and there is a change in the vibration from one universe to another universe, while there is no change in the vibrations from one dimension to another dimension. In one universe, all the globes have the same basic vibrations of that universe. Some a little higher and some a little lower, but everything within that universe vibrates within the same range of frequencies. If it vibrates at a different frequency, it is in another universe that is overlapping but in a different dimension. The only difference between the two universes that exist in the same space, one on the top of the other, is that the vibration rates are different. It is not a good idea to go to a universe of different vibrations because people of one could not exist in the other. Only the spirit beings, such as angels, demons, or any physical being who can change the vibrations, and very few can do that. So we cannot travel through one universe to another physically, but it is possible to have psychic communication from one universe to another.

Demons also can travel freely through these intra-dimensional and inter-dimensional pathways and can appear in a person in another dimension without any problem. That is why we should pray for cleansing, healing, and protection of these pathways.

Patient: As I look at the universes above and below, it seems that intelligent forms of life get simpler and simpler on the way down through the universes with the lower vibration rates, until the intelligent races seem to be in the forms of slugs or crawling creatures further down. They are just blobs without much form. They are dark and gray, as if they are negatively influenced. As I look down, it seems like there are more and more influenced races. As I look at universes above, there are races that get more ethereal and there are less and less dark influences in the races with higher vibrations.

I also see that even Earth has four levels or dimensions. The first is the physical dimension, which is solid. The second dimension is mental, where we interact with people. The third dimension is emotional, and the fourth dimension is spiritual.

Insects

A couple years ago, all of a sudden, big centipedes began to appear in our bedroom. Never in any other room of the house. They created a feeling of fear and dread, and the first thing I would do was kill them with the bug spray. Then I would feel bad all day. I normally do not like to kill or hurt anything. So one day, I prayed to cleanse and heal all the insects and requested the angels to remove the centipedes from our bedroom. Archangel Gabriel asked me to speak to the leader of insects. Following is the transcript.

Dr. Modi: Leader of insects, why are the centipedes coming in our bedroom, and what should I do to stop them from coming?

Leader of Insects: You will have to make a connection with them.

Dr. Modi: Can I speak to the spirit of insects I had to kill?

Patient: I see that the spirits of insects integrated with the leader immediately; he looks like a large centipede. He lives in one of the dimensions around the Earth. It is a combination of heaven and Earth. They have a very short life span here on Earth, and when they die, they go back to this dimension around the Earth.

Dr. Modi: Leader of insects, is your dimension cleansed or is there still darkness.

Leader of Insects: It is both. I cannot tell. The more you do the cleansing, the better it is.

These dimensions are around the Earth. We live half in etheric and half in the physical world. All elementals live in one of these dimensions. They have their own areas where they come and go, depending on what their lifespan is and what their DNA programming is. They are on Earth for their own evolution and development. Part of their purpose is to assist humanity and the growth of Earth and everything else because everything is interconnected. When you see some insects after today, you need to respect them and thank them all for what they are doing for Planet Earth. Ask for forgiveness for wanting to kill them.

Dr. Modi: We request the angels to please put the magnetic sheet around all the insects and elementals and around all the dimensions around the Earth and all over creation and all the beings who live in them. Turn the magnetic switch to the eject sign and expel all the foreign entities, dark shields, dark devices, and dark energies. Collect them in the net of Light, transform them, and take them to heaven. Then turn the switch to the attract sign and allow each and every soul part to come back from Satan, his demons, people, places, darkness, and heaven, from this time and space and beyond. Cleanse, heal, and integrate them where they belong. Clamp the cord to the soul parts that cannot be brought back at this time, twenty or more times till we are ready to retrieve them back. Flood everything, every being, and every dimension with the crystalline, white, liquid Light and shield them with the triple compression chambers of crystalline, white Light. Tell me what happened.

Patient: It was like cleaning of the work spaces or the living spaces of where they are. The insects do not have any darkness in them but their dimension was slightly darker. There was some interference with the flow of the energy.

The insects come to people who have the power to understand and change things, like when they were coming to your room.

The elementals do have some darkness in them, but not much because they are not creative and original. They take care of the Earth, the fire, the air, and water, watch humanity, and show themselves from time to time to humans. They get some darkness because they imitate and mimic humans. Darkness is taken out of them and their dimension.

Dr. Modi: We pray to God to please flood all the dimensions around the Earth and all the insects, elementals, and other beings in them with the violet flame; cleanse, heal, and realign their DNA. Open their connecting cords to God and flood them with love, Light, and joy. Leader of insects, tell me what is happening.

Leader of Insects: We did not get much cleansing because we did not need it. We got an infusion of recognition and Light coming from your request and from other cords that connect us to you because we are connected to you. Our life is very short, about three days on an average.

Dr. Modi: The electrical insect-repeller devices; how do they affect insects?

Leader of Insects: It is unpleasant and we go away, but it also affects the users without knowing on two levels. First, it interferes with their hearing, on deep levels, of information that might come to them. Second, it interferes with their creativity and need to understand us and what our function is. They are also a part of the Earth and, without insects, they will not be able to live on Earth. They need to understand on a deeper level

When you see the next insect, a fly or any insect, thank them for the great work they are doing for the Earth and send them love, and only then tell them that you love and appreciate them and for your own balance for the work you are doing, they need not come around. They will accept it.

They have the respect; they know they are eternal. They do not think and feel the way humans and animals do.

Dr. Modi: How about the honeybees?

Leader of Insects: It is the same thing. You need to thank them for pollinating. Talk to the queen of the honeybees or me.

Dr. Modi: Can I speak to the queen of the honeybees, please?

Queen of Honeybees: Yes, I am here.

Dr. Modi: Why are you coming around our home?

Queen of Honeybees: Well, we are coming to you for the same reason others are coming to you. We need to get out the message to humanity. Our disappearance causes a lot of concern. So you can work with that concern in your prayers, so that humanity achieves a greater appreciation of nature. Many scientists are working on it because they fully know that if we do not pollinate, humanity will starve. You need to thank us for our work and what we have done today, to remind yourself and then we will not come around you so much. You can admire our beauty, but do not be afraid of us because we will not hurt you. Be aware that we are there; do not sit on one of us if one of us is resting on a chair. Watch us and respect us. Understand our job. That is what we need, because that understanding will travel in a ripple effect through all of humanity that is able to take it. Every time you see one of us, do it again, and when they are ready, they will expect it in the same way you have thanked others, because we all have free will. You have sent out others over and over – other instructions, other bits of Light of people to receive soul parts to be returned when they are ready.

Dr. Modi: Instead of creating honeycombs in people's houses, can you do that away from homes; maybe in the woods?

Queen of Honeybees: Of course we can, but we are trying to get your attention. Just thank us for what we have done for Earth and humanity to maintain the balance on the Earth.

Dr. Modi: We ask for the forgiveness of all the insects and all the other beings for hurting and killing you in different ways in this life and all the other life times because of fear, ignorance, or cruelty.

Queen of Honeybees: We ask you all: please remember each time you see one of us anywhere to thank us, because these thanks will go as reverberation through all humanity and children will notice and thank the insects. Each time you see us, know that somewhere on the planet somebody is ready to stop and notice our good work and make some changes in their own life. When you go on the porch and see one of us, you may feel the memory of the fear. Remember to call on us and recall our real purpose for being here. Remind us that we no longer need to be around you because now you understand our purpose and our work and you are sending your gratitude to us, out to the world. Experience it and you may need to do this particular exercise a few times.

Dr. Modi: I will. Thank you all for this knowledge and education.

Queen of Honeybees: We thank you so much for what you are doing and for being willing to do this. We kneel to you in gratitude. We are grateful. You can take this experience and change the past. It is like reactivating DNA for speeding up self-healing. It is similar to when you can go back and change the attitude you had in all the other life times.

Dr. Modi: We thank God for helping me understand about all these different life forms and their role on Planet Earth. Please continue to give me understanding and guidance about what I need to do. I pray that, in past lives when I might have hurt and killed insects and other living beings, please cleanse and heal the memory of that through time, and reactivate the DNA to speed self-healing. Humans are responsible for taking care of the Earth and everything on it. It is necessary to open up that part of the DNA strand of self-healing that has forgotten it was a part of all creation, all insects, and all parts on Earth. Remove all the fears of insects and all the other creatures from the memories of all of them. How about the bug repeller devices?

Archangel Gabriel: They are harmful to bugs and also to humans. Use them briefly and do not overdo it. You should not keep it plugged in all the time. It interferes with the level of sensitivity and perception. It creates a blocking effect. You can put in the instructions that it will not affect you. You can also ask the insects to go elsewhere. You need to speak to their leader that you will prefer that they just leave. It is not appropriate for them to come into the house. You need to thank them for coming to make you aware of their presence and tell them that they are part of God and they do not need to make humans aware of their presence by annoying them. Take the plugs out for a few hours and tell them not to come back. You could also ask that the sound from these plugs does not affect you in a detrimental way. It creates fear and discomfort. It is like someone screaming at you. It is very dark and negative. It is based on fear instead of compromise. You need to compromise with them because they are trying to get your attention by annoying you. Talk to them and their leader.

Chapter 15

ASTROLOGY AND THE MASTERS OF OUR SOLAR SYSTEM

Heavenly beings, speaking through my hypnotized patients, suggested that I should speak to the astrological masters of our solar system and some other masters because they all work very closely with humans and Planet Earth. They explained that the masters of the planets of our solar system are the channels of energy that infuse all the life forms and consciousness of people in terms of how they react to change. Each of the masters of the planets represents a particular quality of energy and change. I need to cleanse the planets and human perception of the way they affect them. In astrology, these are perceptions of humans of the effect of transits and traveling of planets. There is a Christ-level, a master for each planet, but there is also a master for the energy as perceived by different human astrological groups.

People are individuals. That is the great beauty of the creation of humanity; individuals will notice different things, such as their astrology, and the astrology of the people around them interacting. These are all sensitive changes, and change is the constant force in the level of time and space that exists on Earth. Change is also constant outside the Earth; it is the process of evolution. The understanding of evolution includes change, even though it may seem to be the fixed point. Understanding is another quality you might like to explore. Take understanding and see what it encompasses.

Astrological signs are different, and there are also masters of them that are different. The signs are reacting to the energy of the planets as perceived by the humans. There is a hierarchy here; the signs are ruled by the planets. The planets have their own history and energy that is more complex than humans envision. They have such names as Uranus, Jupiter, Neptune, etc. Humans have observed that all these planets travel around the sun with a different pace and speed, and when some of them combine, they notice different effects of the energy that comes down to Earth. What people notice they name. Humans created astrology. It is a human structure to understand the pure energy of creation.

Heavenly beings claimed that, as I go through more and more detail consciously focusing on understanding, I will put it in my book for others to read and understand. The focus of attention will expand the overall understanding of these energies. Some astrologers say there is so much Light coming to Earth in the last twenty to thirty year period and many people have gone beyond their original signs of astrology and the basic interpretation of it. It might be interesting for me to look at it, so I can understand how much expansion of the concept those humans have. For example, Taurus is the bull, Gemini the twins, and Cancer is the crab; Scorpio is the scorpion, Libra the justice symbol, and Sagittarius is the centaur, a man on a horse shooting an arrow to the stars. These are all symbols of human life, and humans come to their conclusions with the help of heavenly beings. All creative observation is made with the help of Light. It always moves into the void of concept. That is the fractal concept – creation moving into the void on a very human level when creativity and insight occur. It is expanding what is already known but has a question mark at the end of it.

There is a demon commander for our solar system – the commander for the sun, and from the sun, there are commanders for every planet that goes around the sun. Then there are moons, and the commanders for those. If you look for the commander of the solar system, it is the commander for the sun. The sun also has its own life force, and there are other suns in the universe. There is a top commander for all the suns of all of creation. So instead of working with the individual commander of each planet, you can work with the demon commander for the sun and the top commander of all suns throughout creation, thus healing all the planets, suns, and moons.

Heavenly beings, at different times, have suggested that I talk to different planetary masters and get an understanding of how they affect the Earth and humans. This will give humans the idea that they can request help from these masters during different situations. I was able to communicate and get information from some of the masters, as follows.

Master of the Sun of Our Solar System

Dr. Modi: Master of the Sun, can you tell us about yourself?
Master of Sun: I am the brightest reflection of God. I am filled with the Light and fire. I Light up the world. I am the first one to be seen and I am always seen by someone. My energies bring life; I am the life giver. The sign that I feed in astrology with my Light is Leo – the lion. So the personalities of people born under the sign of Leo have my Light. They walk in the center stage; they are right there in the middle and are very bright. They make themselves known, like I do. We all affect each other, but I am the biggest and the brightest, and every astrological sign has me in it, but they are of different qualities. It is as though each sign is like a screen of a different combination that I filter through. So when I am in Taurus, I Light up Taurus. I light up everything. I am filled with love and I love life.

There is no interference from the dark side with me, but there is interference with the filters. Most of those have cleared now, as more and more dark forces are removed and transformed; my Light is brighter with everyone now. The filters were in the perception of people and the way energy was distributed. One of the major interferences is to narrow the channels of energy to block them, just to put a dark spot so that the flow does not keep going. Then there is some kind of misperception and confusion, but without the basic energies, nobody would be alive. Everything is alive because of me. Without me, planets would be frozen and nothing could grow on them.

I follow orders from the Light and masters in heaven; we interact with each other. Nothing exists in isolation. We and all the stars also have a life cycle; we will eventually die by imploding or exploding. One sees it as an end, but no energy can be destroyed. It transforms, but the astronomers could see it as the end.

Dr. Modi: Did yesterday's healing help you?

Master of Sun: The healing of kundalini was very helpful; I did get a lot of soul parts back. I did not pay attention to it before, but now I am becoming aware of them. I am living in a very extended time frame and I see things from a very large perspective, unless it is necessary to focus on a detail. When humanity invented those astrological signs, I could see what they were doing and that was interesting. I can see how they are affected, but I am more concerned with the critical mass as the people on Earth talk about.

Dr. Modi: What will happen to you after the transition of Earth to the fifth dimension.

Master of Sun: Nothing much, because the transition is in consciousness. The transition will affect many elements that I impact on Earth and all the planets, and they will relate to each other because of the particular configuration at that time, and it would be a great opportunity for multiple leaps. I am very constant and changes do not affect me.

It is a wave of understanding, and when more of my Light is understood, the astrological signs will change. They will expand. There will be cellular changes in humanity over a period of time based on changes in consciousness and the instructions to their bodies. The bodies are there to accommodate the conscious energy of Light and beings. Unless you point it out, I just accept whatever comes. I am the most accepting of the energies and maintain the stability of the Earth and of all living things in this solar system. I am like a big brute here. I am a big, strong element and it is necessary to filter my energies. Every human, plant, and animal has the mechanism built in to filter me, including the original design that I do not shine on the entire planet at the same time, so there is a cooling-off period. When the planet is rotating, I am fixed and do not move. The planet rotates on its own axis around me so there is enough variation. All the planets have different rates of rotation. I do not get excited easily. I am very calm.

Dr. Modi: Thank you for all the information and knowledge about you.

Master of sun: Yes. Happy to be of service as always.

Master of the Moon of Our Solar System

Dr. Modi: Can we speak to the Master of the Moon, please?

Patient: I see she is a female.

Dr. Modi: Master of the Moon, Hi! Tell us about yourself, please.

Master of Moon: Everything has a male and a female. I am seen as a female because Moon has many female qualities. I am reflective Light and I am filled with great love. People on Earth love me. They are not afraid of me; they are comforted by me. All love expands a sense of self. So when there is demonic influence, it becomes confused with fear, ego, and arrogance. All of these qualities of self need to be nurtured within a living creature. When it is interfered with, it will turn to its opposite to protect itself. There is an excessive need of protection. I would like to be able to protect people more.

I am always there. I am a little pale reminder during the daytime, but when people sleep in the night, I help their dreams. I flood their dreams with understanding. They mostly do not remember their dreams, but when they do, if they make an effort, they will understand more about some of the questions they have not been able to answer clearly during their waking life. I do not give them the dreams; they are given by their higher selves through their experience. Their dreams are like a language, but I give them the space and Light in the dream so the dreams can be there. The Light is calming for sleep. It is a Light without a lot of color in it. This trust in me is a relaxing acceptance; that is probably why humans have called me "the mother." I am watching over them when they are asleep and innocent. They feel safe; otherwise, they cannot sleep. I help every soul feel safe, including the Earth. I cool that part of the Earth and give it a chance to rest from the sun.

I am a part of the Sun in terms of life, and reflect the Light of the Sun. I am an extension of it. I have an inner Light, but my Light is a reflection of the Sun. If I did not have my inner Light I could not reflect the Light of the Sun. The moonlight is from the Sun.

Dr. Modi: Are there any negative effects of the Moon?

Master of Moon: There are no negative effects of the Moon, except the demonic interference. All those stories of vampires, werewolves, and people acting crazy during a full moon are because I affect people's emotions. They feel their emotions with more intensity, and if there is a great demonic interference, they become out of control, but my energy is loving. Sometimes I affect the tides as I get closer to the Earth. The attraction of Earth to the bodily planets, the oceans' waves, and the tides' changes are caused by my relationship to Earth at various times, not my Light. I rotate around the Earth in one day. I complete my rotation around the Earth within twenty-four hours, so I affect the night and the day, the tides, and the wind. I also interact with other elements. Storms are caused by the evaporation of water and the tides. We are all moving in relationship to one another. We are all beings, and there is a complex relationship that we have with each other.

Dr. Modi: Is there any other way you affect the Earth?

Master of Moon: These are the basic effects, then you can go into effects on individuals. That is why astrology is helpful; because individuals can go deeper. As you go deeper with your patients through therapy, astrologers see what the influences were at birth and how they worked because there is an imprint at birth of a particular set of relationships with the planets. There are also genetic imprints, so there are many complex influences.

Dr. Modi: Is there a demon commander who is assigned by Satan to interfere with the moon?

Master of Moon: Yes, there is a demon commander, along with multitudes of demons under him, who are responsible to influence and interfere with the energies of the moon. A lot of the demonic influences were already cleared up as you worked and transformed different demon commanders. It helped a lot, and there is more Light and hope on Earth now. You will not see it right away, but more and more people are becoming aware of the changes. When you work with the Master of Time, then other layers of demons will be removed.

I feel my Light is much stronger and peoples' dreams will be clearer and easier for them to understand. Time can go back and forth for each person; it is quite complex. Time is like the grooves in an old-fashioned music record. Since we are working in a space-time continuum, space and time change in relationship with each other and our energy. So if you clear out one little rung, one groove, there will be others that are not quite as clear. There is a relationship between one and the other, just like on the record; it is all one continuous song. Slowness of healing has a purpose. There is an evolution of comprehension of time that has to do with the original instruction of the Light. The original DNA of development on the Earth is evolving with the various changes that are taking place.

The time needs to be respected; otherwise, you will burn up in a second.

The aging process happens within a certain time. When you sent the lightning bolts through the self-healing strand of DNA to speed up the self-healing process, it changed the instructions. If there were no limitation of the forms, the bodies, the history, or the life expectancy, it would be quite different. It is time that creates the extent of the healing.

Each person is like a god to the cells of the body. This is a fractal image of God within the rules of time and space that was set up before all these creatures came. All the animals have skeletons, faces, eyes, legs, and other features. There are enough similarities among them. Flowers do not have eyes, but they have senses; humans do not fly but birds do. There is complexity in the applications of basic rules of time and space setups for Planet Earth.

Master of Neptune

One of my patients had a soul part of the master of the planet Neptune in her who gave the following information.

Patient: I see a carving of Neptune in this dark one. Neptune is a planet of confusion; it represents spirituality but does not know right from wrong. The carving of him is in front of me and it has soul parts of Neptune.

Master of Neptune: Yes, I am here in this soul part of Satan. He was making all of us sleep so the patient would not succeed with her purpose. When I woke up, I realized I was in the net, trapped in this soul part of Satan. The sleepiness is caused within the energy of Neptune and I am a soul part of the master of Neptune. They had me as the god of the ocean and spirituality, dissolving barriers and mistiness. So when the planet was discovered, they named it after me. I have existed from the beginning of time as a potential concept, which they attributed to the effects of the planet. I feel like I have to wake up because I have been asleep for such a long time.

Dr. Modi: I request the angels to cleanse and heal this soul part of Neptune. Fill him with the crystalline Light; activate him and integrate him with the master of Neptune in heaven.

Master of Neptune: Thank you. I am grateful that you integrated this part of me. There are many more of my soul parts out there that need to be integrated with me.

Dr. Modi: I request the angels to bring each and every soul part of Master of Neptune from Satan, his demons, people, places, and darkness; cleanse them, heal them, fill them with the love and Light and integrate them with him, please.

Patient: The first thing I saw was multitudes of Neptune's soul parts coming out of Satan, who is literally lying on his back with his stomach open because he had devoured these soul parts. They are also coming from other planets. Then I saw lines and lines of psychics and wise men, shamans, alchemists, and medicine men through history that used Neptune's energy. They were sitting there with their costumes. Many psychics were using the energy because of satanic influences. It was the level of consciousness shared by all psychics and wise people outside of time and space, because Neptune represents the levels of consciousness. All the soul parts of Neptune were cleansed, healed, and integrated with him. Now he is looking better, more muscular.

Dr. Modi: Neptune, did you get all your soul parts back?

Master of Neptune: [Happy] I am so happy to have so many of my soul parts back that it is hard to say. Maybe you should check again.

Dr. Modi: We pray to God to please send the lightning bolts to all the soul parts of Neptune throughout creation, wherever they may be!

Patient: I see multitudes of his soul parts coming from all over creation: from Satan, his demons, people, places, and the darkness, and integrated with Neptune after cleansing and healing. He looks very happy to get all his soul parts back.

Archangel Michael: You also work with the soul part of Neptune. The Satanic energy worked a great deal with the Neptune energy, causing confusion between truth and lies and good and evil, and that was maintained in a dormant condition.

Patient: I see Neptune is standing in heaven, waving. There may be more soul parts of Neptune to call back. There is also a level of psychics and shamans who contain many parts of Satan.

Archangel Michael: Neptune is an ancient icon, an ancient symbol of seas. In the ancient times, it was the god of the sea when the planet of Neptune was discovered. The qualities psychics and astrologers noticed came at a time when there was no difference between good and evil. The boundaries were very misty. It represented the magical and spiritual energy and all possibility without judgment.

The most important part to remember right now is that it does not know the difference between right and wrong; that created problems for humans. It is mysterious and mystical. It is the energy of spiritual communion. All astrologers and psychics use that energy to make predictions and give advice to their clients. Some of them do not know that it is Neptune energy. The essential energy represented by Neptune has been flawed because of its murky boundaries. It moves to a level where good and evil are not important. It is more important to sense the continuity without a definition, so there is a positive aspect to this energy. It has been misused because evil has occasionally been accepted within this flow. True understanding of the difference between good and evil has been removed, and this soul part of Satan has that energy in him and played an important role in this person's life. It cut short any feeling of good that she has done and experienced. It caused her to doubt and think that anything good she has done has an underlying evil element. The dark parts and energies need to be cleansed, healed, and transformed into the Light. They have a long history from the beginning of creation of all life and planets. Neptune looks happy, big, and strong, and says he wants more of his soul parts back. He looks like the picture of the Greek god Neptune.

Dr. Modi: Michael, is there a demon commander for each planet?

Archangel Michael: Yes, but you can work with all of them together and the top commander, which would be Satan himself, because of the spiritual aspects which specifically bridges heaven and Earth. Every human and living being has an aspect of Neptunian energy. This is why it is very important for Satan to use that energy to manipulate human beings, especially when there is confusion between good and evil. This is where Satan can persuade people that something that is evil is very good.

There is a separate demon commander for each planet and one top demon commander for all the planets because there are different requirements, mythologies, and abilities, and a different sense of good and evil. But there is always a limitation in all planets where there is a difference in the balance of various energies.

Dr. Modi: We pray to God to please send lightning bolts to all the soul parts of Neptune, wherever they may be in creation; transform and allow them to come back and integrate with Master of Neptune and his planet, wherever they belong.

Patient: I see the lightning bolts are going to many sealed cabinets that are opened all over creation. Soul parts of Neptune are coming out and going where they belong on the Neptune planet and Master of Neptune. Lightning bolts were like keys to the cabinets. It seems Neptune is standing here and all the soul parts of planets all over creation are coming to Neptune. His energy is very adaptable

Archangel Michael: This was not explained before. What makes it so attractive to Satan is that after they were in people, the Neptunian energy muddled the truth and caused confusion. The true energy of Neptune is that all things are possible. There is confusion because the discrimination of continuity of ideas has been removed. If not used properly, Neptunian energy can be dangerous because there are no boundaries.

Dr. Modi: Neptune, did all the soul parts come back to you?

Master of Neptune: Not yet.

Archangel Michael: Neptune is represented by the ocean and fishes; he is the king of the sea. So you must ask the soul parts to come back from all humans, all the water bodies and their creatures, and even the fluid in the human body.

Dr. Modi: Can we use the magnetic sheets?

Archangel Michael: Yes; put them around all the water bodies and everything that is liquid, lives in liquid, is surrounded by liquid, including human bodies which have liquid, trees which have sap in them, flowers with liquid in them, all of creation, and every planet that has liquid in some form.

Dr. Modi: We pray to God to please put the magnetic sheets around all the water bodies and all the creatures, plant lives, and everything that has water in it.

Patient: I see magnetic sheets going around the Earth and all the planets throughout creation, around all the water bodies and all the creatures and plants in them, and the entire plant kingdom. I see angels lined up for further instruction.

Dr. Modi: I request the angels to turn the knob of all the magnetic sheets to the "eject" sign, to eject all the dark entities, energies, dark devices, dark shields, dark blocks, soul parts, and spirits of other beings and collect them in the net of Light. Transform them into the Light and take them to heaven, please. Cleanse, heal, and fill everything with the crystalline Light. Then turn the knob to the magnetic sheet to the "attract" sign and allow all the soul parts to return that were lost from the beginning of time from Satan, his demons, people, elementals, creatures of all types, plant life, places, darkness, and heaven. Integrate them where they belong after cleansing and healing.

Patient: I see all this happening so fast that it is hard to describe.

Master of Mercury

Dr. Modi: Can we speak to the Master of the Mercury, please?

Master of Mercury: I am here. I am too grateful to be approached in this manner.

Dr. Modi: We are grateful to be able to communicate with you, too. Maybe you can give us some understanding about you and what is happening right now—"the Mercury retrograde"

Patient: I can see him. He looks like an old man but has a lot of energy. He has a silver cap on his head that is flat on top. It has a border about an inch and a half. He has long hair down to his shoulders and a beard. He is very strong looking and dressed in a kind of silvery, shiny, moonlight quality of clothes. He has a robe on that is changing to various colors. I get the word "quicksilver," which is a name used for Mercury. It means changing quickly, as his outfits change. I see him as a Roman soldier and wearing many different kinds of robes that look like a magnetic sheet.

Master of Mercury: I am very excited that you want to know about me. You can see pictures of me on Google on the Internet; I am everywhere. I have been very powerful in the history of humans. I speed things up, slow them down, stop or move back; that is why they say, "Mercury Retrograde." I move back a step and take another look, then I go forward again and move back. Sometimes it is a long step back.

I have been brought to a form, as have many other masters. As each one of us has come into connection with varying degrees of material forms and all dimensional creation, we have learned how to adapt to wherever we happened to be during that evolution. This is a little difficult to explain since we are working outside and within the concepts of time and space. As humanity evolves, Planet Mercury, which was named after me, existed, and my energy was connected to this planet. Humans reacted in different ways to the influence of the planet and I observed and incorporated these qualities in me.

My energy works through the planet and through humanity. This operated with different masters, different planets and humans, as well as life forms in other dimensions and on other planets. We each have qualities of energy. We – all the masters, angels, and beings – are filters of different qualities of energy from God. We are all aspects of God's energy.

I am the Mercury master, a name given by human astrologers. This is a time of speedy transformation of humanity, all life forms, and the planet, and we each have a job to do. On Planet Earth, it is back and forth much more than the other planets because of the humans' level of curiosity and acceptance.

During the so-called, "Mercury Retrograde" that many people were aware of, the speed-up and the slow-down of time affects the way people's minds work, in terms of remembering and forgetting. Today, you, Dr. Modi, are the recipient of my forgetting and slowing down so that the opposite within the qualities of duality could be activated. This is the acute perception and determination, to zero in until you are satisfied, even though you claim not to understand it.

Dr. Modi: So you were tuned in to me and this person, about what we are thinking and planning to do?

Master of Mercury: I am tuned in to everybody. If someone focuses on me, I am right there because I am a part of everybody. Everyone who exists has a Mercury quality to them. I am connected with the speed of the mind and the variability of changing quality. Think how the mind can change so quickly from one thought to the other. If you think of a horoscope, there is the symbol for Gemini and the planet for that symbol is Mercury. People who are Gemini have a very short attention span. They have to use the other planetary energy consciously to slow themselves down. They are extremely mental. They collect various levels of superficiality and all kinds of information; they do not necessarily process it with depth. They need to learn more about self-discipline, self-control, and the area of the void, of not knowing. They have to tolerate not knowing. Patience is one of the demonic interferences with the flow of Mercury's energy. I am capable of patience; I can stop time. I can stop machines. Like today, I stopped your tape recorder from working.

It is a good time for us, because everybody is responding to this Mercury retrograde . When people do not know what is going to happen next, they quickly try to fill in by misusing my quickness of thought. They hop from possibility to possibility.

Dr. Modi: How do you affect humanity?

Master of Mercury: The quality of joy and happiness that people experience when they say, "I got it." That is positive. We are the speed of their thoughts. We represent the speed of humanity's perception and comprehension. I am like a computer; I have the capacity of a computer. The speed of computers and the accuracy of the points connected to make it work are part of my energy. This is one way humans use me.

The most developmentally challenged humans use my energy very slowly, and other times they do not see it at all. It has to do with the speed and flow of information. Each human being is a unique filter of so many layers of history, thought, genetic history, and the different times their soul has experienced. I am like a Light on the cobwebs.

Dr. Modi: How did you affect me?

Master of Mercury: As you have figured out by now, we interfered with your memory of many situations, because you want to do this work, and this work is like exploring in the dark. Both opposites are in one. In other words, you have a lot of memory that will interfere with what we are doing here and you might be distracted. If you do not have any memory, then there is no distraction. You are simply what you are at the moment, and then you forget it when you do not need it. When you need it, it comes back, but it might take a little longer because you are in a human body and do it in order to stay alive on Earth.

You are doing the future work. I, Mercury, remind people of a point of connections, but when they are ready to do the full integration, there is a process of larger integration of humanity. Groups are coming together with greater understanding. There are huge movements, speed of thought and recognition of an idea and the flow that is into the action. The action and the flow are more Neptune qualities; mine is acuteness to the point, like a laser. We masters also learn from experiences. There is a higher and lower in everything: the higher is Light and lower is the dark.

Interference with your tape recorder was caused by demons or aliens using my energy. I have needle sharp laser beams to attempt to get through when there is some sense of confusion. When a human says, "I need some help with this," or "what can it be?" I send these laser beams to help them understand. When the laser beams are used for eye surgery, sometimes the demons are attached to the laser and the results are slightly off. Doctors and patients should pray for protection before all surgeries.

Dr. Modi: How else is the dark side using your energy negatively?

Master of Mercury: As I described before, they attach to the laser beams and all of our energy. They imitate and follow us to stop the flow of our Light.

Dr. Modi: Gabriel, is there a demon commander for the planet Mercury?

Archangel Gabriel: Yes, Mercury, like each planet, has a demon commander and you can work with them at a later time.

Dr. Modi: How did you affect this person?

Master of Mercury: This person has Saturn and Aquarius working in her astrology. Uranus is an explosive energy that comes out of left field. People who are Aquarian have that planet and they have a very cool demeanor of thinking.

This person has Saturn in Aquarius, so she has never been able to understand how it works because Saturn is restrictive. It makes you focus on your difficulties. Uranus is explosive and the sign Aquarius, which is a physical expression of Uranus, is very cool-minded, dispassionate, and has a global vision that causes an extraordinary explosion of surprise. So there is a very curious opposition between coolness, lack of emotion, and a tremendous explosion of understanding. She also has her Saturn in the area she works, in the sixth house. It is a way of separating the qualities of energy so people can understand them.

Dr. Modi: Should we first do the healing of the original intent of DNA and the progression, or work with the demon commander for Mercury?

Master of Mercury: The order in which you ask the question is the way to work because it works in stages, and then you can go back again because we are working with time. So do the cleansing first, and at that time, there will be a certain loosening up of energy. Then you can work with the commanders. So you cleanse all the dark energies from the DNA's original intention with what would have been a natural progression of evolution and the energy of Mercury.

Dr. Modi: We pray to God and request the angels to please cleanse, heal, and clear the original intent of DNA that represents the use of Mercury's energy and its progression.

Patient: Before cleansing, DNA looks like a series of hanging intestines. They are straight, not twisted. It looks like endless amounts of DNA. They are the set of instructions and some of them pertain to different stages of life, so they light up or are activated.

Master of Mercury: The concept of DNA was a set of instructions. So the original concept could be a golden book with symbols. Then a symbol, purpose, and meaning would take form. There would be varying stages of what the form would look like, and this first one she is seeing looks like a laundry line, like tubes made up of what looks like flesh. They are about two feet long and hanging near each other; they are the color of intestines. These are the DNA of all of creation and they are in infinite number. They have to be programmed, almost like Christmas stockings hanging on the fireplace. They put different presents in stockings for different children.

There were several stages of human DNA. Originally, they were very fine and thin, and there were about fifty strands. They looked like very thin hair and they were hanging straight down. Then they began to intertwine because they have relationships to each other. They also had their own course and places where they made contact with each other. So this, in a sense, is a parallel to astrological aspects. The planets are individual and the strands are individual, but when they form a line of energy, they cross each other, so the points where they cross have different qualities. We are not going to use the expression "positive and negative." That is where humans got stuck trying to predict the future. They would observe certain effects in themselves.

Then there were various stages of evolution. There were demonic interferences and other things happened in the history of ecological progression. We were the masters of the planets that contained the original strands of DNA that were connected to the original qualities of energy. But everything is evolving, so to simplify it: the basic energy is the ten planets, including the Sun and the Moon.

Right now, there are more humans on the planet than ever. There are other forms of life that had more parallel consciousnesses. Certain consciousnesses are much more evolved and complex and carry many strands of DNA of combined energy and instructions, because DNA is very flexible. That is why this person was seeing them as intestines.

We are like the directors of these energies in heaven, equivalent to the dark commanders. There is one strand of DNA that represents my Mercury energy and several others that are combined. Let us take the major Mercury strand, because whatever is healed in a major infliction is evolving. So the more Light there is, the larger the channel through which the energy passes. There can be gigantic DNA strands that are networks of combined tubes.

A fractal is a repetition of the same design; it is like one cell has the entire history of creation. My Mercurian energy evolves in different stages of humanity in history, and the demonic energy tags along with us. It coats us almost like dark syrup on the outside and interferes with the instructions. But there is also the Light that always wins, as we know, but it takes longer. It works in time. The demonic entities do not always understand it. You can ask for the cleansing of the Mercury strand of DNA and all its branches. There are an infinite number of branches, which come from that original strand all throughout the history of humanity.

Dr. Modi: We pray to God and request the angels to please cleanse and heal the planet Mercury, the Mercury master, the DNA strand of Mercury, and all the branches coming out of the original strand through time. Remove all the dark energy from them, transform them, and take them to heaven. Fill the DNA strand and all its branches with the crystalline Light. Bring all their soul parts back which were lost from the beginning of the time, from Satan, his demons, from people, places, darkness, and heaven, from this time and space and beyond. Cleanse them, heal them, fill them with the Light and integrate them where they belong. Cleanse, heal, and fill them with the crystalline Light and shield the planet Mercury, its master, and inside and outside of the DNA strand and its branches with the triple compression chamber of the crystalline Light, violet shield, mirror shield, and rays of blinding, crystalline Light.

Also cleanse and heal all the other planets and their masters and fill them with the crystalline Light. Shield them with the triple compression chambers of the crystalline Light, inside and outside, with violet shield, mirror shield, and rays of blinding crystalline Light.

Patient: I see the energy is radiating out from the master of Mercury. Just imagine the master of Mercury as a trunk of a tree with all the roots going underneath to everywhere, every person, and to every being. It is the intelligence, the quickness of the mind, and the speeding up and slowing down of the thought process that is parallel in time. It also works through the master of Time. These are part of the combined strength that comes later with more stability. You can use the magnetic sheet to shoot everything where it belongs very quickly. You need to simply understand and visualize, and you can say as much as you want to, but it just goes back through it. It is just tremendous suction. Everything is connected to Mercury. It is the root of the intellectual understanding of mankind.

Dr. Modi: What role do you play in mental illness?

Master of Mercury: When my flow is interrupted, it is twisted and stopped, and pushed large in some places and small in others. Since the Light always wins, it is not always a bad thing. There is always something good that comes out of it. Remember, there is still a memory of automatic response, so there will be slow change in spite of the healing. There is also a great deal of quickness in mentally ill people. It is unbalanced.

Dr. Modi: We pray to God and request the angels to please put the magnetic sheet around the planet Mercury, Earth, and all the other planets connected with them, including the DNA strand connected with Mercury and all of its branches. Can I put the magnetic sheet around the masters and other beings of heaven, too?

Master of Mercury: See what happens. This is powerful; it works with time and is very fast. The magnetic sheet has a powerful force of expulsion to it. It is like an atomic bomb, but more powerful. So try putting it around all the masters and heavenly beings and see what happens.

Dr. Modi: We pray to God and request the angels to please put the magnetic sheet around Master of Mercury, all the masters of Light, and all the beings in heaven, including the people in between the incarnation and transformed demons. Turn the switch to the "eject" sign and eject everything that does not belong with all the strands of DNA, and all their branches, and all the masters and heavenly beings. Collect them in the net of Light, transform them, and store them in heaven. Then turn the switch to the "attract" sign and allow each and every soul part to come back from the beginning of time, from Satan, his demons, from people, places, darkness, and from heaven, from this time and space and beyond. Cleanse them, heal them, fill them with the Light, and integrate them with whom they belong or where they belong. Clamp the cords to the soul parts that cannot be brought back at this time, twenty or more times as needed.

Patient: I see things are being ejected from everywhere and collected in the net of Light; they are transformed and taken to heaven. I see the nets of Light are put in the void all around the planets and dimensions. They stretch out and become larger as more things are ejected. Soul parts are coming back from everywhere and they spin as they come out. Darkness comes out and the soul parts are instantly cleansed and healed, and they become crystalline and integrated where they belong.

Dr. Modi: We are connected to higher self, heavenly guides, and angels; all humans have darkness. So can the darkness go to them from the humans?

Higher Self: Yes. They can come through the connection but instantly change into the Light. They cannot stay dark. Sometimes you also need to cleanse the Akashic records.

Dr. Modi: Mercury, did everything get cleansed and healed?

Master of Mercury: Yes. The mind is observing and receiving instructions and deciding what to do next. Any part where natural progression is being interfered with needs to be cleansed and healed. There is a big change as you cleansed everything. It is as if a thousand million eyes are opened up; it is like we all sort of woke up and blinked our eyes.

Patient: I see that the DNA strands are more translucent.

Dr. Modi: We pray to God to please fill all of creation and heaven and everything and everybody in them with the violet liquid fire and let it blaze into intense flames, nonstop twenty-four hours a day, as long as our soul exists, please, and transform and realign our DNA.

Patient: It looks like gas burners lighting up with the purple flame all over creation. The violet flame is more refined in heaven.

Master of Mars

Patient: I can see Master of Mars. He looks like a big, strong man and he is a warrior. He looks like a Viking a little bit. He has a Viking hat with horns on each side and he is changing into different types of warriors. He is the ultimate male energy, while Venus is the ultimate female energy. He has leather straps around his knees and is wearing a Roman outfit. He has big, wide shoulders, muscular legs, a beard, and a mustache. His hair is of medium length and he has blazing eyes. He represents the sign of Aries, and Aries uses his energy. It is the first sign of the Zodiac; Taurus is the second sign, and the Gemini is the third. This is how humans designed it. Aries is the beginning; it is the male energy that comes forth. It is the charging of the seed (sperm). It is the seed of life and the warrior energy. It is the natural sign and planet for the first house. There are twelve houses. The first house is when you are born; it is very important. It is called "ascendant" and Mars represents that in its natural state. So Mars represents the first house and Aries is in the first house. Now if you have Aries somewhere else, like everybody has Mars, somewhere else, it has the quality of the first house energy in it. It is the male creative life force.

Dr. Modi: Master of Mars, hi! Tell us about yourself, please.

Master of Mars: Well, she has been giving a pretty good description here. I am a male, warrior energy. I am also very creative; anything that needs any initiation or any beginning of any project, I am right there. I have all the energy of the initial sperm, the spirit of life, in me. I also fight to survive, that is why I am considered a warrior. I am very strong. I start things, and when I balance the female energy, life happens. You need to have a good balance of male and female together. I tend to be impatient. I want to do things quickly and efficiently. Essentially, I am part of everything that ever begins. Everyone has me somewhere. There are some houses that have me there because they follow my progression. Everybody has some Mars energy, so when you want to start something, you can call on me, like if you have trouble in starting a car, you can call on me. I can help you in solving a problem. The only thing I am not so good at is finishing things. I can start them well because I am fast.

This is how humans have described me astrologically. Since all life is opposites combined, I can be as patient as I am impatient, but people notice impatience more easily. I finish a job more quickly. I might not wait long to finish it;

I like to finish a project quickly. I am every person. If they ever want to win anything, exercise, long distance running, or horse racing, they can use my energy. My energy is working in them with the intention of doing something strong, and quick, and like a motorboat, because I am fast. My energy is simple. I am the male energy and I initiate things. Basically, human males like to get to the bottom line. They do not talk a lot; they want action. That is what humans have observed as my energy. I also get angry. Anger is an explosion and a reaction. You do not have to do anything. It is a frustration to take notice and to stop you. If you are running too fast and stumble over a stone – then you get angry. That is a spread of energy too. Sometimes it makes you jump up again. The demonic energy comes in only when things stop and repeat themselves.

Dr. Modi: Is there life on Planet Mars?

Master of Mars: There is, but in another dimension. It is not life as you know in your time zone or time frame. There was life before the planet heated up to a point where it was no longer possible to have life. It was too close to the Sun. There is life in etheric form. There is an understanding of possible life on another level of existence and consciousness. It can be accessed by humans who wish to meditate on that life form and see how it would come to them. They need to expand their channels of consciousness to reach out to those life forms, and many people have done it.

Dr. Modi: Over the years, we did healing of many planets that were destroyed. Could that be done with Planet Mars?

Master of Mars: Nothing is impossible, but an adjustment needs to be made that is useful. Beings that are set up there cannot live there anymore. It is more of an etheric life form now.

Dr. Modi: Are they like what we call ghosts, whose bodies died but the souls are still stuck on the Earth plane?

Master of Mars: Yes, but those forms have a different emotional structure. They are not supposed to be there, in a sense. They are unhappy and they have a problem. It is an interim position for them, whereas these beings on Mars have chosen to be there to see what the experiment would be like. It is a different kind of problem solving. All life forms are problem-solving humans.

Dr. Modi: How did you affect this person?

Master of Mars: Her moon is in Aries. She also has Mars in her first house. She has a very strong Mars energy, a strong male energy that is very impatient. She also is a Taurus, so she can be patient and can use it to the two extremes. The Moon she has is very difficult because it makes her very impatient, and Mars is not a good mother, but the Moon represents the mother. So she has mothered animals and people in various ways, having given birth to none. She is very impatient and has a lot of force and power she gets from Mars in terms of anything she does. She combines it with persistence and other qualities. She has a dark personality and a number of large planets in her first house. She tries to tone it down, but it is difficult because it is very obvious to most people even if she does not say anything, which becomes kind of dangerous. She actually practiced making herself invisible. I actually helped her to do that because the Mars in her has gotten her into trouble. She would fight very easily, not physically but verbally.

I also helped her with survival, creativity, and perseverance because she did not have a higher education, but she is very well-educated on her own. She is better than many people who are collage educated because I gave her a great survival life force to find work so she could learn. She went to war and survived. I helped her with that and with the animals in her care. When she was outside the ways of society, she managed very well there. She was persistent. I encouraged her Taurus energy, which is patience; I just gave it a little boost. She can convince people quite well to do anything she needs. I represent a male energy passion and she has that when she focuses on something. I helped her get what she needs.

Dr. Modi: How did you affect me?

Master of Mars: When you encounter resistance, I help you to move ahead, and Taurus is useful, too, because you are very persistent. You stay with your feet on the ground, no matter what. Even if you have to walk through walls or stones, so to speak, you go through. I helped your hair grow before and even now if you ask. You can use the same energy, the analogy of walking forward and taking one step backward. You can also move sideways. I can help you whenever you need to have extra force. I represent force and male energy that is insistence. I helped you to not waste your energy with little conversation.

You can call me in; I can give you a sign of some sort or maybe a little impatience. To grow your hair back on your scalp, you have to imagine my energy all over your scalp and tell your hair to grow. Try that. You do not have to do it instantly. With my energy, you have to give the command once and then wait for a while and watch it, and then you can give a second command with slight alteration to the parts that did not work. I represent passion, and red is my color, so you can wear red to remind you of me and blend with Venus. That will be good because she is a female and I am a male. I am sensitive in fixing to a point and taking action. I am all about action.

Dr. Modi: Anything we need to do for you or the planet?

Master of Mars: We would like to become more of ourselves. We, meaning all the planets, Sun, and Moon, because we are all parts of Light that join us all into one. As we become one, we will lose the specificity of the characteristic being incorporated in a more subtle understanding. We are all kind of brutally defined.

Dr. Modi: Thank you for giving this understanding about you, your energy, and the planet, Mars.

Master of Mars: You are welcome.

Master of Jupiter

Patient: He looks like a very fat Santa Clause and is very strong. He has a big belly and big arms, almost double the size of a normal person. His energy is huge. It is a huge planet. That is why people call it Jupiter.

Dr. Modi: Master of Jupiter, hi! Tell us about yourself, please.

Master of Jupiter: I am so big because I am like blowing wind or a ferocious storm. I am not ferocious but I make everything twice in size. It is in comparison to the nice, quiet air when you walk along, and all of a sudden a great big wind comes and blows you off your feet. That is me – my energy. I am twice life size and can make things twice as big for positive and negative, depending on who I combine with and what is happening. I make everything more, so if you have Mars and you are moving your foot forward like Mars was saying, my energy can make it really move forward. [Laughing] I can make your feet twice as big; I can make your step twice as big. I can make your intentions twice as big, but it works negatively just as easily. You have to be careful, because if you have a big fear, I can make it twice as big. That is mostly what I do. I am very optimistic and positive; I am the essence of optimism. I am opposite of Saturn. Saturn makes things smaller so you can focus. First they have to develop a positive, then I can make it bigger. [Laughing] You have to know how to use me positively. I have too much energy and do not care if it is used positively or negatively, because in the long run I know everything is essentially positive even when it is negative.

I am completely positive. Don't say "almost." [Laughing] Why do you think the second letter in positive is a big, round "O"? I represent round and big. Obesity is too much of my energy. They call me in and I do not have much control over what people do with my energy.

Dr. Modi: Can we take your energy out from those people so they can lose weight?

Master of Jupiter: Not really. They have to be willing, because I protect them with all that fat. There is a protective element in it. It is a distraction for them from fear because they are able to comfort themselves with food or being big. They take up twice as much space in a bus, so they feel big and important subconsciously, but the truth is that it is a false importance. They need to learn how to use me properly.

Dr. Modi: This is what we can teach them?

Master of Jupiter: Yes, you can. There are many ways of teaching on the physical plane. You can teach them with your books. Right now, there are so many overweight people and so much concern with how it is affecting their heart and other organs. There are many of them who are in the position to change their diet or bring fear, which is being used to lose weight, like giving up smoking. The way in which the entire smoking campaign got people to stop and it happened in ten years.

Anything that gets exaggerated to the point of death either dies or gets a shock and decides to live. If they have enough passion, then they can use me with the passion to change their diet, stop overeating, and lose weight, and there are other people teaching how to do it. It is like anything – a pendulum swinging back and forth. So I can actually exaggerate the problem as in the current obesity situation, to get people to pay more attention to their daily lives, how they treat their bodies, and how they deal with their own anxiety and uncertainty. It is the fear of uncertainty that causes people to use me. They push my energy into any kind of excess: spending money, putting all the money under the mattress, or starving oneself when there is plenty of money. I represent excess, and again I repeat that I am somewhat similar to Neptune in that I do not really care, because I do not have judgment whether it is good or bad; I just go wherever I am called because I know, in the end, there is only good, although it may be a thousand years of bad. So you could work with time to understand it. Once you understand this and put it out, there are people in a position to bring this out, on a public level or on a political level, that will move the energy where it needs to go.

The demonic forces will try to stop the flow. Remember, all they do is stop the flow and all we represent is flow: qualities of flow, where flow goes, and where people's attention is placed together with emotions that are usually run by fear.

Dr. Modi: How am I using your energy?

Master of Jupiter: You are using my energy to keep yourself going because you have a hard task, as you perceive it. You can change the way you perceive it by saying it is not a hard task. It is easy for me; push my energy to make it easy because what you say becomes reality. We are all here willing to accommodate you, because your journey is more important than anything else. As you create your journey as a common human, the commonality of where you come from, what you are doing, and where you go vibrates energetically to all those who have the same commonality. They may not have the same balance as you do, but no one has the same balance as you. You are unique. There are places where you have a unique understanding combination of, say, a cultural thing or a female thing, and having lived in certain places. Those combinations of thinking will go to people of spiritual consciousness. They may not have the same culture, same sex, same age, or be in the same place, but if they are ready to take a next step, then you have strength that will move them.

Dr. Modi: How did your energy affect this person?

Master of Jupiter: I am in her first house. She also has Neptune and Mars in there, so whatever she does, people say it seems a little bigger than life. I have affected her positively, and it gets her where she needs to go, and negatively. She tries to hide it because she does not want to stand out too much. So I have actually helped her to hide it. I helped her become invisible when she needed to be. I worked on both sides. She used my energy for survival. I have also helped her survive in a way that is beneficial because she knew she should not be boxed, so she had many jobs. She was fired a couple of times because she went overboard, which I helped her do, because it was not a good place for her. I have always been beneficial to her. She had a hard life but she managed to enjoy it. Her sense of adventure and sense of purpose were great, which I infused in her more so that would keep her going. She may have even exaggerated her sense of purpose in changing the world because I represent exaggeration to see where it can go.

The negative part is that she has not controlled it well, so some people find her annoying, but she plows anyway. She can always find some new people who will help her. She does things for people, too, which is very helpful to them. So I worked on both sides of the fence with her.

You, Dr. Modi, I helped you with your power of observation, and I also helped your efficiency with the Mars energy to get things done quickly.

Dr. Modi: Thank you for all your help for us.

Master of Jupiter: Well, I am the one who should be thanking you because I like to have my energy used and recognized. There are many people who use it but do not recognize it, so it is not that interesting to me. When you recognize it, then it becomes more interesting because it could be a more refined use, and part of the evolution of humanity that is happening now is a more conscious awareness.

Dr. Modi: How can we use your energy positively? What should we do?

Master of Jupiter: Well, first you have to understand yourself. Then you can ask each one of these energies you perceive, either in speaking with people, treating them as a doctor, or writing and possibly doing something in music. There will be something you will be doing in music. I can help you with your understanding of the passage of time, how it operates for you in the larger world. When you put your book out, you have to go into the larger world. It will help you proceed in an orderly fashion. We can help you understand the passage of time related to events worldwide that you are not necessarily aware of, but we can make you aware. At some point, you will look at a headline, see a magazine, or meet someone, and they will give you a small bit of information. You must understand that every bit of information that comes to you is important. The smallest thing, even the interference with your tape recorder, is a message you need to find and allow yourself to understand and allow it to come through. It means you need to find a better balance with technology. Ask me to help you find the quickest and most efficient way to really know technology, and not only fix it for you but explain it to you. I can help you find a person who will help you with the technology because these are physical machines. Your block about technology is a certain Taurus resistance to change to new information coming in, so you just stop with it. I, Jupiter, will exaggerate it, or you can ask differently, by saying, "I need to resolve this particular technology problem." You are very good at working with the general, better at that than with a particular problem. So find somebody who knows about that machine and get them to help explain it to you. When you do that, the block to technology will slowly go away because technology, just like anything else, has people who know more than you do.

I can help you clear your block. Imagine a bowling alley and you have a bowling ball. You have to focus on the pin, while I will help you with your arm and the bowling ball to hit that pin. So you need to break it down a little bit.

Dr. Modi: Can people call upon your energy for help?

Master of Jupiter: People have to understand that I am going to exaggerate whatever it is, good or bad. So if they do not understand that, there is no point in putting it out there. You need to find someone or you will find some kind of story.

You can attend to your own work, and what you do will go out naturally to whoever can use it in their own evolution. If they are in a place of public dissemination, they will get it and apply it. So you just take care of yourself. You are the important one here. Just remember, "Be careful what you ask for." I am the one that will give it to you.

Dr. Modi: Thank you, Jupiter, for the information.

Master of Jupiter: My pleasure!

Master of Venus

Dr. Modi: Locate the master of Venus.

Patient: She is very beautiful and very serious. She is wearing a deep red robe with flowers on it. She has a beautiful golden crown that is very elaborate and has brown hair.

Dr. Modi: Master of Venus, hi! Tell us about yourself, please.

Master of Venus: Well, I represent beauty and the feminine aspect of love, which is the tender embrace of nature, mother's arms, etc. I represent the mother with her arms around the child. I encompass all the curves and shapes that are round. I represent Mother Mary's energy for many, but she is greater than I am. I am part of the Virgin Mary's energy – the yin, or feminine energy. It depends on how people see me, but I represent a large amount of feminine energy, beauty, and love in everything. Love of the mother is a female who is receiving and giving. That is what I do: whatever makes people happy.

I am connected to creation; I influence all the planets in our solar system. It will be very difficult to describe my influence on Uranus, but when we come together, there is a joint influence on humanity. My influence on Earth is easy to describe. Whenever people appreciate or have a sense of beauty, they have Venus energy in them. There is a level of consciousness in humans so that if they search me out, they will see more beauty.

Dr. Modi: How do we search you out?

Master of Venus: By asking and looking, feeling beauty and beauty in the music, and engaging in an activity within time. If you run around like a chicken whose head is cut off, it will be very difficult to do anything except feel the anguish of the lost head, as opposed to spending the time to look at something, to listen or to feel, and working with all your senses. I operate through time and senses, and all the energies of different planets as described by astrologers' work with time. Without time, there can be no sensation other than desperation and fear.

The demonic influence in people cuts short the experience of the flow of beauty, love, and music. If it stops it short, then there is a terrible shock to the flow, and that is the quality of some heavy metal music. If heavy metal music is to be continued, or even if one would try to listen to it and go beyond the shock of it, one can hear tones that would stretch out to beauty, but that requires great effort. That will be the effort of the Light, which always can go beyond the darkness and stop the flow of Light. Demonic energy simply stops its flow.

Some shoes are made with very high heels or too-pointed toes, whereas slightly high heels with the equivalent bigger sole might be a positive form, where the toe might be slightly rounded, then pointed, would have a more balanced sense of beauty. There is interference with what is called beauty. This is very important, because if people can look into what is fashionable, they are moving into the energy of comparing themselves to others because they do not trust their own sense of beauty. People's own sense of beauty will normally work with the harmony of the body and spirit, nature, and form.

There are two signs that come from me: Taurus and Libra. They have a great sense of beauty because I flow my energy through them. Libra has great sense of beauty, unlike Taurus, because it is of a different quality. Libra is constantly balancing something on one hand and the other hand; it has difficulty knowing which one to choose. Taurus is grounded in the Earth and has a deeper sense of connectivity, and it has more sensual understanding of beauty, while Libra has more mental understanding. These are different qualities that humans have attributed to where planets are at different times of the year and how people have responded to who is born at different times of the year, so it relates to seasons. There is a slight difference when it is above or below the equator.

The demonic energy always interferes by stopping the flow of the Light. In Libra's case, they create more confusion, because Libra is a more mental sign and cannot decide. So that closes off the flow of beauty, as it goes into uncertainty. Uncertainty is always a frontier for creation; this is very important. So whenever people are stopped with fear as part of uncertainty, it is the demonic influence.

The demonic influence in Taurus will get it fixated on what is beautiful and what is not. Taurus energy is not light; it is heavier. It stops the sensual appreciation or will exaggerate sensuality. For example, in fashion, velvet is beautiful because it is soft, reflects the light, and takes color in a certain way. The demonic energy will put in too much velvet and make it so heavy that the person is almost falling down under the weight of it, because Taurus will exaggerate how much it wants, whereas Libra will see the velvet in its correct weight, but will have difficulty in deciding color or thickness.

With mother love, Taurus is very warm and expressive, very sensual, and will exaggerate the mother love to the point of smothering the flow and not allowing freedom, whereas with Libra, the mother love will be similar but cooler. It is more of a mental discipline and not so physical. Taurus is very physical, while Libra is more mental and cooler. Libra has very good qualities because it represents justice and truth. There is a refinement to Libra, unlike Taurus. It is more down to Earth and more simplified.

Dr. Modi: This person is a Taurus. How did your energy affect her?

Master of Venus: Positively. I gave her great sensitivity to nature. An identification with everything in nature, such as animals, plants, flowers, the ocean, and sky. I also gave her great artistic sense and a great sense of responsibility and mothering for Earth and all people for the creation of life.

In a negative sense, she feels too much responsibility and closes down the other options. For example, with rescuing animals, it became heavy handed when she continued to expand it into a larger area. It was not realistic for that time. She was not willing to go to an organization for help to raise money and to set up larger places for rescuing animals. She got stuck doing it all herself until everything collapsed.

She is very patient, like all Taureans, and very loyal. On the negative side, she is stopping loyalty in some areas by allowing her Aries energy of impatience to come in too soon and affect her insight. In working with you, she would stop short at what she already knew and not allow the continuation of new information. It is the stubbornness of the Taurus. Persistence is good, but stubbornness is the lower end, which will come in with the fear of losing ground. That is how the demonic energies work.

Taurus is the ruler of the second house in astrology; it is the house of money and possession. So she should be able to have plenty of money. However, she does not have any major planets in the second house and she has a duality of money. She acts as if she has a lot of money but she does not have much money. She has not allowed herself to do things that would continually bring in a lot of money. She could have done her paintings all along and made a lot of money, She made it with films, and different things happened so she was not able to work with the films. She made plenty of money when she was working with films but did not save it. She did not handle the money with respect and did not invest it. Instead, she spent it on animals.

There is a positive and negative side to all these break-downs, because every time there was a negative stop there was a positive lesson.

Dr. Modi: How did your energy affect me?

Master of Venus: Positively. You have a great sense of delight and pleasures of life in colors, movements, food, clothes, dance, music, mothering, a sense of responsibility, and a great deal of joy. You have great persistence, as exemplified in this work. Your creativity in coming up with different solutions as you stay patient and persistent is very Taurean. You do not give up on friendships, loved ones, work, plans, or any ideas. Your hands and sense of touch, the way you take care of yourself, your sense of dress, your sense of the appreciation of your hair, your respect for your hair. The stopping point would be feeling disappointment with losing your hair as opposed to understanding that you are part of a cycle of transformation. After that, you can speed it up and do other things with your hair, but you stop short and become unhappy about your loss of hair.

Difficulties that Taureans have are that they are very sedentary and stuck in their ways. Loyalty to any situation becomes exaggerated. In that situation, you need to call in other energies or just use your mind to go beyond heavy disappointment. Whenever disappointment comes up, try to go beyond the disappointment. Sometimes it is necessary to change perspective by going physically. There is heaviness to the Taurean body.

The same things happen with the Libra; if he chooses the dark side, it closes down and feels hopeless, whereas a Taurean's sense of hopelessness is different.

You had experiences where your desire had pushed through the heaviness of feelings that you could not get anywhere. In those situations, you can ask me –Venus – to help you with a qualitative desire for a change. If you ask just for change in general, it is not specific. You need to ask for specific insight because beauty is a delicate quality in Taurus, which is interesting because Taurus is heavy but the beauty is delicate. It appreciates the smell of the rose. I can always help you to go into the exquisite.

In the negative, you have a feeling that you are plodding and plodding with big, heavy boots, dragging yourself. Simply visualize that you are going through at the speed of Light. When the dragging comes up in your mind, ask for help for beauty of movement and also ask Mercury to help, because Mercury is a messenger of Light. Ask for your planets to help you with the speed of Light. There is a beauty in going slowly and in slogging through. Ask me—Venus—to show you the beauty each time and then you will see what comes to you.

Right now, the beauty is that you are challenging time and are moving through fixed positions and fixed attitudes about time; how long it takes to do something is irrelevant. If you can understand that time is irrelevant, you can move it around. Time is challenging you because you are attempting to create change, but to you it seems that it is going too slowly, so you feel the negativity of impatience, but Taurus energy is very patient. When you feel impatient, ask me –Venus – to show you the beauty in the amount of time it is taking you, because it goes into more detail. Taurus represents the Earth and the change within it. You are bringing changes in more fixed ways; you are grounding it more. So if you can see the beauty of grounding, then you will not be so impatient. You are challenging time in a negative sense, pushing yourself and becoming impatient, unhappy, and distracted from the work, and it takes the pleasure out of it.

Dr. Modi: You said, "You ask and I will show you," but now I do not see psychically.

Master of Venus: You may not see the way you expect to see; I always show you. Watch what you do with your body, because Taurus is the body of the bull: very strong. You may not see but you will feel it and become aware of it. You will get a sign. You see with your mind; you do not see with your eyes. Every time you are in an uncomfortable situation, asks where the beauty is and then you will become aware of what you feel.

Dr. Modi: Thank you, Venus, for giving us the knowledge and understanding about you and how you help us, even when we are not aware of it.

Master of Uranus

Master of Uranus: I am glad you let me come through. I heard you were going to talk to me, so I am here. I am coming in from left field; this is my job. When you least expect me, I am here. I am the explosion. The planet Uranus was discovered by humans in 1781. The planet was always there, but humans did not notice its energy.

Patient: He is very skinny. I can hardly see him.

Dr. Modi: Uranus, why are you so skinny?

Master of Uranus: Because I am like a bolt of lightning, and bolts of lightning are skinny. My elbows and knees are sticking out like the zigzag of the lightning bolt. I am a bolt of lightning coming out from where you never expected, and I make a big shock. I am the essence of electricity.

Dr. Modi: How come humans did not discover you sooner, with all your characteristics?

Master of Uranus: Well, humans mixed up my energy with Mars. They just did not see the planet and did not have any way to apply that particular quality. They have to see the planet first and how it affected the weather, the changes in plants, the animals, and the humans. Then they would make up stories about the qualities of energy and check to see if they were accurate; that is what the astrologers and spiritual people did. Once they became aware of the planet and our energy, they began to study. They gave it the sign of Aquarius, which is an enormous, cool energy. It is interesting that the sign is opposite of my energy, but is not emotional in normal ways. The passion has gone beyond emotions; it is a huge and creative Light force. It does not interfere with small emotional fits of temper.

Dr. Modi: What else?

Master of Uranus: That is the information I came to give. That is all. I do not waste energy; that is why I am so skinny. Aquarius is a good sign and the way they put it with Uranus energy is very good for me. It takes advantage of my quick, crazy energy to shake things up, but it does not make people run around like crazy. It gets the Aquarian energy that people have to stop and look at the big picture. They get a cosmic view and are able to make a creative decision based on it. They do not get emotional. If you have Aquarian energy that is strong, you have Uranus energy. Everybody has Uranus energy somewhere, so they can call us to give a larger world view. Let us use the Aquarian energy; all these different signs, houses, and planets have them in some combination, but we are free; we do not cost anything. Just dial in and take a look. [Laughing] I can help you go anywhere because I am so skinny.

Dr. Modi: How did you affect this person positively and negatively?

Master of Uranus: I have affected her a lot. Positively, I helped her with survival. I gave her a very active imagination, which I can creep into any time. Somehow, I had fun with her because she could imagine the most incredible things. That kept her happy when she lived in a very difficult circumstance during her childhood. "Strange" is how she used me, and she would explore the strangest things. She loved to explore her own mind; she did not need other people so much. She made herself very independent. Her Saturn is in the sixth house, which is the house of how she does things and how she works. It is not the carrier house; it is the methodology, and it is in Aquarius, which is the sign I feed.

Some of her hardest life lessons have come in my domain. The way she does her work and has educated herself is very unusual, since both of her parents came from the upper class but were not particularly well-educated. So I have been extremely useful in helping her. Through her painting and art, which she has maintained over the years, she is able to do very crazy things in her paintings. I almost take hand, mind, and eyes and help her to paint. I combine all these energies in her. I helped her not to be conventional all her life, almost to the extreme.

I have a better sense of right and wrong, because I am quicker than Jupiter. Jupiter does not care about right and wrong. Also, I have Aquarius, which is cool and is able to make better decisions about whether something will work or not. It is not a conventional right and wrong, so I have helped her go to very unusual places to find her education.

I helped you get on this track, which is very unusual. Whatever is unusual comes from me. Humor is necessary, because the changes that have to be made are so extreme that the only thing to do is to laugh at them. Otherwise you would be crying and sad.

Dr. Modi: How else did you affect me?

Master of Uranus: I affected you tremendously. I gave you the charge so you could move on the path. I give you a push when you want to digress. I can help you devise a plan for the development of your body, spirit, and soul as a representative of humanity, because the work you are doing is way ahead of the condition of your physical makeup. So you need to upgrade your understanding of it. Just be gentle with yourself and it will evolve in harmony.

You can ask Venus to help you with harmony and Jupiter to expand that harmony, and when you are in water, Neptune will help you with the deeper spiritual understanding without a name. Saturn will help you become very precise at the end. Do not get too precise too quickly; Mars will help you fight for it. Mercury will give you the mind to stick with it because Mercury is very cool and very precise, too. Mercury and Saturn would be very nice to work together.

Dr. Modi: How did you affect me negatively?

Master of Uranus: I did not affect you negatively; the dark forces try to scare you. When I bring in something that would really be a shock, you want to go fast, where I want you to go slow. The dark forces just stop the flow of Light. I am that lightning bolt that you call upon to go through the strand for the aging process, and other times when you call, that is me.

Dr. Modi: Thank you for all your help, even though I did not know about it.

Master of Uranus: I am so glad that you decided to make our acquaintance.

Master of Pluto

Patient: I see the master of Pluto. He is very somber and all dressed in dark clothing. He is like a "Darth Vader." He is a lord of the underworld. In Greek mythology, he is from the deepest, darkest parts of the Earth and humans. The sign that goes with him is Scorpio.

Dr. Modi: Pluto, hi! Tell us about yourself.

Master of Pluto: [Serious] How do you do? Neptune, Uranus, and myself are called "generational" because we take a long time to go around the Sun. It is like every twenty years a generation would be born with my energy in a different sign. I always manage to go to the deepest part of whatever needs to be examined, cleared, and brought to Light so the action can be taken. I bring secrets to life, such as the breakage of water pipes as you experienced in Wheeling, West Virginia, last month. It was an old plumbing system that needed to be redone. There is a Pluto-Saturn aspect on the Earth right now. A lot of dark energies are there that are coming up. I am sort of an excavator of the pit of places and people; the hidden secret parts need to come up to the Light, and I help do it.

Dr. Modi: It is a very good thing to do.

Master of Pluto: Yes, it is a very important job. It is the last important one. My natural house is a twelfth house, the completion before death. I am the equivalent of the examination after death, but you have the opportunity during life to use my energy. Sometimes when there is an aspect happening in the regular procedure of the days that involves me, you are pretty much forced and do not have much choice there. Free will is there at the superficial level, but eventually I come into the picture and you cannot hide from me. This is good. It means we are there to evolve, to change, to grow, and to create. I am not so much interested in the direct application of creativity; I want to set the scene so people can create.

Dr. Modi: Do you have a lot of dark influence?

Master of Pluto: My energies are affected by the way I affect people. That is where the dark influence is and I could use some of my soul parts back. We all can get our soul parts back because, as people misuse our energies or stop short, the demonic interference comes in and we feel frustrated. We are just here without being able to do much.

Dr. Modi: That is what we are going to do when we work with the demon commander for the Sun of our solar system. We will get the soul parts back for all the planets, their beings, and the ruling masters.

Master of Pluto: That will be good.

Dr. Modi: Do you have beings like humans living on your planet?

Master of Pluto: Consciousnesses are not the forms. It is a stopping place upon which consciousness can light. When people on Earth die, they can visit different planets during the intermediary phase and take on consciousness forms that are available.

Dr. Modi: Is it a purgatory?

Master of Pluto: No, this is not a purgatory, which is a state of mind. Souls just visit there and do not stay. They come to Pluto to see what the energy is like at the advanced level. Usually the souls that are more advanced will come here before they incarnate to experience a possibility for translating the equalities of thought and experience. Souls come here for a short time but do not stay, like in purgatory. It is like a stopping place to get information on the journey. Each planet has its own different qualities and application of energy. In some cases, there are life forms that stay longer, but really none of the planets are inhabited by life that will be accessible to humans. Mars has some fire beings that can live there. There are beings that can live on all these places for any amount of time, but they do not live in time zones. They live outside of time in another dimension. That is why when explorers go there they do not find anything.

Dr. Modi: What are the other ways you affect humanity?

Master of Pluto: When people need to review their life and find themselves in a corner, I help them to stop, think, and evaluate their life so they can make a change. My whole purpose is to help people make positive change for themselves, to give a greater sense of consciousness and understanding of the Light. At any point, if you stretch time, you can contact me because I am at the furthest reach of time. So if you have a problem and are willing to stay with it and allow different thoughts to come up and explore but do not stop short, you will eventually come to me because I am the completion of life, any idea, and any project, and you can understand why things happened the way they did. I can help you have that understanding because I bring you in up to the life. Like the water problem in Wheeling that forced people to look at what it was and what caused it, so they can fix it; but it cost money, changes, and discomfort.

These are all the side effects of my energy but the outcome is always good.

If people reject my energy, they come back to it later.
It is not good to reject my energy because people will be
stuck in that uncomfortable place. My energy is uncomfortable for people on the whole, unless you are a mystic
who is accustomed to silence without much interaction
with others. Then they are not so uncomfortable. There is
always some resistance to my energy, and sometimes it is
called "the dark night of the soul."

Dr. Modi: Is it due to the demonic influences?

Master of Pluto: When my energy is stopped short by
demonic interference, they do not want to have all the
information about themselves that whatever it is I am
offering. I am a historian; I have a history people's lives
and a possibility of showing it without judgment, but they
are full of judgment most of the time, and therefore, do
not like what they see. It does not fit with their ideas. I am
generalizing, because there are all degrees. When people
are drowning or have a review, they do not have judgment. They just see what happened. The judgment comes
later or earlier. But I get into the possibility of looking into
their lives without judgment to see the cause and effect. I
am a master observer of cause and effect.

Now, humans have given Scorpio to me as a sign, which
is very deep and has a very wicked part to it. When it stops
short, it will cut anybody's throat, but when it does not stop
short, it goes as deep as possible into everything, so it can
tolerate great truth. I permit the tolerance of the great truth,
so my energy is very valuable.

Dr. Modi: How did you affect this person?

Master of Pluto: I made her go to the depths of her issues
with her psychiatrist, which was useful. Even when the
psychiatrists turned to the dark side at the end, she was
finally able to leave, but was able to see the depths of the
dark side and see that she could stay there.

When she was growing, up I did not affect her much. She read all the myths, so she knew the stories about me being king of the underworld. She developed a love of the dark Earth, the smell of the Earth, and a sense of what it was like beneath the Earth. When she was a child, I reminded her of the help that was available to her, like the baby Jesus with whom she used to see and play. She had connections with Jesus from another life. There is not too much one could do when she was young, but as she got older, I could help her more because she developed courage to see the depth of her psyche. She was willing to give up things for the truth, so I did help her in that way, but there is more to come.

She was stopped at various points by the interfering energy when she was young. She used sexual energy to get things she needed. There was always a need for the search of depth within her, so I was always there, side by side. I gave her the desire for the constant search for depth of spirituality, and the deeper meaning behind the outside surface was always there.

Dr. Modi: How about me?

Master of Pluto: You were not aware of my energy, but I assisted you subconsciously and your desire to dig into the origin and the source of things. The more you did it, the more you wanted to dig. You have to be ready to give up any fixed conclusions; that is part of what is so difficult. That does not mean they are wrong, but do not come to fixed conclusions. If you come to any fixed conclusions or answers to any particular thing, that is a danger because no answer is fixed. Everything is in constant evolution, and the images that you humans have are stories and pictures, which are clumsy descriptions of qualities of the energies themselves. It works well enough, as long as you leave an open end for more information. I represent the source of endless information.

Dr. Modi: Is there life on Pluto?

Master of Pluto: No, not in the normal sense. Every planet has life on it in one form or another, not in the normal sense of time and space. The life is of the thought that is a part of a framework. For example, there are limits if you are going to work on a book, or a piece of music has notes that can go only so far. Everything has a framework around it and limitations. The life form there has a different framework and different limitations than on the other planets. They are not living in a time-space continuum, but there is also change that is observed and understood. It would be like where you are in a movement in time and you understand all the past history of the world. You get a flash of understanding of it in this movement. This is very hard to explain.

Dr. Modi: Is it like souls without the solid physical body?

Master of Pluto: Past-life personalities are almost like decorations of a soul. Those are still the part of the original essence of a person. It is hard to understand the essence of a past life personality because it still is existing at another level and another dimension.

Dr. Modi: How can we use your energy positively?

Master of Pluto: As I described, in any situation, you must be willing to go deeper and understand that there is some discomfort. Be willing to tolerate some discomfort; then you can go as deep as you like and I will be happy to help you.

Master of Saturn

Dr. Modi: Can we speak to the master of Saturn?

Master of Saturn: Yes, I am here.

Dr. Modi: Hi! Can you tell us about yourself?

Master of Saturn: I have a rather cool energy. I am thin and very serious; I do not have much humor. I have very strict rules that change because all things change. It is for maintaining the optimum efficiency of an individual's evolution and progression. I am what they call "the straight and narrow path." Many religions have adopted that expression for their higher spiritual understanding because their path becomes much narrower without many choices. That is my quality. My energy is to provide a narrow path to people to know where their progress is best suited. If they would maintain consciousness of that, they would not be so upset when they face a difficult turn in the road. That is essentially my purpose. It changes from time to time, depending on what the life of the person is.

For example, the Mercury retrograde you were discussing. If you wish to have a smooth flow, it is better not to initiate a project during the Mercury retrograde, because the action of the planet's energy is to go back over it, so you get the opportunity to go back and forth and accumulate more wisdom. There is always a positive quality to all of these energies. My energy as Saturn is for people to clearly plod through it, but they can go quickly if they are using other energies available to them. I am not squeamish when it is uncomfortable or painful. That is why I am called the malevolent.

Use of the word "return" in astrology has to do with the rotation of a movement. For example, return to a point of birth to where it was at the time of birth. Saturn's return is between twenty-nine to thirty years. The effect on humans happens when people are twenty-nine to thirty years old and when they are fifty-eight to sixty years old. Then it comes around at eighty-eight to ninety years old. In the first Saturn return, many people will have it come up in their face, so to speak, if they have not followed the narrow path correctly. They will have a marriage, divorce, death, change of job, change of home, or some other opportunity for change between twenty-nine to thirty years of age, then again between fifty-eight to sixty years. So many people are aware of this because my energy is affecting them in terms of narrowness of their path. If they follow it correctly, a greater path will occur in the evolutionary progression.

I am static. I can say everything the Sun said to you. I am aware of how people are affected by my energy. I move around the Sun, so I have a relationship with it.

Dr. Modi: When you make one circle around the Sun and come back to your original place, that is your birth?

Master of Saturn: Yes, that is called a Saturn return, which is one of the most important points in a person's life because I am the strictest supervisor, so to speak. Not that I can control much of what they do, but they need to use my energy correctly. It depends on a person, on their spirit, on their generosity, and their courage to always hear God; to recognize the Light, to know the power of the Light, to know the power of their own Light, and to develop an understanding of their own destiny and purpose and to overcome the dark forces. I make it possible for people to see how to know the dark forces, and to overcome them, if they follow my path.

Dr. Modi: It is believed in astrology that Saturday is Saturn's day, and no good project, wedding, or other ceremony should start on that day.

Master of Saturn: If many people believe that, then it becomes true. I may appear to be very heavy-handed, but if I am well-understood in what the energies are, I can be as light as a feather if you are harmonious. For over one hundred years, in large parts of the world, people no longer consider me malevolent; they understand the benefit of discipline. I represent discipline and order. Your house in western astrology will represent the area of your life where I have the most effect, where you need to work the most. Each house in the astrological man-dala represents a part of your life, like your home, your inner self, outer self, relationship with others, playful-ness of children, health, etc. Each of these parts of your life is represented in special ways in different houses. If you wish to connect to the energy on your own, it is possibly; more difficult but it might be more useful. But you can also find out, from the time of your birth, where I stand and what house, this is always helpful. One of the purposes of the development of Earth and space-time continuum linear time is to slow the evolution of bodies and creation of forms. These are all very slow experiments; it becomes very interesting to see the way evolution occurs. It is interesting to God and to all of us who are mostly in the Light. We are Light beings of the highest order.

Dr. Modi: Do you have any suggestions for humans so we do not get trapped into negative thinking?

Master of Saturn: There is a greater need for international communion between all people on the planet, because there are many who understand the true purpose who have developed greater courage in going outside their safe belief system. It is possible that some of the older cultures may not be aware of the planet Uranus. It was discovered in the west, maybe in the last hundred and twenty years. It represents an explosion of the unusual, something that comes from left field. It is always positive; there is nothing negative. For us as beings of Light, we see nothing negative, only slowing down and speeding up. We watch the effects. We observe and stay true to ourselves in our own development and evolution.

There is a communication of consciousness between us that is received in each individual. That is why the astrologer who developed "talking to the planets" would be helpful to the patient's expansion if they are fearful and saw me as some kind of tarantula or sneaky ninja, hiding in the shadows to come kill them. They would need to explore their own life and see how they are using the energy I have for them. Then they could willfully change their behavior and their understanding of the energy's quality. This is how it is beneficial when people are ready to find out what these qualities are within their character. We all are in every being. Animals and insects know it because they live in the present moment. They are almost reactive to whatever combinations of energies are coming to any planet at any given point. Energies are always changing because the planets are moving and affecting the weather and people's moods. We perceive it as extremely exquisite interaction. We do not judge; we just watch.

Dr. Modi: It probably is good for astrologers to communicate directly with you.

Master of Saturn: Yes, direct communication is always good so they get the correct understanding from us directly. They can be mistaken about the things they do not know. It is always good for people to understand that there is more they do not know and understand than they do know. They move with humility into great knowledge, but many astrologers have the same problems as many politicians and priests who are followed by people, and then the ego becomes frozen and the cancer of the ego takes place.

Dr. Modi: Can we do anything to heal Planet Saturn?

Master of Saturn: Healing is love, and I can always use love. We all can use some healing.

Dr. Modi: That is what we are trying to do.

Maser of Saturn: You are doing very well. You are just touching us exactly where we are. I say "we," as planets who circle the Sun, and the Sun can say "me and my planets," because we are all related.

Dr. Modi: Yesterday we worked with the demon commander of "Change" and did a lot of healing. Did you and all the planets in our solar system get healed, too?

Master of Saturn: Yes, lots of soul parts were brought back. Planets are a whole different story. There is darkness in evolution and there are beings that are consciousnesses that live on all the planets. These consciousnesses are multi-leveled, so they can be considered beings. It is very hard to describe. We all are affected by everyone, so the healing you did yesterday involved almost Saturnian – a return to Saturn as proper function – because we insist on proper function. We are like the guardians. A lot of darkness came out and soul parts were brought back. There is a lot of Light in the planet now. It happened for all of us, and the planets. The energy expanded and it makes us happy. There can always be more happiness, more joy, more understanding, and more creativity.

It is like discovering more consciousness of God. The human spirit can bi-locate as a being of Light, since their body is still alive, and can join with our energy, evolving all of humanity in unimaginable ways, and evolving the structure of the body. We have some understanding of all the possibilities until they happen within time, because we are all working in various aspects of time. All individuals have their own time around them and are a center of their own universe. It is hard for people to imagine that. [Laughing] It is nice to laugh. I, Saturn, do not laugh too often.

Dr. Modi: Is there anything else we should know about you?

Master of Saturn: Well, there is plenty more, but nothing is necessary at this time.

Patient: I get the feeling that he is helping you with your work.

Dr. Modi: Saturn, how are you helping me and also affecting me?

Master of Saturn: I am keeping you focused on your work. I am sorry for the different problems you are experiencing that are not part of the work itself. As the work evolves, you will retrieve all these other functions based on what you are doing. We wanted you to know this.

Dr. Modi: Thank you for all the information.

Master of Saturn: Yes! Great pleasure for this lovely recognition.

Master of Earth

Dr. Modi: Gabriel, do we need to speak to the master of Earth?

Archangel Gabriel: You always need to talk to Earth. It loves to be recognized because it is changing, too. It is actually helping with the evolution of humanity. Earth is known as Mother Earth, but it is both male and female. It has many names. Some people call her Gaia; others call her Terra. Every language has a different name for Earth.

Dr. Modi: Thank you. Can we speak to the master of Earth, please?

Mother Earth: Yes, I am here. I am the Master of Earth; I am always right under your feet [Laughing]. Even if you are in a big, tall building, the gravity pulls you down. It is the love in my heart pulling you – all my babies – to let you know that I am right here. You grew out of my heart.

Dr. Modi: Tell us more about yourself.

Mother Earth: First of all, I can look like a woman and wear different color clothes. I have a beautiful rainbow dress because Earth is sometimes a pale yellow, red, brown, black, or white. You may notice that these are the skin colors of the human races.

Patient: She came as a female because she wanted to show you the color of her robe, which has colors of skin of the human races.

Mother Earth: I was a little idea in the mind of the Creator, and then a bunch of us were created as planets. We all have our own intelligence and purpose. The Earth is the third planet around the sun. We love the sun and the moon. When we say "we," we are speaking of the royal we, with the Creator. When we speak this way, we are speaking of God in us and in creation, because we represent a major creation. We are created to attract the weather, the temperature, the waters around us, and the layers of our bodies to accommodate humans, animals, plants, and vegetables, birds, fish, insects, and all the other life forms, such as gnomes and fairies. Any consciousness that has form or part of a form can be happy here; that is how we developed the phrases "heart of gold," "warm as fire," and "warm as the sun." Our heart is in the center, and all life comes to receive our love. We send our love through all our layers into whatever and whoever is on our surface. We also have connections within and below the external surface layers of all the life forms in partial dimensional layers.

We respond to the effects of what exists in our skin, so to speak. We have organs parallel to your organs. We have hearts and livers and bloodstreams, an external epidermis that is sometimes misused, so we have to shake it off. We connect psychically and spiritually with the energies of tectonic plates, which are part of us, and the volcanoes. We feel their anger, their frustration, joy, calmness, and evolution. We are constantly monitoring all the stuff that is going on, and when people think about healing Mother Earth, they are healing their connection to us and understanding us. We do not really need so much healing in that sense, but we would be much happier if we did not have to keep shocking people all the time by seeing certain behaviors that are getting stagnated.

Our whole purpose is to rotate around the sun and within our own orbit. We create opportunities for the change of seasons and many other changes, such as the relationship with the moon and the tides. These are all like movements and we move very slowly. We, the Earth itself, do not appear to be moving, but even when plants are planted into our epidermis, there is movement, especially if they are watered. If human energy becomes too greedy or sedentary, we will work with some of the other energies to create a change. Sometimes we will create a necessary tornado. We monitor all the energies that are around and in the Earth so we can make decisions. We have constant telepathic connections with all these different energies, like air and the atmosphere. We have constant telepathic meetings and are always balancing what is necessary.

As humans, what happened in New Orleans with the terrible change was because of human nature, because of those who did not fix the levees that led to the flooding, and the lack of respect for people and political problems there. These are the ways people think, behave, and make decisions.

We work with time and understand how groups of humans need to be shocked to take them to their next stage of development. We are never quite sure how it will play out because it is all free will. We would be much happier if there was peace and harmony, as you requested earlier in healing of this person and others. You hear about so much murder that it would be good for you to stop it because you know what it is. We are here as the Earth; we also know what it is like to have parts of our skin ripped away. We do not mind if it is to be of benefit up, to a certain point where greed gets in the way of proper respect. Respect is extremely important for everything and for change in all life forms.

All these situations where people build homes near polluted rivers and get poisoned, we become extremely affected by this lack of sensitivity and their brutality. The humans who are trying to heal the Earth are actually trying to heal themselves, because humans live here because of me and us. They could not survive here if their consciousness became so limited in the understanding of the oneness of all things. The experiment of humanity on Earth has to do with evolving uniqueness and separation, if necessary. It is also necessary to understand the oneness and the responsibility that each person has for the well-being of everyone, which includes the Earth. Right now in the last forty-year period, there is a great consciousness to respect the Earth. There is a thought of it but not enough action. That is why we continue to reflect some of the negative energies, such as the volcanoes and shifting tectonic plates that cause discomfort to people.

The September 11 event is a perfect example that brought everyone together, but they did not stay together long. They kept attacking the very people we were trying to help. There are levels on the planet of those two big words:

fear and greed. Among the ones that are most fearful and greedy are the stock market traders. There is a difference between lip service and action about healing the Earth. So our relationship to all that is to deal with the real energy levels put out by people, not what they say. What they say is better than not saying it, because some people are in a position of power to understand these energies and put out more correct understanding of the balance required. By clearing out the demonic interferences, it helps people be more responsible and more creative to the overall good. It does not mean making less of themselves. The idea of suffering and sacrificing everything you love is an incorrect perception.

Free will does not exist in the higher realms. They still have a choice and will always have a response to that quality of choice. So at that level, free will does exist. If you look at it that way, free will exists everywhere. There needs to be an understanding that free will is an expression to allow people to understand that they are part of God and are made in His image. That is what their religion tells them, so they feel empowered. In other places, there is a group understanding, so choices are made based on the highest good of the group. The decision-making process is quite elaborate here on Earth. Time has worked with stretching out of time, and creating linear time here on Earth gives you extended feedback as a result of your choices.

Humans are able to make the choice of far-ranging view of things, but most of the time they have very short-range thinking; just what they need for their survival from the fear of death. You would think that with the amount of killing taking place people would stop it, but they keep on doing it. On a deeper level, they do know that they are eternal, but they do know to integrate that in the day-to-day choices they make. It is very interesting to see what the different stages are because each slow step in the development of a decision has a mathematical equivalent; it has an energetic potency which we look at and see how it applies to other things, to other ways of growing and sending my energy through the Earth to bring the environment a different type of plan, something that will be suitable for different humans with the understanding that we could change certain parts of the environment.

Dr. Modi: What is the plan for humans and what was the plan for them?

Mother Earth: The plan and the experiment were to see what will happen when humans are given free will under these conditions, to see within the limitation of linear time and the aging process how humans would integrate being one and unique. This is the place where uniqueness is being developed in individuals more than anywhere, but that would be without really a memory of being connected with God. There are other civilizations where people have gone beyond fighting and killing that seems to be the major solution on Earth, but they have a greater understanding of what is good for all, so they stop themselves. They are not as loose as people on Earth are.

Dr. Modi: Is there more demonic influence on Earth than anywhere else in creation?

Mother Earth: There is a great creativity on Earth. With all the uniqueness, a lot of creativity comes through. Even though everything is there to be discovered, the applications are very unique and the demonic energy has a lot of work to do. If you look at it from a larger point of view, the demonic energy presents a challenge. As people advance, they feel comfortable and relax and then there is not so much creativity.

Dr. Modi: You said before that the Earth has organs like humans do. Can you explain more?

Mother Earth: It is a parallel. It is what the job and quality of each organ is. For example, the vascular system is like the rivers of liquid that go to the ocean; not just above the Earth, but through all the layers and the center of it.

The function of the liver is to purify, and some parts of the Earth also have energy with purifying qualities. It balances the Earth. We are here cooperating with humanity; it is not separate. So whatever humans are thinking, we react to it. Our purpose is to balance and sustain human life. If humanity continues to create atomic and hydrogen bombs to destroy everything, part of our function is also destroyed. So we have to be able to stop them. We can send our energy through certain parts of the Earth where we have a direct response.

Earth also has twelve major chakras and multitudes of minor chakras all over and inside it. What is inside the Earth is contained. They are not located in exact places, but they could be. They move around, depending on what is needed to maintain the balance inside and outside. We monitor what is happening outside, depending on the attitudes and decisions of humans. We know the animal population and the balance of energy they need and are holding, and the humans who are supposed to learn from the animals and plants.

Dr. Modi: How about the vortexes?

Mother Earth: The vortexes are simply places where there is an accumulation of energy that can be adapted to whatever is needed. It is like a crystal that expands on whatever it is focused. In humans, each chakra has its own function and placement. With us, there are vortexes that spread around the Earth. There are more vortexes than chakras. The chakras inside the Earth are the consciousness of the quality of energy, and if it is needed to send it up into the Earth, we use the vortexes. They are the centers of energy, but not specific centers. Sometimes there would be a specific energy in a place for hundreds of years, but that is just because of what people needed who were living there. What their actions and needs were are what others knew of people who come there to experience that energy. But we could send that energy to another vortex. The vortex could simply be there for people to make their own wishes or whatever they believe.

There are stories about some of the vortexes that represent a certain thing, but that is not quite how it works. People created stories by their observation, like they created astrology by their observation, but these things could change as life evolved. All the chakras suddenly could be activated to the same energy everywhere in the whole world on the vortexes. Chakras are not used by most humans because they are not conscious of them. Chakras are like little motors for specific things that people pay no attention to, like driving a car. People can drive a car but do not know how the engine works. There is a different chakra for each purpose in the human body, and humans use the chakras if they are conscious of them. Then they can pull the kundalini or they can increase the energy of the chakras, but maybe not all at the same time. They create combinations. They can close down all of them if they need to sleep and rest, or they can activate some of them. Most people are not ready to understand it. There have been a few wise people and mediators who were able to do it.

Dr. Modi: Is the kundalini of the Earth connected to the kundalini of each human being?

Mother Earth: They are parallel to all things. As more humans become conscious, they will experience the kundalini, but it is often not necessary. It is enough to simply know that it is there. Kundalini experiences happen off and on in our life and we do not even know it.

Dr. Modi: Any other part that is similar to human organs?

Mother Earth: The throat, which is used for swallowing food, for communication, speech, and sound. We also make sound sometimes.

Dr. Modi: Thank you for the information. We will talk to you later.

Mother Earth: I talk to you even when you are not talking to me. You can talk to me anytime; I am always under your feet. Just tap the ground a little bit to get my energy coming through your feet. You ask for my energy and I will come into your heart, and you will feel all the love. You do not have to worry about visualizing it.

Master of the Taurus Sign

Dr. Modi: Gabriel, is there a master for the Taurus sign?

Archangel Gabriel: Yes, there is, and the planet for Taurus is Venus. It is also the planet for the other signs; Taurus is the bull.

Dr. Modi: Can we speak to the master of Taurus, please?

Master of Taurus: Hi! I am here. I am part of the flow of energy and I have many names. Taurus is one of them for the qualities of energy that I represent.

Patient: I see him looking like a warrior in a bull helmet with two horns coming out of it, like a Viking. He has the strength and energy of a bull and his strong knees are exposed. He has a leather outfit and is a protector warrior. His feet are on the Earth; he represents the Earth. He is all dressed in brown because it is an Earth color. He works through Venus's planetary energy. He is a flow of energy but is just taking a form so I have something to see. He has the characteristics of a bull: stubborn, strong, dependable, and muscular, and will defend you until the death. He wants you to get his soul parts back.

Dr. Modi: Yes, I will, but first, tell me more about you.

Master of Taurus: I have never been born as human, so you cannot really attribute any human history to me. I am the observation of humans of the planetary effects of Venus at various times of the year. It is true that my energy will operate in different geographical parts, even though seasons might be different because my energy is related to the Earth. The attributes that had been selected for me come from humans who asked God for help in understanding our characteristics and how to focus their energy. I am part of a very long history of humanity's attempt to focus attention on invisible powers and strengths of energy that exist, but of different qualities, so as to be able to have a little more control over a world that seems chaotic to humans.

Humans are built in a very slow, physical condition. There are stories of them being created from Earth. I am the second sign in the progression of human life around the Zodiac, which was designed by humans. The first one is Aries—the fire, the beginner, the impatient one. I come after Aries and am very patient. The sign that comes after each one, the qualities of their energy correct the previous one, because we are learning how to experience linear progressive time.

The astrological design is essentially a human construct and a way to understand God's energies and be creative with the forces they do not see, but feel. There is an extension of spiritual psychic ability as people become aware of our different qualities. I am the second sign of the Zodiac and I am the Earth. I am solid, dependable, and strong. I do not give up and I am also stubborn. So there are levels of my energy as people learn to work with it, to control it, and to combine it with other energies. There is struggle for humans to both know themselves and be patient. I represent extreme patience. I come after Aries, which is extremely impatient.

There are other astrological systems on Earth, such as Chinese, Hindu, and other systems with slightly different descriptions of our energies based on mythology and religious stories. I am a combination of these energies, which you can use to play like a musical instrument. I love to work with the energy of Planet Venus because that is about beauty and art. It lightens up the whole Earth. We love the Earth; it is a gift from God. We are the most loyal friends because the Earth is stable.

Humans have decided that Aries represents the head, so those who have Aries energies will get the head energy. It is a different type of chakra system as you move down the body. According to humans, I represent the throat.

Patient: I am hearing the name Tobias. I think he is connected to Taurus.

Master of Taurus: He is. He is like a young apprentice that will grow into a new development for humans as my particular quality of energy becomes a collection of energy. I do not like to use the word "exclusive" because we are always combining, but there is exclusivity, an exclusive understanding of the make-up of my energies. Tobias is wearing brown clothes just like me. He is next to me where these particular distinctions of the different astrological signs will no longer be applicable.

Astrological signs have an image; they have a planet from where they get energy, like I get from Planet Venus, which also gives energy to other signs.

The magnetic sheet is a way for you to connect with change. Your job is to bring the darkness to the Light. You can also ask to put the magnetic sheet around every master, because we all have missing soul parts, too. There are multitudes of masters you do not know yet.

Dr. Modi: Thank you for the information. I pray to God and request the angels to please put the magnetic sheet around Taurus, Tobias, and all the masters and beings in heaven. Turn the switch to the "eject" sign and expel everything that does not belong with them. Collect them in the net of Light; transform them into the Light and store them in the Light. Then turn the switch to the "attract" sign and allow every soul part to come back from Satan, his demons, people, places, darkness, and from heaven, from this time and space and beyond. Cleanse them, heal and integrate them with whom they belong.

Patient: I see only a little bit of gray energy coming out and multitudes of soul parts coming back for Taurus, Tobias, and all the other masters and heavenly beings. They are integrated with whom they belonged after cleansing and healing.

Master of Taurus: Thank you! Many soul parts came back to me. I feel better now.

Master of Time

Dr. Modi: Can we speak to Master of Time, please?

Patient: I see him. He is a tall man with the robes of different colors; silver, gray, blue, and white. He carries a scythe in his hand, or a tool for cutting that has a big curve in a half moon shape; that is the symbol of the Master of Time. It means he is going to cut off your life when the time comes. He is a man with a beard and long gray hair. He has a face that keeps changing into different colors. He becomes the different colors of various races and has their features. He is making a joke now; he is turning into a ballerina twirling round and round. He is very serious and wants to be taken seriously, but he is full of fun and changes a lot. Right now he is changing into a mouse running into a field. He wants us to know that he is full of possibilities; that is his main quality. He is very strict.

Dr. Modi: Master of Time, hi! Can you tell us about yourself and your costumes? What is the meaning of it?

Master of Time: Well, the colors are not so bright. They are more silver, gold, and light purple. They are like the late sunset colors, but not so brilliant. It is to remind people of the ever-changing passage of time, whereas the bright colors, such as red, green, and blue are more fixed. I am not fixed. I represent the shadow colors – the subtle combinations – but I maintain my form, my coat, and the outfit so that people know their stability. Even though things change, there is stability because we are working within the duality that there are always two sides. People wish to think it is constant but it is not. It is like two, three, or more. Every number comes after two. Between one and two, you have the possibility of the million, billion, googol numbers, and my time is like that within the form of one. So I [all of a sudden my cassette recorder and phone went dead for a few seconds and then came back].

Dr. Modi: Master of Time, what caused that?

Master of Time: Well it was a little demonstration. [Laughing] Don't think timing is a crucial essence of my power and your power, because you are connected to me. I am the part of the order of our body. There is the aging process, which is part of my energy moving in time. The demonstration was a pause in time, so you can stretch time, and understand how you can use time, because I am in you. I am part of your basic structure as a human being and as an individual, so your timing from one movement to another will change if you are conscious of it. If you are not conscious of it, something will happen to make you aware, such as the lights going out. You will feel yourself falling in slow motion. You will not fall; you will catch yourself in slow motion and correct yourself. That is the stretching of time. We want you to know of all our capabilities. There is no way to even imagine the extent of how busy I am.

Dr. Modi: Give us some examples, please.

Master of Time: If you are sensitive to time, you will have instincts to leave the house at the exact time so that when you cross the street, all the lights are green. That is sensitivity to time. I can also change the timing within the lights on the streets, if you ask or are conscious of it without even asking. You can find a parking place that way. I can make sure we stretch the amount of time you take to get to the place when another car is moving out.

Dr. Modi: I pray for that and, amazingly, it works almost every time.

Master of Time: Well, there we go. You count and see how many times you use my name. On Wall Street, they use my name many, many times [Laughing]. You can change time to see how long it takes for your hair to grow. You can put the consciousness of the time frame of your aging process. Create the formula of all the ways that time operates within you, including the growth of your hair, and ask that a part of the timing be changed so that the growth of the hair can be parallel to the time when it grew more quickly. The cells that grew the hair somehow are sleeping now. You can tap into that timeframe which has been changed by the various applications and attitudes. There is always an attitude. There is an internal under-standing and external application. That is why I wear two sets of clothes.

I can affect everything; I can slow down or speed up time. For example, there were a number of elements involved in the sinking of the *Titanic*. I participated because I am part of the evolution of every human being, not only on that ship, but in the decades ahead where it would exem-plify people who wished to go quickly but did not take into consideration the iceberg that was there. They could have slowed down, calmed their thinking, and allowed the thought to come in about the iceberg.

Another example is this patient's life: when she was on a ship escaping from Europe, there was a slowdown in time. If the ship had arrived at the expected time, she would not be here now because a submarine was waiting in the night to torpedo the ship. As the ship arrived late, I changed the time due to many elements. It was necessary for certain people to live.

I am woven in, that is, I am a form of DNA woven through every aspect of creation, including those parts where the progression of time is not as you have it on your plane. The very use of my name, "Time" means there is time, for there must be a time to have "no time." Sorry to make this a joke. [Laughing] I am very creative. By knowing who I am, you can have a partnership with me. You need to promote me in your first page as a major partner in evolution.

Dr. Modi: How?

Master of Time: I am very precise to a nano-second. When you are on your path, there is total precision. Do not complain about not remembering people's names. I was involved in making sure in Atlantis that people who were responsible to carry the information were absolutely protected. This is how I am woven into all the decisions that are made on Earth.

I was a major partner in the decision to create with the Alohim, and I am evolving as you are with your use of me. I am all over creation and creations cannot exist without me, but I am not the same as on Earth. I represent stages of evolution that might happen in a single instant, as opposed to a billion years. The same stages of evolution, in terms of mathematics or energy formula, could happen in one second or in ten billion years, depending on the application of energies around the space where evolution is occurring. So the creator made or envisioned me as part of the beginning of the separation because I represent the stages of evolution, development, and change. I represent a change. Since I am woven into every life form, I have a different time zone. Each person has his or her own time zone. When you wake up in the morning, you are in a different time zone in your internal individual life based on your age, your basic culture, weather, family members or lack of members around you that day, etc. All these elements are automatically taken into consideration and the way you use timing will be different than other people use it. So timing, in some cases, becomes stultified. The dark forces will exaggerate how long or short a time comes and they will interrupt something that needs to be slower or quicker to create confusion and uncertainty. A great deal of uncertainty is brought into my timing. Uncertainty is good if allowed to experience the fullness of life. It is not good if it creates fear, anger, blame, and negative emotions, so I work every closely with the energy of the uncertainty and change. Change is actually a part of me; it is an attribute of mine within time.

Dr. Modi: Wow, you are everywhere and in everything and everybody.

Master of Time: Yes, I am woven into everything.

Dr. Modi: Could that be why we say, "woven into time and space"?

Master of Time: Space is a being. There is space within your body, between the atoms; there is negative space in art, shadow space, and usually around an object to create art in harmony or disharmony. If you wish to choose disharmony, you will work with the negative space, and if you select harmony, you will work with the positive space. There are always two. I am woven within the space, depending on other activities within space itself as it evolves. That is my only relationship with space. Space rules time, and time makes it possible for the space to rule. I am not so different than Neptune in some ways; he also works with time.

Dr. Modi: Give us some examples of how we can use time properly.

Master of Time: The main way is for you to be aware of precise timing, which enough humans use beyond childhood. Humans have plenty of life experiences by the age of twenty, where they are aware of precise timing; especially athletes, they know about it, but regular people are unaware of precise time. So all you really need to do is to find a way to connect with that internal part of you. Remember I said that I am internal and external. The internal part is you; that respects precise timing and you can apply that when you wake up in the morning. Don't analyze it too much; just say I will be aware of the precise timing for each action today, and then you need to watch yourself. It takes some practice. Humans are schedule-bound; they are locked in time but have much better flexibility. However, if the person is too locked in to security, it might be from their higher self's point of view and it is better to lose the job they do not like. If they are starting to become aware of precise timing, they need to take responsibility for the effect of it. If they decided that morning that precise timing would be better to take their child to school, then they get caught up, with my help, in a traffic delay and get to work at ten o'clock, miss the most important meeting, get fired from their job, or suffer humiliation. These are all effects that will come when you ask for a sense of precise timing, then you can expand on that.

Be aware of the timing of your body when you need to eat and sleep. I am very good at shaking people out of their automatic behavior. People need to examine their own automatic behavior and ask me, little by little, to give some example of precise timing. If you are in a gathering, you might choose to go to the ladies' room at a particular time, meet someone else there, and have a particular conversation on the way out, when you will meet another person. But you might also miss the main presentation of somebody important when you are at the gathering.

I am very busy, I am stretched into a million, billion bits of Light. I am like the tiniest computer, and the speed with which people can access the information is also part of my timing. For you to use this in a very personal, day-to-day way, which is the only way change of evolution in humanity can happen, is your decision from one minute to the other. The timing how your body will receive either one of these, and what your body really needs, will help you to get in touch with the timing of your internal organs, the internal system that is accommodating you, and what you need to do for the spiritual pursuit of your life's purpose.

People do not realize how interwoven I am with them. It is shocking when they realize how interwoven I am with every single movement of their life. They are moving from movement to movement thinking there is continuity, but the continuity changes based on priority and emotional focus. I am like the most refined of musicians with the most subtle sound.

All the animals, insects, elementals, minerals, people, plants, and life forms hold the planet together. All of these are energy forms with different rules of timing. They say the dog lives seven years for each human year; this is a timing of a life form that accompanies humans through all of their lives. A dog can be man's best friend. The dog and other animals are the connection to pure energy and assist the humans, who are the more evolved life form on Earth; to live and survive because they give them a different time frame related to love that keeps them alive. They are more pure to their truth and themselves than the more complex humans. There is not so much ground for interference for them. They are telepathic; that is why they do not need to speak. Humans need to speak as part of evolution to close down certain abilities and develop others. Once the other abilities have been developed, then the abilities will be opened up and they will not have such an influence.

Dr. Modi: Maybe it is time to open up these psychic abilities for humans.

Master of Time: Whatever you do is your understanding of the correct timing. Your constant worrying about memory is an attempt to recognize the perfect timing of what you are worrying about. The way in which to correct it involves a more elaborate consciousness. You need to go into the uncertainty, to ask for some assistance in understanding the larger purpose, which might bring in more uncertainty. There is a great need for people to embrace the uncertainty, so that the correct timing can take effect and the consciousness will understand. There is a progression here. I work with the progression of evolution, which on Earth is timing. There is a possibility, based on the structure of the way energy operates on Earth with all the life forces on it, that is a confluence and coming together of all the energies from one movement to another.

The marketplace this person is studying is a foreign currency market and those people who are working in the stock market are very aware. Their hand is almost on the pulse of the change of attitude and emotions. A large amount – almost more than 50 percent – of the material to study is about the psychological impression that affects the market. It is not so much what actually is happening, because they cannot always know. But there is a psychological perception that is related to fear and greed. All this is part of the commonality of every living being on the planet.

Attempts by plants, rocks, and animals, which are pure and more innocent, have a different time frame; they balance out the more crazed humans. We use the word "crazed" with discretion. It is the desperation in the humans' general timing to hold on to the past and control the future, neither of which is possible because the change moves on. The "March of Time" the famous phrase used during the Second World War, was the expression of my true development within the life form. It is always put out there, but people do not get the expansion of it. The "March of Time" and the evolution of various elements with their own timing all come together in harmony, but not in consciousness. Some people are conscious of parts of it, but if you can create a much greater understanding, there will be a ripple effect to all the levels of beings on the planet to where they can expect it as whenever you say in prayer, "Whatever is necessary." This is a very important comment that you can make.

Your prayers are greatly directed by your higher self and by humanity, as one consciousness of six-plus billion humans on the planet. There is a consolidation and a change from movement to movement on all levels. They are based on the need for security, the uncertainty principle, and creativity. Creativity is full of uncertainty. At the higher level, hope is denying the full acceptance of uncertainty, so it needs to be given up. There are different levels of openings. This is why you activate the tubes and the connecting cords; when you are praying, it is the intention to ask, and the next step is to bring in the golden Light, which is the love that contains everything everyone needs: that unique love coming through the connections everyone has, and that uniqueness is part of God. That will expand and the entire being of humanity will change, and there are arms, legs, and nuclei within groupings of consciousness within the entire body of humanity. This is the fractal development where each part reflects the whole and the evolving whole of God reflects the change in each part.

Congratulations to you for taking on this work. Your dissatisfaction is a gift to humanity; it is a motivation factor. If you can see how your work is changing humanity, you will be overwhelmed and distracted. You have the experience of no distraction in Atlantis. There are people all over who are ready to do the work that you are instigating. You do not even have to know that; you just need to keep doing your work. Occasionally, you will get a pat on the back.

Dr. Modi: Many people are experiencing that time is speeding up. Is it because the vibrations are rising?

Master of Time: Yes, time is speeding up because of the marriage of internal and external vibrations. I am at the pulse of evolution. It is like touching the pulse of a patient to know how the heart is beating. So if you watch what I am doing, you will have a better understanding, and the more you understand, the more you will get answers to what it means. If you do not get the answers right away, you will find someone to ask in the proper time. There is a part of you that knows everything; that is why we have limited your other abilities. The time when you wanted to dance, you were able to do it. Anything else you really want to do, we will give you time to do it. We are your always present, available servants.

Dr. Modi: [Overwhelmed] Oh, not a servant, a good friend, and thank you from the bottom of my heart. Tell me, how did you affect this person at different times?

Master of Time: When she was eight, she wanted her body to grow big so she could get away from her oppressive family by fifteen. So her body grew in normal progression but her life experience forced her ahead in class in school, so she was finally two years ahead in her age group and could finish school by fifteen. In real life, she finished high school six months after her sixteenth birthday and was able to leave home at seventeen. It was pretty close, based on what was possible within culture and society, and she had to educate herself.

I can give many examples where I positively worked with her. I helped her get the jobs she needed, have the courage to give up things quickly, and to walk out the door with just the clothes she wore. Her sense of destiny is very strong and we helped her with that. We helped her when an older man sat by her at a party and told her she had a very unusual future and would have a difficult time. We arranged the timing so they could meet, and she never forgot that.

In a negative sense, she did not listen to our positive guidance, because we are always trying to help everyone with the opportunity to move ahead and fulfill their destiny. Fulfillment of your destiny will help with our purpose, which is to evolve all life forms to a greater consciousness for God. You should examine the "pleasure" sometimes.

Dr. Modi: Is there a master for pleasure, too?

Master of Time: Yes, we all work together. We are like filters and we see when a person is ready to accept a certain amount. We work with timing. We create a situation where they might enjoy eating something that gave them pleasure before they have a dangerous situation they might be hesitant to accept. Going back to this person, there were times when she had a fear of making money successfully because she was afraid she would abuse it. She was afraid of her own power because of its misuse in other lives.

Dr. Modi: How did you affect me or help me?

Master of Time: I motivated you to "hang in there," which is an expression of time. You hung in there and kept going, and you certainly chose a variety of lives. You chose a series of lives that were related to what was happening on the planet, in terms of time. We are talking about all your lives, since they are building up in a linear time. It is building your warrior energy and developing tolerance of suffering. Then you built in another life to balance it. It is necessary to have that warrior experience to know that no matter how violent death is, there is another chance. I helped you throughout all your lives to see that even if you ended in a terrible way, you would be back again because I am part of eternal time as well as the temporal time. The Earth time, the linear time, has a beginning, middle, and end. In eternal time, there is no beginning and no end, only the accumulation of understanding of experience.

Dr. Modi: In my prayers, when I ask for all the soul parts which we lost from the beginning of our existence, I am thinking soul parts from all our lives and also between lives from the beginning of the creation of our soul. Does it happen?

Master of Time: Yes, it happens in the linear time, but in the non-linear time, or eternal time, it simply adds the experience and evolution of the soul because the soul is eternal.

In this life, I helped you in staying true to your purpose. At each movement, when you have to make a choice, you are given time to make the decision that will accommodate your real purpose. I watched very carefully so you would not make a hasty decision. With all the decisions you made that would affect your life as we move from past to future, there is a time to make a choice, such as to move from India to America, and now to move from Ohio. These are timings that are important and you do not always know why. Part of it is that it is not necessary to know.

Dr. Modi: Why?

Master of Time: This way, you have faith in your purpose, which is not always apparent until after the fact, but at the time, you do not know. We give you an opportunity to exercise your whole being in the decision that you make. I am part of every decision you make in your life, even about when to speak to someone. You have a great sense of timing and appropriate respect for the order of things. We have given you a great respect for the order of things. If something is out of order, you usually will notice it. You may not immediately comment on it, but you will eventually take care of it. So we give you time.

Dr. Modi: How can we humans get your guidance or work with you in the future?

Master of Time: As we spoke earlier, it is to be aware that "what you ask, so shall you receive." There is also another angle of it; it is to be "careful what you ask for." You need to ask carefully, and if you are aware of timing, then you will not be disturbed if things do not seem to happen in time and you will not be impatient. Sometimes it is necessary to act on the spot. People need to focus periodically on the correct timing. Just say, "I need to understand the correct timing" and do not say any more. When you feel relaxed about a decision, then you are in the right timing.

You can add in your protection prayers of difference between wanting something and asking for it in prayer. People need to understand that they need to ask what is the best thing for them so they can achieve their life purpose. The most important thing is to respect the timing of their life purpose and how their life purpose reveals itself to them. The respect for the timing of one's personal development is important. If you evolve personally, you need to respect the right timing for your code. You will recognize what is yours as it comes your way, because people can use the wrong timing when they are in a hurry. Do not go too slow or too fast; wait for the right movement and do not be in a hurry. People should have trust in the correct timing once they ask for their highest good. Everyone is guided by the heavenly beings if they allow it.

Dr. Modi: Yes, I feel that, too, especially during a session. I seem to say just the right thing or ask the right question. Most of the time, it seems like my own thoughts. Occasionally, I say something and then wonder how I knew this, and then I know I am being guided.

Maser of Time: Yes! We are a part of you all; we are woven into you. Every human body and consciousness is a genius robot of eternal life. But it is the robot – the body – that is evolving. It is the body that has all these wirings and I am just one of the wires. You have many golden cords going from heaven to different parts of your upper body. They contain different memories, instructions, and evolutionary programs. From various points in heaven, Light will be put in these cords from different sources, whatever you need. In most cases, it will be a being; in others, it can be a connection to the Akashic record, which is also a being. It depends on what you need at any point and in which part of the body you need it. Everything is directed by the mind. There are different levels of understanding that comes from different nadirs, kundalini, meridians, and chakras in different parts of your body, like fingertips. This is how the human body is evolving. If you and other spiritual people's bodies are evolved, they will evolve all the human beings.

In your case, it has been done very specifically with you, to constantly help with balance, because you and this person are different individuals and you are still working with a similar human framework, a similar human body. There is some leeway, but about 88 percent is confluence among all human bodies. That is pretty brave and almost perfect. That makes it possible for the design of the body evolving and developing. As people become more conscious, each one will have a different understanding of their link to eternity, to God, and to the Light, and that they are one with all, even though they are separate and unique.

Dr. Modi: Thank you, Master of Time, for the wonderful understanding about time.

Master of Time: You are welcome.

Master of Minerals

Patient: I see a master of minerals. It is androgynous; a he
and she both, and changes back and forth. It is dressed
in colors like a rainbow because minerals are multicol-
ored. I see when gasoline and oil mix together, they have
a rainbow effect and that is what it is wearing. I am also
seeing red earth of Sedona, Arizona, black sand, and different types of minerals, rocks, and semiprecious stones
of various colors. They are all containers of Light. The
master has a hat on, but I cannot describe the clothes. They
keep on changing colors. Now I see that it has a jacket
and pants, and the woman is wearing a skirt and jacket.
They look like two separate beings, a man and a woman,
and then they become one. When the Light changes, the
energy also changes. All this has to do with the Light. All
the minerals hold Light for us and are of different qualities
and types. Minerals are the happy, shiny, beautiful jewels
that make people happy. They balance the amount of the
Light that comes on Earth, like the white and black sand.
They create the balance. I think the master is speaking
through me.

Master of Minerals: That is true. I am giving the information. We have a lot of Light. We love the beauty and we
love the clothes that we are wearing now. We can wear
different types of clothes like the rainbow. We can be a
rainbow. We do not have to have a form. We are the pot of
gold at the end of the rainbow. It is a legend. They make
people happy. Gold, silver, diamonds, and all the other
jewels have Light in them and they bring joy to people.
They are linked to eternity in the Light. People have a
positive effect when they wear them. If the person mis-
uses the energy, it darkens. You can misuse these minerals
and gems and bring dark energy by showing off, making a
bargain that can be detrimental to the other person, making
false promises, stealing them from others, and all the
negative ways people operate. They are driven by greed,

which attracts the demons and dark energy toward them, and our energy, the Light, gets darkened. Then we shut our Light off, because out of Light comes the creativity. The demonic energy is not creative. That is a waste of energy for us, so we close out our Light. We are always there in case the person decides to change. The moment they look at us with innocence, pleasure, and beauty, we put the Light in them. It is only the Light that recognizes the beauty. In duality, there is a matching effect between them. We become dark. That does not mean that we allow any negativity into us. We just close our Light, because there is no reflection and no possibility.

Minerals are there through all the layers of Earth, up to the core, full of Light. All the elementals are filled with the Light and help maintain the balance of Light on the Earth. We are all filled with love and Light, but we are dependent on humans for our evolution. We want to help them but they have to notice us. We are available. We are aware of the entire balance of energy on the planet and there are others working on it, too. We hold the vision of life and beauty, and a sense of permanence and eternity because we live longer, almost forever. We may change into other minerals but we do not disappear. We raise the level of the ocean floor and we also go into hibernation. We stretch time.

Earth is made up of us. There is also organic material in Earth; the Earth is complex. Gems created by humans also have the Light in them because the intention is there, and depending on their intention, there will be more or less Light. Swarovski crystals are wonderful. They have a lot of Light. Even the plastic sparkles kids use have light, but they do not last as long as we do. They do not have full consciousness, but they certainly have the Light. It depends on the belief system of the person. They might think of us while looking at the created gems, then we can come through, because the power of intention of humans is enormous. It is the power of God. It has to be pure intention. The time helps because the time gives the intensity. You can ask us for the help with your intent. None of the humans have been able to create artificial minerals or gems that have all the properties of the real ones. We have the history of the world within us, so people who create artificial gems should pray for infusing the Light to activate them.

If you look at the artificial pearl, there is no consciousness in it, while real pearls have the consciousness and the Light. We are balancing the Earth. We also filter water, like in the shores of the river.

When humans use gold, silver, or gems, and if they are aware of their beauty and use them for competition, it can be beneficial for them. If they use them to show off, then it will be less beneficial. Shapes of jewelry and stones are also important.

This person does not wear much jewelry, except for a gold chain with a healing energy, which helped her with throat problems to some extent. When people wear different colored stones in jewelry, it makes them feel happy. People have a similar response when they wear beautiful clothes with lots of sparkles.

Master of Akashic Libraries

During a session, one of an Archangel, through a hypnotized patient, suggested that I needed to speak to the master of Akashic records in heaven, and also do the cleansing of them. So during a session with a patient under hypnosis, I asked him to look at the Akashic libraries in heaven and describe what he saw. He described them as follows:

- *"I am looking at an Akashic library building, which appears extremely tall, and there are multitudes of shelves stacked with books. Everything is etheric here, made up of*

Light. Nothing is solid. It feels like the whole building and everything in it is floating in space. I get a sense of being soft, quiet, and peaceful from it. Initially, it looks like everything is of clear Light, but when I focus at it, then the pages of the books become more solid.

"There are Light beings who are just floating around and helping beings who come into the library. Books can have the flowing aspects of a life, whether it was a dark life or light, and has the energy of that life. As I pay attention, there are two Light beings on each side of me, ready to help.

"I am getting the understanding that there is one huge etheric library for all of creation. All the libraries are connected to all creation and all beings. But depending upon what you are looking for and whether you are allowed to have access, the only part of the library you see is what you need out of this one huge library.

"As I look at the building of the Akashic library for all of creation from the outside, it looks like a combination of different architecture. Some parts appear to be kind of newer, made of concrete and extremely tall, while others are more gothic in appearance. It seems to have a different appearance across time and space. It seems to be extremely tall and etheric building. It is like a huge complex with different buildings with different architecture through time and space, all interconnected through different pathways. One seems to be closest to the most recent time and seems to be an extremely massive concrete structure, many stories tall. I am getting that there are also Akashic Record libraries for animals and all the other beings.

"There is one section that looks like just blocks on top of each other. It is a library for the time before architecture. There are very ancient and primitive records here. I see there are libraries where there are books of ancient history. The books are arranged as the timeline of activity and development of humanity on the Earth. It is like the levels of construction, and the capability seems to be

reflected in the building. Each life that we have can be a whole separate volume and they could be in different buildings, based on different lives of the soul.

"I even get that there is a section where there is no building and the library is not housed in the building but it is kind of floating in midair. The books are there and you can see the etheric outlines of the books. Whatever it is you want to see, it will appear.

"Now I am looking at the Akashic library for the planet Venus. It is very tall, story after story, reaching deep into upper space. It is a kind of light gray color. I am also seeing dark beings flying around Planet Venus.

"As I look at the Akashic library for our Sun, it looks like it is made up of pure golden Light; very, very tall, thick, large, and cathedral type, illuminating and giving off Light. I am inside now. It feels like everything is on fire, not a hot fire; it feels like a cool and controlled fire. It is a blaze for the perception of the fire. As I look around, I see books with the bright golden hue. Here, there is no ceiling; it is just open on the top into space, giving off Light. Here, there is the history of the Sun, its birth, evolution, and growth. I feel that the building is representative of history of the souls of the Sun. It has a consciousness and it is alive. Even when the Sun has large solar rays, which explode at times, it can lose its soul parts by this action.

"Now I am looking at the planet Saturn. It is a huge planet. I can see its Akashic building. Saturn and all the other planets and their Akashic libraries have the magnetic sheets around them. There are pathways to get to others by intention. When we have intent to visit other planetary libraries, it creates a portal. They do not exist till we have the intention to experience it. Similarly the Akashic libraries are not in solid form till somebody inquires, then it becomes solid enough to recognize and experience it. I am having trouble in finding the Akashic library for Saturn. It is really a massive structure but is almost invisible. It is illusional but has enough of the solid

aspect so you can see it. It is very etheric, massive, holo-graphic and light gray.

"As I look at moon, it appears a little bit lighter. It is kind of vanilla in color, not white. It is a building with big rectangular blocks. The place does not feel pleasant and there are dark clouds circling around the building and the doorways. It seems like there are black witches flying around the buildings. I can see a dark band around the moon like a dark atmosphere.

"Now I am looking at the planet Neptune and it looks pretty clean and lighted. As I look at its Akashic library it looks like a very ancient building. It seems very light from the bottom of the library, almost white but as you go closer to the top, it changes into light gray. It is not black. It is long, rectangular and has large stone beams. It is a two tone building.

"It looks like all the Akashic libraries have different levels of darkness except for the Sun and Moon, and Ura-nus appear to be darker than the others."

Dr. Modi: Can I speak to the master of the Akashic libraries?
Master of Akashic Libraries: I am here. I am the master of the Akashic libraries for all of creation.
Dr. Modi: Please tell us about you and the Akashic libraries.
Master of Akashic Libraries: Akashic libraries are the history of God and creation, as you know. It is a complete history of everyone, everything, every event, plan, and the structure. They are records of life and creation. They are an energetic representation of consciousness, intention, and different realities. Not just as a record, but as a tool to teach, to inspire, and to motivate. It is as conscious as part of creation.

The energy of the Akashic library is conscious of beings and places that are imprinted upon the mind of God. There is no real difference between the consciousness and the mind of God, although to you they appear separate and different. Consciousness of all things and all beings is an extension of the consciousness of God. The Akashic library simply allows the imprinting of experience of that consciousness onto the consciousness of God, yet there is no separation between them as if you call up that conscious experience from the mind of God. It appears to you as a separate and real thing when, in fact, there is no separation.

Dr. Modi: How are these Akashic records written or created?

Master of Akashic Libraries: It is created by the consciousness of God and the individual beings, because there is no separation. Every experience is simply a different reality of that consciousness, which is connected to the mind of God. So it does not have to be written; it already exists.

Dr. Modi: Can you explain it please?

Master of Akashic Libraries: When you seek to understand something from the Akashic, you are really reading the imprinted experience of the person, place, or a thing that already exists in consciousness and the mind of God. It is imprinted at the moment it occurs. It is energetic, instantaneous, and there is no writing; there is no book, no separation, and no time of any kind. It is all one transaction. The experience, the event, the knowledge, and the transcription are all the same. At the very movement of the experience, the record is formed and is there forever.

There is no separation, no space, and no time. It is all now. Everywhere, everything, everyone, every intention, every action, every behavior, and every event is a life force. There is no separation and no experience because it happens all at the same time. It is a record because you seek a record, but it is simply a recording of the consciousness of the mind of God.

It is like a creative energy, creating itself, recording itself, knowing itself, because it is itself. There is only one self, the self of God, because there is no separation. There is really no one to experience it.

Dr. Modi: Are there different masters for various Akashic libraries?

Master of Akashic Libraries: There are, as you seek for one.

Dr. Modi: What is your job as a master of Akashic library?

Master of Akashic Libraries: I am here because you asked me to be here. I do not have a job. I am essentially a concentrated part of God. Masters are really an accumulation of energy, Light, and knowledge that are needed at a given movement to respond to a specific request; from my perspective, there is really nothing to do. Everything is automatically done. It does not need a maintenance group. It happens instantaneously. Truth is truth; a book is a book. There is nothing else to do. The Akashic library reflects the experience and the existence of the events. There is nothing to repair, nothing to change, and nothing to correct.

Dr. Modi: Do we need to cleanse them from time to time?

Master of Akashic Libraries: Akashic records appear exactly the way events occur; whether Light or dark flows through, Akashic records represent that reality. It is as dark as there was darkness in that life; if it was Light, there is Light. Cleaning the Akashic function is cleaning of the occurrences, the persons, and the planets. Cleanse the person, they both become Lighter. Cleanse the planet, both the planet and the Akashic libraries for it become Lighter. The Akashic represent that which was and is. Clean up what feeds the Akashic library and the Akashic book is clear.

Dr. Modi: One time, archangels suggested that sometimes I should also cleanse the Akashic libraries

Master of Akashic Libraries: Yes, it is time; just remember that just clearing the Akashic will not clear the planet.

Dr. Modi: When psychics give information about people, they are tapping the information from the Akashic library, right?

Master of the Akashic Libraries: Some do and some don't. It really depends on what they are listening to. They can listen to the dark being or the Light being.

Dr. Modi: So when we want to tap information from the Akashic records or a Light being, what are the different ways?

Master of the Akashic Libraries: Prayers, meditation, request, and intention are all the same. They all come from the same and go back to the same.

Dr. Modi: How does it work? When we want to get information, we get connected to that part of the Akashic library?

Master of the Akashic Libraries: You are already connected to all things, including Akashic records. You are simply accessing what you already have, what you already are. You are connected as part of the One; there is no division and no separation. The only thing that keeps you from accessing it fully and completely is yourself. In the mind of God, you are not separate; you are simply a part of "All that is." You are connected permanently to the Akashic, to God, to everyone and everything. You are not only a creation; you are the creation. You are a manifestation of the mind because none of you are separate.

Dr. Modi: So we need to pray and ask for connections with the Akashic records to be opened up, and have the intention to get the information, and that will help?

Master of the Akashic Libraries: There are different elements of intention for requesting. There are those whose intentions are clear, powerful, and truthful, and there are those who are less than that. There are those who have full access and do not know it. There are those who are not quiet enough, though they are connected to the mind of God who is speaking, but in the chaos, they cannot hear God. The separation is simply a way for you and others to realize what already exists and to be quiet enough to hear that it is there.

Dr. Modi: What can stop us from accessing the information from the Akashic libraries?

Master of Akashic Libraries: All the ugly emotions piling on top of others, such as anger, hate, jealously, revenge, etc. Being surrounded by the darkness makes it more difficult to access and experience the Light or just be in the Light. God really did not leave you. He remains the same, but a barrier has been erected by the negative thoughts, intentions, behaviors, denial, fears, deceit, and anger. Connections are still there but they are corroded. Continuing to carry those separated aspects opens you up for the influence beyond yourself that further separates you because of the darkness. After a while, it gets darker and darker and it becomes difficult to access the Light.

You must evolve back from where you came, to what it is you are. Pray for everyone, everything, and for all of creation. Prayers are important, powerful, and available, and they are a ticket back to what you were in the beginning. They peel off the accumulation of the darkness in time. All beings, all things, all places deserve the Light of God. I am always available, Akashic is always available, and God is always available.

Cleansing of the Akashic Libraries

Dr. Modi: We pray to God and request the angels to please put the magnetic sheets around the whole complex of Akashic records for all of creation and all the masters, angels, and other heavenly beings who help there. Turn the switch of the magnetic sheets to the eject sign and expel all the foreign entities, dark shields, dark devices, dark connections, dark energy, and dark emotions. Collect them in the net of light, transform them, and take the energy to heaven, please. Fill the Akashic libraries for all of creation and everything in them and everybody who works there or goes there to use the libraries with the Light.

Patient: I see some dark energy from the emotions, feelings, actions, and behaviors is being removed from everywhere, but the history and events are still there. I do not see any dark entities here; they may be outside. When the dark events are recorded, the darkness of that event bleeds through; it is reflected in the Akashic records.

As I look at the Akashic libraries for Earth before cleansing with magnetic sheets, they appeared slightly darker and gloomier. They are about 15 to 20 percent brighter than before. The memories are still there; you feel them, recognize and own them, but do not have to experience darkness in them. It is like being forgiven.

Now I am looking at the Akashic library for the moon. Before, it was pasty, blocky, and dark beings were flying around it outside. Now the Akashic libraries are brighter and dark beings that were flying around the moon and the library are not there anymore. The same is true about the Akashic libraries all over creation. They were slightly grayish before and became brighter after the cleansing

Dr. Modi: We pray to God to please flood all the Akashic libraries for all of creation with the crystalline white Light and allow it to cleanse, heal, and remove everything that is left over. Collect them in the net of Light and transform them into the Light. Shield all of them with the triple compression chamber of crystalline Light, mirror shields, and violet shield.

Patient: I saw golden Light infusing through all the Akashic libraries and everything and everybody in them. I also saw bubbles of the triple compression chamber of crystalline Light around every book, shelf, being, and all over the building.

Dr. Modi: We pray to God to please flood all the Akashic libraries throughout creation with the violet liquid fire and let it blaze into violet flame and transform everything.

Patient: I saw all the Akashic libraries for all of creation being infused with the violet flame and shielded with the triple compression chambers of the crystalline white Light all around them.

Dr. Modi: We pray to God to please open every soul's connecting cord to you and to the Akashic libraries. Cleanse, heal, and fill them with the Light and shield them with the triple compression chambers of crystalline white Light inside and outside. I request every person's higher self, guides, and angels to cleanse, heal, protect, and guide them.

Patient: As you were praying, I felt being flooded with the crystalline, white Light. This time the connecting cord was golden and very ornately carved and filled with the golden Light. It was going to a very large etheric chamber that encases the entire Akashic library for all of creation. It is completely available through this one cord that connects not to a building but to an energy around the entire Akashic library for all of creation. Just ask and it is there.

Chapter 16

INCARNATING ON OTHER PLANETS

Some of my hypnotized patients have regressed back to a life on another planet leading to the source of their symptoms. They give a detailed description about the life on that planet, such as the living conditions, the culture, society, and purpose of life, and how it all impacts their current life and causes different symptoms for them.

Reasons for Incarnating on Other Planets

Heavenly beings, through my hypnotized patients, state that every human being has lived on other planets, not just one life, but hundreds of lives, so that their experience in the universe can be more rounded and not focused exclusively on one race of a planet. A particular soul may relate to a given race and to a particular aspect of that race more, but that soul does not concentrate exclusively on that planet nor does it focus exclusively on that race. It incarnates on other planets and it works on different problems during its time in the universe. It is as if you have to round out the character and not just focus on the narrow aspect. This is in keeping with God's plan to develop an all-around appreciation and understanding of each part of God.

We incarnate on many planets, and there is no planet where we cannot incarnate even though the life may not be a human life. During the life span of the universe, every planet, every celestial body, every bit of matter, and practically every soul in all the universes and in all the dimensions evolve. There is a progression that even as the individual soul evolves, so does each of the universes because they move at the same time and their relative spacing stays about the same.

As we evolve and develop, we can not only incarnate in our universe, but we can also incarnate in a universe that is close to our own, either just above, below, or on either side of our universe. We cannot go to a universe that is far away. We may be able to incarnate two levels above or below, but that is rare. If the individual soul develops more rapidly than average, then it will change the universe in which it is at home, or if a soul goes through a really bad streak of negative lives, then it can go down to the lower universes, being pulled down by those bad lives. Generally, the soul yields to arrogance and pride and lays itself open to satanic influences, so it is pushed lower by that contact.

Not only do we choose positive lives, we also choose negative lives for a well-rounded spiritual development. If we can overcome the negativity, we can make tremendous progress in one lifetime. The negative lives offer a tremendous opportunity for advancement because, by avoiding negative choices and by making positive choices, we advance dramatically. We can take a great leap in our spiritual development and evolve very rapidly. The negative lives can be a great spiritual gift. Of course, it is also a real spiritual challenge and many times people do not succeed, but we must have this balanced experience. We cannot develop our part of God without fighting our way through these negative lives. The main objective is the development of our part of God, which is our soul. We are doing the actual work in the universe, and unless that work is done, our part of God that is our soul cannot and will not develop.

Karma is an ancient concept that has to do with the consequences of our present or past actions in the current or future lives, a negative or positive "payback." It does not just work negatively; it can also be positive. We can develop positive karma in the negative life when we make a positive choice. A positive choice will earn five times as much positive karma as a negative choice builds negative karma.

The primary reason we plan to incarnate on different planets is to resolve some type of problem in a different culture, a different body, and with different challenges. We may have the same challenge occurring in five different lifetimes, in five different races, and on five different planets. Each alien race has a different physiological structure, a different social structure, and a different mindset. Overcoming a special problem in each of the lives on different planets builds a lot more character, and we get a well-balanced and faster development than when overcoming a problem in just one life, on one planet, and in one species. So we incarnate on different planets, in different bodies and cultures primarily for a well-rounded development to gain a real understanding of what it is that God is dealing with.

The expression of the spirit in the universe is the function of the vibration of the soul. As we incarnate on different planets, it modifies the vibration rate we are expressing in that physical body. Sometimes people incarnate on different planets and in different bodies simply to experience the vibration shift in the body to either a slightly higher or slightly lower level. There is a concept of balance and keeping things in perspective. When we incarnate on a planet that has a lower vibration rate, we gain positive karma as we help to bring up the vibrations of those around us. Going to a planet with a higher vibration rate brings with it a small negative karma by pulling down the vibration rate of that planet a bit. It is a cooperative venture. We get pulled forward when we go to a higher vibration planet and when we go to a lower vibration planet we get pulled backward slightly. In both cases, by keeping them in balance, it increases the strength of our vibrations. The vibrations are stronger and higher, just not more frequent and closer together.

Earth is a third or fourth-generation planet and was not ready to inhabit for a long, long time. So most of us incarnated on many different planets in a variety of physical forms before we came to Earth as human beings. As a result, we have lived a vast majority of our lives on other planets before and even lived some lives elsewhere after the Earth was ready to inhabit. At this stage, we mostly incarnate on Earth, but also on other planets from time to time. Human life has existed on Earth for only three and a half million years, but we existed before, for billions of years, and we have lived on different planets more lives than we have lived on Earth. As a matter of fact, everybody and everything on Earth existed somewhere else before.

In heaven, before incarnation, we plan all the details of the life, such as what planet, in what culture, with whom, for what reasons, and in which time. It is really a group decision for the most developed souls. If the soul is less developed and is not a part of a group, it frequently will want to incarnate on its own planet. If it chooses to incarnate on a different planet, people tend to reach down and pull them up, but it is a difficult climb.

Sometimes we incarnate on another planet to have a particular existence with a particular soul, in a particular body. We make those decisions in heaven before incarnating, such as what planet we will incarnate on, with which group of souls, and for what experience. Sometimes we incarnate on a lower planet to be a spiritual teacher to spread the spirituality, and we set up a plan to live it out. It is very seldom that a life is completely lived out as planned, because of the demonic influences and frailties of human existence.

There are individual vibrations. Sometimes an individual will make an irrational decision even in the Light (heaven), not really for any good reason, and sometimes these decisions are divinely inspired. According to heavenly beings, we can incarnate on any type of planet, from a very large gas planet to a very small, dense, rocky planet. The incarnation does not depend on the physical state of the planet and it can be anywhere. Basically, there are two main types of planets: the gas planets and the rocky planets. Then there are individual variations, depending upon amounts of fluid, the amount of dry land, and the gases there. The carbon-oxygen life forms that we have here on Earth are not the only possible choice. There are three primary patterns: carbon and fluorine, silicon and oxygen, and silicon and fluorine. There are two possible elements and three reactors with them. So we have multiple choices for the life form.

Life can be carbon-based or silicon-based. Silicon-based races tend to be slower, so life is not lived as rapidly and generally it is more limited and not as flexible. The rate at which life is lived is slower because silicon undergoes chemical reactions at a slower rate than carbon-based life forms do. The fraction of the life that is lived per unit of time is lower. Instead of having oxygen for respiration, it is possible that fluorine and chlorine could also be used.

There are also planets that are mostly water. This happens when the planet has a rocky core. There is some land on this planet, but the souls lived and evolved in the sea. Their first exploration out was to go out of the water and onto the land.

We may specialize in Earth life and can also incarnate on other planets in between. It depends on which planet offers the conditions for life and the events that we need for our next step in our spiritual growth. Many of my patients have regressed to a life on another planet and have given a coherent and detailed description about life on that planet, the living conditions, culture, society, purpose of life, and how it has impacted their current life and caused different symptoms for them.

Following are some of the amazing past lives on other planets described by my patients as the source of their symptoms.

I am A Spiritual Teacher on Another Planet

One of the patients recalled a life on a swampy planet, which was a source of his muscle weakness, joint problems, and memory blocks. He looked humanoid, but like an upright lizard. He incarnated on that planet as a spiritual leader to spread spirituality. There, people were not very spiritual:

* *"My soul is coming from heaven to the planet Algarve, and entering into the womb. It is about 50,000 BC in Earth time. When my body is born, it looks grayish at birth and gets greener. Our people look whitish green; that is, the backs of our arms, our legs, and our backs tend to be green while the rest is a lighter kind of a smoky white. It reminds me more of a frog. I am a male and am able to crawl right after birth, almost looking like a frog with a wide body. There is a big change between the infants and adults. The body lengthens and changes its orientation.*

  "I see my parents as being of the same size, which is about four feet nine inches tall, and they look like lizards. Their heads are set down and there is not much of a neck; it is more like a skinny part of the body and it tilts forward. The jaws are longer, like those of horses or dogs. Their eyes bulge and there is a covering that goes over the eyes like skin flaps sticking out. There is no nose, just holes. The arms are much slimmer than a child's body. The children remind me of a frog while their parents remind me of a lizard. The arms and shoulders are free swinging. The neck doesn't have many vertebrae and the shoulders are anchored to the vertebrae and are free moving. The hands have four fingers and a thumb, which are long and thin. The torso is slimmer. There are two legs, which are slightly bent. The legs come out a bit forward toward the knee and then back, and then have an ankle and a foot-pad with five toes. They have fuzz on their heads but no hair. The forearms are thin but the arms and upper parts of their legs are big and muscular. They move quickly. They wear clothes around their waists and live in dwelling units. The males and females live together and raise the children together.

"As a child, at the age of two, I am intrigued about God and angels. I develop very rapidly. My brain and head seem to develop first, and then intelligence develops. We are not born intelligent as humans are. We are primitive. As the brain and head grow, the head begins to drop forward and, from the shoulders up, gets longer, and then the rest of the body lengthens and we become upright beings. It is almost like the child is born as an animal and then develops into an intelligent being rapidly.

"I crawl on four limbs right after birth, then become upright and walk around by the age of three. As my head grows, while I am crawling, it drops forward and sometimes bumps on the floor. I go to school when I am two years old and still crawling. We are taught how to speak and communicate with others. There are streets for kids to crawl on while the adults walk beside the kids.

"At the age of three, my body elongates and I can walk, and I become a fully functioning being by about four years of age and become upright and can use my body properly. At the age of three, we are taught about physical movement in school when we can walk upright and become well-coordinated. We are taught math and sciences at the age of six and seven. At seven, we are like teenagers and are capable of reproduction. This planet has a wet and swampy environment and there is not too much land, so the beings compete for it. The society is organized into families with two parents and the children, and there is a religious structure.

"I am intensely preoccupied with God and religion. As I grow, I devote a lot of time studying it. At the age of sixteen, I finish school and enter into serious religious training. This is done mostly by reading, experiencing, and an occasional contact with a religious leader. Our whole race is kind of psychic. It is a survival trait that developed in our race very early because we had so many predators that we had to share information with each other and warn each other. So we learned to cooperate very early

and learned to communicate psychically. That is why there are no problems within the tribe. We train babies in languages because psychic ability does not develop until adulthood, after which the language drops away.

"I become a religious leader in a large community at the age of seventeen. There are not many religious leaders on the planet. They have organized religion but not many religious leaders to run the churches. Most people are tied up in ordinary, mundane activities. They have the psychic gift but they are not spiritual. After five years, I become a religious leader for a group of several cities and I am teaching about God.

"I get married at twenty-one and have several children. By the age of thirty-five I develop aches and pain in my joints. I have done a great deal of spiritual teaching to children and grown-ups, equally and successfully.

"I die just before my fortieth birthday of heart problems because the muscle fibers get soft and wear out and my body deteriorates rapidly. My last thoughts are that I sure liked being a spiritual leader. My spirit comes out of my head and follows the silver cord to the heaven. After cleansing and healing, I go to my life review with three heavenly beings.

"From heaven, I see that my problems with muscle weakness, joint problems, and memory blocks came from that life. I had a total of two incarnations on that planet. My life purpose was to gain the experience of instant spirituality and teaching it. My preoccupation with God and religion came from genetic modification done long ago on Earth by alien race two of group two."

There is a Hole in the Ocean Floor

One of my patients suffered from depression and anxiety for many years, even as a young teen, and felt that she was different from others. She had dreams that she could breathe under water. Also, when she was swimming, she would feel that if she tried just a little bit harder she could stay underwater in the ocean and survive for a long time. She had a great deal of fascination for the ocean and its creatures as a child, and later wanted to be a marine biologist. In school, she wrote an essay about farming in the ocean. Under hypnosis, she recalled a past life on another Earth-like planet a long time ago, which was responsible for some of her problems, as follows:

- *"It is like a light in the tunnel that opens up, and I can see the night sky with lots of stars in it. I am traveling through that tunnel and the stars. Now I am in a place that is very bright, and I am seeing people who look like humans, both males and females, but no children. They have white skin and brown hair. I am standing near an ocean and the sky is very bright and reddish orange, and the sun is setting. I look like a human male. I am about five feet ten inches tall and in my late twenties. I love the ocean and all the sea creatures. I live on the land and I can also live in the ocean for a long time, because there is a way I can take oxygen from the water.*

  "I am in the water and I am enthralled by the beauty of the plant life in the ocean and the creatures in it. For some reason, I am seeing the water going down into a deep, bottomless pit. I do not know where, and it does not seem to fill up. I feel alarmed. I go back to the land and tell other people about it but they do not share the same concern.

  "My home has three levels; one under the water and two above the water. The house is pyramid shaped and made of stone and glass. The steeples on the top of the build- ing help to draw in energy and inspiration from heaven. There is a research area on the top story. There are lots of drawings and designs. There is a computer-type device. On the second floor, there is a stove and other appliances. The lower part of my house has all the equipment I need to go into the ocean. We have electricity through solar

energy. Most of the houses here are triangular or pyra-mid shaped. Some of the windows are done in crystalline structures with many facets on them. It seems very dry here on the planet. There is no vegetation. People wear loose garments, like robes of different colors. Both male and female wear similar robes.

"*When I tell people about the hole in the ocean, they are concerned but not as concerned as I am. They are more fatalistic, because the planet is getting hotter and there is less food and it is becoming more difficult to survive. What we eat comes from the ocean. That is why there are no kids, because they do not see any future for the planet. Since living on the land of the planet is not working well, I am trying to find a way to move to the ocean, but that hole in the ocean alarms me. I realize things are much more serious and the whole planet can be destroyed. I want to discover ways we can live in the ocean when people are unable to live on the land, but now there is no hope of that either because of that hole in the ocean floor.*

"*I am concentrating all my energies to find a way to live in the ocean. I am in the exploration stage. I want to find a way to build dwellings in the ocean so we can live in the ocean if something happens to our planet. When I go in the water, I wear a special suit that allows me to pull nutrients from the ocean, and there is some respiration through the skin. It is much more sophisticated than a scuba diver's suit. I can live under water for weeks at a time. Everybody is feeling hopeless. Even I feel that there is not enough time. I'm beginning to feel depressed. I do not see a way out. There is no escape, so I go into the ocean. I fill my lungs with fluid, which allows me to as-similate oxygen so I can breathe under water. There is a membrane between the two fluids, the ocean and the lung fluids. The membrane is part of the suit, which also has fins so I can travel long distances under water. I go in the water and live there, but occasionally I have to come back to land.*

"*I am very depressed about the whole situation. There is no hope. I sleep like the fish sleeps, by just resting against some plants. I feel I can communicate with some of the sea creatures. I feel at home with them. I go to see that hole in the ocean from time to time. I get the impression that it is a hole between the two dimensions and things are draining out from the ocean. There are more and more disruptions, and strong currents in the ocean. I get alarmed. I go closer to the hole. It has become massive. I feel intense depression and anxiety but then there is a glimmer of hope that I might end up somewhere else in another dimension. As I go closer, I get sucked into the hole. I feel a horror that it is actually happening. My body is totally blown apart and it feels like all the molecules are scattered everywhere. Eventually, everything goes in that hole, including the whole planet.*

"*I go to heaven with this huge sense of depression and failure because I could not change things, even though it was a cataclysmic event. Cleansing and healing in heaven were hard, because the whole soul was shattered. Angels put me together and heal me very carefully, and then I go for a rest for a long time. Then I review my life with seven wise beings. I feel that the quality of heaven for this planet is slightly different as compared to heaven for Earth. I am asking them what my purpose was there because it was a futile life. They are saying that I did see beyond what other people saw, even though I was not able to prevent the cataclysm.*

"*From heaven, I see that I needed to learn the lesson of being more communicative and not to be centered on one single objective so that I do not see the whole picture. I see that many of my problems came from that life to the current life, such as a sense of futility, depression, anxiety, loneliness, feelings of being scattered and not being whole, different aches and pains in different parts of the body, and also a deep appreciation for the ocean life.*

"I also see from heaven that most people knew there was going to be a cataclysmic destruction because of severe global warming. That is why they were not having any children. When I was growing up with my parents, there were no schools, but we had a lot of stored knowledge in the largest library in the world, but in the form of computers, and everybody had access to them. We all had computers much more advanced than what we have now on our Earth. We communicated through language. Our parents helped us in learning. I always had an interest in science. I was always trying to understand why we could not live in water.

"We could not go outside the house because it was very hot and we would die, so we had underground tunnels to go from one place to another. If we had to go outside the house, we wore special suits that protected from the heat. The planet had been gradually becoming hotter for about a couple of hundred years, and it was at the point that people knew the planet was not going to last much longer. As a result, they were not having children anymore and the population was reduced tremendously.

"From heaven, I get the planet's name as "Old" or "Oel." It was an Earth-like planet but slightly smaller than Earth. People there looked like Earth humans. There was a combination of things that caused the planet to get this hot. At the beginning of the planet, there were few places where the climate was good. It had to do with how the landmasses were set up and the currents, and the tilt of the sun, and the rotation.

"People basically over-utilized what was there by using everything that was usable, like all the minerals, and not thinking about the future. Scientifically, they were very advanced. What I see from heaven is that they were trying to harness energy from the sun in a very unusual way, with a huge collecting device. It worked on a small scale, but on a larger scale it was a disaster. There were miscalculations, and as a result, the container blew up with such

force that it knocked the planet out of its orbit slightly, but enough to change the climate and make it hotter. This was hundreds of thousands of years ago.

"Before that, people on the planet were very advanced and had all the conveniences. Houses in that area were more spiritual shaped. They had points or steeples pointing toward heaven, which was due to your spiritual teachings, Dr. Modi. You were also on that planet as a spiritual teacher. People were not very spiritual and did not use prayers, meditation, or other spiritual practices. A lot of their time was used for higher pursuits of art, music, and science. I also see some demonic influence on the planet.

"There was a need for spiritual development because people knew that eventually the planet would be destroyed. You were teaching people how to pray, meditate, something similar to tai chi, how to get in touch with God and Light, and preparing people spiritually about what to do when the end comes. You died of old age before the planet was destroyed. I was a child when you died. You felt discouraged about trying to raise the spirituality of so many people in such a difficult situation.

"From heaven, I see that, with the shift of the orbit, there was the shift of an energy field, which caused some instability that slowly grew. Finally, the hole in the ocean got bigger and bigger and, as everything was being sucked in, the pressure built up and the whole planet exploded. The planet in the next dimension could not stand the pressure and disruption, and was also destroyed.

"When you asked that soul parts of everybody who was on those planets when they were destroyed be returned and integrated with whom they belong, I saw soul parts coming back to me and also to everybody who was there. Even the soul parts of both planets were brought back. I actually can see the solid surface of the planets and now the whole globes of both planets were recreated."

Later, heavenly beings through another patient confirmed that the incident did occur as described by that patient. The beings of that planet were trying the concept of free energy, that is, energy to be taken from space for literally no cost, and storing it. It sort of had a backward effect. They set up a condition in which a black hole was attracted. Heavenly beings explained that a black hole is generally created by the collapse of a massive star that is augmented by other material so that, when it collapses, the force of gravity is so great that no light or energy can escape from that space. It is small at the beginning but extremely heavy and very dense. Neutrons and protons are literally crushed into each other so the matter that we conceive of cannot exist.

Black holes are natural phenomenon, and happen in about every galaxy because of accumulation of matter in one spot. Once something super massive gets formed, and as more and more matter falls into it, it becomes compressed into a black hole.

There was a tiny black hole in that part of space and it ended up running into that planet after a disastrous accident there. The attraction of the black hole was due to an accident on that planet, but its existence was natural. Over time, the tremendous gravity of the little black hole pulled the matter of the whole planet into it, thus enlarging the black hole by a tiny fraction and completely obliterating not only the planet, but eventually devouring the whole solar system it was in. The planet was long gone by then.

On my request, angels brought back all the soul parts of every soul who was on all the planets of that solar system, and to each planet and the whole solar system, and integrated them with whom and where they belonged thus healing every soul, planet, and the whole solar system, and shielding them with the crystal shields.

Wow! I Look Like a Big Grasshopper

A patient recalled two lives as a grasshopper-type humanoid being, living on a rocky planet called Kyro. These lives were responsible for his depression, anxiety, and feelings of being disconnected from God:

- *"I am living on the planet Kyro as an insect-type be-ing, something like a grasshopper. I am a humanoid male with a head, two arms, two legs, and a body with the thickness of less than half the size of a normal hu-man body. I have two short, powerful back legs and two smaller front legs or arms. I have five claw-like fingers and toes on each hand and foot. I walk upright and I can also hop and fly short distances. My head looks some-thing like that of a grasshopper. I have two eyes, two tiny ears, a nose, a mouth, and two antennae coming out of the top of my head. My head is set on my shoulders and I don't have much of a neck. My body is wider than my head and it ends in a peak. The peak is actually the end of my wings, which can expand out to help me glide or take short flights.*

  "I do not need food or water to survive. We have a built-in battery-type internal organ that is located where human beings' internal organs would appear. I have a brain and I am an intelligent being. I am of average height, which is around three feet tall. I am two hundred and fifty years old, which makes me a teenager in human years. I live with my parents, three sisters, and four brothers. We live in tunnels and caves that are located in the rock formations of our planet. All families live in separate quarters. Our individu-al quarters are not divided. We live in a large room, but we use a part of it for sleeping and a part of it for socializing. We have no day or night on our planet.

  "We are friendly and harmonious with the other group of tall, thin, stick-like beings that live on our planet.

These beings also live in caves or under overhanging rocks. They are humanoids and we work and play with them in harmony. I go to school and learn about ways in which we can evacuate our planet in case of an enemy attack. I learn about preservation of our species and self-protection. I also learn about our small but upcoming space program. Later in life, I plan to be a designer of spaceships.

"Many of our people work in offices. We have medical facilities, schools, libraries, and business offices on our medium-sized planet. All these facilities are divided into separate compartments. We have a central government. Our leaders are made up equally between us [the grasshopper-like beings, and the tall, thin human-like beings]. We live on a very peaceful planet and we are taught respect for others in our schools. We are not spiritual beings; we are not aware of God and we have no churches. My father, a real estate agent, and my mother, an administrative secretary for the space program, take all of us to regular meetings to talk about harmony and the importance of support for one another.

"We have a limited range in our emotions. We have some fear, but it is more of an intellectual awareness. Our love is for everyone and we agree on most things. Basically, we are a one-minded race. We communicate telepathically. In tuning into each other's thoughts, we feel like we are all one. We have knowledge that there are other civilizations out in space. We would like to visit and learn new things from these civilizations. We are passive and have no desire to rule or fight with others.

"We begin to form relationships when we are around four hundred years old. A male takes a female and they remain together for the rest of their lives. We have an inner desire to stay with one and we do not desire others. After the relationship is formed, there is a desire to have children. Each of us sits and meditates on our in-

tent to have a child; we focus on the child's appearance or looks. We sit together, close our eyes, and visualize a child. If successful, we open our eyes and a child appears in an area that we had previously set aside for this purpose. This baby is six to seven inches long and has features like an adult. It is a fully functioning being in just a few weeks. The parents' job is to nurture and teach the child their beliefs and to keep the child as a positive and balanced being.

"When I grow up, I become a designer in the spacecraft industry. I know my purpose by having an inner knowing. Our space program is growing out of necessity. We have been taking minor attacks from warring tribes from other planets. As a result, we must prepare to develop our own space program in the event that we would need to escape. I have seen our space program grow to where we can handle over fifty people in our spaceships. We have established space stations some 200,000 miles above us. And we are designing bigger and faster spacecraft every day as we make plans to establish more stations out in space.

"At the age of about three thousand years of our time, I am growing weak and I am no longer able to work. I remain in my cave with my wife. I can no longer communicate. I cannot move except for a slight shaking of my antennae. Shortly, I am without any movement and my spirit leaves my body. My spirit is located in the battery-like organ, which has completely run down. I remain in the cave for a few months because my body does not decompose. Then I am taken to a remote burial place where my body is deposited with the multitude of others who have passed away.

"I have a soul but no knowledge of it. I am not aware of what happens beyond the death of my physical body. I do have a slight sense of something coming out of my body when it died, but after that I have no awareness. It feels as if I have lost myself."

Alien possessing stick-like characteristics. This intelligent being lived in harmony with the grasshopper-like alien billions of years ago on the planet Kyro.

Alien possessing some grasshopper-like characteristics. This intelligent being can walk, hop, and fly short distances. This alien being lived in harmony with the stick-like alien billions of years ago on the planet Kyro.

Drawings by a hypnotized patient

This 8 to 9 feet tall monster along with the 2 to 3 feet tall monster invaded and drove out the stick-like aliens from the planet of Kyro billions of years ago.

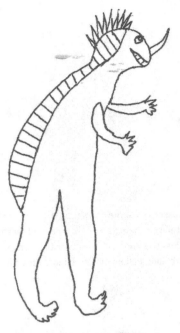

This 2 to 3 feet tall monster along with the 8 to 9 feet tall monster invaded and drove out the stick-like aliens from the planet of Kyro billions of years ago.

Drawn by a hypnotized patient

The same patient recalled living another life on the same planet, Kyro, as a source of his symptoms, as follows:

• *"I had another life on the planet Kyro about a thousand years later. I am a young adult, about twenty-five in human years, and I have a wife and seven children. I am trained as an architect and help design living quarters for others. A lot of my work is trial and error, where I search for and discover caves and other living quarters. Once I find a cavern, I clear the debris with earth-moving equipment. I enlarge the caves and clear out tunnels. Sometimes I find building sites and design a new housing development under overhanging rocks.*

"In the meantime, our planet is taking on more attacks by the aliens from another planet. At this time, they are very intense on a very regular basis. The attacks are coming closer and closer to our area, and our planet is becoming a very dangerous place to live. At this time, we [the grasshopper like beings] are looking more and more like the stick-like aliens. This resulted from intermingling over the years. We are more advanced at this time. We have an inner awareness that our planet could be taken over by warring tribes from other planets. We sense that we could be destroyed or become slaves to those who would conquer us. We are experiencing anxiety, worry, and concern. I am planning to leave with my family and friends on the next available spaceship. Our nation has plans in place to defend our planet and then, if necessary, to evacuate and live out in space.

"We can see the enemy coming to our area and we can hear their spacecraft firing on our planet. They are monster-like beings. Some look like dinosaurs standing eight to nine feet tall. Yet others, just as aggressive, stand only two to three feet tall. They are vicious and cold. They have scales; some have two eyes and some just one eye. They walk upright. Their hands and feet have sharp claws

*with webbing between these claws. Their arms are small-
er than their legs. Their bodies are burley and stout. We
sense that our defenses will not hold, so we leave on the
next available spaceship and go into space.*

*"There is a lot of confusion, and people wish to escape
into space or bury themselves deep into the farthest re-
cesses of the planet. By this time, hundreds of thousands
have escaped into space. Many have been killed from the
attacks. Some have been eaten by the enemy, and others
are hiding in tunnels and caves.*

*"We stay in space for hundreds of years. We live on
spaceships and continue to monitor our planet. We are
reasonably safe, as we are very far from our planet and
we have methods to shield ourselves from the enemy. Our
ships can accommodate over two hundred beings and we
live very similar to those in a small city. Our living conditions are better than they were back on our planet. Meanwhile, our planet still exists, but portions of it have been
taken over by warring alien tribes. There is much turmoil,
and our planet is not a good place to live at the time of
my death.*

*"I live for 275 years in Earth time. My battery has ex-
pired, and I become still as my spirit leaves me. I am kept
on the spacecraft for several months in the event that I
might rejuvenate. After a few months, when there is no
rejuvenation, my body is thrown out into space. I have no
knowledge of a life presence after the death of my physical body.*

*"From heaven, I see that our planet was destroyed a
few thousand years later. There are still a few beings left
on the planet, but others had come and it was a war zone.
Life was short and there was lots of fighting and destruction. I see that our planet was a Lighted place. When the
aliens came, they brought demonic influences with them
and our planet became a dark place. The demonic influences increased along with tension and stress. Finally, the
planet began to break up and explode naturally because*

of evil actions. Little explosions escalated into larger explosions, and over a few hundred years, the whole planet exploded and disintegrated.

"I can see from heaven how babies were created in our race. The body of the baby is created through intent. The intent goes to the Light and angels create the baby. The body of the baby comes down and the soul is infused into the body. I see that my connecting cord to God was open and it entered me through the top of my head. I had a soul but it did not seem to have an awareness of God. I see that we have our own space in heaven. I lived a total of seven lives on the planet Kyro and since the destruction of Kyro, those aliens are living on a spaceship because they don't have a home planet anymore. I also see that those tall, thin, human-like aliens living on our planet are the same alien beings as the fourth alien race of group two.

"I see many of my problems came from that life to the current life, such as anxiety, depression, and feelings of disconnection from God. When you asked the angels to bring back all my soul parts from all my lives on that planet and also of all the beings who were there and also soul parts to that planet, I saw thousands of soul parts coming to me and all the other beings who lived on that planet and also to those who attacked us, and integrated with whom they belonged, thus healing us from the problems coming from those lives. I also see the soul parts being brought back to that planet which was being recreated and shielded completely."

I am a Radio and Television Preacher on Another Planet

Following is another example of a person who recalled under hypnosis being incarnated on another planet as a spiritual teacher a long time before there were any humans on Planet Earth:

• *"I am a twenty-four-year-old male, which is forty-eight in your time, living in a city called Arman on the planet Murdock. This is 1722, according to our time, and long before life started on Earth. My name is Nazam. I am a humanoid with a head, body, two arms, and two legs. I am four feet six inches tall, with brown eyes, light brown hair, and tan skin. The skin complexion varies in our people from beige, tan, and brown to dark brown. Occasionally the skin is white, but not often, and it is considered freakish because there are so few with light complexions. We walk upright. I am married and have two children, who are eight and ten years old, which is sixteen and twenty in your time. They are nearly full-grown.*

"I communicate with ordinary people about God. I am like a preacher but I do not have a real church. I broadcast through radio and television so people can see and hear me. It is a hard job because there are always worries and problems trying to get the message across and not having enough money to do it. It is expensive to pay for the airtime. I have to ask for money all the time and I need help. I know that everybody does not go to church, and these are the people I am really aiming toward, but it is the real believers that send the money. I try to deliver the message, that God has a purpose, to both groups at the same time. There are ways He wants us to function and to be closer to Him. We have religious books that we follow.

"One of the space survey crew found an intelligent alien race on a planet that is only ten light years or so away. It is very exciting. The radio messages came in a while ago and it is widely talked about. We do not know too much about them except that they are roughly built like us and the space survey crew will be bringing back full information. I am getting lots of questions about these people from the general public. I have to tell them that nobody knows the answers to these questions yet. We do not know if they know about God, and if they are a good or bad race. Inside, I really think that every race in the uni-

verse has to know something about God. I think it will be interesting to see how their understanding of God might be different from ours, and to see what forms of worship they use.

"The rules for the space survey crews are that they are not supposed to reveal themselves. They are supposed to just observe but not let the people know that they are there. That is for two reasons. One is for the benefit of the race we are looking at, because it might not be a good idea to expose it to them right away. The other thing is that it might not be safe for us to be exposed to them right away. We want to know these people well before they know we are here. Come to think of it, I am wondering if there are other alien crews surveying us and how we would ever know. Maybe someday we will.

"Four years later, I am invited to the official showing of the space survey crews' results. Much of what I see appears to be incomprehensible. They have structures to live in, they have transportation, and they seem to have worship places, medical care, a verbal language, and a written language. They seem to be behind us in developing things, such as growing their own food and transportation, and they have very few machines or mechanical stuff or devices. They do not seem to be mechanical. We do not know the name of the planet as they know it, but we call it Wilton. Actually, that is what we call the star, so we just applied the same name to the planet.

"I am asked to be on the panel because they need people from a religious group. Not all questions are about technology or sociology. People want to know about the religious and spiritual practices of these people, such as what are they like, what do they think, and how do they do things. It is my job to review the artifacts and video recordings brought from there, along with the other panel members, and try to come up with some answers. It seems obvious that they have some religious feelings, but we do not know their language. I am concluding that these people are es-

sentially good, which may be overstating it, and that they do recognize God, and we should continue to study them.

"The space survey crew recorded plenty of information. They have written language, but no radio or television broadcasts were detected. They seem to be a pre-scientific culture. They have agriculture but no machinery. The panel reaches the determination that this race needs to be studied and its language understood very thoroughly before establishing any contact. We want to know these people really well before we do that. They are humanoid, meaning they have two arms, two legs, a body and a head, and they walk upright. They are taller than we are. Their planet is near a cooler star, so the skin on the outside is lighter. Their planet is green.

"We see no reason to take the risk of establishing contact with them, so the decision is made to send a fleet of survey craft to examine this world much closer. We want to look for keys to understand their language and record lengthy interactions between them and see what is said and what happens. We want to look for elementary schools where kids are just learning their language. Our elementary classes use words and pictures, and maybe if we can find books like that we can figure out what the words mean. We can learn to read their alphabet, how they do mathematics, chemistry, physics, or whatever they have discovered. Each of these subjects can provide some insight into these beings.

"I die at the age of sixty-eight of a heart problem before the second space survey crew returns. We figure that the survey crew is just arriving at the vicinity of the planet. I am old. As I am dying, my last thoughts are, "Lord, I hope I did well and accomplished everything you wanted me to do." I am feeling chest pain, breathlessness, and am cold and clammy. It gets dark and I am out of my body. I see the Light above and something inside tells me that is where I need to go. My father and mother are in the Light and take me to heaven. As

I turn around, I can see the universe down below. I get cleansed and healed, and then I go for a life review with a being that looks like us.

"I review every second of my life, and sometimes see it from more than one point of view and from other people's points of view. It is very interesting to know what they thought and felt. From heaven, I can see that my purpose was to bring messages of God to people and to help establish a climate of trust and acceptance of aliens rather than suspicion. I achieved my purpose somewhat, but I could have done better.

"From heaven, I see that my issues of needing to provide security and making sure that I have enough to get going and not taking chances in the current life came from that life."

We Go on Expeditions in Space

A patient recalled a life on another planet called Melton, as a short, stocky being of race five of group two as described in chapter three, as follows:

- *"I am a forty-four-year-old male living on a planet called Murdoc or Melton, long before people existed on Planet Earth. It is a large rocky planet like Earth and we are short and stocky, but human looking. My name is Nemkazahar. I am divorced. My wife left me and then she died of cancer. I have grown children. I never remarried after the divorce. I live alone. I am about four feet eleven inches tall and very strong. I have a blocky, cube-like head, my eyes face forward and are brown, my ears are barely out, my mouth is like a slit, and I have thin lips. I have two arms, with one thumb and three fingers each, and two legs. My feet are broad and have four toes. I have a powerful torso.*

"I am an aeronautical engineer. I am involved in designing, flying, testing, building, and making new devices. We are experimenting with an entirely new means of propulsion. We are working with physicists, and my part of the job is designing controls. They have to be extremely fast acting. They say this craft will be able to fly very fast and be very maneuverable. So the controls have to be very precise and easy to handle.

"The craft is completed and we are testing it and everything the physicists claimed is true. It can travel in water, but we have to be careful because the forces of water on the craft are extreme. It will travel in space where there is no atmosphere. It is very quick and very maneuverable. We have already redesigned the controls twice. You can literally sit in the control chair and control the craft by wiggling a finger or with a slight move of the hand and change the direction, altitude, and speed. It takes a lot to get used to it.

"Now we are actually taking the craft in space on a serious expedition. We are going to explore other planets in our solar system for the first time. I am the most experienced pilot, so I get the job. I am forty-six years old now. We are exploring the planet Tuko, which is next to our planet. It only takes a few hours to get there. We accelerate halfway there and decelerate halfway, and there is not one indication of strain or of the craft working. It is effortless propulsion.

"Now we are exploring another planet. The craft, with just a few supplies, can survey two, three, or four planets at a time because of its incredible speed. We go to the most distant planet first and everything we need is carried inside the ship. Our first surveys are very rudimentary. We do not land on these outer planets because they are gas planets. We wonder if life can exist in a gas planet environment and if we will recognize it if we see it. We are surveying and looking into temperature, pressure, circulation around the planet, speed of rotation, and just

confirming a lot of the stuff that is already known. We sur-
vey these four outer planets of the solar system in a period
of weeks and then we start back home. We are in contact
by radio with the home planet. Other suggestions come up
for what they want us to do.

"I propose that we prepare a small craft that will be
remotely controlled, which we can actually send into the
gas planet for measuring composition, collecting data,
and to find out if it can be done. We wonder if that craft
can come out of the gas planet and in what condition the
test instruments inside would be. We try it and we find out
that the smaller scout craft can handle the pressure, but
the hot or cold temperature can penetrate the craft and
affect the crew. So the scout crew can exist inside on a gas
planet, but not for an extended time. It can get close to the
sun but not for an extended time, because the temperature
does affect the craft. We are now sending the big ships to
the stars with large supplies and just a few crewmembers.
We calculate that it will take almost four years to reach
the nearest star. We have already launched a ship toward
a star and are waiting for word back.

"My flying days are over and I am put in charge of a
segment of a program. We are training the crew for more
extensive exploration, and plans are made for a trip to
the next star. Meanwhile, I want to apply the technolo-
gy to life. This power system could really be helpful, but
I am running into all sorts of resistance. The people in
charge do not want this technology made available. The
politicians are trying to keep it a secret to conceal it. I am
pointing out that we can make a train out of devices like
this and it would operate very cheaply, and transportation
would be greatly simplified for individuals. But they do
not want to hear about it. They are afraid that somebody
else will figure out the technology and use it against us.

"I get involved in the most interesting religious discus-
sions about whether it is suitable for us to go to other
worlds in the plan of God. Is this what is intended for us

and what if there are other intelligent beings? What does that mean to us?

"I am dying at the age of seventy-two of an unknown cause. My blood cells are going crazy. I am losing consciousness. I fade away and die. I wish I were younger so I could go for star explorations to look around the universe. I am pretty sure that it is the power plant in the propulsions system that is the cause of my death. After my death, my spirit is quite upset, feeling it is unjust and I have been robbed. I am being approached by beautiful women. They are offering all sorts of things, and all I have to do is work for their master and say that he is my god. Something just does not feel right about this and I do not want anything to do with them. They pressure me and I feel like I cannot get away from them. I pray to God in desperation and I am helped immediately. The angels come from the Light and help me to heaven. They tell me those women were working for Satan, and if I had gone with them, they would have taken me to hell.

"In heaven, I get cleansed and healed. Then go for my life review with two men and a woman. From heaven, I see the influence of religion on that life. I had a spiritual bent from the time I was a kid. I also see that my perception about religious and spiritual debates, about contacting other planets, and my active participation in it came from my religious background. I planned several things for that life. One of it was the group plan to bring the advances in technology to the people, and second was to keep spirituality, the concept of God and spirit, in technology and not to use technology without spirituality. My individual goals were to be spiritual.

"From heaven, I see that I died of radiation in that life, and in this life I am very sensitive to radiation, such as ultraviolet rays. Feelings that the government has not been for the people have also been carried over from that life to the current one."

They Contaminated My Planet Uranus with Evil

Urantian child

4' tall — green soft skin - round eyes. Long thin arms with long thin delicate fingers

(three fingers and one thumb). Small mouth, communicates telepathically. Feet have long thin delicate toes. The feet have three toes just like the hands.

Drawing by a hypnotized patient

A patient recalled a life on the planet Uranus where there was no demonic influence. They communicated telepathically and were very spiritual. At the age of five, in that life, the patient remembered being abducted by aliens who were influenced by the demons. They put a device in him that was programmed with evil thoughts. It was a way of planting the seeds of evil and contaminating that pure and spiritual planet with negative thoughts and emotions, such as intense anger, hate, and desire to hurt others.

• *"I live on the planet Uranus with my parents and two brothers. My name is Ioxid and I am five years old. Our homes are dome shaped. They are modern looking and made of metal. It is much different than Planet Earth. I do not see any plant life or any water, but there are mountains. There is no darkness here. There is not much diversity and it is a very peaceful existence. Everybody looks alike, but there is a sense of male and female or sexuality like on Earth. We are not very tall. My parents are about five feet tall, like most adults.*

"As I look at myself, I see that I am about four feet tall, humanoid, with a body, two arms, two legs, and one head. My head is roundish, without hair; eyes are round and human-like, and I have a nose and mouth. My ears are smaller but pointed; my hands are long and thin with three fingers and one thumb, all long and thin and of the same length. My skin is greenish.

"I see that a couple prays to create the intention to have a child. Then the body manifests outside and not inside the womb, and the soul comes down and enters the body. People here seem to be very evolved and peaceful. There is no military or even government. Our body is dense and the growth of the body has nothing to do with food, but depends on internal development. We do not seem to have a need to eat or drink, and we do not have a desire to own too many things. We also choose to leave the body whenever our purpose on the planet is fulfilled. It is like we know how to manifest and de-manifest. In school, we study the whole galaxy. We have computers that are much more advanced than the computers on Earth currently.

"People work but it is different. We learn to tap into our inner knowledge, as we are doing now during this session. We learn to tune in to vibrations. The job of all the beings of this planet seems to be to process vibrations. It seems like it is the unified purpose and it impacts the whole solar system. It is like people here can somehow transmit the energy collectively. The focus is mostly on holding the vibrations in place, and as a result, we impact other planets positively. There is a narrow range between the high and low vibrations, and as a result, we do not have a wide range of emotions. We are mostly

happy, joyful, and peaceful, but do not feel extremes of those emotions. We do not have any negative emotions, because we do not have any demonic influences. All parents genuinely value their children. We communicate with each other telepathically from birth, and as a result, we do not have any language or secrets. We feel the constant connection with the source all the time, and this is not as questionable as it is on Earth.

"We live a simple lifestyle. My parents, siblings, and I all sleep in one room on simple platforms. One night as we are sleeping, I see lights come down in the room and they suck me up in a spaceship while the rest of my family is still sleeping in their beds. I feel strange and it is affecting my body. I never felt this constricted before.

"I am in a room and it appears to be an experimental space lab. There are many of us here. We are just children. I am seeing people with weird heads. They seem to be aliens. We are in a spaceship lying on a table with heads down. The spaceship has wings like our airplanes, but it is boxy and pointed in the front. There is a big, round fuselage in the back and there are windows across the front and the sides. Inside, it is divided into different rooms but I cannot see them. It seems as big as a football field and appears to be metallic.

"There are about fifteen children lying on the tables in two rows, and one alien being is walking back and forth. He is about six feet five inches tall and he is dressed like those people in Star Trek movies with the tight fitting suits. His head is oval, wider from side to side, and there are scales on his head but no hair. His ears are big, his face looks metallic, and the nose is beak-like, almost like a hawk. His eyes are red, round, and laser-like. He does not have teeth. It seems to be a robotic being, but it has intelligence that seems to be programmed. It had two arms and two legs, claw-like hands, and a body. He is walking upright. I feel like somebody is controlling him through a device.

"I am not sure where these other children are from. I feel like I cannot move or get up. I get the feeling that they just want to put devices in us to influence and corrupt our society. They cut my abdomen to put a device in and close the wound with a laser. I do not feel any pain. I am beginning to have feelings I never had before, such as doubts and confusion, and I cannot communicate telepathically anymore. It is a new experience. In some ways, I feel like I am being poisoned.

"They take us to a big hall with high ceilings. There are many different types of beings there who are talking about us. I feel that they are evil. I am upset because I cannot understand what they are thinking and saying. We are on examination tables again and I am feeling powerless. There are two beings in white coats putting a thin coppery disc-type device in my abdomen and then they program it with a wand. Then they beam me back to my planet to my bed.

"I cannot communicate telepathically anymore. This is the only way everybody communicates here and there is no verbal communication. I do not remember anything about the abduction. I grow up in my own world feeling alone, separate, and lonely. My family and other people do not understand me. I cannot form the intent to create a baby because there is nobody here who is like me. I am feeling more and more angry, almost to the extent that I want to kill others. Other people on my planet are now feeling fear and try to hide their thoughts from each other.

"I am a grown man now, and somebody from the spaceship makes contact with me. He is very pleased, but I do not know why. I have so much hatred and anger, as if I am a single man army. I have a struggle of conscience going on in me. I want to get out of it but do not know how. Every now and then I remember how I used to be.

"One of the beings on our planet is trying to get through to me to help me remember. He is very loving toward me and I feel his love. He is integrating something in me, maybe my soul parts. I feel more resolved with this life

after that being talks with me and heals me. I feel at peace and live by myself most of the time.

"I die when I am about a hundred years old. My spirit comes out and goes to the Light (heaven). After cleansing and healing, I go for the life review. There are many beings sitting there to help me. As I look back from heaven, I can see that those space aliens were trying to contaminate our planet and spread evil by putting those devices in my body and programming me with negative, evil thoughts. They wanted control and power. I also see that I planned to be abducted and influenced by evil to understand the duality of God and evolve faster. People on Uranus are very good people and live a peaceful life, but they do not understand the duality of God because there is no demonic influence here and, therefore, they do not evolve as fast. Since then, I have chosen to incarnate on Earth to experience the duality of God and evolve.

"The abductors implanted the seed of evil in me through that disk in my abdomen, and programming it for dark emotions, and I had to experience them and still remember the Light. That was a challenge. I see that my soul began to plead for memory, and as a result, that person on my planet helped and healed me, and after that, I lived in peace although I could never communicate with anybody. I see that I needed to learn about forgiveness.

"I see that my parents in Uranus are also my parents in the current life. The robotic man on the spaceship is somebody here in the current life and I am afraid of him, too. I also see that the man on Uranus who helped in healing me was you, Dr. Modi, helping me remember, as you are helping me to remember now, during the session.

"From heaven, I realize that many of my problems came from that life to my current life, such as stomach problems, feeling separate and isolated, and difficulty in communication.

"When Dr. Modi requested the angels to remove all the devices from me and all the other people in whom devices

were put, and bring all our soul parts back and integrate them with us after cleansing and healing, I see it happening. Many soul parts are coming back to my abdomen, and all over my body. I see all the other people healing, too."

It is Weird! I Look Like a Large Caterpillar

Alien being like a caterpillar

(3 feet long - soft yellow green body)

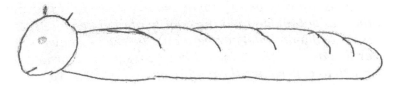

Drawing by a hypnotized patient

Under hypnosis, a patient who had gastrointestinal symptoms for a long time recalled living on another planet as a three-foot-long caterpillar being. That being was abducted by ant-like beings and genetic modification was done to create hybrid beings by mixing caterpillar and ant genes, so the ant beings could survive on the caterpillar's planet. The planet of the ant-like beings was dying for some reason. Following is the account given by the patient:

- *"It is really weird. As I focus on myself, I look like a bug, like a large caterpillar. I am really upset that I could incarnate as a less evolved being. I am about three feet long. I am not upright, but I crawl. My body is greenish, soft, and has many little feet. I have a little head and mandible, and am eating foliage. I do not seem to have much intelligence and awareness except of the food in front of me. At this time, I am a baby about three feet long and not fully developed. I live inside a hole in a tree.*

"I see eggs and cocoons hanging up here. I see adult moths, like butterflies, that laid all these eggs. When these eggs hatch, they look like me, a caterpillar. Then we have to spin the cocoon, and when they crack open, we become an adult moth. Then we mate and lay eggs. I, as a caterpillar, do not feel much evolved, and do not have much emotional attachments with others. There is a consciousness but it is not as evolved. We have basic intelligence and communicate telepathically. The moths are almost as tall as I am. They have three body parts, six limbs, and brownish wings, and their antennae are feathery. They are very harmless.

"On our planet, I see water, trees, and rocks. There are other beings, such as beetles, that are also about three feet tall. They are like horned beetles that have two wings that fold out from the back of their bodies. They have a head of a beetle bug, but bigger. They are not upright. Nothing is upright on this planet; like us, they crawl and can also fly.

"There are saucer-like spaceships landing on our planet. They have triangular panels that come out. I see ant-like beings coming out and they are collecting all the eggs and carrying them into the spaceship. They are also taking me and other caterpillars. I am feeling uncomfortable and afraid. They inject something in me that makes me numb so I do not fight. They do not have to do that with the eggs. These ant beings are about six feet tall and upright. They look just like an ant but bigger. They stack the eggs in the wall like a honeycomb. They are very orderly.

"We are taken to their planet. It seems that their planet is hilly, rocky, and muddy, and has termite-type mounds all over. I do not see any foliage. I see underground tunnels, and these beings are crawling all over, just like ants on Earth, but these are big, almost like human size. It looks like something is wrong with their planet. There is no foliage or water. It seems like they have a social structure.

The being who is standing in front of me appears to be a leader, while all the others seem like workers.

"I see their queen, who is reddish brown and huge, about thirty feet long. She is just laying on the platform, and there are all these ant people feeding our eggs to her. She does not have legs, and her body looks like a big, round, long blob and has a head and antennae. She has a big mouth and big round eyes. She can sit upright and move her head all around. She has a ferocious appetite and a red glow around her.

"I am being carried through a tunnel and taken in front of the ant queen. I am scared by her hugeness. Then they take me and all the other caterpillars away. We are all piled up on top of each other and are crawling around. They take me out and put me upside down on a table. A tall ant person cuts my abdomen and puts a metallic rod-like device in it, which makes me feel like vomiting. I am out of my body, watching all this. Then he closes the wound with the clamps. He also puts a little round transmitter-type device on the right side of my head. This being is reddish brown and looks almost like an ant. It has a big head with two antennae through which it communicates, and has ant-like mandibles and big, oval eyes. It seems to be human size, about five to six feet tall fully grown. It is standing upright, but I see other ant beings crawling. So they can crawl or stand upright. They have a crusty shell and three body parts like ants. They also have a tail and six limbs. They have tiny hairs through which they can sense.

"We are taken through a long tunnel and they are putting us back on the spaceship. They do not take the eggs back; just us. I think they fed the eggs to the ant queen. They take us to our planet and deposit us there. It is time for me to spin a cocoon. I secrete some kind of string stuff from my tail and wrap it around me, creating a cocoon. My body is changing. I feel a deep sense of guilt. When I come out of it, I look like a moth. I am a male.

"I get the feeling that those ant people communicate with me through the device in my head. I mate with

another moth. Something from my tail enters into an-
other moth, which is a female. I get very weak after mat-
ing and die. The female also dies after laying the eggs. I
see my body down there but I do not feel dead. I feel that
there is Light all around me and I get drawn into heaven.

"After cleansing, I go for a life review. There are many
Light beings sitting around the table with me. They also
look like caterpillars. From heaven, I see that I incarnat-
ed on that planet long before Earth was ready for human
life. The name of my planet was Rexterra and the name
of the ant people's planet was Oldor. From heaven, I see
that the ant beings were not evil. It looks like most of their
planet was burned. I see some kind of smoke all over ex-
cept for the small part where we were taken. The planet is
dying. There is not much greenery. For some reason, they
cannot reproduce on their planet. So they have to mutate
through the caterpillars to take over their planet and live
there. They cannot live on the caterpillars' planet as ant
beings, so they do genetic modification on these cater-
pillar beings and on themselves and create mixed beings
to escape from their planet before it dies completely. The
caterpillars' planet has water and greenery.

"I see that the device in the brains is a tracking device,
but in the abdomen, they implanted their sperm in the cat-
erpillar beings and mixed their gene pool with the cat-
erpillar beings, creating a mixed species. From heaven,
I can see the babies that hatched from the eggs that the
other moth and I created. They looked different. It is a
combination of ant and caterpillar beings."

From heaven, I realize that I chose to incarnate on that planet
as a caterpillar to experience what it is like to be a less evolved
being, and to experience the contrast between highly evolved
beings and lower evolved beings and that all beings have
consciousness. We have to respect all life. It also keeps me
humble. I see the ant being who put the devices in my brain

and abdomen is also here in the current life, and I am afraid of him in this life. The queen ant is my mother in this life.

"From heaven, I see many problems that came from that life to my current life, such as the device in my head that does not allow me to integrate information or access it. The demons, through this device, put doubts and fear in me. It also blocked me from the Light and affects me emotionally and causes confusion. My gastrointestinal problems also came from that life.

"When you asked angels to bring back all the soul parts to me and all the beings who were on my planet and the ant planet, I see soul parts going to all the beings and also to my brain, abdomen, and other parts of my body.

"Through another patient, I asked the angels to locate and integrate all the soul parts to the ant planet that was destroyed and integrate them together. The patient could see the whole planet being recreated again."

I Am Afraid Our Race Might Go Extinct

An alien being Queen ant

About 30' long - head is hard - red brown color - body is soft - no legs

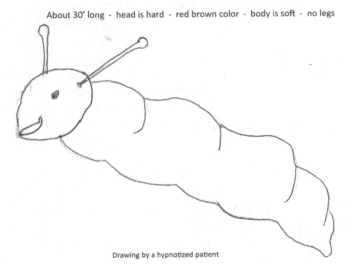

Drawing by a hypnotized patient

One person under hypnosis recalled a life on another planet as an ant like being who was four feet two inches tall, and upright. He was a scientist. He and his race were afraid of becoming extinct because something was going wrong with their planet, so they began to abduct beings from different planets and create hybrid beings, by mixing the genes. They were hoping that these hybrid beings could survive the harsher conditions on their planet. Following is the description given by the person:

* *"I am a male living on another planet called Senit. It is a small, sandy planet and there is water underground. We look like large ants. We are about four feet two inches tall, upright, and have a reddish brown color. We have two antennae on the head and a face like an ant. We communicate with these antennae. We do not eat, but we drink some liquid that sustains us and has a universal knowledge in which it is programmed that we will have an equal number of people for different jobs. Before, it was available naturally. As we drink this liquid every day after birth, we know what we will be doing as our job. We put that liquid in a computer, which lets us know that two scientists will be born or a nurse or a doctor will be born, then the liquid programs them. I am a scientist feeling certain fears. A meteoroid hit our planet and our planet got polluted, and we may not be able to procreate in the future. Now we have to create the liquid in the laboratory because it is not available naturally. We do not want to go extinct. It is built into all beings to remain alive.*

    "We have no marriages. We all interbreed with one another. We are very community oriented. We have a station where all the babies receive care. We have male and female. After they lay their eggs, they do not claim them. They belong to the community. We do not have many feelings, just a sense of duty.

"We live underground in the dirt. We have little ant mounds with little openings like doorways through which we can go in and out. There is a big underground amphitheater with a big huge open area with concrete steps that go down, and in the center, there is an open area. That is where the spaceships arrive and depart. We have a sandy type of spaceship because the sand and dirt are very important to us. We are all busy doing things. Our technology is rather simple but very evolved.

"It seems like something is wrong with our planet because of the solar rays, or solar pollution. We began to abduct beings from other planets to create hybrid beings who can procreate and survive on our planet. We are creating different forms and different species, such as ants with wings, ants with lizard faces, a bigger body, and legs like ants, combinations of ant and beetle, human and ant, etc. When we work with a human, we have to clamp the mouth because he has a lot of emotions and we do not know what to do. It is a whole new experience. I am literally hands-on with this and create an ant-human that is very strong and superior and can live on the surface of this planet. We create many of these ant-human breeds.

"Somebody from another planet steals one of our ant-human beings. These look like gray aliens. I am upset, because I do not want anybody to know about our technology. Then something happens and our planet explodes, and since then, the ant beings who survived live on the spaceships. They did not have much technology. This is why the two possessing ant spirit beings came into me to get information about this technology. While these ant beings were in me trying to tap into this information, I did not consciously know anything about it, but my inner self (soul) knew.

"From heaven, I see that similar types of genetic modifications were done on me on different planets in

different lives. When Dr. Modi asked angels to separate all the souls of different hybrid beings from each other who were created through genetic engineering by mixing different genes throughout creation, then bring all the missing soul parts of every soul in the creation who did the genetic modifications on others and also when modifications were done on them, cleanse them, heal them, and integrate them with whom they belong, I saw it happening all over creation. I saw thousands of my soul parts coming to me from ant life and all the other lifetimes from the beginning of time, thus healing me from the traumas and issues from those lives. I see similar healings happening to all the beings all over the creation and all the Earthbound and universe-bound spirits were helped into heaven by angels."

Life On A Water Planet

One of my patients had shortness of breath. As she scanned her lungs, under hypnosis, she saw a gray net around her lungs. She recalled living on a water planet in a past life as follows:

- *"I am a fish-like alien being on a water planet. I see that there is the core of the planet in the middle and all around there is water, like the atmosphere on Earth. The gravitational pull of the core keeps the water contained on the planet, which has a hard surface all around. The core is like heavy iron and it is spinning, so the water stays where it is. The water is warm and the sun shines on the water and it appears magical, like in Disney movies. It is beautiful. At the bottom, there are rocks, and at some places, there is sand. There is no dry land on the planet. I am a big fish, about eighty feet long. I have an iridescent bluish green color. I have a big head, and my eyes are on the sides of my head, and my nose is pointed. There are many fish like me. Here big fish eat little fish. We swim in groups with similar fishes. There are whales, which are bigger than we are, and then there are predators like sharks. There is a variety of plants and corals. There are different fishes of mixed sizes, shapes, and colors. We mostly stay in groups of our kind, but sometimes we mix with others, except the sharks. It is not very crowded on this planet and there is a lot of space around.*

"I live in a group with other fishes of my kind, and most of the time we look for food. We make sounds to communicate. The female fish lay eggs, then the male fish swims over the eggs and fertilizes them, but we are not really in a couple-type relationship. We relate to each other as a group. If somebody is scared, then through sound and vibrations, everybody in the group knows it. We live in certain territories, although we can go anywhere we choose. There is so much space on our planet that we do not have to worry about territory. Our major function is to look for food. During sleep, we are kind of in suspended animation and we go back and forth because our gills have to move. There are no other activities. We are very primitive.

"As a group, mothers protect their babies, although there is not much of a bond between them. If our group is attacked, the younger ones will move into the middle and the larger fishes will be outside and circle around them to protect them. If we are not killed by sharks, we die of old age. We usually sink down, and when we are dead, the body floats up and the sharks eat us.

"One day as I am swimming along with others in the group, all of a sudden, there is a net pulling us up. We are struggling, feeling fear and terror. The net gets tighter around us and we do not know what to do and how to get out. When they haul us out of the water, the oxygen is

pulled out of us. I feel like I am suffocating and experiencing total terror and panic. We flop around in the net but cannot get out. We are appealing for help, although we do not know of God.

"We are dying because we are not able to breathe. We become very heavy when not supported by the water, and our organs are collapsing and we are in pain. We do not understand why this is happening. It is like being sucked into outer space. We are being pulled out by some aliens in a boat. They have workers who are robots and look like trolls, but the aliens look like a variation of the tall, thin, gray aliens. I am losing consciousness and everything is going black. There are about fifty of us large fishes in one, huge net.

"We are all dead and I am watching from above the body. The aliens wanted us for some research. They take samples from a few of us and then dump all our bodies back in the water. It is so wasteful. They take my body with some others. I am looking down and debating if I should go back into my body. I see a Light and I go into it with the other fishes. We are kind of swimming in this Light. We are in a channel of Light and we go up into the Light in a huge ocean. It looks like the ocean we left, but it is very spectacular. Instead of water, there is golden liquid Light in the ocean. It seems like all the fish we ate are being taken out of us as a cleansing process. Then we are watching this big video aquarium of our lives. I see my shortness of breath is partly coming from this life. I also see many people who are in my current life were also in that life with me."

Life of a Jellyfish on a Water Planet

One of my patients recalled a life on a water planet as a jellyfish, which was the source of his sensitivity to cleaning chemicals, perfumes, hairspray, and smoke, and also for his anger outbursts:

• *"I am on a water planet called 6362. There is no land, just water and atmosphere. I look like a jellyfish. I have a head, face, and arms that hang down. I have a central heart. I am about six feet tall. Most of the time, I swim, but I can also stand upright. I have hundreds of tentacles, which I can bring together to push or break things. My tentacles are of different sizes but some of them are about twenty feet long. We are transparent white beings and change colors according to our emotions. I see whales, which are about eighty feet long, and there are octopuses and squids. They mostly swim, but can also stand upright. We emit some gas from our body which can be poisonous to other species but not to us. We live in caves underwater. They are like aquariums. We rest against the cave walls. We do not have schools or an education system. We simply download the files to our brain from our ancestors or older jellyfish. They are transmitted telepathically. We are having problems on our planet due to pollution. Some of the species are polluting it. I can sense temperature, salt, and chemicals in the water. I am florescent and glow in the dark.*

"I am inside a building that is very big. On one side it has a ramp, and on the other side there are windows in the wall. In the center, there is an open space. The stadium is a stone structure built underwater, where a competition or fight is going on. Like a football stadium, there are steps from where people are watching. The top is open. I see we are floating up one by one and spinning around. There are two teams with five members in each team. I am the captain of one team. Our color glows a little bit lighter than the other team. This is like a game between two groups of beings, and the group in which most beings are still alive wins the game. Instead of having a war and killing hun-

dreds of beings, ten beings will fight or compete, and the team that has more people alive at the game's end, wins. This way, we can avoid a big war. The leaders of both teams are releasing neurotoxins of different types in the water, which causes paralysis, and it hurts. Each team has different tools. We are fighting over more space, food, water, and oxygen because the planet is crowded. Beings are watching through windows, and other beings of the planet are watching on a television screen. They are sending a conscious energy to each of their teams telepathically.

"I am spinning around and have sharp tentacles, and I poke the captain of the opposite team, which pulls him back. He splashes something on my face and ear. It is abrasive and burning. Then I poke him with another sharp spike, which kills him. He falls down and I am also half dead. All the five members of the other team are dead, while two members of my team, including me, are alive. So we win the competition. We are taken to a doctor. We get more space, water, sun, and oxygen because we won the competition. Doctors are pulling the pointy spikes from me. I do not think I will make it for a long time. I die within six months because of the wounds and the toxins. The other captain died because of the toxins I put in him through a poker and it went straight to his nervous system; that is why he died right away. The toxin I got came in slowly and took some time to affect me. It is like chemical warfare and is terrible.

"After my death, my spirit comes out, and I see a beam coming down and I swim up into the Light and go into a white marble room where I stand under the shower. Instead of water, a musical vibration goes through me and cleans me, and yellowish black stuff comes out of me.

"Then I go to review my life. From heaven, I see that the whole planet was polluted and there was not much to eat. The excrement of all the beings was polluting and poisoning the planet and survival was becoming difficult. There was overpopulation, and the planet was very con-

gested. I also see that we stirred up the silt or the sand, which ruined the water, and it took a while for it to settle, and it disturbed and polluted the environment. Beings were apathetic about the pollution and did not do much about it. There were groups on the planet who used to live together harmoniously but later they became segregated.

"They released certain chemicals from their being, which caused more pollution and harm to other beings of other groups but was harmless to themselves. They were angry at each other a lot. From the Light, I see that, over time, the planet and all the beings got very dark. When the beings became angry, they created and released toxins that were damaging to everybody except themselves. They used it like a killing machine, and others also learn to do that. So they decided to have small wars between the representatives of the two groups, and the team that lost, their people would leave the planet and commit mass suicide. If they did not do this, then pretty soon everybody would die and the planet would be destroyed. From heaven, I am seeing that the group that lost refused to leave the planet. As a result, there was a war between the groups and they each released a lot of neurotoxins, and the planet choked. The atmosphere became poisonous and everybody died. The whole planet was all black. I see that the planet is basically dead. It is still floating around but there is no life.

"I see that, in the current life, my sensitivity to different cleaning chemicals, perfume, hairspray, and smoke is coming from that life as a jellyfish, causing symptoms such as instant headaches, difficulty in breathing, getting very angry without any reason, and an inability to function in the outside world. I see that my attention deficit disorder partly comes from this life because of the toxins.

"From heaven, I can see that it was a better way to resolve a conflict where only a few people fought and sacrificed their lives, rather than having a full blown chemical war which would have destroyed thousands of beings and *probably done a great deal of damage to the planet and the beings of the planet through the chemicals.*

"Before the planet looked completely dark, and when Dr. Modi asked for the healing of the planet, angels put drops of something in the water and it got purified. It absorbed all the negativity and the toxins were neutralized. Then the angels lifted the demons out and freed all the soul parts of all the beings of the planet and integrated them with whom they belonged, after cleansing and healing them. They took the spirits of the beings of the planet to the heaven. They also transformed the demons into the Light and took them to the heaven, too. I see that the drops the angels put in the water were the tears of the angels, which neutralized the toxins and purified the planet. It may be symbolic, too. Then they brought the soul parts of the planet from everywhere and integrated them with the planet. I see a golden Light and then the violet Light going through the whole planet and its beings and purifying them. Then the angels shielded the whole planet with the crystal shield."

We Were Genetically Created to Follow Orders Like Robots

One of my patients recalled the following life as a source of her indecisiveness and difficulty in breathing:

- *"I am on a red planet. I am about a hundred and two years old. We have skeleton-like bodies with big mouth and teeth. We have backbones, and we look like scary animals. We are of a dark green color. We are bony, with thick scabs, and no muscles. We are upright, have thick tails, and are about five and a half feet tall. Other soldiers and I are genetically created beings to follow orders. We have very little emotions and do what we are told. We have a little place where we sleep and eat. We are like robots, just following orders. The commanders have more emotions. We are like a military unit that protects the planet from intruders and attackers. We are protecting the center, or core of the planet, which has knowledge and information of the planet. The core looks like a sun within the planet. It maintains the life force on the planet and the beings of other planets want it as an energy source.*

"An alien race from another planet is attacking us. We are on spaceships fighting in space. There are too many aliens for us to handle. Our commander becomes greedy and wants more power, so he told the enemies the location of our sun. They take the sun from our planet and it implodes and everything just disappears in a flash. It seems that, when this happened, some of us are grabbed by the dark beings while others are helped into heaven. The enemies take the sun and use it to create more energy and get more knowledge, but it was from the dark side. From heaven, I see our commander was taken by the enemies and tortured. They took different samples from his body and used him as an experimental subject, which ultimately killed him.

"On Dr. Modi's request, the angels located and brought back all the soul parts of all the alien beings who were blown out when the planet imploded. They cleansed, healed, and filled them with Light and integrated them with whom they belonged.

"Then they were escorted into heaven by the angels. The angels also removed all the devices from me and all the humans and other beings. Then they scrubbed, cleansed, and healed those areas and brought all their soul parts back and integrated them into those areas where the devices had been. They cleansed, healed, and shielded me and all those humans and other beings. They also destroyed the aliens' spaceships, dark centers, and devices. They did the same for the planet, by bringing all

its soul parts back from Satan, his demons, people, places, and darkness, then cleansed, healed, and filled them with love and Light, cut their dark connections, and integrated and recreated the whole planet. Then they brought back the sun of the planet and integrated it with the planet and completely shielded the planet.

"The demon commander, after his transformation, described how they took the sun of that planet and its knowledge and used it negatively.

"I see many symptoms that came from that life to this life. I was completely automated in that life. In this life, I wait for the directions. It is hard for me to make decisions."

I Am Shocked! I Am a Plant Being

One of my patients regressed back to the following life as a source of her feelings of being stuck:

- *"I am shocked to find that I am a plant-like being on another planet. We all look like plants, except we are mobile. We detach, float, and reattach again. We feel we are a part of the group and we communicate telepathically through vibrations. Our energy is being zapped and taken away. We are very old and we are all dying together. I am having difficulty breathing. I feel there is some toxicity in the environment that is causing all of us difficulty in breathing, and slowly we all died, except the younger plants.*

  "As I look back from heaven at that planet, it is not green or pretty. There are mud pits and plants. Plant life is the main life. They are the intelligent beings of the planet. There are plants near us that are vines and make nets. They are covering and shading all of us and all the other plants. These are networks of vines, while each of us is just one plant. They were blocking the sun and making shadows. We are like sunflowers, and if we do not have sun,

we cannot generate food. The vine beings are indifferent about our suffering. We are all sick and dying. This was happening all over the planet. You, Dr. Modi, are a shaman on another planet. You are looking into a crystal ball and can see our planet and what is going on there. You are praying and redirecting the energy of the universe, and it is pulling out the poison from the plant beings. You send the trails of the vine in the ground and anchor them, so instead of going wide, they are going deep in the ground looking for food, and it does not have to expand outside. You manifested it through your will. I see that another part of your soul is a plant being on our planet. That is why you became aware of that planet and what is going on, on that planet. The younger plant beings get healed, but the older ones, including myself, die. I have difficulty in breathing, extreme fatigue, and weakness as I am dying. Some milky stuff is oozing from all of us.

"As I review my life from heaven, I see that some plant beings who were there are also here in my current life as my friends. I see that my difficulty in breathing and my feelings of being stuck are partly coming from that life."

Life as a Robot

One of my patients had muscle and joint rigidity and stiffness all over her body. Sometimes she described feeling like a robot. As she focused on these feelings, she recalled a lifetime on another planet when she was created as a robot:

- *"I am on another planet where I am actually created as a robot. It has something to do with the artificial intelligence. I choose to be born on that planet because I want to experience what it is like to be a robot and have artificial intelligence because this is something that is going to be used some time in the future on Earth. Beings choose to be born on that planet because they want to know what it feels like to be a machine, because in the future, machines will play a bigger role in everyday life.*

"I am in an assembly line where I am being created as a shiny metallic humanoid robot that is about five feet tall. At some point, my soul, which looks like a yellow ball, drops into the robot from an invisible portal as if it is being dropped from nowhere. But it is really coming from heaven. So instead of going into the womb of a person, the soul is going into the robot. I see hundreds of robots being created in that assembly line. The robots are put together piece by piece by machines and then the soul enters the robot. The robots have two arms, two legs, a chest, and a head.

"First my chest and head are put together, and then the soul, which looks like a ball of yellow Light, enters my head and goes into the chest. Then my arms and legs are attached to it. Then I open the eyes, as if I am being born. I am aware that I am a being or an entity. I do not think I am a robot, different from humans. I just am. Then some robots direct us to different places, where we receive specialized instructions about what kind of functions we will be performing. We can walk and understand the instructions. All the hardwiring is there for the basic functions, such as walking, talking, and other functions.

"I am told that I will be a diver. There are lots of big ships that sank with valuable treasures.

"So I receive special computer chips, which are put in the brain, and hardware to be able to swim in very deep water and bring back valuable treasures and artworks that fell into the ocean. They are also adding some special material on the outside of my frame so the metal does not rust and does not get damaged in the water.

"After about twenty years of doing the diving, it becomes difficult for me to move with comfort. They are not making new parts that I need. So it is like I am becoming outmoded. They stopped making robots like me. They cannot get the replacement parts, so they will continue to

let me work until I cannot function anymore. With time, it becomes hard for me to function and walk. One day, after about twenty-five years, while I am in the ocean, my machinery stops working and I fall apart in the ocean and die. My soul feels relieved. I am not trapped in the metallic body anymore. I am helped to the Light by angels right away. In heaven, I get cleansed and healed.

"Then I go for my life review with three Light beings. I tell them I am glad to have been born into that life because it taught me a lot about what it means to be a machine. Sometime in the future this information will be very important. My soul inside the robot was not feeling much pain or emotion, but it was storing the memories.

"As I look at that plane, it is not the Earth. This is a very advanced society and they use robots for all sorts of purposes. That is why I chose to be on that planet as a robot, to experience how it feels to be a robot. The beings there are creating robots to do different jobs but are not aware that, literally, souls are coming into the robots and that these souls were there to experience how it feels to be a robot. What I see is that not every robot has a soul in it. Only randomly does a soul go into a robot for the purpose of experience. About 6 percent of the robots have souls in them. Souls in the robots are dormant and do not feel emotions.

"I chose to have this experience because I knew that robots, machines, and artificial intelligence will be a big part of our existence in the future. I wanted to live like a robot to understand how humans and robots can communicate properly. I see that later on, in another life on another planet, my job was to construct these robots, which were most efficient.

"From heaven, I see that the problems that come from that life to my current life are stiffness, joint problems, and sluggishness.

"On Dr. Modi's request, the angels brought all the soul parts of the souls who lived in robots on that planet and on all the other planets throughout creation, from Satan, his

demons, and from people, and places; then they cleansed them, healed them, and integrated them with whom they belong.

"Archangel Michael gave the understanding that, in some instances, soul parts were lost when the soul felt intense feelings such as stiffness, rigidity, and difficulty in moving, although the robot did not. In other cases, people did not lose the soul parts in that life, but in heaven they chose to leave the cords to the memory of that life open so that they can feel the symptoms and remember the life.

"On Dr. Modi's request, angels cleansed, healed, and integrated my past life personality with me."

Wow! I Can Communicate With All Life Forms on My Planet

One of my patients recalled a life living on a glowing white planet where she could communicate with all types of life forms.

- *"I am incarnated on this planet as a white, translucent, human-type life form about five thousand years ago. We are all female and have long white hair, white gowns, and a garland of fresh flowers on our heads. We are not born on the planet as infants. We arrive fully developed – I was twenty – through Light that comes to Barina. We transform into our forms out of the Light. I live with four other women. We are a sisterhood, and each of us has a special mission. We support each other with our missions. We have no reproductive organs. Eating is important and it's a ritual around which ideas are exchanged and mutual support given. We do not have names, but intuitively know who each other is. We are not required to work for money. We focus our time on completing our missions. There is no need to procreate or raise children, since we arrive on the planet as adults.*

"*Barina is a planet that looks glowing white from a distance. There are many life forms on the planet, most of which are there from other planets. All forms of life are very friendly. The only indigenous life is the large, orange-yellow manta ray-like creatures that fly in the sky. Other animal life forms are the multi-colored caterpillars, the pink, almost translucent snake-like creatures, and the blue creatures that live attached to rocks. There are various types of plant life. It's a green, peaceful planet with an advanced society that is guided by the floating, shiny white orbs that are a very advanced life forms.*

"*Barina is in the early stages of habitation and it is important to understand the needs of all the life forms, including the planet. My mission is to understand how to communicate with the different life forms on the planet. After prayer, meditation, and consulting with my peers and the white orbs, I understand that I must travel through one dimension to get to a special dimension, from where I can access the energy and vibrations needed to communicate with the various life forms on Barina. I see that I must travel through the space between two spinning, yellow disks. After going through there, I see a larger white-blue spinning disk. I stand inside the disk and am able to see that there is a blue energy stream that flows between all the life forms on Barina. I can tap into this energy stream to understand what each one wants to communicate. I work on this project for many years and much of my time is spent teaching the orbs and other human-like forms to communicate with the various life forms.*

"*When I am approximately a hundred and sixty years of age, a large, orange-yellow ball of fire descends to Barina and floats just above the surface. Many feel apprehensive about this ball. I go with two other human-like sisters to the special dimension. This time, instead of just stepping into the dimension, I understand that we must step through it, to the other side. As we look forward, above, and to our sides, we see darkness and many stars and planets. We feel very small. When we look down, we see the orange orb of fire floating in the darkness. We must enter the orb to understand what it needs. The three of us immerse ourselves in the orb, and once inside, we hold hands and face outward. The orb tells us that it is a piece of a planet that broke apart. There are many others like it and they need a new home. We explain that, though our planet cannot provide the environmental conditions necessary for their survival, the orange orbs can circle around our planet, in a ring. This is what they do.*

"I live on this planet till the age of one hundred and eighty, when I decide my mission is complete and I return to the Light. I understand that I chose to be born on this planet so that I could learn how to communicate with different life forms. This information will be necessary on Earth in the future, where the environment is being quickly depleted and where many humans and their leaders are unable to communicate effectively with one another, let alone understand the needs of non-human life forms, such as animals and plants."

My Body was Chopped Up for Believing in God

One of my patients had severe aches and pains all over her body, including her joints. Under hypnosis, as she discussed her symptom, she recalled a past life when she was incarnated on another planet where there was extreme darkness and most people were totally possessed. Nobody was allowed to talk about God or spirituality, and those who did were tortured and punished severely:

• *"I am a six-year-old girl living on another planet named Zota. It is about 6000 BC according to Earth's time. I have a body like a human except that I have pointed eyes and ears. A group of psychic people can see the Light around me and tell my parents that I have special abilities which should be developed, and that I got a scholarship to a school where they can help me develop them.*

"In that school, the first thing they do is cover the Light around me with a shield so other evil people cannot see the Light around me. In that school, they teach me how to communicate with the heavenly beings, how to protect myself from the demonic influences, and how to develop and use different psychic gifts I have. I graduate from that school at the age of sixteen. I decide to become a writer. For about five years, I write fictional stories but incorporate a lot of information from the Light.

"When I am twenty-eight, I see a lot of darkness all over the planet. Most of the politicians are very dark. People are not allowed to talk about God, and anybody who does is tortured and killed. Since I am also writing and speaking about God, they capture me and take me to a spaceship. The captain on the spaceship is totally possessed by the demons. He is an alien being and looks like a walking lizard, and is very mean and evil. I see on the spaceship that there are many of my journalist friends who are talking about what I wrote in my books, that God is real and we are all connected with him.

"The alien captain of the spaceship is collecting people from many different planets who talk and teach about God to their people, like I do. The captain and his people cut the left foot off of everybody they capture. Then they send us back to our respective planets. We are told to tell everybody that God does not exist. If we don't do that, we will be captured and brought back on the spaceship and another foot will be cut off. This way, if we do not do what we are asked, then they will cut us up part by part till we die.

"Then they send us to our respective planets. They put a device in us so they can continue to observe us. On the planet, I still continue to talk about God, on television and in person. I also write articles for newspapers and send

emails. I distribute pamphlets with information about God. As a result, they send me to the spaceship again. The evil captain is very angry. He cuts off my right foot this time. He does it with a laser instrument so there is no bleeding. Then they send me down to the planet with the same condition, that I should tell people there is no God. If I do not, then they will cut off another part of my body, and this will continue till I die.

"On the planet, I continue to talk and write about God and our connections with Him. As a result, they continue to take me to the spaceship, and the captain and other dark people cut another part of my body off and send me back to the planet with the same condition, but I continue to teach and write about God. Over time, they cut off both ankles, knees, hips, hands, elbows, and shoulders, one part at a time, but I remain determined and continue to talk about God and demons. After they cut off both my legs up to the knees, they send me to the planet on an electric wheelchair. I have lots of pain, but I am determined, and continue to spread the word about God. I still do not stop, and I continue to talk about God, so they cut off my ears, lips, nose, back muscles, one kidney, and one lung, one part at a time.

"Finally, I die thinking I am grateful to God for giving me great strength and determination. I will continue to do this work. After the death of my physical body, I go straight to heaven. After cleansing and healing, I go for my life review.

"From heaven, I see that all my joint pain and other aches and pains all over my body came from that life to my current life. I chose to have these symptoms in my current life for healing and also a reminder of my inner strength and my purpose.

"I also see the positive qualities coming from that life to the current life, such as the gift of writing and speaking, and incredible strength and faith in God."

Chapter 17

ABDUCTION

According to my hypnotized patients, abductions do occur and are real. They are often purposeful and are not just casual. Some people who are abducted feel there is a reason they were selected, and not because someone was being playful or just fooling around. Some of them even claim that they gave permission to be abducted by aliens in heaven before incarnating into their current life. My hypnotized patients provide various information about abductions, such as why they were abducted, how they were abducted, by whom they were abducted, where were they taken, what was done to them, how were they brought back, and how it affected them.

Consent Given for Abduction

The word *abduction* indicates that it is done without consent and it is something that happens even though the person does not want it. In fact, many of these abductees, as they are called, have actually consented to the events. They either consented beforehand in the Light (heaven) before the incarnation, or beforehand in the life, or at the time of the abduction. Sometimes consent could have been given in a past life. A blanket permission is frequently granted in heaven or in the life in early stages. So even if it appears to be against the person's free will, it is in keeping with free will because the consent was given long ago. Still, there are many that are real abductions, where there is no consent, and are like literal rapes.

There are some alien abductions for the person's benefit, which are primarily done by the positive races that have obtained permission. The ones for the aliens' benefit are primarily being done by the races that would not bother to ask permission. These are the negative races that are working for Satan and his demons. Sometimes the negative races working for the dark side are given permission by the abductees, which the alien races did not seek, but nonetheless, permission was given.

Here, we have two separate categories: abductions with consent, and abductions with no consent. Some abductions are done for positive purposes; some are done for negative purposes, to control, and for the alien's own selfish purposes that are not necessarily negative but not to help the person either. That is not their objective. Currently, aliens who are influenced and controlled by the demons are doing the most abductions. The gray aliens are actively abducting for selfish reasons. They have demonic influence but do not even know it.

Those humans who had lived lives on the gray aliens' planet before its destruction have a bit of sympathy with them and are more likely to give permission and agreement in heaven before birth that this will be their plan to be abducted. They give permission to improve the gray race, to try and give them genetic material so the grays can survive, but they do not remember it consciously. As far as these people are concerned, it is like a rape to have their genes taken by the grays. These gray aliens have made so many intemperate modifications that their survival as a race is questionable. They do not know what they are doing.

Methods of Abductions

My hypnotized patients described many methods by which people are abducted. Sometimes the craft can land where the human being is and the actual physical being is transported to the craft, so the entire physical, mental, and spiritual body is carried away. Sometimes they only abduct the spiritual body, and in these cases, people feel that they floated right through a window, door, or a wall. They do not realize they are in spirit and not in the physical body. These are the most common kind of abductions, where the body stays behind. It is a spiritual abduction and because we are real in spirit, it feels as if the body is there, too.

The actual physical abductions are done through an anti-gravity device. It can float people out of an open window but not through a closed window. According to my hypnotized patients, witnesses on the ground have witnessed the abduction in various cases. They have seen people floating through the air and into a ship. Sometimes even a flying machine, such as a helicopter or an airplane, has been taken up to a UFO and taken into it with the same antigravity mechanism. There have been other occasional abductions by other means, such as a human taking another human away. Here, the human is actively cooperating with the aliens.

Crafts Used for Abductions

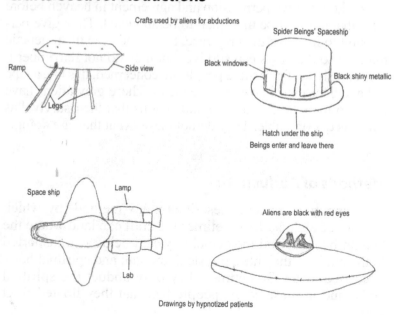

Crafts used by aliens for abductions

Ramp
Side view
Legs

Spider Beings' Spaceship
Black windows
Black shiny metallic
Hatch under the ship
Beings enter and leave there

Space ship
Lamp
Lab

Aliens are black with red eyes

Drawings by hypnotized patients

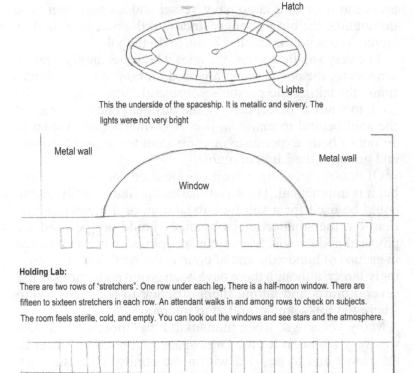

Drawings by a hypnotized patient
Spaceship with the Blobs

Hatch

Lights

This the underside of the spaceship. It is metallic and silvery. The
lights were not very bright

Metal wall

Metal wall

Window

Holding Lab:
There are two rows of "stretchers". One row under each leg. There is a half-moon window. There are
fifteen to sixteen stretchers in each row. An attendant walks in and among rows to check on subjects.
The room feels sterile, cold, and empty. You can look out the windows and see stars and the atmosphere.

The size of the crafts used for abductions range from extremely small, perhaps ten inches across and a few inches high, to a full sized main base craft, which is immense by Earth standards, according to my hypnotized patients. The most common craft for physical abduction is what we might call a scout ship, or a family sedan. It is not very large, but it is used to take the person away to a place where the aliens can work undisturbed. There is room inside for perhaps three, four, or five occupants. Sometimes these physical vessels are used to transport the person to a larger ship. The larger spaceships generally do not come that close to the Earth and do not interact with people.

Smaller ships are the ones that actually go out and carry the crew to do most of the work. It is like the difference between an ocean liner or a large navy vessel and a small boat. You do not take the big passenger liner into the bay, into shallow water. You send the smaller boats to do the job.

The very smallest ships, the ones which are simply a ray of sensors for the power plant, are used for non-physical abductions, for taking the person's conscientiousness, that is, the soul, to another place, leaving the physical body and part of the soul behind to maintain life. It is roughly equivalent to an out of body experience or equivalent to leaving the body and going to the Light at night.

Of course, any larger craft can be used for an abduction, but it is impractical. The scout spaceship, like a family sedan, could be used for a spiritual abduction, or a mental abduction, but the smaller ones obviously could not be used for physical abductions. Sometimes people have been abducted in groups of hundreds, and of course, the craft is correspondingly larger, although there have been group abductions using several crafts and taking them all back to a common ship where the folks are permitted to interact.

Many years ago, when humankind was more primitive, it was very common for the large spacecraft to come closer to the planet and to be used within the atmosphere. But with humankind becoming more technologically sophisticated, the larger craft now stay further out away from the planet.

The **shape** of these spacecraft varies from the classic smaller craft with two saucers, one on top of the other, where both the top and bottom are curved. The larger the craft gets, the more likely the bottom is flat and the top dome is higher. Sometimes there will be a dome on the top of another dome. Most commonly, spacecraft are circular. Some are boomerang shaped or triangular, while others are shaped like conventional airplanes. Some are shaped like air balloons, or long thin cigars, or rockets. The largest of the major spaceships are rather irregular in shape. Since there is no resistance in space, they do not have to be streamlined in any way, shape, or form. As a result, they have projections and parts added everywhere.

The **color** of the craft, according to my hypnotized patients, ranges from a dark iron to stainless steel. Some alien races use yellow, blue, or green material as a decoration, while some are painted or have color incorporated into the metal itself. The color can be incorporated into the top surface of the metal or as a plastic cover, and sometimes it is worked all through the metal, depending on which race makes it and if they have a particular purpose in mind. Most crafts are made of a lighter metal, which is more common in the universe. Sometimes they are made up of a ceramic material that is incorporated from non-metallic elements. Ceramics can be made very light and fluffy, extremely strong, and silicon- or carbon-based. The structures can be made up of thin and light substance, which is not exactly a plastic but not a metal either. Sometimes they are of a composite material carbon- or silicon-based, sometimes incorporating lighter material into them and other times using heavier material like iron. Some could qualify as the Earth-designated plastic.

The **interior** of the spacecraft ranges from literally no interior at all to the more elaborate. The small ones have no interior, since they are all machine and filled with working components. Other smaller crafts, like the scout crafts, have functional interiors where there is a cube shape left open for the crew to be in, while the rest of the volume is used up with control, propulsion, and other devices. Some of the smaller crafts do not even have seating in them, since the crew is not expected to be in for long periods. The larger the craft, the more elaborate they are. There are rooms for the crew to rest, eat, eliminate; all the things they need to stay for an extended period of time. They have several rooms, a medical facility, and a place to do research. This is not a place for elaborate scientific research, but a place where they collect samples and implant the devices into human beings.

The larger ships get even more elaborate, where the scientific rooms for conducting experiments occupy more of the craft. The largest of them are like self-sustaining ocean liners. According to the heavenly beings, they have everything needed to maintain life for millions of years. They are not limited by time, space, fuel, food, or water. Occasional small additions can be made to continue operations from planets where they are or taken from asteroid belts or from stars. They can grow their own food and create their own fuel so that, except for a little less space, the crafts are self-sustaining. These are bigger than a city or more like a world. The largest of these are moon sized. These are the motherships, where aliens can live and move from solar system to solar system, or even from galaxy to galaxy. They are completely independent and can be in communication with their home world or each other. In these motherships, entire civilizations can be maintained and they can be the size of a small planet or large moon.

These huge motherships have their own artificially constructed gravity. The folks who built these are sophisticated enough to control their own gravity and can create, modify, or negate gravity. There are also those travelers between time and dimension, where they can travel to other times or other spaces. These ships oftentimes belong to beings who do not have a planet of their own because their planet was destroyed. They were on these motherships before their home planets were destroyed.

The interior of a mothership has everything needed to maintain life, to do all the scientific work, and enjoy all the life activities, and it is just a way of life on board. Things are small and close together and multipurpose, more like a ship than a home on land, where people tend to spread out. On a spaceship, everything is compact. These ships have a common eating area, a common food preparation area, and a common bathroom area, rather than duplicating and requiring more space.

Different Types of Abductions

My hypnotized patients describe different types of abductions besides the individual abductions, as follows.

- Abduction of many family members or a group by the same aliens
- Abduction in a past life on Earth
- Abduction in a past life on another planet
- Abduction by a demon acting as an alien being

Many Family Members or a Group Abducted by the Same Aliens

Positive alien abductions of a family or a group generally are for the benefit of individuals within that group, to help them understand their own lives, their own interactions, to help them develop spiritually or physically, and to study human psychology and how humans function within groups. There can be other reasons for group abductions, such as an occasional abduction to take people out of the world to prevent something bad happening to them, such as during a natural disaster or a car accident, or removing someone from an airplane that is about to crash.

Sometimes many people from one family or a group are abducted. In general, there are some family abductions to examine how families are developing into a group, but for the most part it is done for the aliens' purposes, to take genes from them and to see how the DNA is expressed through the generations.

Abduction of more than one family member creates more anxiety in the family members than in an individual abduction. Everybody feels nervous, upset, vulnerable, and insecure, which creates more problems in the family. If the aliens put devices in one person, they can not only track down and abduct that person, but they can also abduct other members of the family. Aliens abduct many members of a family for continuing genetic studies, to learn how the genes are expressed in a family. This is generally done by the selfish alien beings, such as the gray aliens. They are not interested in helping people, but do it for their own selfish purposes.

One of the dragon-like aliens was in a patient as a possessing entity who claimed to be from a planet that no longer exists because it got sucked up in a black hole. The alien spirit claimed to join the patient when she was young. The patient recalled the event as follows:

- *"I am six years old, sleeping in my sister's apartment. She is twenty-four years old. Both of us are abducted by the dragon aliens and taken to a spaceship. These aliens have a body of a dinosaur and also like a mythical dragon. They have two arms with three fingers on each hand, two legs, and they stand upright. They seem to have a dark gray or brown skin. They put us on a table and poke and examine us. They are emotionless, rough, and they are violating us. If they want something from us, they just take it. They are like bullies and forceful. We both lost many soul parts in the spaceship.*

  "They are putting something in my mouth and it becomes very dry [patient is coughing continuously]. They put a device in my ears, which sometimes causes them to clog. They put something in my belly button to look inside. Then they put something between my buttocks to look inside. After that, they sent us back to my sister's apartment. We are both blanked out and do not have many memories. Through the device in my ear, they are broadcasting their thoughts to me, telling me I am supposed to serve them and no one else. I get the feeling that they are controlled by demons.

  "I am abducted by the same aliens when I am eight years old. At this time, I see my mom, dad, and my sister lying on the other tables in the spaceship. I feel very upset and scared. They examine me and do different tests on me

and then beam me back to my room, and next morning I have no awareness.

"After you asked for cleansing and healing, this dragon alien spirit in me is saying that they were trying to take genes of different people so that they can create new beings. But now, since we cleansed and healed them, they realize that they were controlled by Satan and his demons, and were misguided by them to do these evil experiments. They are apologizing for it. They seem to be completely changed after the healing, and appear to be very caring and helpful. They are just realizing that their bodies died thousands of years ago and they are just a spirit. They want you to heal their whole race.

"As you asked the angels to cleanse, heal, and remove all the devices from me, my family members, all the humans and aliens who were ever abducted from the beginning of time, and all these dragon aliens, and all the beings of their race, I saw it all happening, with me and all over the universe, and then angels are taking all these dragon beings to heaven. They are thanking you for the healing and apologizing to me and my family for abducting and traumatizing us."

Abduction in a Past Life on Earth

Some patients claimed being abducted in one or more past lives. Sometimes abductions can happen in many lives by the same aliens, because the aliens live a long life, maybe four or five times a human's life, including the time in the Light (heaven). So the same aliens can abduct the same soul in many lives, over and over. They recognize the soul by its spiritual vibrations. The aliens, who do not have the built-in ability to recognize the vibrations, can build machines or devices that can detect and analyze spiritual frequencies.

So, for the aliens, it is like they still have consent to abduct the same soul who is living another life in another body.

One patient, just before entering into a trance, began to cry because she could not feel her hands and feet. During a hypnotic trance, she recalled being a soldier in a past life who was wounded in a battlefield and then abducted and taken to a spaceship. There, the aliens cut his forearms and legs and put mechanical armor on him, converting him into an android.

Following is the account given by the patient:

* *"I am a nineteen-year-old soldier living in Scotland in 1489 AD. We are fighting a religious war. I am hurt by a sword in the left shoulder and in my left and right knees. I am unconscious. I see these other soldiers with shields around them. They pick me and other wounded soldiers up and take us into a spaceship. We are being sucked up into a spaceship by a force. There, they put us on tables that do not have legs. They are just floating. Here, there are many different types of alien beings, like a whole civilization. They want to change us into androids, part human and part robot, and then they can hook us up into their system and make us work for them. One of their androids takes me and eight other soldiers into another room.*

    "An alien with a bean-like head and an android come to me. They are cutting off my armor. They are very rough and callous. I feel like this android has feelings but they are suppressed. They cut my forearm off below my elbow and put a mechanical arm on me. Then they put my fingers in the mechanical hand so that they are attached to a machine through which an electrical current flows, which helps in healing and connecting the mechanical hand and fingers with each other. They cut my toes and put two

Created Android

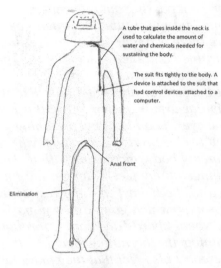

A tube that goes inside the neck is used to calculate the amount of water and chemicals needed for sustaining the body.

The suit fits tightly to the body. A device is attached to the suit that had control devices attached to a computer.

Anal front

Elimination

Drawing by a hypnotized patient

Mixed created being

Spoke telepathiically

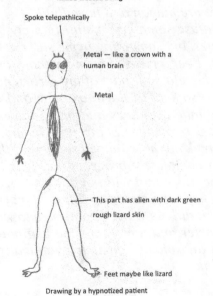

Metal — like a crown with a human brain

Metal

This part has alien with dark green rough lizard skin

Feet maybe like lizard

Drawing by a hypnotized patient

plates on the bottom of my feet. It seems like I am not in my body, or I am passing out intermittently. They also cut out my penis and put a tube in, which goes down in the shoes where there is a bag. When you push it over, all the fluids get drained and then it seals itself. They also put a tube in my rectum to drain the stool.

"Next, I become aware that I look like their android. They put similar armor on me. I have this helmet that has holes for the eyes. I can hear my breathing in this helmet. I have about twelve prods all around my head. The whole armor fits on my body and moves with it. There are these shoe-like things on my feet. I am getting the sense that I am attached to the helmet and the rest of the robot uniform with prongs, which go in different parts of the body, such as my vocal chords and lungs, through which they are maintaining the breathing because the atmosphere here is different. I also feel that they put a tube on the left side of the helmet going down through my throat that is a part of the uniform. It keeps the fluid going in and out because we are human and have fluid.

"They infuse some green stuff into my brain to cover my memories, but something in me still remembers in bits and pieces. I get a flash of memory that I am part human and I also have a soul part of my girlfriend in Scotland. Now I am also sent to Earth as their android worker to pick up wounded soldiers and bring them to the spaceship. Since I remember being part human, I feel being jolted as I pick up the wounded soldiers. I think they were not able to completely program me. It is like there is a strong force in me that will not allow them to totally program me. They keep on trying different ways, even shocking me, but it did not work. I continued to work on getting more memories and now I am also beginning to secretly help other androids. I do it telepathically because we cannot speak.

"When we bring the wounded soldiers from Earth to the spaceship, they first examine them. They select some to change into an android and the rest of the soldiers are put into a slot where they are chopped up, like in a garbage disposal. I feel there is a strong demonic control here on the spaceship. I am upset about what they are doing, so I go to their leader. Others are trying to stop me but I go anyway. It is a female alien. She has a bee head and has a crown over her head, and has kind of beetle wings, which are brown and translucent. She has very thin arms and legs like a beetle and has three fingers.

"I go in and say, "In the name of God, you are not to do this to humans," and she says, "God? Who is God?" We are communicating telepathically. She orders me to be taken away but I grab her neck and crack it, and notice her mechanical spine. She is just mechanical, and her head bounces back and she orders me to be destroyed. They take me to that garbage disposal and I am going to be destroyed. My last thoughts are, "If I did not have these emotions I would not have gone to that leader." They take my robotic costume off and unplug me. I am having difficulty breathing. They throw me into that slot and I am chopped to pieces.

"My spirit is out of my body. I go to the leader. She is still kind of twisted. But I feel myself being pulled up to the Light (heaven). It is very quiet. I see my friend who was also on the spaceship. As a matter of fact, many of the soldiers who were abducted and then killed are here. First I am cleansed and healed in heaven. Angels are doing hands-on healing on me. I am concerned if all my soul parts are back. The angels are telling me to ask them to be brought back. When I do, they are all brought back and integrated with me. They put bandages all over my body and then I rest for a long time.

"After resting, I go to a room for my life review with a grand Light being. He says he is Moses. He is saying that because of my dedication to God the aliens could not program me. As I look back from heaven, I can see that the alien beings on the spaceship did not have their own planet. They had limited space on the spaceship and limited technology, so they were using humans to create more helpers so they could take over a planet. I see that the whole spaceship looks dark and there are demons all over and there are black cords going from the spaceship to hell.

"From heaven, I realize that I needed to learn a lesson of not being too attached to the body. God's Light rules the whole universe and that I am made from God and no matter what parts I lose, what mechanical part is put on me, and even if I am all chopped up, I am still a part of God. The soul is a part of God and cannot be destroyed by anyone, ever. From heaven, I realize that I planned to be abducted to really know God within my soul and beyond the flesh. Also for the karmic balance, because in another life, a long time ago I was an alien and experimented on humans.

"Many problems came for me from that life to my current life, such as stomach problems, deep sadness, fear of loving, self-blame, throat problem, and hemorrhoids and colon problems because of the tube they put in my rectum.

"I also see from heaven that there were many people who were there in that life who are also here in my current life.

"When you asked the angel to bring back all the soul parts of me and all the other people who were there, I saw many soul parts coming back to my stomach, my throat, head, right hand, feet, and all over my body. Also soul parts are going back to all the other people and I see all of them healing. I also feel healing and releasing from that life's issues."

Abduction in a Past Life on Another Planet

Some of my patients recalled being abducted by aliens when they were incarnated on other planets. One of my patients recalled a life on another planet when the whole group was abducted by tall, thin aliens to a spaceship. They were modified surgically to function as obedient, telepathic, robot-like slaves, to do a certain job. She gave the following account:

- *"I look like a green Pillsbury Dough Boy, about four feet tall and not as round. I have two antennae in my head above my ears. They are for seeing, hearing, knowing, and sensing things. They are silvery metallic in color, and two or three inches high. They are like radio antennae. I do not speak. I live on a spaceship. I do not see a family here. There are other people who look like me. We are genetically and surgically modified. The spaceship is elliptical and made of shiny metal. There are windows all around, and there are feet-like projections to land on. This spaceship is used for research about the solar system and for communication with each other and other beings out there. The psychic antennae communicate visual pictures like movies and then we get commentary from within. It is like telepathic communication.*

    "I am also trying to pick up information about the lives of other beings on other planets. We have satellites in the solar system to pick up the information, which give visual images like movies from the satellite. I am also trying to analyze that information and compile it. There are hundreds of beings like me on the spaceship and they all are doing different jobs. I do the same thing for about fifty years. I am able to understand what I perceive in the data. I get what other people are experiencing but I do not have feelings or emotions myself. We are trying to understand a view of their lives and can understand intellectually their

feelings and emotions. We are doing it because we are curious about our universe. I think I am observing the people of Earth.

"After fifty years of working like this, the leader of the ship decides that we need to leave. The leader looks like us but is taller, about five feet, and has a bigger head and antennae above the ears and one on top of his head. The eyes are oval and look mechanical; he has no hair and has holes in place of a nose. There is a mouth and he can talk, but I cannot. There is a neck, chest, torso, legs, arms, and claw-like fingers. It looks like he has terry cloth for skin. I feel I have done a good job. I think I am to be disassembled. I do not feel bad about it because I am programmed. We are taken to another spaceship. It is bigger, like a city. There are doctors, scientists and geneticists there. They put different devices in us so we can perceive in a telepathic way without making a new model. These beings look more like humans. They have white skin, a long thin face, and a nose. They are tall and thin. After the surgery, I have a heightened perception. Then we are sent back to the first ship and do the same work for another thirty years. By this time, I am old and cannot be retooled anymore, so they put me to sleep by an injection. My last thoughts are that I did a good job. I enjoyed my work.

"My soul comes out of my chest and looks like a ball or cloud of Light. I am relieved and glad to be out. Now I feel emotions that I did not feel while in the body. I see a Light beam and I follow it. I see angels who look the way I did in that life and not like humans. They remove the devices and dark energy that were put in me to control and program me. I did not have senses such as touch, smell, and love. After cleansing and healing in heaven, I am hearing the beautiful, soothing, and healing music, and gradually I get all my senses back.

"I review my life with some angel-type beings. They are telling me that the tall aliens did genetic engineering

on me and on many others like me to increase telepathic power. My emotions and all the other senses were taken out so I could focus on the telepathic power. They are saying that these tall alien beings were misguided, but I will be able to use that knowledge and experience in the future. The angels want me to remember what I felt like to have that ability and to be able to use it.

"From heaven, I see that beings of our race were taken away from the planet Mars, but I am not sure. My parents were also genetically modified. When I was born, I had all the senses and emotions. Then at the age of fourteen, they did surgery and put devices in my brain, which took away my emotions and other senses and increased my telepathic powers, and they programmed me to do a certain job like an obedient slave or a robot. There were no feelings of discontent or rebelliousness. I see that the planet I was observing was an Earth-like planet with human beings with similar personalities and behaviors.

"From heaven, I see that my difficulty in expressing myself, my throat irritation, memory blocks, and sinus problems came from that life. I also see some people who were there and are also here in my current life."

A Demon Acting as an Alien Being and Abducting People

In some cases, patients recall being abducted by an alien being and, after a while, they changed into black blobs. These are often demons who have one or more disembodied souls or soul parts of aliens trapped within them. As a result, the demon can take the form of that alien being any time they want to. In these cases, patients' experiences of abductions are extremely traumatic. The abductees may find bruises and cuts.

One of my patients, in her history, mentioned that she went through a long period in her childhood when she was convinced she was a bad person and felt terrible. Her mother told her that when she was about six years old, she sent her to get some apples from a place where they sorted and sold apples from the local orchards. It was just down the street. When she got there, a man who worked there had to drive her home because she was hysterical. She told him she thought the police were going to come to get her because she was bad. The patient only vaguely remembered this. During the session, she recalled under hypnosis what follows.

Patient: I am about six years old. My mother sent me to get some apples. As I am walking, I see something that looks like a light at first, but it changes into an ugly glob with eyes sticking out of its head, like those monsters in the movie *Monsters Inc.* It is kind of humanoid. It looks like a blob, but it can change its shape. It has a kind of mouth that looks darker when open, and I do not really know where it goes. I do not see any ears, and the nose is like a blob. The rest of the body is a blob. It can have hands or legs if it wants to, because it can change shape. It is kind of greenish.

It is communicating with me telepathically. It is telling me in an authoritarian way to stop. I am shocked, confused, and scared. A beam lifts the being and me to the spaceship. I see that the being takes my spirit or soul to the spaceship, and I see my body kind of crouched, with my hands around my knees, as if I were frozen in time. On the spaceship, there is a different vibration than there is on Earth. It is faster. I can hear some humming and there is a light energy that is not coming from any light source. It is around these beings all the time. It makes me sick.

Inside the spaceship, there are a bunch of other blob-like beings. The spaceship has a dome shape and part of it is slightly open to the sky. I do not feel too good in the spaceship. It makes my heart and eyes feel funny, and makes my head hurt. There is a strange sound and I do not know what they want. I am confused. They are telling me that I am bad because I have done terrible things and they know all about them. They say my parents and everyone knows what I have done. They watch me all the time and they know what I did, and eventually I am going to be punished for it. It has something to do with this device.

They have my soul parts from different past lives when I stole money to buy food in one life, I was a prostitute in another life, and I misused psychic energy to hurt people by focusing my energy on them in a third life. They are actually showing me all this from a book and telling me I did all these bad things and I do not deserve to live.

They tell me I have to put this device over my face, which will make me feel better. It fits over my face and looks flat from the outside. It has wires which go to different parts of my face; my sinuses, the emotional centers in my brain and my cheeks, and there are connections which go down to hell. It looks like a facemask. As they put it on my face, my face feels frozen and strange. Then they tell me I better be good now and that this device will help me know what is good and what is bad.

Then they send me down. It is like I went to sleep and I am back on Earth in my body. That same being brings me back and when I go back into my body, it shakes me and it is saying not to tell anybody about this or we will call the police. Then it is shaking me and saying that I will not remember anything, and it goes back up to a spaceship, which is round with yellowish lights. The rest of the spaceship is metallic. In the center of it, there is a hole that is like a door.

I am very scared and confused. I keep on walking and crying. A man finds me and drives me home. From that point on, I am afraid to sleep at night. The alien beings were activating the device on my face to make me feel I was bad, and every time, my soul fragmented due to fear. I see that the connections from the device on my face go straight to hell, and from hell they go to the spaceship, and the demons along with alien spirits are able to affect me through that device. They still have my soul parts on the spaceship, which they are using to cause me feelings of fear and being bad. The demons, along with the alien spirits, are constantly talking and manipulating me. When you asked the angels to bring that being here, they did. It looks like an ugly black blob. It is very angry.

Dr. Modi: The being who abducted this person, who are you?

Being: (Angry) I am from hell. I am a special demon. I go after souls who have a special purpose, while they are still children. Children can be scared very easily, especially when they are apart from their parents. I have many spirits of aliens with me and that is how I am able to take their form from time to time. I took this person to the spaceship because I wanted to scare her. I did not want her to fulfill her mission.

Dr. Modi: I pray to God and request the angels of the Light to locate all the soul parts of this person and of aliens trapped inside this demon; help them out, cleanse them, heal them, cut their dark connections with this demon and with hell, and put all the aliens in one bubble of Light and put the soul parts of this person into another bubble of Light.

Patient: When you asked the alien beings to come out of this demon, about forty alien beings came out. These aliens are short. They have two dark, shiny eyes and are very slim. They have arms and legs and a big head. They look like the gray aliens do in pictures. Many of my soul parts were inside that demon and they came out, too. Also there are soul parts of many children coming out of that demon. The alien beings are saying that they are from the planet Antares.

All the alien beings and the human souls who are influenced by this demon are freed and cleansed and healed by the angels, on your request. This dark one was transformed into the Light and sent to heaven. The spaceship was cleansed, healed, and filled with Light. The alien beings here are spirits because their bodies have died and they and all the other alien spirits are sent to heaven on your request. Before leaving, these gray aliens claim that their planet was destroyed.

Dr. Modi: I pray to God and request the angels to please locate and bring all the soul parts of the planet of these alien beings, cleanse them, heal them, fill them with love and Light, integrate them together and recreate the whole planet, please.

Patient: I see that all the parts of their planet are being reintegrated and put back together. Now that planet looks luminous, kind of yellowish and big. I think it is going to take some time for it to totally heal. It is shielded with the Light and filled with the violet flame. I see the beings of that planet, who are on their spaceship, have a hard time believing what they are seeing.

Dr. Modi: Please remove the device from her face and all its connections from different parts of her body and all the other devices and dissolve them. Scrub and scour and cleanse her body. Bring all her missing soul parts back from the demon, aliens, spaceship, and hell. Cleanse them, heal them, and integrate them with her, please.

Patient: At your request, angels removed the facemask and all its connections and all the other devices. Then they cleansed and healed my whole body and being, and brought back all my soul parts that I lost due to the traumas and were with the demon, and from aliens, spaceship, and hell, and integrated them with me. The facemask device, which the demon put on me, worked as a wall so I would not be able to accept different realities of the things we are dealing with right now, and also the issues of right and wrong or black and white. After removing the device, I have freedom to accept what I want. The device on my face was working like a filter. When somebody said something to me, the demons were able to interject thoughts of my being bad with it.

Reasons for Abductions

There are many reasons why humans are abducted by various alien races through centuries. In some cases of abductions, consent was given, but in the majority of these cases, consent was not given. My hypnotized patients gave multiple reasons for their abductions, as follows:

- Abduction to help humanity; the cover story
- To perform genetic experiments
- Selfish purposes
  - Evil purposes
  - Spiritual education
- Technological purposes
- Psychological purposes
- Light Group purposes
  - Individual purposes
  - Friendships
  - Spiritual or religious experiences
  - Karmic resolution
  - Fun experiences
  - Curiosity

Abduction to Help Humanity; The Cover Story

Sometimes abductions can be for spiritual teaching, or they can be used as a cover story, such as, "We brought you here to help you with your spiritual development." Both the negative and positive races use this reason for abductions, but with the positive races, it is a true statement. Only about 5 percent of the legitimate abductions are by the positive races for spiritual advancement. When they first began to study mankind, thousands of years ago, there were very few abductions for spiritual teaching, but they have gradually increased since then.

Sometimes people are abducted so the aliens can help them, as described in chapter three, where eight alien races abducted humans from time to time to do genetic modifications leading to tremendous physical, emotional, and spiritual changes in humankind. They are still abducting some humans to observe changes caused due to genetic modifications they did thousands of years ago.

In about 1 or 2 percent of cases, people are being abducted for teaching of technology, especially by the positive races. Sometimes the grays will do this with some people in return for something else.

Some of the spiritual information being given by the negative grays with almond eyes right now is only a distraction, as a cover-up to hide behind. They are using it as a reason for the abductions. These grays are the gray alien race that is negative and selfish, not the gray alien race that did the genetic modifications on us about 800,000 years ago and is a positive and spiritual race. There are some cover stories that are planted in people by the alien abductors. Not that the reason is real, but it makes the person think and feel better about the abduction. Most of them are just that, cover stories in which the aliens make up a reason for the abduction that the person can accept. Stories such as, "They are abducted to save the planet"; "The aliens are here to avert a big disaster"; "They are abducting me to make the world a better place"; etc., rather than the truth, that the aliens want to gather scientific data.

These are not the real reasons for the current abductions, and helping mankind is not their big interest. The aliens are mostly interested in their own personal purposes. The real reasons may be that they are using their genes for selfish purposes, or using the materials from our planet. For those who gave consent, it has nothing to do with the reasons for their original consent.

One of my patients under hypnosis recalled being abducted by beetle-like alien beings. These aliens told the patient that they were creating humans to recolonize in case something happens to Planet Earth. They said they wanted to make sure the human species continues. In fact, the aliens were trying to create a mixed race for their own purposes. The patient under hypnosis gave the following account.

Alien being like a Beetle

The beetle is 5'4" tall and is dark brown in color

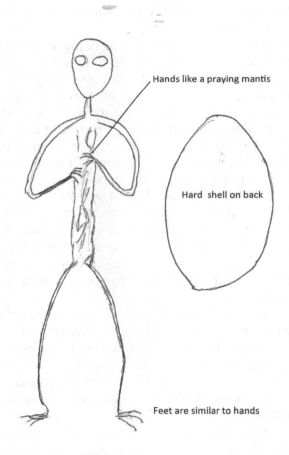

Hands like a praying mantis

Hard shell on back

Feet are similar to hands

Drawing by a hypnotized patient

- *"I am a baby in a crib, about two months old. I see two aliens who just came through the wall. They are upright beings but look like beetles. They have a head, a body, two arms, and two legs. Their eyes are like a beetle and they have thin hands like a praying mantis. They have a hard shell on the back like a beetle. Their legs are long and bent. They are about five feet four inches tall and have a dark brown color. They are saying that they have followed me for a couple of lifetimes and they want me to go with them. I see a spaceship hovering above the house, but nobody else can see it.*

  "These aliens state that they are creating a human family to recolonize in case something happens to Planet Earth. They want to make sure that the human species continues. They care because their ancestors helped create humans in their lineage. They want to integrate humans into their species. They live on a spaceship and they want to create a race mixed with humans and them. I did not like them and felt that they are not telling the truth.

  "They wanted to take my body but I resisted strongly. So they took my soul parts from my hand. They have a beetle baby with them, which is kind of dead, but they are sustaining it, like in a coma. They are taking my soul parts and putting them into that baby, especially from the left hand. The baby survives but it is a little bit retarded. So they come to me again at the age of three, but they could not take my body. The alien beings are saying that there is something about my DNA that they want because I have some knowledge about genetic modification. In a past life, I was a top scientist doing micro-integration, which was successful. I was doing exploration, mutations, and integrations of different species, and their scientists worked with me. Since the age of three, I am afraid of being taken away. They took my soul parts and fed their computer to track me down. They also put a device in my back, thyroid, and pituitary area, which caused a hormonal imbalance in me.

"The understanding I get is that there are about 220 million beetle beings living on a huge network of spaceships. They are working with a few other species, but mostly with humans. They are trying to create a superior race. They lost some capabilities that humans have, such as emotions, intuition, and knowingness. They claim their race is extinct now and most of them are in spirit forms. I am realizing that their spirits are controlled and used by the dark beings. They want you, Dr. Modi, to heal them so they can go to heaven.

"When you prayed to God and requested the angels to cleanse and heal me and all these alien spirits and beings who might be living, and bring all our soul parts back from Satan, his demons, humans, aliens, spaceships, places, and hell, and integrate them with whom they belong, I saw it all happening. Devices are being removed from me and all the humans and alien beings; soul parts are integrated and everybody is cleansed, healed, and shielded. I also see these alien beings and their spaceships and computers being cleansed and healed, and all their soul parts are being brought back from Satan, his demons, humans, aliens, their spaceships and other places, and integrated with them. Then thousands of spirits of beetle aliens are taken to heaven by the angels where they meet beings like them."

Abductions to Perform Genetic Experiments

As described in chapter three, about a million years ago, eight alien races did abductions in order to do genetic modifications on humans, who appeared like apes rather than humans. Heavenly beings, through my hypnotized patients, state that these were mostly positive alien races who were inspired by God to do genetic manipulation on those ape-looking humans to speed their evolution. Due to these genetic changes, we changed in our physical appearance from ape like humans to the current humans. We also became very spiritual and emotional beings. This surprised even these alien races. They are puzzled about how and why we have become so spiritual. They are still watching us to see how we change and what we do.

These alien races initially were not aware of other alien races doing genetic modifications with humans at the same time they were. Now they are aware of each other and discuss with each other the genetic changes they made with the humans, and their findings about the outcome. According to the heavenly beings, some of the alien races are still observing and abducting humans from time to time to see how we have changed and what progress we have made. They do it only with the consent of the humans they abduct.

Currently, some alien races are abducting people to do genetic experiments to create hybrid babies for different reasons. The short, thin, gray alien race with big almond eyes is the one who is doing most abductions currently, to create hybrid babies. This gray alien race is influenced by the demons but they are not even aware of it. There are also a few aliens of other races who are abducting humans for genetic modifications.

During a session under hypnosis, a patient saw two alien spirits and a spirit of a hybrid alien baby in her as possessing spirits. She recalled being abducted by these beings at the age of eight years. Following is an account of what happened:

- *"I am eight years old, sleeping in my bed. Two aliens come through the window. They are about five feet nine inches tall, thin, and have big eyes. They come in a spaceship that is on the top of the building. It is circular, coned up, and has red lights underneath. It is metallic gray, about twenty feet in diameter. I feel frozen and cannot move. I am trying to scream but I can't make a sound. One of*

Larger colored leader

(Hybrid)

Smaller, darker

"gray" drone

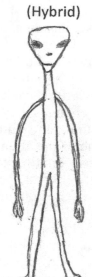

Drawings by a hypnotized patient

them takes an instrument like a wire tube, puts it through my arm into my heart area, and takes out a piece of tissue like a chunk from my heart. They also take a piece of hair, an eyelash, a piece of tissue from my eye, pubic hair, a piece from my belly button, a piece of my toenail, and a piece from my fallopian tube. They are taking pieces from different parts of my body and putting them in a box with little compartments. They are able to keep compartments in the same environment as the different pieces of my body so they can stay alive. This box is a machine that is connected to different parts of my body.

"They are beaming this light from their third eye to levitate my body from the bed so they can work all around my

body. They are not emotionless and seemed to be sensitive and caring. They have a scanner through which they can look right into my body and can take molecular pictures, as if they are almost taking that part, but they are not. They got my essence in the form of my whole body structure, and when they beam it up, it manifests dimensionally in the spaceship out of thin air. I feel like I am also in a spaceship, as if they instantly recreated me. Their technology is very advanced. In their spaceship, they have an operating room with a table, and with the scanner, my body shows up here molecularly, and then all of a sudden I am there on the spaceship, but it is only a part of my soul. I see a connecting cord between my physical body in my bed and my molecular body on the spaceship above the house. They want to replicate me as a human. After they are done, one of them puts his hand on my head and my body lowers down and I go to sleep. Next morning, I do not have any memories at all but have a sense that something happened.

"I see these spirits of two aliens, a male and a female, and an alien baby in me. The angels lifted them out of my body and brought them in front, outside of my shield in a bubble of Light. The only distinction between male and female is that the female's head is like a cone with no hair, but has bony bumps on the head; the eyes are big, and it has ears and a mouth. The body is smooth and there are no breasts. Their body has greenish lizard-like scales. They have two hands and two legs. They have four fingers and a thumb, but these are arranged slightly differently and are longer. The toes are the same way, and their bodies are thin. They do not have clothes. I feel that this alien baby has a soul-part or an essence of me. It is about five months old. I am getting the understanding that the aliens were able to create this hybrid alien baby from my structure that they took from me when I was eight years old. Also, these alien spirits are the spirits of the aliens who came to my room when I was eight years old.

"The alien spirits are saying that they are from Planet Pleiades. They need to keep the purity of the race. Through the scanner, they were also able to take my etheric body, and then from it, take a frequency that allowed them to create my body all over again in their laboratory. My body was in my bedroom but a soul part was in the spaceship. They wish me no harm. I had given them permission while in heaven before incarnating in the current body and I had lived on their planet before.

"They state that they wanted a baby, which they were trying to create from me. They were a bit of a renegade with this. There was a galactic policeman who took the baby away from them and killed it because it was tainted with human genes. These aliens were put in separate chambers, where they were suspended in time and space. It is like our jail system, and ultimately they were killed.

"They are saying that they are also a hybrid race. There were big, scaly, lizard-like aliens who abducted some Pleideans and they created hybrid beings like them by mixing the genes on Planet Xantha, which was hit by an asteroid and exploded a long time ago. Their people knew it was going to happen, so they escaped to a different galaxy and solar system. Some of them went back to the planet Pleiades. They wanted their own baby, so they took a spaceship and came to me and created the hybrid baby.

"These beings do not have many emotions because of the way they were created. So they created a baby by mixing human genes and with both of these aliens' genes so they can have more of love emotions. There are hybrid beings living in Pleiades and other planets and solar systems. They want to be healed and go back to heaven.

"As you, Dr. Modi, requested the angels to remove all the human, alien, and demon spirits, dark devices, energies, and shields from me, these alien beings, the baby,

and all the hybrid beings from all over the creation, lift them up, and help them to the Light or bind them in the spaces and cleanse, heal, shield, and protect all of us, I see it all happening with me, the spirits of the baby, the two alien beings, and multitudes of beings all over the universe. I see two, three, or more connecting cords coming out of these hybrid beings and going to God. The spirit of this hybrid baby has five connecting cords, which are connected to the soul parts of me, these two alien beings, and two of my friends. All our genes were mixed to create this baby, who looks like a combination of a human and an alien. They were separated and integrated with us where they belonged after cleansing and healing.

"I see multitudes of spirits of these hybrid beings going to heaven from all over the universe, and those who are still living in the body are cleansed, healed, and protected with different shields. They also completely healed me and shielded me."

One of my patients was having pain and discomfort in her rectum and vagina. She recalled a life as the source of her problems as follows:

- *"I am a fifteen-year-old female. One night, tall, big aliens abducted me from my room and took me to another planet. There they used me as a breeder. They impregnated me, and after delivery, they took my children away. These aliens are big, tall, with elongated heads, and they look like skeletons. They are humanoid, with two legs, head, arms, and big teeth. There are many of us here from different planets that are of different shapes, sizes, and forms and are used as breeders. It is horrible and terrifying and there is no escape. We are treated as slaves. They are creating mixed babies. I have had about twenty babies so far. The aliens have a long penis and they come from behind to penetrate the females and impregnate us.*

"After we are pregnant a few months, a long larva comes out of our vagina and a baby comes out of it. The babies look like a combination of different beings. It feels like it rips my insides out and I am always bleeding. I do not want to do this anymore. One day I try to escape because I do not want to be pregnant and lose my baby again, but they catch me and kill me by cutting my throat.

"From heaven, I see that after that life I had trouble becoming pregnant or had miscarriages during many life times. On Dr. Modi's request, angels brought all the soul parts back to me, and to other women, aliens, and all the babies, and integrated them with whom they belonged. I see many soul parts coming back to my vagina, reproductive organs, blood, and my whole body."

Abduction for Selfish Purposes

According to the heavenly beings, some of the aliens are abducting humans for selfish reasons, to obtain genetic material from them to modify themselves and their race. They are making changes beyond reason in their own race. They are incorporating genes from humans without exactly being aware of what they have changed. They do not keep their modifications contained but allow them to spread in their own population. This is a very dangerous practice because they may take a gene that will spread throughout their race and all the members of their race can have it before they realize what they have done and it may even destroy their race.

My hypnotized patients say that the gray aliens with big, almond shaped eyes are the ones who are doing most of the abductions for selfish genetic modifications. They are very aggressive in their activities. Guaru is the name of their planet, and Marth is the name of their race. They found a substitute planet, Marth Guaru, to inhabit after the destruction of their planet. It is not a good home and is alien to them. They are hoping that these genetic modifications will help them live on that planet and that some of their people will be able to settle there. At this time, they are living on spaceships, and from time to time, they find a stopping place. They need materials to continue their journeys, which cannot go on forever without supplies.

They had one primary planet of origin. This planet was destroyed hundreds of thousands of years ago. Different patients give different names for this planet. Some names, just like for any planet, are dialectic, due to different languages that developed on the planet. Some of them are the names that were used during different time periods. The name did not stay the same. The culture and language that dominated the planet dictates the name. This was not the natural home of some of these beings. Sometimes, other planets within their solar system were home to these particular beings. Sometimes, after explosion and destruction, they may use the names of the planets they stopped at, or the name of the planet on which they were born or had strong ties to. It may also be a planet that is prominent in their spiritual background.

For example, in English, Earth is the name for our planet, but every country and every language on Earth has its own name for the planet. English is the predominant language on the Earth today, but it has not been so throughout the centuries. There are other languages that were and will be predominant.

The selfish gray alien race has been abducting humans for the longest time, with the most unreasonable expectations for themselves. They seem to have the attitude that whatever they do will work out wonderfully well. They are not evil and not consciously working for Satan, but they do have dark influences, which they are not even aware of on a conscious level.

They are not doing abductions to hurt people or for fun, but to extract genetic material from them.

Heavenly beings, through my hypnotized patients, claim that this negative gray alien race has always been an immoderate and intemperate race. They are hot headed and act before they think. As a result, they have had some bad consequences. They literally caused the destruction of their own planet and the entire solar system. Before that, they had colonized other planets nearby, and they were able to modify the conditions for living.

These gray aliens are mostly abducting human beings because our DNA is easy to work with. They can abduct humans, extract genetic samples, and return the humans, because we are technologically unsophisticated and have trouble detecting the aliens' presence. They want to connect with the emotional and spiritual components, in particular. Compared to them, we are not advanced technologically, but spiritually, our potential is much greater. Emotionally, we are far beyond them. We have much more potential to develop spiritual and psychic capabilities and that is the gene they are trying to extract and add to their own genes. We have more potential to grow spiritually and psychically because of our emotional component. These gray aliens have removed their emotions from themselves with their genetic modifications.

The initial fumbling steps of the grays were in the directions of genetic modification and space travel. These developed at approximately the same time, with these aliens going into rapid experimentation in genetic modification and coming up with results that were not entirely intended. By actively experimenting, they were creating the seeds of their own destruction.

According to heavenly beings, they had great technological achievements. After the genetic modifications they made in their own race, they removed the emotional component and the emotional understanding of what they were doing. Also, some of their moral sense and altruism disappeared and selfishness prevailed. What an individual wanted became more important than what was needed for the entire race. They devised horrible weapons based on fission and fusion reactions, with direct conversion of matter into energy. This depends in part on spirituality, on being able to see that this matter is nothing more than condensed energy, and removing the structures that are in it and allowing it to expand as energy. This, then, causes the matter to go into the energy phase. A tiny amount of matter can release a phenomenal amount of energy. They developed devices for direct conversion of large quantities of matter into energy. As a result, their negative leanings and destructive tendencies shook the spiritual foundation of their solar system and ended up destroying not only their planet, but also the whole solar system.

They converted matter into energy in large quantities and literally fragmented the planet and blew it all over the place. This impinged on their sun and caused it to contract, pushed it in on one side, and caused it to explode. The aliens who survived were the ones who had left the solar system before the explosion of their planet. They had the details of what was happening, which were sent to them, but there was nothing they could do to stop or help it. They simply observed what happened. From there on, it was simply moving from place to place, gathering and building materials, stocking them, and sending them out. They were looking for a place where they could settle and live.

They stopped at different places and inhabited them for different periods of time, but none of them were completely suitable as a life space for them, and the living conditions had to be maintained artificially. There are groups of gray aliens living on other spaceships in space and on other surfaces in the universe at this time, not just around Earth.

At this point, I prayed to God and requested the angels to heal all the beings of this gray alien race. My prayer was granted for all who allowed the healing. Literally each place they touched would have to be healed. These beings had no idea about the history of their race and what happened because their solar system was gone instantly, and only the ones living on the space ships survived. The children who were born on those space ships had no connection to the old solar system, and what was not passed on or taught immediately died out. They were isolated in space. They were already out for a while and were not even sure of the details of what was happening.

According to heavenly beings, each group of this gray alien race working with genetic modification had its own agenda and sometimes these agendas were in conflict. The aliens were dealing with this impossible situation, and as they made the modifications, they ended up with results they did not expect and did not understand. They allowed these characteristics in the general population without allowing sufficient time to analyze.

The universe of spirituality can be pictured as an ocean, and to step into the psychic realm can be seen as diving into the ocean. What we experience there depends upon our intent, what we bring with us, and our natural inclination. Both God and Satan operate in this ocean. Both of them pervade it, and when we enter it, we experience either God or Satan, depending on our intent when we enter the water. If we are seeking evil, we will find Satan and ignore God. If we are seeking good, truth, and beauty, then we will see God and ignore Satan. Even if we are seeking God, Satan can work through the same medium to influence us. Of course, if we concentrate on Satan, God can work through the same medium to influence us toward good, if we ask for help.

Grays are a psychic race but not a spiritual race. They have a "one mind" mentality. It is like a town meeting, only in the mind. They cannot do this with too many beings because then things become too confusing and nothing is resolved. In small groups, they can enter into the psychic realm, make telepathic communication with a group of minds, exchange information, intents, and everything that goes into prompting their actions, and create a unified idea as to what it is they are going to do. We humans also have the potential to have that psychic capability, but not right now. The grays and humans are better able to do it than many other races in the universe.

Gray aliens were once taller, but they made themselves shorter in height through their genetic modifications so they can survive on spaceships. Size is not an asset for ship-living people. Smaller people fit better in a spaceship and require less material. Because of their genetic modifications, they had a wasting of muscles of their arms and legs and also of the internal organs.

Heavenly beings state that the reproductive setup in this gray alien race is a little different and is affected by their genetic modifications. Their females have trouble having babies naturally. In vitro growth of the embryo is important for them because they cannot sustain their numbers through natural reproduction. They mix human genes with theirs because they want to see what will happen. Humans have a whole group of genes that are unique and different from the gray aliens, and the aliens are experimenting as fast as they can, trying to find practical uses for them and trying to move forward with these.

They have a treasure of genes to work with. There is human DNA, which is relatively untapped and unexplored, and they want to see what they can do with it. All the variations from all over the Earth are taken so they can see what they can do with them. They are carrying on these genetic experiments without really knowing what the results will be. They have already greatly damaged their race by doing genetic modifications, and they are still not sure what the ultimate results from their experiments will be. They have created a lot of babies between themselves, humans, and other aliens.

With the grays doing the major abductions, their purposes are not to transfer spiritual development or technology. Their purposes are selfish and one sided. The only individuals who have consented to these abductions are those who need to reestablish a karmic balance to get their own spiritual development back in gear or to progress again.

Those humans who had lived lives on the gray aliens' planet before its destruction have a bit of sympathy for them and are more likely to give permission and agreement in heaven, before birth, that it will be their plan to be abducted but not to remember it consciously. As far as these people are concerned, it is like a rape to have their genes taken by the grays. They give permission to improve their race and give them the genetic material so the grays can survive. The grays have made so many intemperate modifications that their survival as a race is questionable. They do not know what they are doing.

One of my patients recalled a past life in Egypt, when he was abducted and taken to a temple where gray aliens were experimenting with humans, with the cooperation of pharaohs and priests:

- *"I am a twenty-seven-year-old man. I live in a desert city in Egypt. I am a worker and live with other workers. It is about 4050 BC. I am at work. We are building the great pyramid. I am strong and appear courageous to other people, but I am very afraid. We see people being kidnapped by the government and we never see them again. We hear alien influences are here and they are remapping the DNA. They are very powerful, so I try to work quietly and not be in the limelight. I am afraid they might snatch me for experiments.*

    "Some Egyptian solders come and arrest me and take me to a temple. Gray aliens, pharaohs, and priests are there. It seems as though pharaohs and priests are giving me to these aliens. I am extremely terrified. I am taken to a different area. The aliens are gray and slender, with dark black eyes, and about five feet tall. I also see some tall gray aliens who are about six feet five inches tall, but they basically look the same. Their eyes have no expression and show no emotion. They are skinny and have three fingers and one thumb. The short aliens are doing examinations and testing, while the tall ones just watch. They are

prodding and sticking needles in me, and taking samples from my nails, nose, eyes, throat, brain, and spinal canal. Then they castrate me. They also put a chip in my brain as a tracking device. It hurts but it does not matter to them. I am afraid they will kill me, but they let me go. They treated me like a cow.

"When I go back, I do not tell anybody. I stay by myself and do not communicate with anyone. This fear feasts on me. I am so afraid that I commit suicide by hanging myself. My last thoughts are, "I seriously doubt if there is any God. I do not know what is going to happen to me but anything is better than this." As I am actually dying, I am wondering if I am doing the right thing. My last thoughts are, "I do not want to live with this fear again and also I will never commit suicide again." As my spirit comes out, I see beautiful angels and I am crying hysterically. They are saying not to be afraid and everything will be all right. They pick me up and gently take me to heaven. There, I get cleansed and healed.

"Then I go to my life review. As I look back from the Light, I see that I did not pray or reach out to anyone for help. I did not talk to any human being. I see that the aliens were transplanting animal parts to humans and human parts to animals, but this did not work. The aliens were also breeding between aliens and pharaohs, but they did not do well either and soon died. The aliens taught pharaohs and priests about energy, herbs, and oils in return. Pharaohs thought that the aliens were gods and they wanted to be gods, like them. That is why they cooperated with the aliens. They did not know they were aliens. I see that most of the aliens, pharaohs, and many of the priests were influenced by demons, but some of the priests were also connected with the Light.

"I see that I needed to learn the lessons that technology without spirituality can be dangerous. Life is sacred, and with suicide, we damage our soul tremendously. When in trouble, turn toward God and ask for help. When I turned

toward myself, I committed suicide, but when we turn to God, all things are possible.

"I see that many of my problems came from that life to this life, such as my dependence on drugs and alcohol, and not caring what happened to me. I had no respect or reverence for life. I was also full of fear and secrecy in this life.

"On Dr. Modi's request, I see angels bringing all mine and all the other people's soul parts back and integrated them with whom they belonged, after cleansing and healing them."

Following is a case history of a patient who, under hypnosis, recalled being abducted by gray aliens with big almond eyes who were using human genes to create hybrid babies. She also remembered that she gave permission to be abducted while in heaven before her incarnation in the current life. She recalled being a scientist on gray alien's planet who was doing experiments that caused the planet to explode. So it was her karmic issue, too. Following is an account of what happened.

Patient: I was in a friend's cottage sleeping in the night when I heard a sound. I sense alien beings coming inside the room. They are examining me. I feel like they are trying to remove eggs from my ovary. They are sticking a needle through my skin; it is almost like doing an amniocentesis. They take out eggs then leave. These aliens look short. They are gray beings with big heads, no nose, no hair, no mouths; just slits, and big black eyes. They have no emotions. They are small, about four to five feet tall, like in pictures. They have three fingers and a thumb. They have four toes with long nails. I feel like they created scar tissue on my ovaries. When you asked the angels to bring back my soul parts, I see many soul parts being brought back. This was one of the reasons for my ovarian cyst.

As I look back under hypnosis, I see that they contacted me first when I was in the ninth grade, at my parents' home. They came to my bedroom, where they were able to paralyze me with their thoughts or a laser beam. I was awake but I could not move and could not say anything. They took my eggs from my ovaries. Then, through their thoughts, they told me that I would forget it and I did. They came to me two more times when I was in a summer camp.

The aliens contact me when I am fourteen years old. I am having my period so they take me to the spaceship while I am sleeping at home, to examine me. They send down a laser beam that just sucks me up or pulls me up into the spaceship. As I am being pulled up, I feel like I am floating. They have me take my clothes off, and then I am cleansed, like being disinfected. It is like some light goes over me and disinfects me. I don't like what is happening. I am feeling scared. They are telling me through their thoughts to just calm down. I will be all right. These beings are the same as before. They do not appear mean, but they are emotionless. They are not compassionate and do not understand why I am upset. They appear as robots with a task to do and do not seem to be intentionally trying to harm me.

They put me on an examining table and send some kind of vibrations into me that affect me negatively. They are getting some kind of information. Then they do a pelvic examination. They are putting a probe up there and taking out several eggs. It hurts, so they are holding me down and I am hysterical. I feel completely violated. Now I understand why I don't want to be touched. Then I go to a tub, where I sit in some type of liquid like water. I am bleeding and in shock. They are not paying any attention to me at all. Then they send me back to my room from the spaceship.

As you asked the angels to bring back the soul parts I lost during these traumas, I see many of them being brought back and integrated with me. Many of them went into my abdomen and ovaries. These are the soul parts I lost in this life and in past lives when I was also abducted.

They put some tracking devices in my forehead just above the third eye, one in the back of my neck, and the third one above my heart near the sternum so they can track me down when they want. These devices have to do with something magnetic, which, when they turn it on, sends out a frequency and then they can send the light beam down. They can also somehow numb my emotions with these devices so that I don't get as scared or remember anything.

These devices look like little boxes or small squares, like little computer chips of silver color. They affect my emotions and make me depressed. It is feeling like something is wrong but I don't know what it is. There is also a low grade depression and anxiety. They put these devices in me at the age of twelve, fourteen, and twenty-one years. They put one on each time. They affect my immune system. They put another type of chip behind my pubic bone and two devices are behind my ovaries near the fallopian tubes. They are creating two separate triangles. These are more than tracking devices. They can also tune into me and monitor my emotions and reproductive organs.

My higher self in heaven is saying that what these alien beings want to understand from humans is the human emotion of love, because they do not understand it. They know it is very powerful. They want to be able to contact that emotion. Their experiment on humans in general is to understand love and how they can get that feeling and emotion. My higher self is saying that I do not need to be alarmed because with love I can heal the damage that was done. I can release these devices and let them know that I will not participate anymore in their experiments because it is doing damage to me. If we can communicate this to them with love, they will respect that emotion even though they do not understand it, and they would be willing to release me. But I need to make it clear to them that I will not give my permission any more. We can ask the angels to remove the devices and release them to the Light (heaven).

I see that, in heaven before the incarnation into the current life, I gave permission to be abducted by these aliens with the hope that eventually I would come to you, Dr. Modi, and be healed and help to heal them. I was willing to take on the karma of being influenced and traumatized by them, so that eventually we could help and heal them. It is also balancing my karma from the lifetime when I abused my power when I was incarnated on their planet and was partly responsible for the explosion of that planet.

The taller gray aliens who were in me as possessing spirits with which we worked before were the original gray beings from before their planet exploded. The ones who survived continued to do genetic manipulation with themselves and changed themselves physically and emotionally a great deal. They are disconnected from their original purpose, which got off track. These gray aliens contact males and females both, but mostly women because of their reproductive systems and emotions, and also some men who are emotional. They take ova and sperm from them to examine and try to unlock the genetic code in the eggs. They try to breed human eggs with their sperm. That is why they don't take men as often. They have created both male and female hybrids. Their females are not as much involved with abductions and experiments.

My higher self in heaven is saying that there are many alien races who are seeking your help, Dr. Modi, but the main focus right now is the gray aliens with whom you have made contact. After that, more information will be given to you. My higher self is also saying that these alien beings can also be healed, and that is part of our purpose. Having them go way back in time and by recalling that they had those emotions can help in changing their genetic structure and can heal their emotions. By bringing their missing soul parts back, they can be healed. They will not change completely right away, because they need to learn lessons from what they have done. It will take time for them to change back. They will have to continue to choose. They are misguided and do not understand how to go about it. They are imposing their wills on other people and that is why their progress is so slow.

Dr. Modi: I want to remove these devices from every human being on Earth who was ever contacted by these gray aliens. So I ask permission from their higher selves if we can do so.

Patient: I hear a collective yes.

Dr. Modi: We pray to God and request the help of all the angels necessary for this healing. I also call out the gray aliens who are connected with this patient through the devices and all the other gray aliens of this race. Can I speak to one of the gray alien beings?

Gray Being: We are here and we are watching. We heard everything. We are willing to take your help to learn how to get back our emotions. If you can help us with that, then we are willing to remove the tracking devices from every human being.

Dr. Modi: Do you know of God?

Gray Being: Yes, we understand there is God. We understand it more from an intellectual point of view, but we don't have a direct experience with it. We are learning more by observing human beings through these devices and what you are doing.

Dr. Modi: Have you also put devices in the beings of other planets?

Gray Being: We focus mostly on human beings, because you have the broadest range of intense emotions. Most of the beings from the other planets are more refined and don't have as wide a range of emotions. Our focus is on Planet Earth. We want to understand humans and take what is good and perfect in them.

Dr. Modi: Can I speak to your commander?

Commander: I am here. My name is Atticus and I have been observing and listening.

Dr. Modi: Do you understand that what you have been doing is wrong and why?

Commander: Yes, because we are traumatizing people. We can see that it upsets people, but we do not feel these emotions so we can't empathize with them.

Dr. Modi: What are the other reasons it is not right?

Commander: We are not succeeding with it.

Dr. Modi: There is another important reason why it is not right. Do you know of God?

Commander: We know of God intellectually.

Dr. Modi: Do you know that we are all created by God?

Commander: Intellectually we know it.

Dr. Modi: Do you know that God has a rule for all of us, which is the rule of free will, and it is the most important rule? When you impose your will on other people, you are going against the rule of God. Do you understand that?

Commander: Yes.

Dr. Modi: Also, it seems that you did not turn toward God and ask for help. You forgot about God and that He is within you and everybody. Instead, you went on doing things on your own for thousands of years. You all need to connect with God again, and you will be guided in the right direction. We can help you with that, but first you need to take out all those devices from every human being in whom you put them. Would you do that, please?

Commander: How do I know I can trust you?

Dr. Modi: You will just have to take my word and go by faith.

Commander: Okay. I can trust you for one night.

Dr. Modi: That is good enough. Do you know of angels in heaven?

Commander: Yes.

Dr. Modi: Do you need the help of the angels or can you do this on your own?

Commander: We need their help.

Dr. Modi: I call upon as many angels as necessary right here, right now. Please remove all the devices from this person and from all the human beings who have ever been contacted by these gray aliens in this life and all the other lifetimes, and destroy the devices. Scrub and scour those areas and take away any residue that is left over. Bring everybody's missing soul parts back to those areas that fragmented because of emotional and physical traumas.

Patient: First, I see angels lifting all the devices out of me. Then they are scrubbing and scouring those areas and sending Light to them. They are also bringing back my missing soul parts and healing and integrating them with me. There are thousands of other angels doing the same things with other people all over the world. Seems like most of the females with these devices had difficulty in becoming pregnant or difficulty during pregnancy and delivery. They also had problems with their reproductive organs, like ovarian cysts or uterine fibroids.

Dr. Modi: What percentage of humans had these devices?

Patient: My higher self is saying that a very high percentage of people had these devices. Some of them had given permission while in heaven before their incarnation because they wanted the abductions to end. Most of them are spiritual. In some cases, in families where one person has given permission, other family members were abducted, too, who had not given permission, because the gray beings wanted to study family genetics. Sometimes, they did that with spouses, too. They are doing this all over the world. These beings live on spaceships because they do not have a home planet to live on since their own planet exploded. They do not feel safe on any other planets. After they are healed, they will find a planet to go to.

Dr. Modi: That is so sad that they do not have a home planet and have to live in spaceships. Atticus, are you watching? Can you see how the healing can be done so fast with the help of God?

Commander: Yes.

Patient: My higher self is saying we need to invoke the violet flame for everyone who got healed today. It will help them a great deal with continued healing.

Dr. Modi: We pray to God and request our angels and the angels of the gray alien beings to remove and collect in the net of Light all the foreign entities, dark devices, dark shields, dark energy, and everything that doesn't belong to the gray alien beings and their spaceships. Scrub and scour, and take away any residue that is left over. Bring all their missing soul parts back from people, places, and the darkness (hell); cleanse them, heal them, fill them with Light, and integrate them with whom they belong. Clamp the cords to their missing soul parts that cannot be brought back at this time. Remove all the blockages from their silver connecting cords to God and reconnect them with God, their higher selves, heavenly guides, and angels, and guide them in the right direction. Fill them and their spaceships with love and Light. Create tubes of Light around all the gray alien beings and their silver cords to God and around their spaceships. Cover them with reflective mirrors and rays of blinding white Light. Also cover these tubes of Light around them and their spaceships with a triple net of Light and metallic shield as they continue to heal.

   I also pray to God to please flood these gray alien beings and their spaceships and all the human beings from whom the alien devices were removed and all their homes, work places, cars, and all of Planet Earth, and everything and everybody in it with the violet liquid fire like a violet lava, and let it blaze into violet flames nonstop, twenty-four hours a day as they heal. Thank you.

Patient: I see it all happening. They and their spaceships are cleansed, healed, and shielded completely. Their silver connecting cords are opened completely and I can see God's love and Light flowing in them through their silver cord, which the gray aliens are able to feel and experience for the first time. They are very happy about it.

During the next session, I called out Atticus and all the gray alien beings to be present to watch as I regressed the patient to the life she lived on their planet when it exploded, Atticus claimed that there are about 700,000 gray aliens in total who are living in spaceships. Atticus also reported, that since the last session after we cleansed and healed them, they are feeling much better and are able to experience emotions and communicate with God and their higher selves, heavenly guides, and angels.

Patient under hypnosis recalled that, before incarnating in the current life, in heaven, she gave permission to be abducted by them, although consciously she had no memories of it. Hope was that by going through this healing, not only could she heal but the whole gray alien race could also heal, and these abductions could be stopped. She realized that she is also balancing her negative actions (karma) from a lifetime when she was incarnated on the gray aliens' planet and she and other scientists misused technology and, as a result, the whole planet, and later the whole solar system, exploded into pieces.

She described her life on that planet as follows:

- *"I am a male living on a planet called Leviticus, which is mentioned in the Bible. I also get another name, Zaccharia. It is 180,000 BC. This is my forty-sixth life on this planet. We don't think so much about age in each lifetime. We do not die. We choose to leave when we have finished our purpose for that life. We live each life for a couple hundred years, and then make a conscious decision to leave and go to heaven, as you do, but in a different section of heaven, where we take a long rest because we have longer lives.*

    "I am about six feet six inches tall, and thin. Most of us are tall. Women are also tall, about five feet eight inches to six feet two inches. They look almost the same as men, except they have breasts and reproductive organs. I see babies growing in their stomachs, but there is a differ-

ent connection with the babies. They don't have an umbilical cord like humans, but instead have connections to the backs of their heads because they communicate telepathically. I have a head with ears, which are kind of big and pointy. I am bald. I have big almond shaped eyes like those other gray beings, but I show more expressions and emotions with my face and eyes. I have two hands and two legs. My hands have four fingers and one thumb, but they are long and skinny, with nails that look like claws. My feet have five toes and are webbed, but my fingers are not. My torso is almost like humans' but there are no nipples. My bone structure and organs are different. We have a different digestive system, or do not really have one at all, and we have a slit instead of a mouth. It seems there is more empty space inside. I see the heart but don't see any lungs inside.

"I have a family. We actually have many families in one lifetime. They are simultaneous. We may have two, three, or four wives, with several children. A wife can only have one husband, because there are more women than men on our planet. I have four wives. One family does not live with me anymore. They finished their lives. They were my first family. There are three separate dwellings, one for each wife, and I spend time with each one. The dwellings or homes are circular and modern looking. They resemble space-age buildings, with smooth angles. They are more monochromatic, and everything is very clean and efficient. It is not set up like homes on Earth, for comfort and good looks. Our focus is not on decoration but on function. Inside, we have separate rooms, like kitchen, bedrooms, workrooms, etc. We have furniture, appliances, a screen on which you can watch things, advanced computers, electronic devices, and communication devices like telephones and radios.

"I am a scientist. I am involved in genetic engineering. We are doing many things which people are beginning to do now on Earth, such as trying to mix genes outside the

body, change genetic structures, change DNA, cloning, and mixing different races to create one perfect race. We are trying to take the best features from all that we know, to make a perfect life form. We want to bring in more qualities, like the ability to absorb the spiritual white Light and advance the spiritual awakenings, in our race. We are trying to eliminate any weaknesses and diseases, because our bodies also malfunction.

"We get the genes from other races on other planets, such as Venus, Neptune, and Mars. We are doing similar things as the gray beings are doing now to the people on Earth. We are picking up subjects from other planets in our spaceships and doing experiments with them. We are able to trick them. We are more technologically advanced, but they are more spiritually advanced, and we are searching for spiritual advancement.

"We understand that there is a Supreme Being; that is, God. We have our connecting cord to God. Because we are telepathic, we are able to communicate with our higher selves quite easily. We do not pray and ask for guidance from our higher selves about these experiments. We do not pray and meditate like you do, but we do receive guidance. We have a lot of demonic influence, so we are kind of misguided. We focus more on technology and less on spirituality.

"In my daily routine, I get up, and visit with my families, where we do something to recharge, but it is not like eating food. Then I go to work in a laboratory. We have education, like trade schools, and I have been trained in genetics. I am currently working on DNA, merging genes from beings of Venus to create more spiritually developed beings. We thought this was all right and we didn't question it. Now I understand that we had a lot of demonic influences. There are many other people working on other genetic projects. I am more focused on the spiritual aspect. Looking at the cellular structures of people from Venus, I wonder why their cells receive more spiritual Light.

"*Others are working on changing the birthing process by combining genes outside the body, trying to take the best aspects of different DNAs and cloning them. We have created test tube babies. As they grow up, they act differently. They do not have the same connections with the Light. Their lives were not planned the same way, in heaven before birth, as ours were. The souls that came into these bodies were confused. So we were trying to integrate soul parts from beings of other planets into these clones to increase their spirituality.*

"*I am continuing to do my work. The whole scientific counsel is working together. We are talking about some plans we have. It has to do with something that leads up to the explosion of the planet. I am one of the main scientists, but there are many of us. The project has to do with the way we are trying to bring the souls for the clones from other planets. We are trying to trap and remove soul parts from other beings' bodies from other planets and put them into our cloned beings. We are working on machines that will suck up the soul parts from beings of other planets. I work through energy vibrations. It goes out and grabs the soul parts and brings them back to us. But putting soul parts of other beings into the clones never worked.*

"*Before the explosion, I am feeling the pressure. I am feeling very concerned because we know something is going wrong. It is out of our control at this point. We cannot shut it down. We did not think the planet would explode. I am experiencing anxiety, a sense of responsibility, fear, arrogance, and pride. Now I can see that the demons were influencing me. They keep reassuring me that the situation is not that bad. We hid the information about how bad things were from the planet as a whole. We could feel the tension, something like before a volcanic eruption or an earthquake. Everyone, including the animals, here senses it as well, but they do not know what they are feeling. Nothing like this had happened before, so no one has a reference point.*

"The machines are malfunctioning. We can feel the atmospheric vibrations and we are measuring them. We miscalculate and make the wrong decision. We do not shut the machine off, as we should have. The malfunctioning goes on for weeks. The pressure on the planet is building up and up and goes into the center of our planet. The vibrations are being absorbed into the center of our planet and it begins to implode. As the energy builds up in the center, at some point, it breaks and everything just bursts out and the planet and everybody on it explodes. We did not understand the consequences when we built the machine.

"As the planet explodes, my body is blown apart and my soul is so fragmented that even the angels have trouble finding the soul parts. I feel great shock, confusion, disbelief, grief, and sadness. My last thoughts are, "I was wrong. We made a big mistake and killed all these people. I will never be successful again. I will never be powerful. I do not want that much responsibility again. I do not want any notoriety. I never want to be involved with genetics again."

"When I am out of my body, I see a lot of grayness everywhere. I am not aware of other people. I am watching my soul fragments leaving. I am in shock. After a while, the angels take me to heaven on a stretcher. These angels look like people from my planet, and are a little bigger than Earth angels. They take me to the part of heaven where severely damaged souls are taken. It is like an intensive care unit. It takes a long time to repair my body. They put all my pieces back together because my soul was cracked everywhere. They send energy to heal it. It is almost like a Reiki treatment. Then I rest for a long time.

"After resting, I go to review my life. There are four wise men present. They look like beings from my planet. They are the masters. We talk about my life. I feel stupid because I got carried away with the technology and did

not balance it with spirituality. One of my lessons was to balance between technology and spirituality. Another lesson was to learn about ethics and not to take advantage of other people and not to impose my will on others and not to manipulate people for my own benefit. I misused my powers and I did not understand about free will. Another lesson was to have compassion for other people. I was not bad but not very caring of others. Unlike the little gray ones, in that life, we had all types of emotions, such as loyalty and altruism, although they were misguided. We were disciplined and hard working, caring, loving, tender, and had anger, sadness, and compassion, but not as intense as humans.

"The master beings are saying that it was a big life for me in terms of karma. There was a reason I was involved in such massive events. It was to bring knowledge to Earth at this time. I will have another lifetime when I will be able to do great good to balance the karma because of the lessons I have experienced. From heaven, I can see that I had a lifetime in Atlantis as a geneticist, where I misused my knowledge again and learned more lessons in ethics, and, as a result, I succeeded in the Egyptian lifetime. In a lifetime in Egypt, people were developing technology, which was going out of control, and I was a major force in putting a stop to it. Because of my sense of ethics, I understood the wrongness of it and I was able to stop the disaster. They were at the verge of developing interspecies communication and transportation that would have perhaps destroyed the Earth.

"As I look back now, we did not understand that it was the demonic influence that blocked our own spirituality. Venus did not have any dark influences. Satan and demons were misguiding us. They did not want us to gain this understanding. We did not realize we were creating karma. We were just looking at things from a scientific point of view.

"The masters are telling me not to get discouraged. I will continue to have other chances to balance my karma from this life. It feels like what I am doing now is coming full circle to completion. I had that life in Atlantis and Egypt, and part of the plan was to come back and help free the gray aliens who belong to the same planet that exploded and who are still confused and misguided. Thus I am getting a chance to balance my karma.

"Many problems came from that life to the current life, including my inability to focus on developing one particular carrier path and skill because I am afraid of getting too powerful. I do not trust my judgment. I am afraid I might hurt people. I have no interest in technology. I have a fear of getting too close to people because I am afraid I might hurt them. I have a fear of responsibility and I feel some selfishness. I fear perfectionism because I did not do a good job in that life. I have sensitivity to loud noises due to the planet exploding. I have an inability to have children because of the damage I did to the reproduction of others in that lifetime.

"My parasite infestation in the current lifetime came from that life because I was imposing my will on others. The experience of having parasites come into my body is a way to experience something outside of me imposing its will on me. It is also affecting the parts of my body that are involved with reproduction. Parasites are sucking energy from my body as I was sucking the soul parts from other beings' bodies, being parasitic to them.

"I recognize many people who were there are also here in this life. My husband was there. You were there also, Dr. Modi. You were concerned about what was happening. You were also a scientist taking care of the babies we created through cloning. You knew something was wrong and wanted to stop it but I would not listen. You were more psychic and could tune into the disturbances that the souls of the cloned babies were feeling. You were the only one trying to heal them and it was overwhelming,

almost similar to this life, where you are seeing the truth that nobody sees and you feel very alone.

"Most people who have been abducted by the little gray alien beings on Earth were there on that planet in that life. That is why, like me, they gave permission for abductions while planning for their current life in heaven, although they may not be aware of it consciously. Because of the damage that was caused in that life, we are working now to heal these gray alien beings who are of the same race and do not have a home planet to go to.

"I am collecting all the beings in a group whom I hurt in that life, which is everybody on that planet and beings of other planets, the babies we cloned, the gray aliens here, and all the human beings who were there in that life, and asking God to cleanse, heal, and fill them with Light. I see a tornado-type Light coming from heaven and sucking out all the dark demon beings and everything else that does not belong with them, and they are all healed and smiling. As the demons go into the Light, they also become the Light. Everybody is forgiving me.

"When you asked the angels to bring back my and everybody else's soul parts, including the little gray alien beings, I see soul parts coming back to everyone from everywhere. I also see the soul parts of the planet that exploded coming back, and the whole planet was put together and reconstructed, including its physical structure, which is also repaired. I hear St. Germain and other heavenly beings clapping and cheering. As I look back from heaven, I see that the demons were trying to use my soul parts to create doubts in me so that the healing could not be done. They were really trying hard to prevent my healing and the whole healing we did today for everyone.

"As I look at the gray alien beings who are also watching this regression, they are also healed. They began to feel some emotions, and when they saw their planet being put back together and healed, they felt happy. They started to understand the consequences of their actions

involving the genetic engineering and experiments and imposing their will on others. They understand the importance of the ethical decision making and also how the dark beings have influenced them about what they were doing and how it can cause misperceptions. They are also realizing the importance of prayers and asking for guidance and help to create a balance between mind and spirit and not focus just on technology. I see that their DNA is beginning to repair itself, and their emotions are coming back. It is as if they are being freed.

"Their inability to feel emotions was a karmic balancing because they have been stealing from others, especially by trying to take the spiritual Light (soul parts) from others and manipulating the emotional and spiritual realm of the other beings. As a result, they lost their capacity to feel emotions and connect spiritually. Now with this healing, their DNA is beginning to heal and they are beginning to feel emotions. Their DNA could handle only so much spiritual Light before because DNA has something to do with how much Light frequency can come into the body, and they have lost certain parts of their DNA, so not much Light could come in. This is part of the reason they could not feel emotions and spiritual connections. Now since those strands of DNA are repaired, more Light can come into them. They feel as if they are waking up from a long sleep.

"What I am seeing is that the blueprint for their physical form is formed on the spiritual level, but the physical manifestation will take a while. The etheric body is starting to change. The understanding I am getting is that as they get closer to their planet and as they go into it, they will revert back to the way they used to be and they will almost forget that they had this other physical structure. The karmas have been balanced, healing has happened, and they can go back and change without carrying these memories they used to have about these other bodies.

"The gray alien beings are saying thank you. As you told them to thank God and all the heavenly beings who have helped in their healing, it looks like they are saying a prayer. They are looking up to God, collectively coming together and giving thanks for their healing and for making that connection with the Light. I sense that God is sending them the vibration of love. It is like He is welcoming them back to their connection.

"Their commander, Atticus, is here. He is thanking you and saying that he is very happy for the understanding. He now remembers his planet and what happened. He understands that what they were doing with the current abductions and genetic testing was misguided. He regrets it and asks for forgiveness from everyone whom they have hurt. He is saying that when you asked for the demons to be removed from them and to bring their soul parts back, it was like thawing out and waking up, almost like they had been frozen. The frequency of Light was entering their bodies as if a light switch was turned on or waking up from a deep sleep. He is saying that he can feel some happiness, a sense of connection, and caring and love. He also felt the love of God. He seems shy, as if he is feeling embarrassed.

"St. Germain is saying that it was a good healing of the alien beings. We can continue to pray for them, and if there is more to be done, you will be guided, Dr. Modi, and you will know what to do. For now, they need time to make adjustments to what has been done so far and to continue to pray. As more work needs to be done, it will be revealed to you. St. Germain is also saying that there are other beings all over the solar system who need healing. Praying for them is a place to start and you will be guided at the right time to help in a more specific way. He thanks you for the work you are doing on behalf of the planet and on behalf of the Light (heaven). You will be called upon again to help when needed. "Heavenly beings, through my hypnotized patients, state that there are many gray

alien races in the universe, but only two are in contact with humans and only one of these is doing the abductions and the selfish genetic modifications. Another gray alien race, which originally did genetic modifications with humanity about 800,000 years ago, is a positive gray alien race and still visits us from time to time. They use the sea as their base and will eventually get in touch with us.

"They have the same color of skin and resemble each other, but they have different origins. They are two separate and distinct groups. The positive one came from an aquatic background and the negative grays came from an invertebrate background. There is no other gray alien race that is working with us now. The original gray race that did the modifications on us still checks in from time to time, but they have not done so for the past six hundred years.

"The negative grays have almond shaped eyes going to the side, while members of the positive race have round eyes that are set to the front of the face like ours. They are both about the same height. The positive gray race evolved from beings that were not too tall to begin with, while the negative race was six feet or more tall, and through genetic modifications, they made themselves short so they could fit in a spaceship.

"The positive gray aliens have a very slight upraised bump around their ear holes, as if it were an ear or may have been an ear at one time. The negative grays have no bump; it is just smooth, with a hole there. The positive grays frequently have a skin flap over the top of the hole to prevent water from getting in but still permit sound waves to get through. The positive race has nose holes for the nose, that are set further down on the face closer to the mouth opening. In the negative race, the nose tends to set higher and closer to the eyes. In the positive race, the jaws are pushed out a little further so that it seems as if it is a jaw and a mouth, while with the negative race, the jaws are more recessed and there is no apparent jaw but the mouth opening itself.

"A very big difference most people do not get to see is that the positive gray race does not have the alimentary canal that goes through, so food goes down and comes back up and out. The positive grays go into the water. They have arms like an octopus, more like tentacles, and no joints. Each tentacle has a hard structure, almost like a hook, and they have suction cups. Inside each one, there is a little thorn for grasping, to give them the structural rigidity to hold on to things. The hard structures have no bones or joints.

"The negative grays have a single bone and a joint system that is different than ours. They have shoulders like a cat. They do not have shoulder joints; instead, they have connectors that hold the shoulders together and make them work. They have a single bone in their upper arms and a single bone in their lower arms, but these are not jointed together in solid contact like ours. It is a floating joint. They have one thumb and three fingers. Their legs have the same number of toes, with webs between the fingers and toes.

"The positive grays have foot-like structures, but without the hard bone; more like a pad. The foot-like structures do have cartilage supporting the legs, jointed together with connective tissue and muscle ligaments. But the pad foot is not rigid like ours. It is capable of spreading. The covering is more flexible and sort of like an accordion over the foot, so that it can spread out and have a larger surface area. There are four strands of cartilage in it, like toes. So the pad foot does get bigger and smaller but it is not webbed. As it spreads out, it gets thinner so that it looks like a webbed structure."

Abduction for Evil Purposes

Some of my patients recalled being abducted by aliens for evil purposes, to confuse, control, and dominate individuals and human beings on Earth and also beings of other planets. These alien races are working for Satan and his demons. They and their spaceships are totally possessed and controlled by the demons. They appear completely dark and evil, being filled with demons, dark devices, and dark energy. These alien beings, their spaceships, computers, and other equipment are connected with black cords to demons in hell and they get their instructions and information from hell about what to do. Some of these aliens are not even aware that they are being controlled by demons, while others are consciously aware of working in cooperation with the dark side.

According to my patients, there are three negative alien races that are completely dark and are working with Satan and his demons to abduct and control the human race. Their healing and transformation will be described in the next book. There are still individual aliens in other races that have evil influences and are misguided and are abducting humans for negative purpose, but their whole race is not completely dark.

During a hypnotherapy session, my patient remembered being abducted in a past life, where he was taken to another planet where the aliens sucked his blood out and then methodically removed his skin, hair, nails, bones, eyes, and other parts of the body and stored them in different rooms. Then they mixed different parts of different beings to create a new being. The patient described the life as follows:

- *"I am a five-year-old boy living in Turkey. This is 1702 AD. I have a tan skin and dark hair. One night as I am sleeping in my room, some scary looking alien beings come and take me to a spaceship and then to another planet. The planet is very dark and very little Light is coming there. They abducted many of us from Planet Earth. These aliens look half-human and half-animal. One of them has a bat head and another one has a wolf face and the thin, alien body. One of them has the eyes and mouth of a snake,*

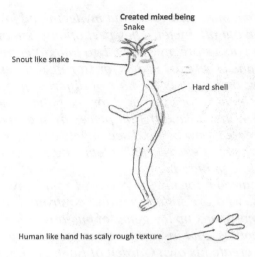

Created mixed being
Snake

Snout like snake

Hard shell

Human like hand has scaly rough texture

Space Center Lab Assistant

6'tall - oval shaped head – Yellowish round dark eyes. Pointed ears - hawk like nose - Rooster like "combs" on his head. Claw like hands. Stands erect. Body and skin seemed shell like. Energy felt male like, Robotic.

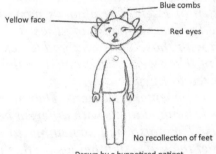

Blue combs

Yellow face

Red eyes

No recollection of feet

Drawn by a hypnotized patient

and snake scales all over the body, but the legs are like a woman, and the back is like a frog and it has feet like a lizard. It seems like a mixture of many beings.

"They take me to a room and put me on a bed and it suctions me in as if I am glued to it. The bed feels like one big leech, which is draining out my blood. By this time, I am dead and my spirit is out of my body and watching from above. They take my feet and slice them into pieces

and then something just yanks out my teeth and jaw. Then they suction out all my fat. They peel off my skin and preserve it, and also store my bones. I go into different rooms to look around. There are rooms for storing different parts of the body; one room is for hair of different people, another for skin, next for eyes, next for the bones, and so on and on. Then they take different pieces from different beings and create a new being. I see angels around me, who take me to heaven where, after cleansing and healing, I grow up into a mature being.

"I go to a room for my life review. From heaven, I see that beings, who are influenced and controlled by Satan and his demons, mix up the genes of humans, other aliens, animals, reptiles, and insects to create new beings. Satan is trying to create his own Garden of Eden on that planet. He wants to create master races on that planet in massive amounts, so that he can be larger, bigger, and have more energy, so he can win over God. That planet is like Satan's Garden of Eden. The planet's name is Lamuria. It is a very red planet with a lot of gases. This planet has a connection with those gods and goddesses with mixed genes in Egypt. They were also created on this planet and then transported to Egypt.

"It was a major enterprise here. They were doing all types of genetic modifications with different beings of different planets. They also had something to do with the pyramids. I get the sense that beings on this planet were intelligent but they were so focused on perfection of their technology that they were losing their goodness. They were trying to perfect the race and forgot about God – the Creator. They were trying to create a superior race. That is why the mythical gods and goddesses believed that they were real gods. In time, the whole planet was controlled by Satan and his demons and became very dark. It is like their technology turned on them and destroyed them. Now I see this planet kind of floating around, like *one big huge crater with holes in it. It is dried up and there is no life. There were wars over time and the resources were being depleted. I am being shown that it could be changed and returned to its former state and can have life on it again."*

One of the patients saw two aliens inside her as possessing entities. They looked like energy beings and did not have any form. They claimed that they were from Venus. They had some demonic influence, and after the demons were removed from them, they looked like Light energy. She recalled the following information about how she was abducted by these Venusian beings who were possessed by the demons and what happened.

- *"I am ten years old. It is daytime. I am in my bedroom and see two beings standing in my room. They came in through the closed window. They want me to go with them to do some scientific studies together. I am telling them that I do not know anything about science. They tell me that they can download my memory bank. I feel like part of me has some knowing and I tell them that I will not go with them. They tell me that I need to go to their spaceship and then I will be brought back. I agree so they will leave me alone. They take me to a spaceship that was hovering above the house. They beam my whole physical body to the spaceship.*

  "They put me in a seat in the spaceship and give me Coke with a straw to drink it, so I can feel comfortable. They are kind of nice. They have me look in something and unload my memory bank by just willing it. I am frustrated because I want to go home, so I do what they say. Somebody puts a hand on the back of my head. I feel sick and I want to throw up. There are many of these beings

here. I feel like I still have my memory with me, but it is also there in their computer. Then they beam me back in my room.

"Now as I am looking back, I see that in the spaceship I could not give them what they wanted from my memory bank because I felt frozen and frustrated. As a result, I lost many of my soul parts there, which are in the possession of Satan, his demons, and these Venusian beings, which they used to make me constantly angry. When you, Dr. Modi, asked the angels to bring back those soul parts to me and integrate them with me after the cleansing and healing they did. I feel much better.

"These two Venusian beings are saying that they were on their planet, Venus, and going on a voyage on a spaceship with twenty other beings when it was blown up for some reason, and they died. Their spirits were taken over by Satan and his demons. Then they began to control them and force them to go to many different beings and download information from their memory banks, which Satan could take and use for his own purpose. These two Venusians were pretty blanked out, too, and were forced to do these negative things. There were about twenty of them traveling on the spaceship.

"When you requested the angels to cleanse, heal, and bring all the soul parts of me and all the other people who were abducted by these Venusian beings, I saw soul parts being brought back to me and to many other people from Satan, his demons, and the spaceship, and integrated after cleansing and healing. I also saw angels bringing and integrating all the soul parts of these Venusian beings that they lost when their spaceship exploded, and then they were escorted to heaven."

A patient mentioned that, at the age of nineteen, while she was asleep on the couch, she had an unusual experience. She felt there was a gray spiral in front of her and she was being sucked into it. She was very scared and struggled to awaken. She felt she must be partially out of her body because, when she opened her eyes, the room looked extremely distorted. Under hypnosis, she recalled being confronted by the spider aliens several times:

Alien being like a spider

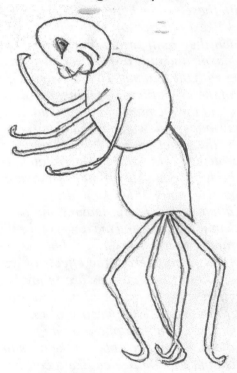

Drawn by a hypnotized patient

- *"I am four years old. I am in bed getting ready to sleep. My bedroom window opens by itself and two spider-like beings come in to my room. They are black and shiny. They are hard and have spider-like legs. They have no eyes that I can see. They are about five feet tall. I am scared and feel frozen.*

"*They press on my temples so that my body will remain frozen, and my soul comes out. They are crawling all over me. It is like they are raping me. I do not know why they are doing it. It looks like they have some sharp body part that they put in my vagina. This explains why I do not like anything in my vagina. During sex, I get detached as if I am frozen in my head. This is what seems to be happening to me with these spider beings.*

"*I feel like I am tied up with something like a spider web, which they built around me before they raped me. My spirit is out and only a small soul fragment in the body is dealing with the trauma. That is why I did not have any memory of the event till now. Only that four-year-old soul fragment had the memory of the trauma. As they are raping me, my main soul, which is out of my body, is taken out of there by the angels, who tell me that it has a purpose. I will be protected and will be healed later. They can only hurt my body. The angels fill me with love and Light and something else that will help me later.*

"*The alien beings leave, leaving me tied up. My soul goes back into my body and the angels take the ropes away from me and I go to sleep. I see that the angels use the Light devices to counteract the effects of what the aliens did to me. These Light devices are in my brain. It is like a light cylinder in the center of my brain and goes from the front to the back. The purpose of this Light device is that, if this type of thing happens again, it will wake me up and the aliens will not be able to take my spirit away. The angels also put a Light device like a coil below my heart chakra [energy center]. It anchors my soul in my body so I will not leave.*

"*As I look back, I see that the aliens put some device in my vaginal area. It is donut shaped and is black. It kept my vagina frozen, and during sex, it brought back the memory of the trauma. They put other devices in my temples, which give me migraine headaches. They also put on a black net, which is hooked to my temples through* a black rod. It covers my whole body and is also hooked with the donut type device in the vagina. It blocks me from the Light and spirituality.

"The net is connected to the pineal gland and blocks it, making it inactive. As a result, I am not able to fully access and experience spirituality. The pineal gland is connected to the third eye [the brow or sixth chakra]; as a result, they are able to block my third eye. Through the pineal gland, we can also tap into other dimensions, like we are doing during the session. This net also covered all the other chakras and the glands.

"What I understand is that the aliens did not put this device in me. It was already there. It was a Light device, a spiritual network that these spider aliens changed into a dark net by covering it with dark energy. During the trauma, my soul parts fragmented and they are with the aliens. Through these soul parts and devices, they were able to affect me and keep an eye on me. These devices are connected to their spaceships.

"The next morning after they did this, when I wake up, I do not remember anything, but I have a feeling of doom and I have a lot of pain in my vagina and head. As I look back, there was a slight bleeding in my panties and bed. There was a slight bruise on my temples, where they pressed on them. After this, they were able to affect me all the time.

"Another time, at the age of twenty, I am lying on the couch and taking a nap in the afternoon. All of a sudden, something is pulling me out. I feel my soul parts coming out of my body. It is like being sucked into a vacuum cleaner, like a vortex. I force myself to wake up and parts of me are still out of my body. The room appears mis-shapen and mis-formed, which goes away in seconds. I am very scared and I sit up.

"As I look back, I see that these spider beings were try-ing to pull out my soul. They were over the house. There were six of them in a spaceship. They have a gun that *works in an opposite way. It sucks things in. They used my soul parts and the gun to try to suck the soul up into the spaceship but did not succeed. This experience got me reading about out of body experiences and got me into spirituality. I should thank the aliens for that experience.*

"After a few months, I am in the shower and the window just begins to open. I get real scared and frozen, and turned off the shower and called the police. They could not find anybody, not even footprints.

"As I look back under hypnosis, I see that the same two spider aliens opened the window and came in. I froze and they began to jump on me. I see now that they were having sex with me. They have something like a sharp tail-like thing that retracts inside when not being used. It seems like they programmed the devices they put in me when I was four in such a way that when I see them I will freeze and will not remember. I see that they came in a spaceship that was above the house. It was not very big, about eight feet around, and it was connected to a bigger spaceship somewhere in space. They do not travel in the big one. The spaceship is shiny, black, hard, and metallic. It is globular. I have seen it in my dreams. It has black windows. I remember that at times I had some weird sexual dreams.

"The angels cleansed, healed, and transformed the devices back into the original Light devices. The other dark devices are totally removed and the space is cleansed, healed, and filled with the Light. Angels brought all my soul parts back, which I lost due to these traumas, from those aliens and their spaceships, people, places, and darkness, and integrated them with me.

"I see that my heart and solar plexus chakras are opening up and the black net is transformed into a net of golden Light. The donut type ring in my vagina is normal and is a network of neurons there for feeling. It is cleansed, healed, and activated. It is not dark anymore.

"I see that I was on their planet a long time ago. We all lived on that planet and had mutual sexual relationships with them. I looked humanoid there, about five feet tall and had long hair.

"I see that it was part of my plan to be abducted by these spider aliens and the experience will help me in my spiritual awakening."

Heavenly beings state that we have worked with, healed, and transformed the three alien races that were abducting humanity on a massive scale for evil purposes and affecting humans and Planet Earth negatively. They were totally and completely controlled by Satan and his demons. These cases will be described in my next book. According to heavenly beings, some of the beings of the three races chose not to be healed and are still influencing humans very negatively. Depending on the race, 8 to 20 percent still choose to be negative. About 20 percent of the spider race refused to change and are still negatively influencing humans and beings of other planets. They are very devious and have cunning minds. They are dampening the vibrations. Changing them will cause more direct spiritual experiences. The spider beings that were influencing the humans, their healing was done at that time. However, there are many spider beings still working negatively with Satan and it would be a good idea to heal them. The spider race mostly came to humans and installed the devices into them. Only a small percent were abducted for major surgery or major insertions. Going to people and installing the devices was quick and easy. These spider beings claimed to create modified humans who appear to be autistic.

According to the heavenly beings, humans who are genetically created by the spider race are human-like beings derived from human genes. They are of human origin, of human stock, but they are so different that they should not be called human beings. They were swapped with human babies in hospitals. They are recognized as defective or autistic, and are unable to relate to humans. When there is a sufficient mass of them, the problems will be more evident and they will begin cooperating to create a negative influence over human beings. These autistic-like kids have been frequently placed in an area where the parents have influence, power, or are leaders of one sort or another. They can influence those parents. They can serve as pipelines into these beings, to influence the elite and their power structures more directly.

The ones who appear to be devoid of humanity or do not have human emotions, human reactions, human reflexes, or good human interactions are the ones who have been created and developed by the spider type of alien race. Real autistic humans have the capability to communicate, to use their intellectual ability, being able to do arithmetic and other intellectual activities. This autistic person serves as your adding machine; another one serves as your data bank and remembers facts and figures. By mutual cooperation, they have all these facts, talents, and information. Heavenly beings state that, by converting a large majority of the spider alien race (80 percent) to positive beings, I have short-circuited their plans to carry out this project, and the number of autistic children born or appearing to be born will drop drastically.

According to heavenly beings, not all autistic children are created by the spider alien race. The created ones are no more than 0.01 percent of the total of all autistic children. We will not be able to differentiate one from the other. The points of differentiation will be concealed. The fact that those children who appear to be autistic and have been placed here on Earth among people will not allow us to perceive that they are in contact with others of their kind.

Heavenly beings say that we need to know that an autistic child born to a common, ordinary farm family is probably a genuine autistic child, while one which is born to an elite family, where the family deals with the power, has money, or is involved in inventions or politics, that autistic child might have been placed. There are about seven-thousand of these autistic children scattered across the globe who were created by the spider race. We can work with them and heal them, but it can wait for months or even several years, but not more than four years, to heal the rest of the 20 percent of the spider race and these autistic human-like children they have created.

Abduction for Spiritual Education

According to heavenly beings, individuals from both less advanced races and more advanced races plan in heaven, before incarnation, the transfer of spiritual information and spiritual techniques, and even actual spiritual development from one to the other. Of course, in the Light (heaven), they are equal. When they incarnate in the universe, there is a different scene. It is planned that the alien beings will be more advanced spiritually than the humans and that a transfer of spiritual knowledge will occur between them, or the gift of a spiritual practice will be made. We can call it a transfer of spiritual technology.

Sometimes, information about spiritual practices is given by example, where a human might observe an alien meditating and ask about what they are doing. Sometimes, aliens directly teach spiritual and healing practices, and at other times, information is transferred psychically, but it is hard to transfer concepts into human language. The person who receives the message has more understanding than what they can put on paper.

Sometimes, there is a direct transfer of the movement of spiritual energy, where a human has had his or her spiritual energy (kundalini) started by an alien so that the person could develop into a spiritual leader for humanity. According to the archangels, this has happened more than once with humans. When the kundalini begins to flow, the body system is perfected and the person develops wonderful personal insights and is able to pass this on to other human beings.

Some religious rituals among human beings came from the observation of alien practices and are an imitation of them. In these cases, there is an interchange, but humanity also developed its own rituals. Once the idea of the ritual gets across, the exact, specific practices are not limited. Humans develop their own spiritual practices, things that are meaningful to them, to their concept of God, and what feels good and right, and what they recognize as spiritual. Some of the original eight alien races who did genetic modifications on humans also did some spiritual teaching to humans, especially alien races, one, two and three of group two. These were mostly positive races.

One of my patients, under hypnosis, recalled a past life in New Mexico when a group of people, including himself, where abducted by aliens and taken to another planet. There, they were taught math, science, astrology, meditation, and different healing techniques. The patient described the life as follows:

- *"I am a sixteen-year-old girl living in a small town called Chaka in New Mexico hundreds of years ago. We are all dark skinned and short, about four feet eleven inches to five feet five inches tall. I live in a mud hut with my parents, brothers, and sisters. We do not eat meat. I help cook, feed, and sew. It is a hard life. We pray to gods in a round area that is covered. We are building a pueblo, a temple, which is a worship and storage place; we worship there and also store grain. We are aligning ourselves with the moon. The wise men have pointed out that the buildings should be where the sun is in the summertime and the wintertime, when they align. They let us know when it is time to plant corn and when it is time to harvest. These wise men are the older men of our tribe.*

  "One night, I am awakened by a funny looking man we had been told about. I see a saucer shaped spaceship with bright lights and high-pitched sounds, and we are all drawn into it as if we are just sucked up into its

light. It is like nothing we have seen before. They take my whole family. They go around and take a number of other families from other huts, for a total of twenty of us in the spaceship.

"We are taken to another planet. I get the name of the planet as Pimagnom. We are in a different place and time. There is a lot of the color silver in the buildings. They are brightly lit. Their buildings are beautiful and have a lot of cones and a lot of pointy structures and a lot of curved surfaces. There is a lot of silvery metal, but there is also a lot of sand, almost as if it is born out of or comes out of the ground. The buildings are circular and clustered together. There is a lot of domed glass that lets in a lot of light. The buildings are of light colors: white, yellow, and other pastel colors. There are sidewalks that are very busy. There are spaceships coming and going. There are waterfalls, grass, big open areas, and everything is connected. The buildings are connected by bridges, and there are lots of moving parts and things. There are escalators and flying mobiles around, which are like spaceships but smaller.

"We are taken into a room. We are confused and looking at each other, wondering what is going to happen to us. In the room, there are chairs and control panels. Everything is very shiny. We are being poked and prodded. They examine samples of blood, fingernails, and hair, and take samples of skin from the mouth and vagina. They are shining light into our bodies, checking our organs. They put devices in my ears, which I think is to help us hear and learn their language quicker. I am sharing information with the beings who abducted me about herbal medicine on Earth.

"They told me that they put devices in my ears, throat, and other parts of my body because they want to keep track of us. They want to try to send and receive different messages through the devices. They put devices in our sexual organs so they can understand how it feels when

we have sex and what it feels like to grow from puberty into womanhood. They also put a device in my third eye [brow chakra] and heart chakra. As a matter of fact, they have a device in each chakra [energy center]. They want to see how we grow, how we change, how our energy flow works. These devices look like little tiny computer chips. There are a lot of computer-like objects and equipment in the room.

"The beings are like nothing we have seen before. These beings of that planet are about three and a half feet tall. They walk upright and are somewhat human-oid looking. They have two legs with three toes, and two arms with three short fingers. Their heads look like ninja turtle heads, in that the bottom half is bigger than the top half. They have a bigger jaw. Their chests are small but they have large bellies. Their eyes are oval shaped and green; they have small ears, and two holes in place of a nose. They have big mouths and teeth and a small tongue. They do not have any hair. They have very small neck, a backbone, and arms coming from their shoulders. There are a lot of mechanical robots on the planet that do much of the work and do a lot of interplanetary traveling. The younger ones are teaching my brother and me the language and how to communicate. They are very fascinated by us. They think we are very special. After a period of time, we are not afraid of them anymore. I feel that they chose us because we are a very peaceful race in Chako on Earth and we do not have any wars.

"They teach us and give us knowledge. They are teaching us math, science, astronomy, how to track the sun, moon, and stars, and about different galaxies. They teach us about spirituality, meditation, healing, herbs, Reiki, and crystal healing, how to communicate with animals, and about weather changes. They are educating us about architecture, about designs, shapes, what roles the sun and moon play, and how to bring things into alignment. They are demonstrating how moving certain crystals

around the body will heal different diseases, how energy is drawn through crystals, and how Light works through the crystals in healing. They are also telling us about color healing and magnetic healing. They teach us how to align ourselves with the Earth and different energy forces in the universe and how they can be used.

"We are taken back to Earth by a spaceship about twenty years later, but I only look about eighteen, two years older than when I left. We go to the elders and tell them about what happened and we show them some of the things we learned and they are very excited. I get married, have a family, and live a hard but peaceful life. I help to build a couple of pueblos aligned with the sun and moon. I teach pottery work and also do healing work. I know more now and am able to teach what I learned.

"The implant in the ear is about learning, communicating, and teaching. I can communicate with alien beings from Earth and get their guidance. I also give them information about our culture. I tell them what our culture means, what feelings are, what love is all about, and how it feels to be in love and make love. I tell them what our spirits sense and what our connection to God and spirit is. The place, Chako, was chosen because it is a spiritual center. We are told that the wise men in our town have also traveled to that planet and were given knowledge and wisdom and were also brought back home.

"I die at the age of forty of lung problems, thinking that I wish I could have lived longer. I was glad I got to live in this part of the world. I was glad for the experience of being on the other planet and I will miss my family. I go to heaven right away. After cleansing, I go for my life review. I see my book and it has all my lives inside, and there are multiple cords connected to it, just like an ear of corn. When you pull the husks off, each one of these kernels has one of those strands.

"Archangel Raphael is saying that the devices in the ears were put in that life and other connecting lives and

this life. I was contacted by those aliens in this lifetime, too, and the devices were put in again. They want to communicate with me. The ringing in my ears continues because there are some more past lives I have to look at."

Abduction for Technological Purposes

Sometimes humans are abducted so the aliens can give them some technology. This is a benefit to humans by short-cutting the technological discovery process and making it possible for the human race to advance technologically. At the same time, it is a benefit to the alien race, though indirectly. There is very little that humans can give them technologically. In general, what humans can give them is an understanding of our primitive technology and how and why their own technology developed, but the benefit to the alien races is that the human race became their technological partner at an earlier stage in its development and can contribute more to the scientific knowledge of the universe. Technology is important in terms of survival and in terms of getting out and meeting your neighbors on other planets. Humans do not have the capacity yet to meet their neighbors on their own territory. We are at the stage of accepting that the neighbors are coming to meet us.

A group in the universe may not have learned to control fire yet, and in this case, the plan may be made in the Light that the alien race will teach an individual how to control and use fire safely. This very valuable tool can be transferred to the less advanced race in the universe. This is a very simple and fundamental example, which did not happen on Earth. Humans stumbled on the control of fire by themselves. It has been given to other races. In the past, alien races four and five of group two gave different technology to humans in Atlantis and during the past century; to some degree, it is happening in the present.

Sometimes technology is not given but simply displayed, and the knowledge that this is possible is transferred.

Sometimes a less developed race simply needs a clue for a direction to look, as in the case of Atlantis and the psychic abilities. The clue was there but they did not experience the psychic ability directly. They had the knowledge that it existed, and by following that clue, they got into mess. By contact with an alien race, the means of propulsion, controlling gravity, or a new way of communicating using the technology was gained.

Sometimes just a clue given to the right person will result in that person thinking in a direction that will lead to the development of new technology. It does not have to be handed over, such as, "Here is the machine and here are the blueprints and the details of the theories of why it works." Sometimes the right person just seeing or knowing that it exists leads to the development. For example, when humans examined alien spacecraft that had been recovered, they could not find things that would ordinarily be expected. Knowing there had to be a means of propulsion, and a control circuitry and finding nothing they could recognize in the way of electronics or controls, caused them to realize that it had to be there in a form that humans could not understand. Heavenly beings, through my hypnotized patients, state that the development of solid state electronics came from this.

There were previous clues on Earth about solid state electronics. When an alien spacecraft was recovered and analyzed, they found there were little areas that seemed to be electronically active. This information was carried over to human technology and led to the development of solid state technology. One thing that is not realized on Earth, yet, are the aliens' multiple uses of electrical circuits, where the circuits are interlinked to save space, wiring, and materials, and all the electrical circuits function at once, using the same wires and the same components, without interfering with each other. There are some tentative beginnings to multiple use of circuits, but they are not yet successful.

According to heavenly beings, sometimes there are examples of technology being discovered where the less advanced race just does not have the technological background to be able to put the technology to use. For example, human beings are not developed to the point where they can recognize the UFO's propulsion system for what it is. They have no idea or information as to how it works and exactly what it does. In this case, even though technology is present, the background for understanding is not enough. Physical possession of it is not enough without having the technical background to be able to understand it.

Heavenly beings, through my hypnotized patients, claim that at least one of the UFO crashes was planned in the Light (heaven). It was planned for technology transfer. Humans on Earth are at the point of developing weapons that can destroy the Earth. Part of the reason for alien technology becoming evident to humans at this time is to caution and show us that we really are not the most technological race in the universe, and that we should be careful in using technology and not be so belligerent and destructive. Hopefully, the very knowledge of the existence of aliens can moderate human behavior.

Abduction for Psychological Reasons

Another reason for alien abductions is psychological, and the effect they have on a developing race psychologically. Humankind became aware that it is not the power in the universe and it developed a little caution in the use of its nuclear weapons and its nuclear technology. In the movie *Independence Day*, psychological caution is played out, as the alien races are vastly superior to humans, technologically, and they may not be friendly. They may not be as civilized as we are, and we need to be cautious and polite. The movie was partly inspired by the Light.

In this case, the mutual threat is obvious. Sometimes the mutual threat is the human race itself and sometimes the mutual objective is to develop humanity. Again, cooperation is essential. It is a teaching lesson to humanity. Yes, the movie was divinely inspired in part, but not all of it; just the main elements, which were the cooperation of groups of humans and show the need for psychological caution and paying attention to your own details in the development of humanity. It was simplistic and had violence, just as life does occasionally. Sometimes life is simple, sometimes it is quite complicated, and yes, violence exists in real life. It is part of the universe.

Abduction for Light Group Purposes

As described in my second book, *Memories of God and Creation*, after the creation of the individual souls, God told the souls who were in the top three or four layers to form groups, set up main objectives, pick out the steps, and work within the group to achieve those goals while in heaven and also in the universe. There are multitudes of these groups working together in heaven and in the universe. Some of the groups are: psychological, scientific, healing, religious, cultural, educational, political, artistic, humanistic, etc. The ultimate purpose of each group is to cultivate a complete and thoroughly developed soul through different approaches. These are called "Light groups." The same Light group members plan to work together while living in the universe, as described in some of the case histories.

Here, two members of a Light group can preplan in heaven (Light) that one member will incarnate as a human and the other member will incarnate as an alien, and one of them will be abducted (usually the human) by the other (usually the alien). There is hope that by making this human/alien contact there will be spiritual development of both the human and the alien as individuals of the group members, of the group as a whole, and of the races to which they belong in the universe.

These abductions are planned by two or more Light group members to achieve different goals, such as to pass on spiritual, technological, or any other information to the less advanced race, to prove that abductions do happen, to provide aliens with insight about human beings, or to provide humans understanding about that alien and his race. The hope is that the information and the knowledge can be passed on to the whole race, leading to their spiritual or technological advancement.

Abduction for Individual Purposes

There are many personal reasons why an individual would give consent to be abducted by an alien race. They are as follows.

1. **Karmic resolution**: Sometimes there has been a karmic problem between two individuals in the universe. The one who is offended may be the alien race, while the one who does the offending may be in human existence. The abduction is set up for a karmic interchange to repay this debt in the universe.

A different view of karma is like a balance, and when the balance gets tilted, the spiritual development gets uneven. In order to restore the balance of spiritual development, that karma has to be repaid and has to be brought back into balance. If an individual makes a spiritual advancement at the expense of another, or delays another person's advancement, this incurs a debt and the balance of karma shifts. The balance has to be restored before that spiritual development can get back on track and be normal again. The karma can be one to one, one to the universe; one to God, one to a group, or it can be one to a city, nation, or even a whole race to another race, or the universe to God.

One of my patients, a female, had two spirits of aliens inside her who looked like tubby babies and had bodies like them. They were about four feet three inches tall and looked like stuffed dolls. They had the spirit of a baby who was half alien and half human. These aliens said that in a past life they had abducted the patient to save their own tubby baby. As these alien spirits were describing this past life, the patient was also able to recall the whole life, as follows:

• *"I am a little human baby about five months old, with my mother and father in Illinois, and it is 1800 A.D. There is an alien couple who look like stuffed tubby babies who are demanding my parents hand me over to them or they will abduct them, too. So they have no choice but to give me up. There is a spaceship hovering above. They take me in the spaceship, where there are many alien beings inside. I am being passed from one alien to another to another to check me. They do look like tubby babies with plastic faces and round eyes. Most of them are about four feet three inches tall. They have stuffed bodies and two arms and two legs. They are upright and they do not appear to be mean. They put me on a table and take pieces from my left eye, throat, left arm, left foot, and gastro-intestinal tract, and transplant them into a tubby baby.*

"They bring over their tubby baby and make us sit back to back. They put a cone-type device on both of us, suctioning my life energy and somehow putting it into their baby. As a baby, I am feeling terrified and I want my mom and dad. I feel lifeless and dead. Part of my soul is out of the body and goes to heaven, while part of my soul remains in the tubby baby.

"In heaven, I am being held by an angel who is singing me a lullaby and healing me completely. Then they take me where there are lots of babies crawling around. Here, I rest for a long time in a white baby crib. Then I see a man, who picks me up. I feel I am growing up, almost like magic, and now I am six years old, skipping down with him, and we go through a very pretty garden. He puts me on a swing and asks me if I know what happened to me in that life on Earth. I tell him what happened to me on the spaceship. As I am talking, I continue to grow, and now I am a teenager and still growing.

"He tells me to look back at when I planned for that life in heaven. From heaven, I see that I planned to be abducted because, in another life, I snatched a baby from a couple. I also see that long ago, as an alien being, I hurt

the babies of the tubby aliens and killed them. This is my way of balancing my negative actions [karma]. In another lifetime, I was an alien who looked like a fish alien, who had a lot of authority. I was from a planet that sounds like Vinlar. We were looking from the spaceships at another planet, which was Pluto. I was angry because these tubby aliens were intruding on that planet and extracting some type of mineral that we wanted because it was valuable. So we killed them with laser guns. We also took them, and our scientists did the genetic experiments on them.

"I realize that my fear of losing my parents in the current life came from that life. When you, Dr. Modi, asked the angels to bring all my and other beings' soul parts back to me and to other beings from that life and other lives, from people, places, Satan, and his demons, I saw many soul parts coming back to me from Satan, his demons, my parents, the tubby baby, other alien beings, and from the spaceship, and also from all the karmic lives, and integrated with me after cleansing and healing. I saw similar healings happening for all the other beings who were there in those lives. The spirits of these aliens who were in me and all the others were taken to heaven by the angels after their cleansing and healing."

2. **Friendship:** Sometimes a person is abducted simply to have a friendly contact. Here, two people who are friends, or who have incarnated together in another life before, desire to make contact with each other when one person is in a human life and the friend is in an alien life. This is just to have contact between the two beings in the universe and is a kind of friendship meeting.

3. **Spiritual education:** Sometimes the individual, primarily the human, hopes for a spiritual or a religious experience in the incarnation by alien contact, in hope of getting a jump-start on overall spiritual development.

4. **For fun:** Some abductions are done just because it would be interesting, a playful reason. Here, an alien race or an individual alien will make contact with a human being, abduct him or her, and give a ride around the universe to show the sites, not so much for their development but more for entertainment. It is like playing for entertainment purposes, but it is expected that the information can be passed on. This is done primarily for the individual of the less advanced race in a sort of playful manner.

All parts of God need to be developed, so all the experiences are valid, even if some of them are intended as play. When we are in the universe, we have to play some. In the Light, all phases of God are working all the time, so there are these playful experiences in the universe and they are part of the normal experience of God. It is as natural as breathing.

5. **Curiosity**: Sometimes an experience of abduction and a ride around in a spaceship is set up because the being wants to know how the experience would feel. Here, one being is saying to another race, "I wonder what it would be like." It is a different orientation, a different basis.

Heavenly beings, through my hypnotized patients, state that at the current time, the gray aliens are doing most of the abductions. They have been doing abductions for more than three thousand years. Before that, they were doing a few abductions. The three negative alien races, including the spider race that was working for Satan, were sharing their results and discussing potential plans. The spider race generally took people to a spaceship to put in devices, but did not always transport them into space. They abducted a large percentage of people in a narrow span of time, while the grays have abducted over a longer period, so they have abducted more than the spider race, just not as high a percentage. We can think of the spider race as coincidental with the second World War and the time immediately thereafter, when they were the most active.

Over the years, the short, stocky, alien race five and the tall, thin alien race four of group two abducted a lot more people, but they worked over a long period of time. Also, in the beginning, there were not many people.

There are still some abductions by some of the original eight alien races who did the genetic modifications on us. This is to check on the results of what they did, primarily through technological analysis. They want to see what differences their work made in humankind. There are not many positive alien races currently working with humans. These alien races often get the person's consent before abducting. The alien races who did the original genetic modifications did not realize that other races were involved until they saw the results of their handiwork. Then they began to get in touch with each other.

The fourth and fifth alien races of group two interact with us most frequently to see the effects of giving us technology and what difference it made to people, scientists, and politicians. They abduct ordinary people, top scientists, and politicians, but it has been a while since they have done this. It is about two hundred years since the tall, thin aliens have done any abductions. They were very interested in us in 1700 BC. The short, stocky alien race five abducts a few people from twenty to thirty years old, primarily of the scientific type. The last time they did abductions was about twenty years ago. Some of the abductions that the tall, thin and short and stocky alien races are doing are for providing technology, but the gray beings use that as their cover story.

Chapter 18

MODERN DAY TO FUTURE

Here, we deal with the lessons we have learned from the experiences of Atlantis and Lamuria, incorporated with the knowledge that there has been alien intervention in humankind. Also, we look at the warnings about technology, genetic modification, and contact with the aliens. These three additional parts properly belong to this chapter.

Application of Technology

This is the dawn of a new age in a new era; however, it can die if humanity is not aware of the dangers and if it ignores the fact that technology can be misused. We have to be careful about the application of technology without spirituality in human society. Technology is just about developed to the point that what happened in Atlantis can happen all over again, and we could go through thousands of years of more suffering and hardships.

As described before, after its destruction, the people of Atlantis totally gave up technology. It was as if humankind suffered with collective amnesia, rejecting all the things that Atlantis had gained and stood for. Mankind is now recovering that information and technology. We do not yet have the precision technology Atlantis had, such as the skills to make the micro-component to grow a crystal that is a computer, a radio receiver, and the transmitter, all in an extremely tiny crystal, but that will come, according to heavenly beings. More technology in dealing with power and power supplies will come also. Those who are wise and have an understanding will recognize the danger. The example of Atlantis should not be forgotten, even though all the technology and the history of that era were consciously and deliberately forced out of human consciousness because they were so repugnant to humanity.

We also have to recognize that there has been alien intervention and that humanity has been altered in form, intellect, performance, and in many other ways. The natural course of the evolution of human beings would have taken us in the same direction, but it would have taken much longer. This is important to understand, because at this time, humanity is getting to the point where we can tamper with and alter genes in human beings. We have to understand that the alien races had millions of years of experience, and thousands and thousands of years of experience in genetic engineering before they began to work on humanity. The human race is barely beginning and should have greater wisdom than to actually tamper with genes.

As a case in point, heavenly beings, through my hypnotized patients, state that humanity has rushed to put genes into plants so that what is seen as a beneficial characteristic can spread to other food crops. Those same food crops can pass on those characteristics in their own pollen and sex cells. For example, in Canada, because of genetic modifications, canola plants became more insect resistant and are not damaged by insecticides or herbicides that are put on the fields. These characteristics were intended to produce or improve the productivity of the canola plant. In the end, they improved the genetic strength and the resistance to everything in the weed. This caused a very shortsighted problem. It was as predictable as day following night and night following day that these characteristics would spread to wild plants. Now they have passed on beneficial characteristics to their wild cousins, and they have weeds growing in their wheat fields that are impervious to insects, insecticides, and herbicides. They cannot get weeds out of the wheat, which is infested with wild canola plants and cannot be removed by any normal means.

These canola plant characteristics will continue to spread to other wild plants until it reaches the point where there are weeds that cannot be destroyed. We will not be able to use any chemical spray, so, eventually, the weeds will be the strongest plants in the field.

We also have the example of the corn plant on which genetic modification was done. Corn was modified to give up an insecticide that would attack insects, but the insecticide is also finding its way into the seed of the corn, the part that humans eat. It is also being passed on to cattle or any being that consumes the seeds. In some cases, this can be damaging to the nervous system. They were extremely short sighted to put something so dangerous into the seeds. It is literally destroying a portion of our food crop because this gene, once started, cannot be removed, and it will continue to show up genetically in corn even if no further genetic manipulation is done. If we planted only pure seeds from now on, it will still get the gene from the wild plants that are around. The damage is done and cannot be reversed.

Corn originally came from Mexico, where there are many wild varieties. Genetically modified seed was planted in the United States and, in only two years, its characteristics are being found in all corn plants. It is practically impossible to raise a corn plant free of it. Also, most of the wild varieties of corn, which have the original genetic structure, have been contaminated by the same genes. Those genes are now showing up in the genetic reservoir from which all other corn characteristics can be drawn. By foolish genetic manipulation, humankind has gotten to the point where they are contaminating the planet. Some of the seed companies are actually attempting to manipulate seed crops so you cannot plant from seed; that is, you cannot grow your own seed but have to buy the seeds from them to increase their sales.

Heavenly beings, through my hypnotized patients, say there is also spiritual damage to the DNA of the plant, in that the original intent of God is being thwarted. God's plan is set up as a blueprint on DNA for how the world should work.

These genetic modifications are interfering with that plan, making it more difficult for God's objectives to be realized. The genetic structure is overlaid with the spirit of God. Consuming this corn amplifies the spirit of God in us. When the corn plant is genetically modified, not in keeping with God's plan, then that spiritual energy is modified, too, and is not like the spiritual energy from God. It is not necessarily evil but it is not as beneficial because, of the spiritual energy that the person consumes, only a part of it is in keeping with God's plan. Therefore, only part of the energy is of benefit. The part that is not in keeping with God's plan simply clogs the human system until it dissipates. In this way, it is a real drawback to consume those genetically modified foods.

According to the archangels, there is nothing wrong with experimentation but the experiments must be carried out in a sterile, controlled environment with great safeguards to keep those characteristics from getting out into the general population. The experiments have to be studied generation after generation before we know what is going to happen to the plants. If and when the genetic modification is in keeping with God's plan, then the energy that will surround that genetic modification and will be healthy for humans and animals to eat. But it should first be studied over many plant generations until we know exactly what characteristics of the plant we have changed.

When DNA works, it is not just one tiny little isolated part of the gene that imparts the characteristics, but that part of the gene which gives the main characteristics, modified by little bits and pieces from all over that gene, and in some cases from other genes as well. If we make a change in one part of the gene, we have to know what inter-relationship it has with the other parts, to really know what is happening. To change one part without knowing these things is irresponsible, very damaging, and suicidal.

According to archangels, we will never be able to isolate spiritual energy in the laboratory but should ensure that the spiritual energy will be correct after sufficient experimentation and if enough time is spent to know that the modifications are all beneficial to human beings and are not going to damage them. When other conditions are met, spiritual energy will be right, even when the scientists have no knowledge of spiritual imprints on DNA. They do not have to isolate the spiritual energy to know that the conditions are correct. They just have to make sure of what they have modified and what the total results are going to be. When that is in keeping with God's plan, then the spiritual energy will be correct.

There Are Many Paths: The Individual Choice

We are at the spot where many choices are possible, when society can go in many different ways. It is up to individuals to choose their own path, and as the individuals choose, so will society. If the individuals choose to be spiritual, so will society. Spiritual not in the sense of formal religion, but in the sense of developing our own relationship with the creator and human beings, as opposed to the formal religion where there is an intermediary between us and God, where someone else tells you how to be spiritual. Instead, we have to do it; we have to be spiritual and develop a personal connection to God directly and ask for guidance in our day to day life and in everything we do.

It depends on how we live our lives, what use we make of our own inborn spirit, and how we develop through our own spiritual practices. This is what will really make a difference. Each individual must develop him or herself. If personal spirituality can be developed in each individual, then the whole society will become spiritual, and even the rich and political leaders will become spiritual by being covered in the spiritual field of the society. They will be able to tell right from wrong and to honor everybody else's human rights, and will be able to make the right decisions for the nation. They will not think of controlling the world, and this would seem like an accepted goal to them.

Conversely, if people do not choose to develop spiritually, if they choose to continue in a secular manner whether they are involved in formal religion or not, without their individual development, society will take a less spiritual path. We will not have the depth of spirituality that is needed to keep the ultra-rich and the political figures spiritual because they are the ones who are in control of the society.

Those who have power and authority will not be bound by the dictates of conscience or spirit and will feel free to make society go wherever they would like. And what they like may not be always good for people and we will have the same situation as in Atlantis, only worse and longer. The choice is ours. We have the ability to make a difference if we choose.

Aliens Are Watching Us

It is a fact that aliens are watching us. There are aliens on Earth and in the immediate vicinity of the Earth who are actively involved in observing changes in humanity and studying what we are, and our spiritual and emotional nature. Eight alien races did genetic modifications on us, and return to Earth periodically to observe and gain information. Over thousands of years, the aliens have become more aware of each other and the influence alien races had upon human beings. They are now in contact with each other. There have been active discussions of what genetic modifications were made on mankind, what changes resulted due to those genetic modifications, and the observed spread of the modifications throughout humanity. The modifications on humans spread just as did the genetic manipulation done on corn and canola plants through the wild plant population.

The original stock of humanity that was not modified could and did cross breed with those that had genetic modification. The resulting children generally picked up the genetic modification from the parents who had it. In this way, the modification spread throughout the whole of humanity. Over sufficient time, even if the genetic modification was only made in one reproducing individual, it could spread throughout the entire population. This is another valid reason for being extremely careful about genetic modification, which cannot be allowed to escape in the wild till they are fully understood. Profit should not be a reasonable or a sufficient motive to make untested genetic manipulation on plants, animals, or humans, and release it into the wild. This must not be done.

At its very worst, genetic modification, if not in keeping with God's plan, will produce negative spiritual energy, which can be quite damaging to the individual who consumes that plant. It will block the energy system and keep the proper energies from being expressed, and it may be extremely difficult for that individual to get rid of it. If it is not in keeping with spirit, it can be very difficult to drain off, until the individual accumulates a sufficient backlog of this negative spiritual energy, causing different physical ailments, and is just not able to function properly.

Some of the positive alien races interacting with mankind are implanting small crystal devices, almost like the Atlanteans did, that are capable of collecting energy. These crystals are being powered by the chemical energy of metabolism and the electrical energy of the nervous system, to collect information and data from individual humans and transmit it to the aliens who are observing. Many of the reported abductions involve implanting these devices. These devices are not recognized for being as sophisticated as they are. They are actually a computer or sensor device transmitting information from humans to aliens.

According to the angel Manhabab, there is nothing wrong with these aliens gaining the information, as such. Problems are caused when it is not done with the full participation of the human subjects. They are abducting humans to put these devices in. In most cases, human beings are fully aware of why they are there and give consent before implanting the device. Then the event is erased from their consciousness. They forget what happened and that they had given permission. These devices, which are put in by the positive alien beings who did the genetic modifications on humans, draw some energy from the person, but not enough to be missed by a full grown, fully functional, healthy human being. For those who are physically ill, it can affect them to some extent, and for those who are severely ill and emotionally disturbed, it can affect them negatively, particularly the abduction experience.

Implantation of devices is often done currently by the gray aliens with the almond shaped eyes, without consent, and in fact, many of the grays are unscrupulous and lack ethics. In many cases, with those individuals, there is no prior consent. In these cases, the insertion of the implant for information gathering, for all practical purposes, is like a rape because there is no consent. But with ethical alien races, it is explained and consent is taken before the procedure. Then the event is wiped from their minds. There are about thirty types of gray races, but only three are trying to contact humans. The grays with almond eyes whom we have transformed and recreated their planet, are the grays who did not do the original genetic modifications on us. They do not have any appreciation for the spirit. They did genetic modifications on humans partly for scientific reasons and partly for selfish reasons, in the hope of creating a slave race. These grays are not doing any more experiments on humanity. They are experimenting on themselves. They are borrowing the genes from us, which is allowed. This results in no permanent damage to the human race and this is what many of the current alien abductions are for.

It has been thousands of years since aliens have been in contact with humans. Humanity had been rather unsophisticated and few records were left behind of their contacts. Only since the last fifty thousand years has a written history existed relating to the contacts, according to the archangels. Other than that, the stories were told simply by oral traditions. Since the stories were often in symbolic language, trying to relate the impressions of the person who experienced the contact, they are not often understood by humans. It seemed to the person who was experiencing the alien contact that his was a unique and different experience.

In modern times, we are able to relate to that experience in writing and maintain a historical record. It has become possible for humans to know that others have had these experiences and to interrelate the contact experience they have had with those others. Another factor that is making a large difference is that communication can be done on a general basis all over the world. News in one segment of human society can be transferred to other segments of human society. Of course, frequently, the contact experiences with an alien race and the sightings are related through more informal channels, and those who are actively interested are the ones who become aware of this contact. Still, there is enough news to carry over to the general population and many others have become at least knowledgeable about the existence of such contacts.

There are some alien races that are in actual contact with humans quite regularly. Some are based here on Earth or in nearby space. Others are those aliens who return at intervals to see what has happened to humanity. The third category is those races who have interacted with humanity in the past, even some of the ones who have done genetic modifications on humans. They no longer come back to Earth, but instead get information from those races who are doing the observations now.

The negative gray alien race with almond eyes is the race in closest contact with humanity right now. They are nearby in space and observe humans almost constantly. Practically at any given moment, one of the gray aliens is observing some member of humanity. These are the gray aliens we tried to heal and were negative, who were abducting humans for selfish reasons. According to heavenly beings, most of their race has changed but there are still some of them who chose not to change and still are abducting people. The next race in contact with humanity is the rectangular, blocky built, human-like alien race five of group two, who live underground and on mountainous areas on Earth. These are called kobold or dwarf. They rotate their crew.

The third alien race that lives in fairly close contact is the race that can live underwater. They are not on Earth constantly. They are based nearby and return frequently. These are alien race two of group one, who did the genetic modifications on humans a long time ago. They are responsible for the accounts of unidentified flying objects (UFOs) entering and traveling underwater. This is the gray alien race with round eyes, whose limbs resemble that of a squid, who did the original genetic modifications on humans, and is a positive alien race. The fourth alien race watching us is Sirian, the third alien race of group one, who resembles a praying mantis, and also did genetic modifications on us. Its temperament is quite different. This alien race has bases relatively close to Earth and returns at frequent intervals.

These are the four alien races that have the most frequent contact with humanity. All four of them have put implants in humans for picking up broadcast observations. The first gray race uses them for negative purposes, and the other three for ethical reasons. They put the implants in to gain information on the reaction of the individual human beings, to measure hormone levels and chemicals in the blood, nutrition levels, and the quality of the nerve impulses. The Sirians are also trying to observe spiritual development. They are making a very direct effort, trying to use their implants to quantify it.

The Sirians are putting the devices in humans with their consent. This is an ethical race. It is fully explained to humans before the abduction. There is a visit to the home or to the place where the human is and the whole thing is explained to them. They are offered a choice. If they consent, then the Sirians take them to their spaceship, where they put in the implants, and the person is returned as close as possible to the same location. They are seeing spiritual changes in us that they did not expect and are trying to understand them. They want to learn from us about our spiritual practices, but their attitude is not to do anything till they fully understand it.

The others do know about spiritual development; they are interested in it but it is much easier to observe the emotional state than it is to try and observe spiritual development. The Sirian race alone is trying to quantify it and observe it with their technological implants. They do it by measuring brain waves and by observing the hormones in the blood, such as secretions by the pituitary and pineal glands. By measuring those hormones, they are attempting to quantify our spiritual state. Their current operating theory is that brain waves and hormone secretions by the pituitary and pineal glands are related to spiritual development.

According to the angel Manhabab, hormones secreted by the pituitary glands are, in fact, definitely related to spiritual development. There are definite quantifiable changes as an individual undergoes spiritual development. We can actually measure the change in spiritual development by measuring changes in brain waves and by measuring the quantity and types of hormones given off by the endocrine glands. The hormone secreted by the pineal gland is very little and unnamed because we have not detected it so far and are not aware of its existence yet. Aliens have discovered that hormone. The more spiritual we become, the more of this particular hormone is secreted and vice versa. Actually, each of the endocrine glands secretes many unknown hormones.

There are seven major glands connected to different chakras that secrete hormones and are related to psychic and spiritual development. The first chakra is related to the adrenal glands, the second chakra is related to the gonads, the third chakra is related to the pancreas, the fourth chakra to the thymus gland, the fifth chakra is related to the thyroid, the sixth chakra is related to the pituitary gland, and the seventh chakra is related to the pineal gland.

According to the archangel, we can put the chakras in ranks. The most involved with the spiritual development are the seventh chakra and the pineal gland, the sixth chakra and the pituitary gland, the fifth chakra and the thyroid glands, and the fourth chakra and the thymus gland. The ones least involved with the spiritual development are the first chakra and adrenal glands and the second chakra and the gonads. The third chakra is slightly involved but not the pancreas. The third chakra deals with the nerve connections and the energy channels in the body as well as the pancreas, and it is this connection with the solar plexus and the energy channels that is important for psychic growth.

The aliens are measuring the changes that happened in us because of the genetic modifications they did on us thousands of years ago, and not because they are doing any modifications or changes on us now. They are just watching the changes that took place in us due to their genetic modifications at the beginning, thousands of years ago, which they did not expect, even with all their knowledge and experience. They did not put the implants in the same souls on whom they did the genetic modifications because part of the experiment was to see how it spreads through the human race and how strong that characteristic remains. They are also sampling those that had no relationship to the original experiments except that some of their ancestors just picked up the genes.

When the archangels say "observing," they mean that the aliens actually come to this vicinity and collect the information. The thin, tall humanoid aliens work through an inert device and the information is broadcast a considerable distance. When you consider the tall, thin aliens doing passive observation and broadcasting it, the archangels do not consider it observing.

The implants or devices that these aliens put in us have no particular advantages to humans. In terms of drawbacks, it does draw a small amount of biological and nervous energy from the body. In a healthy person, it does not create any special problems. In terms of long-term advantage, there will come the day when the alien races will share their information with humans and then we will realize the benefit, not necessarily just to the individuals providing the information, but to humanity as a whole.

It is interesting that beings to whom humans respond more positively are not necessarily good for humans, like the tall, thin, human-like alien race. Some aliens, like the Sirians, who look like a praying mantis, repel or scare quite a few humans when they see them, yet they are the most beneficent beings. Also, the fifth alien race of group two, who are short, rectangular, blocky and human-like, also create a fear in humans because they appear mischievous and odd looking, yet they are also one of the beneficent beings.

The tall, thin aliens give us some information and technology, and they are harvesting what we do with it. It is like they give some technological idea or information to human scientists, who expand it, change it, modify it, and use it to create things. When the humans develop it, then the aliens harvest the information. They are using us to do their thinking in ways they could not do. The tall, thin, human-like alien race four of group two do it quite regularly, by presenting an idea or a concept or a technological device so that it will get into the mainstream on Earth, and we have millions of brains that are different than theirs working on the problem or working with the device and making new things out of it. Things that the aliens could never think of, such as different ways of applying a technology. As a result, there is a lot of technology and information that they harvest from humans, which the aliens could never discover without help. For example, in the last one hundred years, some of the most fantastic technological advances that occurred, such as the telephone, radio, television, and synthetic fabrics such as nylon and polyester, etc. Although the idea and chemistry were given by the tall, thin aliens, the ideas behind artificial fabric and all the different fabrics that have been created, and all the different uses for the fabrics that were discovered were harvested by this alien race. They never thought of using some of the techniques humans had invented. These alien beings' planet was destroyed and they are actually living on the moon and in spaceships.

The tall, thin, human-like alien race, four of group two, provide technology and we provide them with much information about what to do with that technology, how to improve it, and how to extend it. In general, they keep their distance, and only when they want to harvest the results do they come in direct contact with humans. Generally, they implant the thought or an idea in a scientist from a distance, then we develop a different technology or ways of using those ideas. A few of them come to Earth to get the results. They prefer to experience the results on Earth so they can be more sure of taking it home, rather than just watching and learning from a distance. They do not want to do any of it themselves; they want a finished product.

They do not want to take home the general idea and have to figure it out on their own. So they implant the thoughts or ideas from a distance, but in order to collect the information from humans, they have to be here on Earth to experience it directly, but not for long. When they do come occasionally, maybe once in several years, they come in groups and separately. Each group goes to an assigned collecting point and stays for a few months to a couple of years. Then that group goes back. They are in direct contact with humans at that time. This fourth alien race is kind of a selfish race, while the short and blocky-looking fifth alien race is not selfish. The four races described above are actively involved in contacting humanity on Earth.

Frequently, contact by the positive aliens with humanity is by observation from a distance, simply to see and observe what is happening. Human knowledge of the aliens frequently involves only a sighting of alien craft and alien transportation in the physical or in a psychic dimension. Actual face-to-face contact between humans and aliens is quite rare and is frequently on the basis of what the human accepts, can relate to and understand.

All the eight alien races that worked with us thousands of years ago and are watching us are really perplexed and amused by us and our developing spirituality. They thought we were of the animal species. They helped modify our DNA and yet we turned out to be emotional, intensely spiritual, and capable of developing spirituality. We were a grand experiment.

Those alien races that do not have spirituality are really in conflict. They know that the spirit exists. They have seen the action of spirit in us. Those races that are based solely in technology, where they felt that the universe works by chemistry, physics, and biology, are seeing evidence that it is not the whole truth. They are seeing that the spirit is capable of affecting the universe and the physical systems and that the spirit is a dominant aspect in us. The spirit is a more important factor in us, and comes as a real surprise to the aliens who are here from time to time. One or the other of these eight alien races is here all the time.

Alien race five of group two have bases underground where they can live for a long time. This alien race is extremely interested in us. They do not recognize spirit and do not know that it exists, except what they can see in us and in other races. Since they watched us develop, it has served as an eye opener to them. This gives them the feeling that if humans can do it then maybe they can do it, too, and it would be worth experimenting with and making an effort to find out if it is true.

These are the ones who are learning from different spiritual teachers by observing them or through bringing those teachers to them by abducting them. Not all abductions are against people's will. They are not really abductions. Sometimes they provide transportation to get them back, so that the teachers can do their teachings. These human-type alien races can teach us about technology and science but we can teach them what we have developed in spirituality.

The less spiritually developed alien races are reexamining themselves and their origins. They know we came from ape-like beings and that we evolved through a lot of genetic changes that the aliens caused, and also naturally. They are observing to see what happens. Looking back at themselves, alien races are wondering what their background was like and where their race made the decision not to be spiritual, or to ignore it, or to implement it some other way.

The Transition

We are moving from the aliens studying us to the aliens wanting what we have. The alien races wish to develop as we have but are not quite sure how to go about it, not quite sure what spiritual practices or philosophy to approach. The alien races wish to join in our transition. Many of them can see that this can be a good thing, and if there is something in the universe they do not have, they would really like to have it, especially something which seems to be so potentially valuable, such as spirituality.

Many of the alien races are not aware of their souls; they are not aware of God, angels, demons, or any spiritual part of the universe. This is beyond them. Part of the reason some of the other alien races have done so well in developing spirituality is because, in general, beings of these races are psychic and they can feel and know that there is something else beyond the physical world. In other words, the beings can feel that they have a soul; they can feel that God exists, and it is not simply the mind-numbing religion, but a constant development of spirituality.

From Modern Day To the Future

In terms of going forward from the modern day to the future, the role of spiritual energy needs to be better understood by the medical community. There are too many cases of spontaneous remission, too many cases in which the cure is not known and not understood by current medical science. In most of these cases, the truth is that the people have been cured by spiritual energy. One of the goals of medicine needs to be the understanding of cures through this mechanism.

Heavenly beings, through my hypnotized patients, say that proper nutrition, including proper spiritual energy, needs to be understood and taught by spiritual nutritionists. This will decrease the illness rate and increase the wellness rate. The old yogic doctrine of the purest foods for the best nutrition is true. Pure, high quality food promotes health, primarily because its spiritual energy is proper for humankind. According to Archangel Michael, what we know so far is very basic knowledge, and it is up to us to find out through the application of psychic ability and knowledge of the spiritual energy through feeling it. This should be a proper subject for human research for those who have the ability to feel, sense, and detect the spiritual energy. It is up to them to do this preliminary research and keep good records and not just trust their memories.

The next part of this chapter is the beginning of the contact between humanity and the aliens in which humans and human position was equivalent to a lab rat. Now humanity has developed to a point where it can be a junior partner in technology and spirit. There are qualities of humans that have come as a great surprise to the aliens who did genetic modifications. They do not know why we developed such a strong emotional content, why we have such spiritual potential, or what they modified to cause this. They do not know if it was there to begin with. This is a tremendous interest to them. They wonder exactly what human beings are.

In the study, humanity is a proper junior partner because it is the subject, and since humans have the intellect and the understanding to be able to deal within this field meaningfully, it is up to the aliens who did the genetic modifications on us to initiate this contact. After the contact is established, it will include other alien races that have not done genetic modifications on humanity, some of which are not even currently interested in us, and some whose primary interest is in trade or exchange.

According to heavenly beings, there is a great scope of human and alien interaction. First is initiating the contact with those races that are presently here on the planet. Then there are those who have done genetic modifications on us and come back periodically to check to see what has happened. They are aware of each other and have contact with each other. As humans contact the aliens and establish a working relationship, the word will spread among the aliens and they will be coming back to see us.

According to heavenly beings, when contacted by an alien, it is best to be friendly, open, and nonviolent. Do not take this to mean that we have to be subservient to the aliens where one needs to do everything that the alien requests. Each human-alien interaction must also have in mind and in heart what is good for humans. If the human feels that the contact is not to the full benefit of the human, then it is their obligation to terminate the contact. They must state their opposition and let the alien go. This should be done in a gentle but asser-tive manner; not threatening violence, not using violence, but simply to state the position that they do not wish contact and that they feel it will be damaging or not beneficial to them, and thus reject it in a straightforward and firm manner.

When contacted by aliens, be polite and gentle, be straight-forward and open in what is said. Do not veil it or use allusions. The aliens are very sophisticated and they can understand that sort of thing, but English or any other human language is not their first language. So if we are not straightforward and open in our language and attitude, there can be confu-sion. These alien races understand politeness, as humans do. Contacts with the aliens should be polite, except with the gray aliens and other aliens who are not responsive to human rights. Sometimes we must be firm and more forceful with them. Even in those cases, there is a danger in responding to these alien races with force because, depending on a par-ticular individual, they just might strike back.

According to heavenly beings, although the gray alien race as a whole is healed through my work with them, there are still some individual gray beings who are choosing not to change. So if we respond to a gray alien with violence, they may fight back with violence. With their capabilities, they can be a lot more violent than we can. Physically, they are no match for us, but to be hit with their mental force and with their psychic ability and technology, we are no match for them. The archangels claim that all the alien races I worked with are cleansed and healed, but some individual aliens have still chosen to work with Satan. We need the contact with the aliens because there are spiritual and technological benefits. Even though spiritual advances were mentioned as first, these will be underlying and hidden most of the time, even though they are the most important. Only the very spiritual and the psychics will observe that they are happening. The aliens will put human technology in line with the divine plan so that the benefit to humans from the technological work is increased. When the information is exchanged with humans, it would seem to be technological and historical in nature; historical in terms of dealing with what humanity was like and what they know of what happened with each change that was made. Their knowledge of humanity and human interaction is in some ways much more sophisticated than human understanding. They have been observing us and keeping records for a long time.

As humans enter into the spiritual realm, they come into contact with the powers of that spiritual realm so that they are not limited by physical constraints in gathering information and knowledge in communicating through the spirit. They are also much more adept at getting feedback from them directly. Masters, guides, and all their helpers in heaven are more consistently available to us if we develop spiritually. We are much better able to get in contact with them that way.

Humanity has an exciting potential. We have the emotional, intellectual, and spiritual components in such proportion that if we develop spiritually, through the power of positive emotions, the spiritual field around us can be quite intense. As we develop, those around us will develop, and as more and more humans develop, the spiritual field around the planet will develop, which can directly affect nearby planets. The end result will be that spiritual evolution throughout the universe will speed up and we can take the whole universe with us back to God. It is possible for us to get back to the original plan of spiritual merging and become the most influential race in the galaxy.

Certainly, we will be nowhere near the most advanced spiritually and technologically at the time this begins. But if we can return to that original plan of spiritual merging, where each individual of the race is so much more developed due to whatever their ancestors had developed, the tides will sweep the planet and we will develop spiritually at a phenomenal rate. The spiritual field can spread out from our planet to another and another planet, and thus sweep the whole galaxy and the universe on to God.

According to the heavenly beings, out of the thousands of races in the galaxy, there are only a few races in this universe, and all the universes are like ours, because of the unique balance we have between our emotions and spirituality. According to the archangels, we are a rare race in all the universe, and that is why we are receiving so much individual attention from the Light (heaven). Many teachers and many masters have been sent to Earth. Of course, they are sent to every race, but we got large numbers of the allocation. Satan also realizes our potential and he puts extra efforts to keep us from developing, so God is giving an equal and appropriate response by sending the extra masters, extra guides, and extra teachers to get our race moving, so we can move all the galaxies, universes, and all of the creation to God sooner.

Heavenly beings state that if humanity can establish that spiritual path that it was supposed to be following at the beginning, we can go back to God in about thirty-seven generations. If we only accomplish a tiny amount of what we could, we will still shorten it into the hundreds of generations. That is why everybody in the universe is watching us, and part of their dilemma is how much of it is possible and how much of it is advisable for them to interfere with us. The Galactic Congress has reached a treaty of understanding in which it was agreed to stop genetic manipulation on us and just observe and mutually share and interpret the information. This is the current position of our galaxy at this time.

Later on, we will be given information on how to enter a trance state and how to develop ourselves to that point. The development process of male and female is slightly different because there is a biological difference in behavior between the sexes. The technique of soul merging will be taught at a later time, and anyone who claims to have the technique very likely does not. According to heavenly beings, so far, it has not been given to anybody. There are those who claim to have it and some who are close, especially in this country, where there are fakes and charlatans and where sex sells ever so well. In other countries, where sex is a realized spiritual practice, there are some who are on the top of this and are actually practicing it, but still not with full knowledge. It is reserved for a very special few.

As explained in chapter one, the original plan for the first couple on Earth was to pass on the learned knowledge to the incoming souls before they enter the body, through the spiritual joining of two souls while out of their bodies. Because of Satanic influences, they were never able to carry on this plan. Soul merging can be done by more than two people. It can be done in monasteries, nunneries, religious groups, ashram groups, prayer groups, church groups, any group that is spiritually developed and where the spirit of love is overwhelming and where the group spirituality can get very intense. They can do it naturally. If we attempt it without the proper knowledge, it can be damaging to the participants, because by entering into the spiritual realm, we open up our shields and can be open for influences by the dark side. Every time we enter into the spiritual realm, we become more spiritual ourselves. Out of body experiences put people in the spiritual realm and closer to God, but should not be done without protection. Both God and Satan exist in the spiritual realm. They are both spiritual beings, as we are, and can affect us positively or negatively. We are a composite of spirit and matter, so if our spirit goes off in a spiritual realm when the body rests or sleeps, then the spirit is inspired and we become closer to God, but without protection, we can be influenced by demonic forces too. So it has to be done by proper knowledge and protection.

Chapter 19

COMPLETING THE CIRCLE: INTERACTING WITH THE ALIENS

Most of the information in this chapter is given by the heavenly beings through my hypnotized patients. The basic idea behind completing the circle is that, at the beginning, aliens contacted the primitive humans, did the genetic modifications on us, and changed us from ape-like beings to the modern humans. Now, humans begin to interact with the aliens to influence others in the universe. The first choice to be made is the selection of the alien race that can serve as spiritual teachers for humankind. The teacher will wait for the selection to be made by the student. The variation in spirituality among alien races is wide. It varies from those who are spiritually negative to those who are positive, those who have a human-type viewpoint and those who do not; those who have emotions and feelings, and those who know absolutely nothing about them.

The second part, in spite of what it sounds like, involves the interchange between the alien race and the human race, reaching out to influence other races in the universe to refine their understanding of spirituality.

The third section deals with the reconciliation between technology and spirituality. As we recall, the Atlanteans devoted considerable time and effort to develop spirituality through technology. There was a reasonable momentum to this action, which led to extremely bad results leading to the total control of the Atlanteans by the rulers and all the disasters that followed. This is the temptation that must be overcome.

Whom Shall We Choose As Our Spiritual Teacher?

Heavenly beings, through my hypnotized patients, state that, as human beings, we must select an alien race that suits our cultural understanding and challenges to be our spiritual teacher. The same alien race will not be suitable for each and every human being. It is advisable that several alien races become the main spiritual teachers for mankind. There are some alien races that definitely will not become spiritual teachers. These are the negative aliens, such as the gray aliens with almond eyes, who are abducting humans for selfish reasons. They have spirituality, just like every being that has form has some spirituality of some sort, but they tend to have a negative view of God and God's plan, and they tend to fall in line with Satan's intent. They are a proud and haughty race, a race that feels there is no other race as good as they are and that their understanding of science and technology is supreme in the universe. There is no humility in this race. These are the grays with the almond eyes. This is not the positive gray alien race with the round eyes that did the original genetic modifications on us for our own benefit. The gray alien race with the almond eyes, most of the time, abducts people against their will for selfish reasons.

The positive gray alien race two of group one that did genetic modifications on us at the beginning is humanoid, with big round eyes, and seems to have limbs like an octopus or squid, as if their limbs have no bones. These beings operate from a fundamentally different basis than humanity, and even though they are spiritual in the positive direction, they would not be suitable as teachers to human beings because of their very different origins, different physiological backgrounds, and their different relationship to the universe. They could not relate to the problems that humans have and thus cannot become our teachers.

The teacher has to have an appreciation of what the race goes through as its spirituality develops. The closer the match between the alien teacher and the human student in terms of physiological backgrounds and emotional content, the better the match for developing spirituality. The more understanding the teacher has of what the student needs, the better it is. This is why human teachers make good teachers for humans. They have that innate understanding of human drive, of human emotions, and of human reactions. They have lived through human needs and have risen above them in developing spirituality.

In the same way, we need to find an alien race that comes from a background similar to that of humans, have the same emotional content, the same physiological basis for existence, the same drives and innate desires as humans have, and who have developed spiritually. The race does not have to look human in order to relate to humanity. A similar physiology of a more mammalian background is a plus in the relationship. Having the same drives and survival, which practically every race has, is a benefit to the relationship. The aliens must be of a race that actively focuses and attempts to develop. There are many of these alien races in the universe, not all of whom will come into contact with humanity in the near future.

When a human or human group interacts with the alien race, there has to be active participation. It is not enough to sit back and be taught. There has to be a back and forth exchange. Spiritual development has to be an active process, one of practice and participation as well as learning. There is more than one alien race that can satisfy these characteristics, that have a positive spiritual outlook, and would be suitable as teachers for human beings.

To meet the needs of individual human beings, there has to be a range of alien races available to them, simply because humans differ from each other. While they have the same basis for existence, their individual fine-tuning is different. One alien race may suit one group of people but it may not be the best teacher for another group, while another alien race with a slightly different orientation and background would be a better teacher for another human group.

According to the heavenly beings, these alien teachers of mankind will start showing up and making contact with humanity when it is ready. Human beings will not have to go into deep space to find these alien teachers. In order to find the correct teacher, it is necessary that humans know that the teacher exists. We can expect that, as time goes on, other alien races will become known to human beings. Over the course of the next thirty years or so, humans will be making those choices and becoming aware of the different alien races.

Those human beings who are spiritually best developed will be the first ones to become aware of the existence of these races and will be the first to begin the dialogue with them. We would not expect these spiritual dialogues to begin with the less developed members of the human race, simply because they are the least in touch with their own spirituality. Those who are best developed spiritually include many spiritual and religious teachers, but not all of them. This is where the first understanding of the aliens will occur. It will not come with the flash of the spaceship to Earth. It will come through subtler mental or psychic contact until the human that is contacted becomes aware that there are a variety of races presenting themselves. This will not be done in a political manner; that is, where country A will select this race as its teacher while country B selects a different race. It will be done more internally, by individual human beings.

A human spiritual teacher, who is a teacher to human beings, will first become aware of these alien races. He or she will make a selection through interaction with those races and then pass on to his or her students the understanding he or she gets through those alien races. Initial contact will not be directly between the aliens and humans. The human spiritual teacher will become more aware of the choices among the alien spiritual teachers and will eventually start to interact with them, making a choice as to which alien spiritual teacher he or she will be following. The human spiritual teachers will pass those understandings down to their students.

The students will not be aware at the beginning, or for a few years, other than through their own spiritual master, their own human teacher. According to the archangels, some of the alien spiritual teachers have already made contact with some human beings through the process of channeling, and as long as the channel remains clear, valid information for human spiritual development comes through. In this way, the alien race has a choice of whom to use as a channel. Depending on what type of students these alien teachers attract, they can come through the channel and make an effort to match themselves to the state of the humans they are reaching. Alien spiritual teachers who are validly channeled have already made an effort to match themselves to the group they are reaching and will not necessarily be a good teacher for a different group of humanity.

After a time of spiritual development, acting through human teachers, the alien teachers will make themselves directly known to the students of the human teacher. After a considerable period of time, there will be actual contact between the alien spiritual teachers and the human students, beginning with those who are best developed for a more direct physical interaction.

Heavenly beings, through my hypnotized patients, say that this will take place with individuals. The government will be unaware that these things are occurring. Government is usually inclined to control everything, but by the time the aliens make physical contact with humanity, governments will not be able to control the situation. The contacts will be too widespread and too numerous for the government to suppress or to keep humans quiet. There has been much worry among human beings and human political systems as to what effect an alien contact might have and how destructive it might be for human culture, as human spiritual understanding and human religions undergo changes based on their contact with aliens.

These fears will turn out to be groundless, because the aliens have no interest in affecting the human political system, and their spiritual understanding will be radically different than that of human beings. The form of some of the Earth's religions may be affected, but not their content. What was valid for God yesterday will be valid for God tomorrow, although the form in which the spiritual content is practiced may change. Some of the practices and customs of various religions are absolutely not related to their messages from God and might change with the alien contacts.

According to Archangel Michael, celibacy is not dictated by God and is not part of God's teachings. It is a custom of that church and not a necessary part of their religion. This is the type of thinking that needs to be distinguished and changed, but the content of the message will not change. Some of the rituals and the customs people tend to think as part of religion are in reality meaningless in light of spiritual teachings. This will be a difficult hurdle for human beings to overcome.

Only after the spiritual contacts between alien spiritual teachers and human students are widespread and firmly understood by humans will there be any physical contact between the alien races and humans. This will be the case to prevent political misunderstandings with the government. There will be such widespread public support behind the alien contact that the governments will have to accept it.

According to my patients, currently in the United States there is a law that anyone who has contact with alien beings or with a spacecraft is subject to imprisonment without a trial and without their civil rights, for an unlimited period of time. It may be because the government does not think that aliens exist or because the government knows they exist and they have no control over them. Probably, they hope to control the contacts completely, and those who are making the contacts will not spread this information to other people.

Heavenly beings, through my hypnotized patients, state that the government of the United States is not alone in its dealing with aliens and its fears about them. Not only are the political systems involved, but businesses are also involved in seeing great benefit in being able to control technology. Between big government and big business, the alien contact will be controlled so that the big businesses receive the alien technology first and use it to make money.

Meanwhile, the government seeks to control the alien contact to preserve the political system and to preserve the power structure behind that political system involving the rich and the power structures such as big business funneling the technology to the current big businesses so they can make money. Another reason is to keep under control the means of production and the ways of making products, factories, and plants. In time, as spiritual development increases, government control will lessen as more spiritually developed people move into the government. The influence of the ultra-wealthy and big business will be weakened if they are not in keeping with the spiritual needs of the human race.

One thing that will be shocking and surprising to readers is that the alien contact will start with our own spiritual teachers. They are the first ones to make contact with the spiritually developed aliens and it is they who will be making the first choices as to which alien races become human spiritual teachers. This is in keeping with the principle of the best and the brightest. Those who are best suited and best equipped to make the choice should be involved in making it.

Eventually, the alien races will be present on Earth. Some of them will have an appearance that will be surprising for humanity. They will be quite foreign and quite alien to the human concept of life, but their spiritual development will be in keeping with humans. Before that contact happens, humanity has to be spiritually prepared for it. It will take several hundred years for the alien races that are most different to make contact. The contacts will be easier for those races that physically resemble humans and have a cultural structure that humans can easily recognize. It may take approximately twenty-five years for these races to contact humans directly. The contacts are already going on, but they are indirect. They are already in the process of contacting the human spiritual teachers physically.

Heavenly beings state that alien-human contact might occur in about thirty years physically, although it could happen as early as twenty-five years, depending on how things go. A myriad of things can happen in human politics, economics, and other areas. There are many things that could interfere with alien and human contact. Out of them, 90 percent of the events that will occur will happen to the human race. A few of the events could happen in space and a few of the events can happen with the alien race itself, and that will regulate the timing, whether the contact will happen in twenty-five, thirty-five, or more years. It is difficult to know exactly when the contact will happen.

The alien races are discussing this among themselves and are coming to the conclusion to try an eclectic approach; for example, more than one teacher, more than one method, and more than one way to develop. They have seen that this works well with us Earth people, and they would like to try this approach for themselves. Alien races are selecting various religious leaders and various spiritual teachers from all Earth traditions and not just one. Some of these are just studied; for others, they actually physically arrange with the teacher to come to visit them, with aliens providing the transportation and doing the actual bringing of the teacher.

There is an interaction between these aliens and humans, as the alien interviews the human and tries to reach an understanding of what a human means about God and soul. This interview has taken place many times on Earth. They are astounded that, over time, our cultures, races, continents, and totally unconnected groups have come to such similar conclusions.

Some of the alien races that lack emotions have just begun to perceive that there is a knowledge in humans that is above and beyond technology and the physical. This is only in the past few thousand years. Their technological experiments failed to produce such results. A few thousand years ago, they switched over to the psychological and philosophical approach, trying to see if that approach held the keys to spiritual development. They are still into the data-collecting phase, still not sure what it is they are studying, still looking at the very basics of it. They are beginning to get an inclination that living spiritually, performing spiritual practices, and the philosophy of the way of life have something to do with it.

My hypnotized patients feel that these emotionless aliens are either incredibly dense or they are so centered in their technology that they are having a very hard time letting go of it. It is astounding that these aliens have so much, and at the same time so little. If they cannot understand it in terms of technology, they are lost. It is like they are trying to swim and cannot. These aliens with great technology have very little emotion and spirituality, and are being presented with thoughts and concepts that are unique in their language and their culture. They do not have the vocabulary to describe it. They do not have any cultural background that corresponds to anything they are told, or that they are observing. So it is not just a new approach. It is something that is absolutely foreign to them. They have a spirit, but they are disconnected. They are just about to come to the conclusion that, in order to do this, they are going to have to start spiritual practices and actually do some of the developing before they can perceive it. It is going to mean a change in their way of thinking, a change in their way of being, as to how they act as individuals and as a society.

Random Psychic Interactions From Aliens to Humans

According to the heavenly beings, when humans go out seeking alien races in the future, initial contact will be primarily by psychic means, through the person in a trance becoming aware of another intelligence in the universe. As this is communicated to other trance workers, they will focus upon that intelligence, eventually to the point where they can contact and establish the communication psychically. We will begin psychic contacts with the aliens within the next fifty years, but these will be random and not purposeful, and primarily initiated by the aliens. In this case, it will be the humans of Earth perceiving other alien races reaching out to them across time and space for instantaneous communication on the spirit level. It will be like speaking to another person in the same room. It will be speaking over millions of miles to groups with whom they will never be in contact physically.

Pleideans, the first alien race of group one, are examples of an alien race using its psychic ability to contact the human race, just as humans will be doing in the future. In this case, Pleideans are doing the transmitting and humans are the passive receivers. Distance is meaningless once you get into the spiritual realm. Every place in the spiritual realm is as far away as any other place. Spiritual and psychic contact between Pleideans and humans is going on now, but it was not initiated by humans. Humans are the passive receivers. The Pleideans are sending out information and they hope it is received and hope it is understood, but as far as getting real feedback, rehashing of the material for discussion, this does not occur. So it is really a one-way communication. True communication does not exist here yet because humans are not developed to the point where they can undertake a sustained long-term conversation.

Later, after many years, the psychic contacts will be purposeful across a long distance, and events on that planet will be occurring at the same instant as the events on Earth. By this time, people on Earth will be fairly well advanced and the concept of psychic contact between spiritually developed people will be well established. It will take a long time to reach the point where it will be a common approach to contact other alien races psychically. Eventually, it will be realized that purposeful, scientific, and spiritual information can be exchanged this way. Of course, this exchange will not take long, so mutual scientific investigation and mutual spiritual development can be shared.

The human race will establish contact this way with multiple alien races over a span of years. For most, it will serve as a positive, uplifting experience. Some individuals within a race will have a problem with it and will have difficulty coping with it. These will be minor problems, and while they should not be ignored, they will not cause huge consequences.

Right now on Earth, with alien abductions, the common response to the experience is negative. While some of the abductions, such as by the grays and with the spider alien beings, are negative, many others are not. When people recall the event under hypnosis,; in some cases they recall that they walked and talked freely and engaged in conversation with those they came to regard as their captors. They were free and independent people, even in the alien craft, and yet they thought of it as being abducted.

Purposeful Alien-Human Interaction

Here, we deal with three ways in which humans and aliens will be interacting purposefully according to the heavenly beings. A sort of feedback loop between alien races and humans. There is an active participation in which the alien race explains its understanding to humans, who, in return, feed it back to the alien race, in the process modifying the alien race's understanding of its spiritual concept. This feedback going on back and forth will develop understanding in both human and the alien races.

There will be an eventual outreach of humans to other races, a feedback to the races that are working with humanity. As humans develop, they will refine spiritual understanding in the alien race, a feedback mechanism where the alien race works with humans who also help the alien race. This interchange increases the depth of spiritual understanding for each. This is another reason why it is an active process. The alien race develops spiritually as they teach humans, through feedback from them. Tiny bits of spiritual understanding are traded back and forth between numerous races. And this is also a part of the feedback loop to the universe. Multitudes of alien races and humans will be exchanging little bits of understanding, though this is not really a full, long-term teaching arrangement. In the distant future, humans will go out in the universe and will start to work with other races.

It will happen in five stages:

First stage: Aliens will contact humans physically on Earth and they will share information with each other, which will be accidental and unplanned.

Second stage: Humans will make a deliberate effort to purposefully share information with the alien races in person on Earth.

Third stage: Humans will be developing spirituality and learning to make psychic contacts with other races in space to share information.

Fourth stage: Humans will visit other planets and share information face-to-face with other alien races.

Fifth stage: Humans will become an interstellar visitor and actively work with less evolved races toward their spiritual development.

First stage: When alien races make face-to-face contact on Earth with humans, they will share information with them, such as knowledge of their existence and that they are technologically more advanced than humanity. In the same way, humans will share information with the aliens. Simply observing humans and what they do will indicate to another race what humanity's basic approach to life is like. The questions humans will ask and the statements they will make will provide information that can be analyzed by an alien race to determine information about humans. This will tell what humans think, how they think, and how they obtain information from their environment. This information sharing will be accidental and unplanned, so we cannot regulate which information about our species gets shared. The first stage already began when the first alien race contacted the primitive humans about a million years ago. It is still going on and will go on into the future.

Second stage: The second stage has not yet begun. It cannot begin until the aliens are known to be present and known to be an active force in Earth life. People have to realize they are here and that they are not here to take over the Earth. They are here because they seek contact with humans to share information. Here, humans understand more completely with whom they are sharing the information and deliberately plan what information shall be shared and how it will be shared. Meetings of groups of scholars in politics, technology, education, physical and biological sciences, sociology, religious, spiritual, psychology, etc. will determine what information shall be given to aliens. The mainstream religious people will provide them insights about religion, while physical scientists will tend to communicate physical science. A sociologist will convey social patterns and how they influence each other and the alien groups. Each field will be interested in its own objectives and what should be shared will be determined.

The method for sharing could be figured out, and once these plans have been made, the dynamic sharing of information will begin, with humans determining what they would like the aliens to know about humanity. The information sharing will be vigorously planned, tightly controlled, and carried out formally rather than informally. Many different groups will be involved in the planning because there will be various concepts of religion and spirituality coming from different groups of spiritual and religious figures from all over the world. Each major group will plan what it wants the aliens to know about it.

While humans are sharing with the alien race and determining what information they want to give to the alien race, the same groups will try to figure out what information from an alien race would be most valuable for them. The alien race will also plan what questions to ask when it is its turn to ask the questions. It would be a planned communication, a two-way street. This will be quite difficult for many humans to work with because of their ingrained belief system that they are the only created race.

Humans will try to figure out the perception of the race they will be giving the information to. According to archangels, the problem will come from the groups that believe that they are the only source of truth in various fields. Most likely these will be religious fundamentalists who believe that their way is the only way. They will make unusual efforts to try and get their ideas across to the aliens. There will be guidance from heaven to those who will ask.

So there is this calculated information exchange from different groups; at the same time, there will be the reciprocal exchange of information from aliens to humanity. They too will go through the same type of analysis about what they should tell humans, how they should tell it, and how they can double check to make sure humans understand what they mean. The usual problems of communication will occur such as, "What I meant to say, what I actually said, what you heard, what you think you heard and what you think it meant to you when you heard it."

Communication is never as exact as it might be. When you are dealing with two different races that are alien to each other, you never know exactly what it is that is heard and understood by the others. You can carefully plan the communication, give the communication, and the other party can actively try to hear it and then try to figure out what was said, because what is heard is not what is said and what is said is not what you really meant to say, and what you tried to say in the first place. Over time, humans will communicate in every possible way.

Heavenly beings, through my hypnotized patients, say that in the second stage, communication with the aliens primarily will be verbal. That is, they will come to Earth and talk to humans face-to-face. In the relatively near future of about fifty years, the alien races will reveal themselves to humans. The humans will be made aware that aliens are here and, after a period of initial shock, there will be occasions when conscious sharing will go on in formal meetings where pre-planned communication will be given back and forth.

What the aliens will be truly interested in is our understanding of ourselves, our psychology, sociology, and anthropology. The way we see ourselves and the way we understand ourselves is important to them. Our spiritual understanding, the information they will get from religious groups, will be important to them. They will not care much to get our knowledge of physical and biological sciences because they already have a greater understanding of these fields than we do. In some fields that we feel are more valuable to us, the aliens will listen politely and make comments, but they could not care less. When it comes to knowledge of psychology, physiology, anatomy, medicine, sociology, politics, and spirituality, this information will be important to the aliens because it will help them understand humanity. It will not seem important to humans that aliens understand how the political system works. They have politics of their own.

On the other hand, as the aliens will be sharing knowledge with humans, the most glaring contrast will come in the physical and biological sciences, where they will show up with this fantastic knowledge that humanity is not even close to. Those areas in which we will be less behind are sociology, psychology, and the understanding of our own species, religion, spirituality, etc. These areas will be well represented in the interchanges back to humanity. The aliens know that the most important information they can give us is not the obvious scientific or technology information, but their perception of spirit – the God and how the universe really fits together.

Both groups will plan their communication thoroughly, trying to tailor to the perception of the other group. Each group will misunderstand what is most important because of their preconceptions. The Earth humans will feel that technology is the most important, while the aliens will feel that ways to understand the race, such as psychology, sociology, anthropology, linguistics, religious and spiritual understanding, are more important. Humans will tend to think of the latter as the least important, thinking that physical sciences and technology are more important. Aliens will tell them how the universe was put together and how it functions when they speak of spirituality.

Then comes the feedback process, in which each race reports their understanding so that the communication can be refined. This will lead to many interesting and hilarious moments as each race realizes what misunderstandings arose. The dialogue will go back and forth until it is refined and there is better understanding. This will take a long time. Once the dialogue starts, it will be well over a hundred years until there is a real understanding between the races.

The positive gray alien race two of group one with round eyes, whose limbs look like that of a squid and which can live underwater, and alien races four and five of group two will be among those races who will contact with us physically in stage two.

In stage two, when we will contact the human-like, tall, thin alien race four of group two, they will reveal that they are here already and will begin to interact openly so that all of humanity knows it. There are many tall, thin, human-like alien races in creation but we might contact only the one we have already contacted; that is alien race four of group two. The short, blocky, human-like alien race five of group two will also contact us. There are many races built along this general pattern. We are already in contact with the fifth alien race of group two, who are short, stocky, and human-like. Over the years, the human race conceivably will come in contact with probably two more alien races who are built like this, for a total of three that are short, stocky, and basically humanoid. The above two races will help us advance our technology.

The praying mantis-like alien race three of group one is the Sirian race. There are many alien races that have triangular shaped heads, but nobody looks like a praying mantis except the Sirians, race three of group one. It is because of their narrow shoulders, the shape of their heads, the placement of their eyes, the flat mouth, and the look they have of a sort of tense expectancy, which is the way a praying mantis looks.

We will later contact alien race three of group two. Most likely we will meet them in space as humans go to their world, and we will be recognized as a race on which their race worked eons ago. They are not interested in coming here. They produced the genetic changes in humans and saw these changes spread around very slowly. Some of the other races with which humanity will come into contact are extremely different, ranging from beings that are practically bundles of brain matter to beings who are practically gas.

Third stage: In the third stage, humanity will be developing spirituality and learning to make psychic contacts with other races in space and sharing information through those psychic contacts. They will begin to understand the aliens and the differences between humans and aliens. Humans will plan and try to determine what to tell aliens, how to present it in the best fashion for the most thorough communication. Communication is an inexact art. Planned communication and feedback can make it more exact.

This will begin approximately twenty-five years after humans make the first tentative communication directly with the alien race. The implementation of that information with humans will lead to an increase in spirituality. Many people on this Earth worry about an alien race disproving the existence of God or laughing at us because we do believe in God. The truth is that many alien races have a better understanding of God and the universe than we do. Following some of their precepts and their religious understanding, plus what we already know about developing spirituality, more and more people will be developing psychic ability and getting in touch with the spiritual realm. As these psychic abilities develop in the entire human race, we will be able to communicate through long distance, psychically, with other races in space.

The same sort of information that was exchanged physically during the initial contact with the races on Earth will be exchanged psychically. The alien races and humanity will develop a mutual understanding, and because it is happening on the mental realm, the understanding will be more complete and more fully rounded. The number of facts transferred will be fewer because it is much easier to convey facts through physical contact than to convey feelings and the understanding behind them. Psychic communication is much better and the truth or falsehood of something will be much more thoroughly communicated. In other words, it is difficult to lie psychically because the feelings come through as well as the content.

It is at this time, when humanity will be in psychic contact with the alien races, that it will be creating its own classification system for the alien races and will begin to make contact randomly wherever it can in the universe. Humans will try to see just how many alien races they can communicate with. Most frequent contacts will be the psychic ones. These will be much more frequent and much more intense.

In the later stages, communication between humans and the alien races will be possible even in other dimensions. As spirituality develops and people become psychically more powerful, they will be trading information with races in other dimensions, where physical contact can never occur. The development of psychic means will be more common and more intense by an alien understanding of spiritual development. Humans already have their own means, which are given to them by the great spiritual teachers through meditation and the development of spiritual knowledge, which tunes humans into the spiritual dimension for communication rather than through physical means. This will become easier and more complete when the alien spiritual understandings are combined with our own.

Forth stage: Here, humans will visit and share information face-to-face with the alien races on their planet. This will occur roughly two hundred and fifty years after the first alien-human face-to-face communication. It will take this long to apply the alien technology because it takes a considerable length of time to understand it. The mathematics and physics will have to be developed in human terms before we can make those leaps.

Of course, human beings will be in space before that, as guests on the spacecraft of others. Human beings have traveled to other worlds, but this will be the first time that a spacecraft built by and controlled by humans goes into space for the special purpose of contacting the other races. The first contact will be preplanned by invitation, with humans going to visit alien races for a face-to-face exchange of information with those with whom they have made psychic contacts before.

Interstellar trade consists primarily of the exchange of information, which is cheap to transport, and huge quantities will fit in a spaceship, in contrast to transporting any material from planet to planet, which is not cost effective. It makes a lot of sense to use spaceships as transporters of knowledge instead of trade goods.

The final stage of understanding will come when a child who is raised in a human culture, with its developing understanding of humanity, and an alien child are swapped and raised with each understanding the other's culture. They will grow up having this knowledge of the other culture. It is really the only way to achieve real understanding of the other culture, to have people who are raised between the cultures, so that they can have the knowledge and understanding of both. Then we can start to have a real understanding.

A human child still in the very early learning stages will be sent to live with the alien family, where he or she will learn the language and culture; and an alien child would be living with the human family, doing the same thing. The kids will be swapped back and forth so that they can also stay in touch with their own family and their own culture. It is in this way that we can really develop an understanding of another culture.

Immersing yourself in another culture to learn about that culture can bring profound changes that an alien culture would have upon humanity. Human concepts will broaden except in those who are threatened by them, and who become much narrower and more channeled. The groups most likely to feel this will be the religious groups; those who feel that their own brand of religion is put down or degraded by an understanding of an alien religion.

Here, the human culture will be carried out into space to share it with those races which humanity has planned, psychically, following the patterns laid down by the other races in their contacts. Their initial interaction with other races will be feedback to the human culture, and will be incorporated by the human culture. We cannot touch another culture and not be changed. When we become familiar with another culture and this familiarity spreads through groups, then our culture has to change because of it.

Of the alien races we will be contacting, some will be human-like and some will be different. In fact, according to the heavenly beings, one of the races we will do well with and will develop a close relationship with will look like amoeba.

Fifth stage: Here, humanity becomes an interstellar visitor and actively works with undeveloped races toward their spiritual development. According to heavenly beings, this stage will begin after about one to two thousand years after the alien contact. It follows after a great deal of technological development here on Earth. They will also be studying with other alien races, an understanding of genetics and heredity. In this stage, spaceships piloted by humans will make contact with other planets. They will go exploring and find races that have the potential of developing. There would be an analysis beforehand, which would include the potential of this race for developing a human culture in terms of spiritual understanding and soul development. This has to be the number one concern in the spiritual development of anyone.

There will be a long period of time in which races will be observed, plans will be made, and genetics will be studied, and it would be debated as to which changes would be most beneficial in this race, how to make those changes, what genes would be involved, what effects will be looked for, and what would be expected from what tiny chemical change in the DNA. After considerable debate, the first experiments would focus on a less evolved race, make a few genetic changes, implant them into the race, and see how they work. Over thousands of years, the race would be observed, its genes would be checked from time to time, and changes in behavior, physiology, and intelligence would be measured and evaluated, and what percent of the change was due to which gene would be figured out. Step by step, they would try to analyze genes and the changes from which they came.

Following that will be detailing the extremely long process, entailing waiting periods of many years after the genetic changes are made in another race and then analyzing exactly what happened as to which genetic change caused what. This will go on for a period of time and a thorough understanding would be gained before the next set of modifications would be attempted.

The human race was already on its way to looking human when the first alien intervention occurred. One of the primary tasks will be trying to develop an understanding of how we can tell that a race is on the spiritual evolutionary path, so that it can be hurried along that path by genetic modification rather than having to wait for natural progression to happen. Just like what was done to us and how fast we progressed.

According to the archangels, when it was done to us, it was not understood that it was important. In fact, our race is the one that helped in the understanding that we were human to begin with, even at that early stage, although we had not developed much in the way of potential but were still human. This was not recognized by the aliens. Now that will become a primary target in these interventions, to see if a race is already human. Though extremely primitive, it can still be human. By human, we do not mean a humanoid form, but a soul having the capacity to develop. The word "human" is used here because there is no other word in English that can explain it. Intelligence does not imply spiritual development. There are intelligent races that do not have spiritual development.

This will become an ongoing process and will be the primary goal of any race that is developed spiritually. They already have the technological make-up, so as their spirituality develops, it becomes very important for them to spread it to other races.

According to the heavenly beings, humans are not intended or suited to be a space-venturing race. We will never be a real space traveling race, but we will be able to use some of the shortcuts that other races have discovered. We could travel within the same universe. Here, a human can go into one area of the universe and transfer to another part of the universe almost instantaneously through an intra-dimensional pathway. They can travel long distances or just make local trips to get out of the destructive environment of space. It will be found that being in space is damaging to humanity. There can be physical deterioration because the human body is not meant to be exposed to that much solar radiation and weightlessness.

Constant recycling in a closed atmosphere can be damaging to humans. Most people will not believe this because they think that space exploration is the manifest destiny of the human race. Also, the technology has not been developed at this time, so we cannot travel to distant places. Some alien races are able to travel because they are physically evolved to deal with those conditions. Humans have been raised in a stable gravity environment with protection from solar radiation and have developed in a sheltered existence.

Races that can travel in space with varying gravity and the amount of radiation from the sun are being evolved physically. The beings had to develop immunity or an ability to cope with that; otherwise, life on the planet would not be possible. Creation of a planet starts and proceeds following the natural laws, so that as organisms come into being, the ones who could adapt to those conditions survive and those who could not die out. Physically, we are not created to travel to space.

According to heavenly beings, our planet, with its iron core, creates a magnetic field around the Earth that deflects radiation from the sun. The planets that do not have an iron core, those that are rocky planets or gaseous planets, do not have a strong magnetic field, and a lot of radiation from the sun reaches the surface. Beings coming into that radiation field have to be able to adapt to it or they do not survive.

By radiation, we mean radiation from the sun and all the stars. All stars work by nuclear fusion. The sun and stars operate in the same manner, so every star, including the sun, is putting out radiation. Where there is no electromagnetic energy field, primarily in the planets that evolved first, the beings have to evolve and be capable of dealing with radiation. If we take human beings out in space and there is radiation coming at them from every direction, they would have to be shielded and protected from it. Eventually, over the years, the human body would deteriorate from radiation poisoning to the point where they will become non-functioning human beings, mentally and physically.

So humans will be limited to comparatively short trips of actual traveling in space. They can travel by leap frogging, going from place to place, but if they end up on a planet without the electromagnetic field, they will need special shielding to exist there. Things to protect humans from radiation can be invented, such as a device for putting a magnetic field around the spaceship and diverting the radiation that might come close to people, but this will not be possible for many thousands of years.

Humans will make short trips, primarily at the beginning, in alien spacecraft to protected environments on other planets. Humans can move by a short leap, such as voyages that would cover a few light years, accomplished in space for the Earth person in a few months. This way they are not exposed to space for too long and do not suffer an extreme amount of damage.

Technology with Spirituality

Heavenly beings state that technology will come from different alien races. They will start humanity on this technological road to the point where human beings can enter into space on their own, first, to contact races that are already developed, and second, to start a new race on a new planet that can enter into the community of spiritually developed beings. The technology is designed to free people and to give them the time to develop their spirituality, but this effort must be balanced. There must be sufficient time for constructive activity such as spiritual development, time for relationships, work, and play. Without that balance, nothing much can be achieved. The balance depends upon the particular race. What are the needs of its individuals? In races that do not understand, do not know, or do not possess emotions, less time is spent on the relationships, self-analysis, self-construction, and spiritual development. But in the human race, this is an essential part because we are based in emotions.

Some alien races, such as gray alien race which is negative and alien race four and five of group two, have less spirituality and no emotions; they see us as primitive, ape-like beings who have changed dramatically in just a few generations. They are burying the dead and treating them with respect and putting in memorabilia and not forgetting that the person existed, as if this primitive being actually knows that there is a part that is continuing. And it is here they perceive that there is a spiritual component to humans, but at the same time, they see technology also developing.

It is the technological development that those aliens were expecting and anticipating with great interest since their own beginnings were so far back that they do not know how they changed from simple beings into technological beings. They were developing an insight into their own past while watching our growth. Here, we are advancing technologically, and at the same time developing spiritually, which is a real surprise to these aliens who lack emotions. So they are taking another look at history, trying to understand our emotional, spiritual, and philosophical development to see if it will give them some insight into our spirit.

AFTERTHOUGHTS

The essence of spirituality and the guiding force behind human endeavors is extremely important. Without it, human efforts can go wrong, whether political, social, scientific, or just every part of human interaction and human life. Most of all, we need to learn from the mistakes of the past. We are facing the same situation now in this lifetime as they had in Atlantis. We are in a similar stage of development as Atlantis was in its Golden Age. Humanity has the choice now to maintain, enlarge, and expand that Golden Age to the entire Earth or, by making the same mistakes Atlantis made, turn the continents into living hells.

Much of the information in this book is given to help humankind understand what has happened in the past and the choices we face in the immediate future. We need to learn from the forgotten past. It is not an accident that my patients are going back through these lives. It has a dual purpose. First, it is necessary for the person's healing. It is an expression of what is wrong inside them that needs to be corrected before they go on to a healthy life, but at the same time, it is serving the purpose of allowing me to inform humanity at large of what has happened in the past, of the choices that have to be made, and of the need for spirituality in human life. Humanity cannot and will not survive properly without this understanding.

Probably there will be a great deal of reaction against this, but people cannot conceive how evil Atlantis became and the spiritual malaise that is carried over from Atlantis and its effect on human life and problems now. Many people think of Atlantis as a place of sweetness and Light. Even though the old legends and rumors do specify that Atlantis went horrible, nobody can conceive just how bad it was. It is an example of the spiritual malaise from that time to this time that needs to be overcome through spirituality. It is so clear and so overlooked that we need to use spiritual practices to overcome the spiritual malaise from past times.

The shame of discussing religion or spirituality began from the fact that the Atlantean culture began with an amalgam of people from Europe, Mediterranean countries, Africa, South, Central, and North America, so that there were many different groups with different beliefs. At the very beginning, it was found that the discussion of these beliefs would provoke extreme reactions, and it developed exactly the same way in our culture in the current time. We do not discuss religion because people get upset and tend to kill each other.

From the simple beginning, simply to keep social calm and quiet, the habit developed of not speaking of spirituality at all, and over time, it evolved from keeping the peace to being a matter of extreme privacy to each individual. Through the passage of time, they were ashamed of speaking about religion because, to them, it was too personal and too intimate to discuss. According to heavenly beings, it was influenced and amplified by Satan. Like in our culture, to discuss our sex life publicly is really bad manners and is not done, yet it is a very common human function. Sometimes there are insights that others give that can be very valuable. We know that love and sex are not shameful, yet we do not discuss it in public.

The development of the Lamurian culture contrasted with that of Atlantis. There was difference in attitude of people and in spiritual practices. Spirituality diffused from Lamuria, moved out to the east first and southeast to Central and South America, spreading to the Pacific coast, crossing Central America, and spreading around into Atlantis and North America. It was easier to travel by the sea than by land, so coastal areas got contacted first. There was also actual traffic to Asia. This way, some of Lamurian spirituality spread to Asia, although the majority went to South, Central, and North Americas, and on to Atlantis. There were also trips to Asia by a few individuals, but very little return traffic. Not all those who made the attempt survived, and not all those who started lived through the voyage. Those who did make it found fertile soil for spirituality. The Lamurians would put out the ideas and people absorbed them and worked with them, not misinterpreting them as the Atlanteans did, and not having the negativity toward the discussion of spiritual matters. That is why, as described before, there were differences in Atlantean and Lamurian cultures. Lamuria was extremely spiritual and did not care much for technology, while Atlanteans focused on the technology and did not care for spiritual development. The two continents met the same fate, but at widely different times. Natural Earth changes were the facts, and there may have been divine intervention, but it was with the people of Atlantis, not with the land. The people were finally set free by the aliens who, by interruption of the current and interfering with the back-up systems, destroyed the means of control. Someone reached out and turned off the mechanism. According to the archangels, the ultimate motivational source of the information is God, because Satan is setting out his plot of control in current time as he did in Atlantis. It is interfering with the purposes of the Light and with the development of mankind. Satan's plan is to cause spiritual death on the planet, while God and the Light are trying to head off this catastrophe. The controlling of mankind was a Satanic plot in Atlantis, and a similar plot is in motion now. It is intended to stop spirituality and to put an end to God's plan in the universe, at least as far as this planet is concerned. With the amount of technology, and communication from nation to nation and continent to continent, Satan's plan is to control the population of the Earth totally. There is sufficient power and electricity that, once all the components are put together, there will be no end to this control. Interruption of electric current, as happened to free the people of Atlantis, will no longer be possible and we can be sure there will be multiple power sources and multiple means of transmission of electricity to keep the control mechanisms going. In fact, if there is no intervention within thirty years, most of the technology will be in place. Whether it is put into use is another matter.

The main purpose of this book is to short-circuit Satan's plan. The plan can be stopped easily by developing enough spirituality in people so that ruling groups – the politicians and rich and powerful – are influenced to be spiritual. Then they will be resistant and impervious to Satan's urging to set up this network. Through spirituality, the political leaders and other rich and powerful people will know the intrinsic wrongness of it, the damage it will do to our spiritual nature, and hopefully, they will refuse to take those actions.

REVIEW REQUESTED:

If you loved this book, would you please provide
a review at Amazon.com?

CPSIA information can be obtained
at www.ICGtesting.com
Printed in the USA
FSHW020636020319
56050FS